THE POLITICS OF READJUSTMENT

SOCIAL PROBLEMS AND SOCIAL ISSUES

An Aldine de Gruyter Series of Texts and Monographs

SERIES EDITOR

Joel Best
University of Southern Illinois, Carbondale

THE POLITICS OF READJUSTMENT
Vietnam Veterans Since the War

WILBUR J. SCOTT

ALDINE DE GRUYTER

New York

ABOUT THE AUTHOR

Wilbur J. Scott is Associate Professor of Sociology at the University of Oklahoma. Dr. Scott received his Ph.D. from Louisiana State University in 1976. He has published numerous journal articles and is currently coediting a book with Sandra Carson Stanley on the controversy over gays in the military.

His areas of expertise are the sociology of politics, social movements, and military sociology. He served in Vietnam in 1968–1969, as an infantry platoon leader with the Fourth Infantry Division.

Copyright © 1993 Walter de Gruyter, Inc., New York

ALDINE DE GRUYTER
A division of Walter de Gruyter, Inc.
200 Saw Mill River Road
Hawthorne, New York 10532

This publication is printed on acid-free paper ∞

Library of Congress Cataloging-in-Publication Data

Scott, Wilbur, J., 1946–
    The politics of readjustment : Vietnam veterans since the war / Wilbur J. Scott.
        p.   cm.
    Includes bibliographical references and index.
    ISBN 0-202-30405-1
    1. Vietnamese Conflict, 1961–1975—Veterans—United States.
    2. Vietnamese Conflict, 1961–1975—Psychological aspects.
    3. Veterans—United States—Mental health.   I. Title.
    DS559.72.S36   1993
    959.704'3373—dc20   93-13488
                                                                          CIP

Manufactured in the United States of America

10 9 8 7 6 5 4 3 2 1

For
Cynthia Kay

and
All my brothers who served in
Alpha Company, 1st Battalion, 14th Infantry,
4th Infantry Division

CONTENTS

FOREWORD

When Wilbur Scott phoned and asked me to write the foreword for this book, I agreed to do so immediately. In addition to being a student of military organizations, I am also a veteran of Vietnam. I was anxious to read Scott's analysis of adjustments to civilian life by veterans of this war, the conflicts and movements that they were involved in, and how they simply searched, and continue to search, for parts of themselves that were left in a faraway land. When I read the manuscript, it fulfilled all of my expectations of what such an analysis of Vietnam veterans should involve.

There have been many treatments of Vietnam veterans in the academic and popular literature. But none of these works bring together, under one cover, the number of issues treated in this book. Even more impressive, the major portions of this book are written with the natural flow of a novel that should make it very accessible to the general population. At the end of the book, Scott brings this novelistic flow together into a theoretical framework so that scholars, particularly of military sociology and veterans' studies, can evaluate the book's contribution to their fields. As a result, Wilbur Scott has produced a work that is an outstanding treatment of the Vietnam veteran.

When Vietnam veterans are compared to veterans of other wars, perhaps the only things that they have in common are that they wore the same uniform, experienced the same basic training, fought in a faraway land, and experienced hardships and problems. The Vietnam veterans' experience has been different, when seen in its totality, in that they were not welcomed home with open arms. When they were welcomed, it was a "lukewarm kind of acceptance." I remember that when I returned from Vietnam, the first thing that we did was to shed the uniform and get into civilian clothes. This is in stark contrast to veterans of World War I, World War II, and Korea, who wore their uniforms to their hometowns, and were received with welcome arms. In a very real sense, this book is about the "politics" that Vietnam veterans developed in order to get the country to come to grips with the Vietnam war itself and the many problems associated with the war.

As the book begins, the reader is given a close-up and personal look at the efforts of a group of veterans who concentrated on ending the war in Vietnam. Scott takes us through the rise and decline of the organization, Vietnam Veterans Against the War (VVAW), the lives of its founders, and their approach to important questions concerning our involvement in Vietnam. In an analysis reminiscent of Samuel Stouffer's classic, *The American Soldier*, subsequent chapters treat the reader to the views of health professionals on the effects of combat vis-à-vis the Vietnam experience. Scott's analysis of the controversy over readjustment programs for the Vietnam veteran is wrapped around significant events of the war, such those that took place at My Lai. His stories also integrate the practice and politics of psychiatry with the reality of post-combat grief experienced by the veterans themselves.

Perhaps no other issue has come to mark the politics of readjustment by Vietnam veterans as has Agent Orange. It was this issue that made all veterans, whether they were active in the veterans' movement or not, identify with problems associated with the Vietnam war. The symptoms of exposure to the herbicide could appear years after service, and a fear of its effects lingers still in the minds of veterans of this war. In informal settings veterans might comment uneasily, "My children are all right, so I guess I was not affected by Agent Orange"; and, when a Vietnam veteran dies at a young age of cancer, people often offer by way of explanation, "Well, you know that he was a Vietnam veteran." Scott does a masterful job of showing how the rise of the Agent Orange issue is correlated with the lawsuit filed by Agent Orange Victims International (AOVI) and the rise of the organization, Vietnam Veterans of America (VVA). His stories show the politics that marked Veterans' Administration policy and the major scientific studies concerning Agent Orange, and examines efforts by government agencies, the military, and veterans' organizations to frame and direct the course of the controversy.

The most moving story in this book concerns the building and dedication of the National Vietnam Veterans Memorial. Although the war ended in 1973, it was not until 1982 that Vietnam veterans were recognized by their country. Like all issues associated with Vietnam, the road was rocky and fraught with controversy. The project was conceived and directed by a small group of Vietnam veterans, and the seven million dollars to construct the Memorial was raised completely through private donations. During the celebration thousands of veterans, some wearing remnants of their old uniforms and some riding in wheel chairs or walking with crutches, marched down Constitution Avenue in Washington, D.C., to mark their homecoming.

For students of military organizations, Scott weaves observations about the impact of traditional military policy on the Vietnam veteran into his narrative. For example, military sociologists have for years looked at the importance of keeping units together so that the demoralizing effects of combat can be neutralized. In Vietnam, the twelve-month rotation system weakened and then destroyed cohesion in combat units. Scott examines how this policy affected veterans as they returned to civilian society.

Also for students of the military, many of the issues discussed in Stouffer's *The American Soldier*, especially the chapter, "The Soldier Becomes a Veteran," can be found in Scott's work. Of course Scott's work is not full of contingency tables showing relationships between selected variables, as was the case with Stouffer's book. But within Scott's many stories one finds a sense of what veterans' issues are all about and what veterans' organizations and concerned citizens should do for soldiers as they re-enter civilian life. These concerns were predominant in Stouffer's work, and form the core of Scott's contribution to the field of military sociology and veterans' studies.

In the last chapter, Scott concludes his stories about Vietnam veterans by developing the sociology of social movements. More than anything, this book is a contribution to the study of social movements, and using the Vietnam veteran experience as data adds an interesting twist to this literature. Scott's accounts of the problems and politics associated with being a veteran, whether psychological or chemical, bring the social movements to life in the book. The analysis shows how personal problems become public concerns, and details the steps by which this process occurs.

Scott's "sociological storytelling" is a great fit with the theoretical discussion near the end of this book. As he builds his theory of veterans' movements, he incorporates the "good war, bad war" distinction and notes the divisiveness this created within the American public and veterans themselves, as indicated by responses to a well-known Gallup poll at war's end. The blend of storytelling and theorizing lends a powerful tool to this book and makes it desirable both to the common reader of fiction and to the specialist reader in the academic world.

I am confident that both sets of readers will find much to enjoy and ponder in this work by Professor Scott. His book should influence for generations our view of the Vietnam war and its legacies, and of veterans of wars and conflicts yet to come.

John Sibley Butler
The University of Texas at Austin

INTRODUCTION

I am both a sociologist and a Vietnam veteran. The writing of this book therefore has been both a professional and a personal journey. I served in Vietnam as an infantry platoon leader for twelve months—longer than the usual "six months in the field, six months in a rear area administrative slot" that characterized the tour of most infantry officers. The Fourth Infantry Division was short on platoon leaders and I never asked to be reassigned. Much of its area of operations, the Central Highlands, comprised the mountainous, triple-canopy jungle of the Annamite rain forest. It was a stronghold of the North Vietnamese Army and, by my recollection, about 40 percent of my company was killed or severely wounded during my year there. We used to say to each other that once we returned stateside, "Everything's gonna be gravy."

I returned home in November of 1969. After a year and a half struggle to reconcile the deaths of my comrades with the controversy over the war and the withdrawal of our military support for South Vietnam, I put the war out of my mind and vowed never to give it another thought or ounce of energy. I remained true to my promise until 1983. By then I was a college professor and sociologist who studied political goings-on that had nothing to do with Vietnam. I was "unaware" of anything relating to Vietnam and Vietnam veterans. I had never heard of post-traumatic stress disorder, Vet Centers, or the herbicide, Agent Orange; I did not know that a national memorial had been built in Washington, D.C. On October 31, 1984, a friend, who would have later become my brother-in-law had he lived, killed himself. An Agent Orange claimant, he had urged me to think again about Vietnam. Over the next couple of years, I slowly began to consider Vietnam and eventually to incorporate it into my sociological thinking and research.

Veterans of all wars must readapt to civilian life once their military service has ended. This calls for several tricky adjustments. They must recover from their wounds, recognize that the strategies of survival in the combat zone are inappropriate in the civilian sphere, incorporate their war experiences into their civilian selves, and re-establish their familial and occupational careers. Veterans carry out some of these adjustments privately within a network of friends and family. Others are carried out in public arenas that process the experiences of veterans and the costs of going to war.

My account focuses on these public adjustments and challenges. This book describes in a narrative style the major social movements among Vietnam veterans from 1967 to 1990. Included are the "sociological stories" of protest against the war by Vietnam veterans in Operations RAW and Dewey Canyon III, the successful effort to place post-traumatic stress disorder (PTSD) in the American Psychiatric Association's *Diagnostic and Statistical Manual* (*DSM-III*), the building of the National Vietnam Veterans Memorial in Washington, D.C., and the controversy within the Department of Veterans' Affairs (DVA; known prior to 1989 as the Veterans' Administration), the courts, and the medical and scientific communities over Agent Orange.

Of course I have many opinions and feelings about these issues. As a Vietnam veteran, I have a deep interest in the subject matter. Writing the book represents my personal effort as a veteran to integrate history and biography and to make some positive contribution within the diverse world of the Vietnam experience. However, I have tried to recount the stories as a sociologist. That is, I have sought to consistently apply an analytical perspective, derived from my sociological understanding of how the world works, in selecting what details to present and in choosing the nuance and tone of that presentation. Good sociology, I believe, helps people make sense of their experiences. I have met my goals both as a sociologist and a Vietnam veteran insofar as what I have written is good sociology.

A Sociological Approach to Veterans' Issues

Nothing has come easy for Vietnam veterans. This is not to say that other wars have produced contented veterans. America's involvement in the Vietnam war, however, was embroiled in controversy from beginning to end. The controversy divided Vietnam veterans themselves and colored the way in which interested parties have viewed Vietnam veterans and their needs. In particular, popular conceptions of World War II, evinced by cultural artifacts about that war and by segments of the American population, including veterans of World War II and Vietnam, provided the contrast for the Vietnam experience. World War II was a "good war"—legitimate, heroic, and triumphant—whereas Vietnam was a "bad" one—divisive, substandard, and shameful. In some quarters, the Vietnam war and those who fought it were found wanting. In others, a just war and gallant warriors were seen as undermined by jaded politicians and generals or by those who opposed the military effort. These lingering sentiments about the war have provided a filter through which the readjustment of Vietnam veterans has taken place.

Problematic conditions, however, do not automatically cause controversy. Rather, controversy and the identification of some conditions as problems result from organized efforts to bring these conditions to our attention. Problems that lack effective advocates generally escape our attention, and problems that we are aware of typically have champions—interested persons or interest groups who have worked hard to place claims about them before us. Effective claims do not necessarily tell us what to think but generally do make us aware of what to think about. This insight tells us that the articulation of veterans' concerns in the readjustment process and the responses to them are negotiated politically in the major arenas of society. There are several categories of actors in this drama. First, there are changing casts of champions who initiate, join, and animate the fray surrounding an issue. Second, there are powerful and effective interests who previously have staked out positions and who continue to have a stake in how the postwar drama unfolds. The task of the sociological storyteller is to identify the protagonists and antagonists, and to detail the drama.

The veterans of any war are persons who share a common fate and may become politically active in behalf of their common interests. They are a potential group because their mobilization during wartime wrenches them from civilian roles and provides unique experiences that set them apart from those who did not serve. However, they are by no means a homogenous potential group, for their experiences also divide them. Distinctions abound, for example, between officers and enlisted men, between front-line combat troops and rear-echelon support personnel, and among the branches of service. The *time* of one's service in Vietnam—the war was very different in 1965–1966 than it was in 1971–1972—and one's feelings about the rightness or wrongness of the war effort provide further divides. The public dimension of veterans' issues hinges on the recruitment of these diverse subgroups and their allies by organizations that seek to define the problem and extract concessions from relevant power structures—a task that would seem simpler for the veterans of a good war than the veterans of a bad one.

The Issues

The public dimension of Vietnam veterans' readjustment to civilian life involves several issues: the question of combat atrocities, the psychological consequences of combat on its participants, the problem of how to commemorate a defeat, and the effects of exposure to Agent Orange on veterans and their children. Sentiments among diverse participants about the rightness or wrongness of the war necessarily color all of these issues. To a significant extent, each issue has its own protagonists and antagonists who have identified problems and competed within varying institutional arenas for dominance. This is not peculiar to the world of veterans' issues, but veterans' issues provide especially clear illustrations of how claims about social problems are set forth, challenged, and defended. Claims must compete for attention and acceptance in arenas crowded with prior claims, and must gain compassion from relevant segments of the public already inundated with "good causes." A good cause is a valuable asset but does not in itself guarantee success in securing solutions to problems.

Vietnam veterans have had trouble establishing their claims. War veterans often are accorded status as holders of special knowledge or performers of a heroic service. However, being a Vietnam veteran, a veteran of a bad war, did not necessarily carry any "privileged" status; often it was as likely to evoke hostility or contempt. In part this occurred because the media afforded the American people access to the war. Television provided a relatively frank look at what war can be like, a view that contrasted sharply with the sanitized versions provided by military censors during World War II. The antiwar movement, including the organization Vietnam Veterans Against the War (VVAW), promoted this contrast in hopes of undermining support for the war. In Chapter 1, I describe the rise and decline of VVAW from 1967 to 1972 and examine the importance of the atrocity issue to VVAW in mobilizing its constituencies. This story depicts competing versions of what war is like and of America's policy in Vietnam. VVAW hoped to erode support for the Vietnam War—and bring the war to an end—by advancing their version of Vietnam as a "dirty" war. This strategy aroused more than feelings about the war itself. It also stirred the sentiment that many Vietnam veterans themselves were worthy of contempt.

Chapters 2 and 3 recount the controversy over post-traumatic stress disorder (PTSD) as a psychiatric diagnosis and the history of legislative attempts in Congress to provide specialized readjustment counseling for Vietnam veterans. At stake here were competing notions of what constitutes the "normal" experience of soldiers in warfare. Previous thinking among military psychiatrists contained two opposing themes: one, that only soldiers marginally adjusted before combat fell victim to "war neurosis," and the other, that war neurosis afflicted well-adjusted troops subjected to too much combat. The American Psychiatric Association's *DSM-II*, published in 1968, contained no entry for war neurosis. Hence, Veterans' Administration psychiatrists and other medical personnel around the country assessed Vietnam veterans with severe readjust-ment difficulties using a diagnostic nomenclature that contained no en-try for war-related trauma. A small, diverse, and loosely organized group of psychiatrists and Vietnam veterans worked to change this. They achieved their goal in 1978 by placing the PTSD diagnosis in the updated manual, *DSM-III*. In large part, they were successful because they were able to gain entry into the writing of *DSM-III*. This allowed them, as official arbiters of disease, to change the diagnosis across the country in one fell swoop.

Legislation for the treatment of alcoholism and drug abuse among Vietnam veterans was introduced in 1971 by Senator Alan Cranston (D-Calif.), a critic of the war. The measure passed in the Senate but died in the House Committee on Veterans' Affairs. Committee members, staunch supporters of the war, disagreed that Vietnam veterans needed special programs. The American Legion and Veterans of Foreign Wars, organizations dominated by veterans of the Second World War, lobbied aggressively against the measure. The Cranston bill passed the Senate four more times between 1973 and 1978, but each time encountered the same fate in the House committee that it had in 1971. By 1977, Cranston's bill emphasized counseling to address PTSD and had the support of the VA's new national director, Max Cleland. In 1979, the House and Senate committees worked out a political deal that allowed the readjustment counseling bill to pass into law. Cleland and his staff designed an Outreach Program to implement the Cranston bill, and by 1981, the VA had established 137 Vet Centers.

The story of the National Vietnam Veterans Memorial is told primarily in Chapter 6. Elements of it also appear in Chapters 4 and 5. The guiding principle in funding, designing, and building the memorial was to sepa-rate the commemoration of those who served from questions of the rightness or wrongness of the war. A small group of Vietnam veterans sought in 1979 to build a memorial inscribed with the names of all American military personnel who died in Vietnam. The principle of separating the war from the warriors allowed the committee to develop a diverse network of individual and organizational support. Nonethe-less, fissures among Vietnam veterans and their allies concerning the conduct and policy of the war jeopardized the memorial's construction. Through negotiation and compromise, the steering committee struggled successfully with the issue of how to commemorate the participants of a controversial war. Dedication of the memorial, now one of Washington, D.C.'s most visited and cherished sites, took place on Veterans' Day, November 11, 1982.

The bulk of Chapters 4, 5, 7 and 8 are devoted to the Agent Orange controversy. The American military sprayed approximately eleven million gallons of the herbicide between 1965 and 1971. In 1977 the VA received the first claims contending illness and disability attributed to Agent Orange, and in 1979 Agent Orange Victims International, a Vietnam veterans' organization, filed a $4 billion lawsuit against the manufacturers of the herbicide. The story of Agent Orange is complex because the issue was introduced and contested in several arenas, each of which developed its own subplots and cast of characters. The VA reacted to the initial inquiries by requiring veterans to produce scientific evidence based upon human subjects before treating or compensating Agent Orange claimants. This encouraged initiatives by interested persons and interest groups in Congress, the courts, and the research communities within the military, federal government, universities, and specially funded cooperatives. Presidents Jimmy Carter and Ronald Reagan established an advisory board, the Agent Orange Working Group, to oversee federal activity about the issue. In 1989—after more than 100 million research dollars, a $180 million out-of-court settlement with the manufacturers, a Congressional inquiry, an additional lawsuit, and a full complement of activity and subterfuge—a Department of Veterans' Affairs committee concluded that certain Agent Orange may, or may not, be harmful to human health. Following DVA guidelines on policy amidst uncertainty, national director Edward Derwinsky gave veterans the benefit of the doubt: the DVA agreed to pay compensation to claimants having the kinds of cancer linked circumstantially with Agent Orange.

Chapter 9 contains a summary of the sociological dimensions of the work. I have compiled these in a separate chapter, rather than interspersing them within earlier chapters, so that the narrative could be presented without interruption. Nonsociologists may this skip this chapter without losing out on the story. I detail there the view of science and the theories of social problems and social movements that underlie the narrative. I develop also a general sociology of veterans' issues and draw particular insights from the Vietnam experience. The story of Vietnam veterans since the war extends and enriches our understanding both of the construction of social problems and of the costs of going to war.

Methods

The narrative presentation of data is not usual sociological fare. Most sociologists are not storytellers. Quantitative studies constitute the dominant research posture and certainly have the appearance of rigorous, scientific work. There is, however, a long tradition in sociology of "qualitative" research and of richly textured description. What makes this type of research scientific is the desire to build a "grounded" theoretical understanding based upon careful observation and detailed description. The term "grounded" here means that theory is enriched through systematic investigation. It is the use of theory for designing and carrying out the investigation, and the examination of data for reflecting further upon the theory, that distinguishes qualitative science from the work of analysts—say, journalists or some historians—who do not consider their work to be scientific.

My theoretical orientation told me to tell the story of Vietnam veterans since the war through the words and actions of the major protagonists and antagonists. In addition, I needed to be sensitive to plot, context, and domain of activity. I did not, for instance, as a sociologist ask questions such as "Is Agent Orange actually harmful?" or "What kind of memorial should be built?" Rather, I asked, "Who says Agent Orange is harmful and who says it is not?" "What kinds of characteristics do these claims-makers have?" "Where do they make their claims?" "How successful (or unsuccessful) are they?" and "Which strategies worked and which ones did not, and why?" In other words, I wanted to know who the drama's instigators were, who made the plot unfold the way it did, and how they did it. By answering these kinds of questions, I hoped to reveal the characteristics and circumstances of successful challenges to the system and of successful defenses of it.

I gathered the evidence for my stories through personal and telephone interviews with participants in the issues, and through newspapers, books, magazines, and archival sources. To identify the subject matter of the study, I looked first for signs of social movement organizations among Vietnam veterans in newspapers, magazines, and other written material. One of the first books I read, for example, was *Long Time Passing: Vietnam and the Haunted Generation* by Myra MacPherson, then a reporter with the Washington Post.[1] I found in it an initial sampling of issues and activists among Vietnam veterans. In 1987, I wrote an article about Agent Orange that was published in April, 1988, in the scholarly journal, *Social Problems*.[2] Afterwards, sociologist John Kitsuse, then an editor of a monograph series for Aldine de Gruyter, urged me to write a book about Agent Orange. I told him I was interested in writing more generally about the "politics of readjustment." This second phase of my research led to the investigation of other topics and the incorporation of personal and telephone interviews into the collection of data.

I developed the list of "persons to interview" using a snow-ball sampling technique. Interviewees were asked to suggest others with whom I also should talk. I conscientiously sought to include both protagonists and antagonists. Nevertheless, the list of those interviewed reflects to some extent availability and accessibility. I interviewed many of those involved in the PTSD issue by attending a meeting of the Society for the Study of Traumatic Stress in Dallas, Texas. I developed the technique of telephone interviewing because interviewees lived across the country and I had limited funds for collecting the data. The section about the Vietnam Veterans' Memorial is based almost exclusively on written sources since its prominence in the book expanded in a latter stage of the project.

In contacting subjects, I always identified myself as a sociologist. During the first few interviews, I worried that the presence of a tape recorder might inhibit the respondents. I discovered that they did not seem to mind and taped all subsequent interviews in their entirety. (Occasionally, a respondent would ask that I not attribute a specific quote to him or her.) Being a Vietnam veteran sometimes helped me gain entry. Frequently, an interviewee was curious about "which side" of an issue I was on. My standard reply was that I was writing a "social history" of Vietnam veterans, that I wanted the respondent to tell me his or her story so that I might understand the role he or she had played in a particular issue. I assembled the story line by integrating the biographies and events, whether gathered by interview or from written sources. This description of the process, however, is all too neat. My theoretical ideas and my understanding of the story line were constantly changing (though the broader theoretical perspective remained the same). It would be fair to say that I did not know exactly what the story was until I got it down on paper.

Acknowledgments

I owe a particular intellectual and professional debt to several of my colleagues. Malcolm Spector was the first to contact and encourage me to write in the constructivist style of sociological storytelling. Had he not done so in 1987, my initial efforts in this research surely would have died on the vine. Subsequently, John Kitsuse was singularly responsible for Aldine de Gruyter's willingness to extend a book contract. He and Joseph Schneider provided warm encouragement and helpful criticism on early drafts, and Joseph in particular gave me the green light to experiment with my own narrative style. Joel Best assumed editorship of the monograph series in 1990 and has lent enthusiastic support. I especially appreciate his nearly instantaneous reviews of later drafts. Among my colleagues at the University of Oklahoma, sociologist Craig St. John and historian David Levy provided sympathetic support and listening ears.

Many others contributed to the success of this project. The respondents entrusted me with their stories and, though we did not always see eye to eye, Michael Sovick of the Oklahoma Agent Orange Foundation graciously gave me free rein in his extensive files. Richard Koffler, Aldine's executive editor, stuck by me even when a I "disappeared" in France for eight months. Finally, my wife Cindy, a public health professional and a pretty good sociologist in her own right, believed in this project many, many times when I had my doubts. To her I am especially grateful.

Notes

1. Myra MacPherson, *Long Time Passing: Vietnam and the Haunted Generation* (New York: Signet, 1984).
2. Wilbur J. Scott, "Competing Paradigms in the Assessment of Latent Disorders: The Case of Agent Orange," *Social Problems* 35 (1988):145–161. Related publications from my research are "PTSD in DSM-III: A Case in the Politics of Diagnosis and Disease," *Social Problems* 37 (1990):294–310; "PTSD and Agent Orange: Implications for a Sociology of Veterans' Issues," *Armed Forces and Society* 18 (1992):592–612; and "Vietnam Veterans Against the War: The Politics of Antiwar Protest," In James Holstein and Gale Miller (eds.), *Research on Social Problems* (Greenwich, Conn.: JAI Press, 1992), pp. 229–253.

1

EXPENDED BRASS

"As far as they were concerned, we were expended brass and not even worth picking up."

Bill Crandell, Vietnam veteran

The first American combat troops splashed ashore in Danang, South Vietnam, on March 8, 1965. The 3,500 troops of the 3rd Marine Regiment, 3rd Marine Division who landed that day had a limited mission: to defend the American airfield there from Viet Cong insurgents. Gradually their mission expanded to defensive patrolling and then to taking the offensive. Correspondingly, the numbers of Marine, Army, Navy, and Air Force personnel swelled to 184,300 by the end of the year. The number of American military personnel in South Vietnam reached a high of 543,000 in April, 1969. Pockets of opposition within the United States to the war effort already existed before the Marines landed, and as American military involvement in South Vietnam increased, so did protest against the war.

On April 15, 1967, a crowd estimated at 100,000 to 125,000 people marched from Central Park to the United Nations Building to demand an end to American military operations in Vietnam.[1] American troop strength by this time stood at about 410,000; approximately 8,000 U.S. military personnel had died in the line of duty. There already were more than 500,000 Vietnam veterans who had served with military units in South Vietnam and now were back in the United States. Protest organizers invited twenty Vietnam veterans to lead the parade. The veterans accepted and carried a banner which read, "Vietnam Veterans Against the War." Following the march, six of them formed an organization by that name. Rather than the traditional veterans' issues of compensation and treatment for wounds, their principal bone of contention was the war itself. Vietnam Veterans Against the War (VVAW) demanded an immediate withdrawal of all American troops from Vietnam; they wanted to "bring their brothers home." They became the first group of

1

American veterans to formally and publicly oppose the war in which they fought while it was still in progress.

In this chapter, I describe the rise and functional demise of VVAW between 1969 and 1972, examine in detail how the "atrocity problem" became the key issue that mobilized VVAW during that time, and comment on the special character of "the Vietnam experience." Vietnam was the first war brought into American living rooms by televised news. Though geographically distant, Americans had a startlingly frank and intimate look at life in the combat zone. Images of Vietnam as "the dirty war" were inescapable; they tainted American involvement in Vietnam with moral ambiguity. Robbed of his "just cause" by rancorous debate over the rightness of American policy, and by the anarchic climate of the counterculture and antiwar movements, even the most gung-ho G.I. found it difficult to successfully present himself as an all-American youth serving God and country.

The story about VVAW raises and examines questions about what war is like. At issue were competing versions of what kinds of violence were justifiable in Vietnam as a matter of policy, and of the extent to which U.S. troops had committed atrocities—acts of violence against enemy soldiers and civilians that were unacceptable under the Military Code of Conduct. In one view, atrocities occurred rarely and American policy was sound; the rare atrocity was the work of the occasional "bad apple" who slipped through preinduction screening or who violated regulations. According to the other view, atrocities were both frequent and the direct result of American military policy. The two versions symbolized more generally how factions of the American public viewed the war.

Early Organizing Efforts

By November, 1967, VVAW's six founders had raised $4,000 and increased their ranks to forty. VVAW placed ads in the *New York Times* and eventually in national magazines such as *New Republic* and *Playboy*. During 1968, the New York City group grew to about 300 members, set up a permanent office, and held regional meetings in other parts of the country.

Sociologist Charles Moskos, Jr., and later military analyst Thomas Thayer, have assessed the tempo of the Vietnam War and divided it into segments.[2] Both describe the years from 1965 to 1967 as a period of relative optimism among those who served and of cautious, qualified support for the war among most segments of the American public. The turning point, they agree, occurred in 1968 with the Tet Offensive. In late January and early February of that year, the North Vietnamese Army and the indigenous Viet Cong of the South mounted a coordinated, country-wide attack against cities and United States military installations in South Vietnam. The strength and scope of the attack dismayed many Americans who heretofore had supported the war effort. In the months before the Tet Offensive, American military leaders had claimed that the Communists were on the verge of defeat and that the end of the war was in sight. The Offensive seemed to show otherwise. 1968 and 1969 thus were years of growing disillusionment with the war among substantial numbers of Americans and of increasingly strident protests against it.

Bill Crandell was one of those dismayed Americans. Crandell had served in Vietnam in 1966 and 1967 as an infantry lieutenant with the 199th Light Infantry Brigade. He had volunteered to go to Vietnam but returned disillusioned. The South Vietnamese, he observed, were reluctant warriors, as if the war were an American problem rather than their own. On his return, he enrolled as a graduate student in political science at Ohio State University in search of answers to questions about U.S. involvement in Southeast Asia. Whatever the initial logic for sending combat troops, Crandell reached the conclusion that the U.S. now should withdraw them. Shortly after the Tet Offensive, he became a regional coordinator of antiwar protest activity for VVAW. Crandell explains:

> Tet was a real changing point for me, because [General] Westmoreland said it was a great American victory. And the premise of . . . the pacification program was that we were going to demonstrate to the Vietnamese people that we could protect them from terrorists. . . . [Tet] demonstrated that we couldn't protect any place, including the American embassy. . . . It just seemed to me that . . . the people in charge of the war didn't have any idea what it was about, and we were going to lose. If we were going to lose, everybody who died from that point on was going to die for nothing! And then the hard part for me was, if that was true, then everybody who had already died had died for nothing! And once I faced that . . . [I said], I got friends over there! I've got to get them home![3]

On March 31, 1968, President Lyndon B. Johnson stunned his close advisors and a national television audience by announcing that he would not seek re-election in the upcoming presidential contest. The war had become too controversial. On May 12, 1968, American and North Vietnamese representatives initiated peace talks in Paris. (Viet Cong representatives joined the talks on November 1, and South Vietnam ended its boycott of them on November 26.) According to Jan Crumb, one of VVAW's six founders, these developments "almost killed us [as an organization] because everybody thought the war would end."[4] The talks, however, continued intermittently for almost four years. All the while, intense bursts of warfare continued as the participants jockeyed for advantage in negotiating a settlement.

Protests against the war received a renewed impetus in the fall of 1969. On September 16, the Associated Press broke a story about an event quickly tabbed the "My Lai Massacre." Eighteen months earlier on March 16, 1968, C Company, of the 1st Battalion, 20th Infantry, Americal (23rd Infantry) Division, had embarked on a search and destroy sweep of a Viet Cong stronghold, My Lai (1), a subhamlet of the village of My Lai. C Company had been in this area before and had taken casualties there. The company mistakenly entered My Lai (4), another of the subhamlets. Anticipating a fight and expecting to take more casualties, they went in firing. The military-age males had deserted the subhamlet, and C Company killed more than four hundred women, children, and old men. Troops on the scene and their superiors hushed up the story until a soldier-photographer, who had accompanied the unit on the mission, returned stateside and sold the pictures he had taken to media sources.

Emerging Ties with the Psychiatric Community

Sarah Haley, fresh with a master's degree in social work, began work for the Boston Veterans Administration (VA) Hospital in September of 1969. Her father had served in North Africa during the Second World War as a special agent for the Overseas Secret Service. As a young girl, she had heard stories about war and atrocities from her troubled father as he drank to forget them. Her first contact with a Vietnam combat veteran took place that first morning at work in Boston. As part of the customary intake process, Haley interviewed a new patient who was very anxious and agitated. The veteran told her that his company in Vietnam one day had killed women and children at a village called My Lai. He himself had not fired any shots. Afterwards, several members of his platoon who had participated in the slaughter threatened to kill him if he told anyone about what had happened, even if they had to hunt him down back in the States. One of them said that he might kill him someday just to make sure that he never blew the whistle.

A few days before coming to the VA Hospital, the veteran had become unraveled. He was easily startled, felt terrified, had fearsome nightmares, and was unable to sleep well. He complained hysterically that one of his war buddies was out to kill him, but had no physical evidence to prove it. Although Haley became aware of the breaking My Lai news story only later, she accepted the veteran's account at face value that morning. However, the other staff seemed unmoved by the substance of his story. Haley recounts that afternoon's staff meeting:

> The staff assembled to discuss all the information and reach a diagnosis and treatment plan. When we met, the intake log already had a diagnosis filled in: paranoid schizophrenic. I voiced concern. The staff told me that the patient was obviously delusional, obviously in full-blown psychosis. I argued that there were no other signs of this if one took his story seriously. I was laughed out of the room. I was told that it was my first day and just didn't understand how things worked. . . . I was aghast. These professionals denied the reality of combat! This clouded their clinical judgment. They were calling reality insanity . . . ! I knew from my father's stories that [this man was] not crazy. . . . That encounter became typical.[5]

In Haley's judgment, two misconceptions clouded her fellow professionals' view of combat. One stemmed from idealistic notions of America at war: American troops fought valiantly and did not commit atrocities. The second had its genesis in the conventional practice of psychiatry: mental health professionals across the country assessed disturbed Vietnam veterans using a diagnostic nomenclature which contained no specific entries for war-related trauma. As a result, VA physicians usually did not collect military histories as part of the diagnostic workup. Many of them thought that Vietnam veterans who were agitated by their war experiences, or who talked about them, suffered from a neurosis or psychosis whose origin and dynamics lay outside the realm of combat.

The backdrop for both of these sentiments was the Second World War. According to Haley, the comparison between World War II and the Vietnam War affected the way many mental health professionals viewed Vietnam veterans who sought help for serious readjustment problems. Haley recalls:

> There was a bias toward Vietnam veterans, especially after the My Lai massacre broke. It was so much easier to blame the . . . [Vietnam] veteran . . . , to romanticize . . . World War II veterans, and . . . [say] they were cut from sterner stuff. . . . Clinicians reflected the ambivance about the war, I mean, they really weren't any different than the regular population. The majority of clinicians at the VA were in one way or another very intimately connected with World War II. . . . They had this sort of noble view of World War II as a glorious fight against satanic enemies and that the World War II veterans were as pure as the driven snow. . . . [Also] we had antiwar clinicians in my agency who didn't want to talk with Vietnam veterans because they were baby killers who should have known better and not have gone in the first place.[6]

In November, 1969, psychiatrist Robert Lifton, an ardent opponent of the war, read an account of My Lai in the *New York Times* while on an airplane en route to the University of Toronto for a speaking engagement. Through Sarah Haley, he later would meet the veteran who had been at My Lai but had not participated in the killing and would write extensively about the implications of the veteran's experience. Lifton had served during the Korean War as a military psychiatrist and was well known in academic circles for his research on survivorship among Hiroshima victims. Upset now by the My Lai story, he vowed to intensify his public protests against the war. He deviated from his prepared topic in Toronto and discussed instead the My Lai story. On December 15, his statement, "Why Civilians Are War Victims," appeared in *U.S. News and World Report*, and on January 27, 1970, he testified before Senator Alan Cranston's subcommittee on the psychological effects of the Vietnam war on veterans.[7]

Lifton argued that incidents such as those at My Lai, inevitable in any war, were especially endemic in the Vietnam War: the same psychological processes—dehumanization of the enemy and psychic numbing— that allow combat troops to carry out their mission of killing combined with features of the Vietnam war to produce a high likelihood of atrocities. He urged readers and committee members to place a good portion of the blame for atrocities in Vietnam on the war itself and upon themselves for allowing the war to continue. For Lifton, the policy implications were clear: atrocities would occur so long as American military involvement continued; hence, the U.S. should end its involvement immediately.

On April 29, 1970, the United States and South Vietnamese military embarked upon a major offensive into Cambodia against North Vietnamese and Viet Cong positions. Within days, college campuses across the United States exploded with protest, and on May 4, Ohio National Guardsmen fired into a crowd of antiwar demonstrators at Kent State University, killing four students and wounding nine others. Previously, fellow psychiatrist Chaim Shatan had arranged for Lifton to speak at New York University. They agreed now to change the topic to the Cambodian invasion and Kent State killings, and plastered posters around New York City announcing the talk. This advertising attracted many people who were not students to the talk, including several VVAW members. From this talk, Lifton and other antiwar psychiatrists formed an ongoing association with VVAW.

As much by happenstance as by well-conceived and executed plans, the New York City VVAW chapter slowly developed a loose network of ragtag, local organizations across the country. The large, heady demonstrations against the war proved to be a ripe organizing vehicle for

VVAW. The numbers of Vietnam veterans who joined VVAW were small, but there were pockets of disgruntled veterans in most major cities and on many college campuses. Many already had formed their own informal groupings. Some groups became VVAW chapters while others retained their distinctive identities. Local VVAW chapters often joined with other larger antiwar organizations in protests and also provided self-help activities for veterans. The exact mix of protest and self-help, and the form that these activities took, varied from chapter to chapter. Still, VVAW remained virtually invisible on a national level.

The Iron Triangle

The most influential body in Congress affecting legislation pertaining to veterans has been the House Committee on Veterans Affairs. It was established as a standing committee on January 2, 1947, when legislation consolidated jurisdiction over veterans' issues previously held by several other committees. Along with the VA and the major veterans organizations—the American Legion, Veterans of Foreign Wars (VFW), and Disabled American Veterans (DAV)—it constitutes what Capital Hill watchers commonly call the "Iron Triangle." The label is not meant to imply that the three are of a single mind but rather that very little in the world of veterans' legislation since the Second World War has originated outside this triumvirate.

Representative Olin "Tiger" Teague (D-Tex.) chaired the House Committee from 1955 to 1973. The most highly decorated World War II veteran in Congress and a long-time member of the committee, Teague had firm ideas about what legislation veterans needed and how the process of developing that legislation should work. Throughout most of Teague's tenure, the Senate did not have a separate committee for veterans' issues. Prior to 1970, the Senate parceled out jurisdiction over veterans' benefits to the Finance Committee and over other veterans' affairs to the Labor and Public Welfare Committee.

A working agreement between the House and the Senate developed the year Teague assumed chairmanship of the House Committee. The American Legion lobbied in 1955 for a pension bill providing a "presumption of disability," and hence automatic eligibility, for all veterans at age sixty-five. The bill also increased the monthly allowances of existing pensions for veterans. Teague opposed the Legion bill on the grounds that veterans' pension allowances should be tied to actual disabilities. Over Teague's heated objections, the Legion bill was introduced out of committee and approved by the House. However, Senator

Harry Byrd (D-Va.) snuffed the Legion bill by allowing the Senate version to die in the Finance committee he chaired. Gilbert Steiner of the Brookings Institution later wrote of the significance of the Legion bill's demise:

> Arrangements between House Veterans' Affairs and Senate Finance soon settled into an agreed pattern. All consequential veterans' benefits legislation would first be acted upon in the House. Then the Finance Committee would move bills that Teague endorsed and drop bills he opposed.[8]

Although the Legion clearly lost that round, it nevertheless stood as a formidable spokesman for veterans. Along with the VFW and DAV, it provided veterans of the First and Second World Wars, and of the Korean War with political clout and fraternal support. However, these organizations attracted very few veterans of the Vietnam war to their ranks. For example, more than two million of the twelve million veterans of the Second World War joined the American Legion, VFW, or DAV, and by 1948, ninety-two veterans of that war—almost 20 percent of the combined House and Senate—were in Congress. In contrast, less than 100,000 of the roughly nine million Vietnam-era veterans joined these organizations during the 1970s. As late as 1978, only eleven Vietnam-era veterans served in Congress. As the 1970s began, Vietnam veterans lacked a national organization dedicated to their interests and had no effective advocate in Congress. In this respect, they virtually disappeared from public view.

The VA is the nation's single largest health care system. During the 1960s, it catered primarily to 12 million veterans of the Second World War, who on the average were in their mid-fifties and had chronic ailments associated with aging that were not service connected. (After the age of sixty-five, veterans are eligible to receive all their medical care from the VA free of charge.) As veterans of the Second World War had aged, the major veterans organizations lobbied Congress for programs and expenditures to meet their changing needs. Though hardly a rubber stamp to their wishes, the House Committee sponsored corresponding legislation, and the VA put it into practice. As a result, 30 percent of patients treated by the VA had service-connected disabilities, and of all medical treatment provided by the VA, 16 percent were for service-connected problems.

As the Vietnam War progressed, the VA suddenly experienced an influx of younger veterans requiring treatment, rehabilitation, and compensation for service-connected, war-related conditions and injuries. Vietnam veterans encountered a system tailor-made to serve the needs of the previous generation of veterans. The Vietnam War had a greater wounded-to-killed ratio than any previous war, producing a large number of traumatized and disabled veterans.[9] This produced strains in a VA health care system increasingly accustomed to addressing the needs of older veterans.

Many clinicians and researchers noticed other important differences. In both the Second World War and Korea, the incidence of war neurosis increased as combat intensified, and as these wars wound to a close and troops began returning home, incidences of war neurosis declined. VA records show low levels of postwar breakdown for World War II and the Korean War. The pattern in Vietnam is the reverse: medical statistics reveal comparatively low levels of war neurosis during combat in Vietnam and large increases in psychiatric problems after the war was over.

The VA under Fire

By all rights Captain Max Cleland, a signal corps officer with the 1st Cavalry Division, should have died in Vietnam. On April 8, 1968, a grenade fell from his web gear as he jumped off a helicopter in a landing zone near Khe Sanh, and exploded as he reached to pick it up. He later described the scene in his autobiography:

> A blinding explosion threw me backwards. The blast jammed my eyeballs back into my skull, temporarily blinding me, pinning my cheeks and jaw muscles to the bones of my face. My ears rang with a deafening reverberation. . . .
>
> When my eyes cleared I looked at my right hand. It was gone. Nothing but a splintered white bone protruded from my shredded elbow. It was speckled with fragments of bloody flesh. Nausea flooded me.
>
> . . . I looked down. My right leg and knee were gone. My left leg was a soggy mass of bloody flesh mixed with green fatigue cloth. . . .
>
> . . . I tried to cry out [for help] but could only hiss. My hand touched my throat and came back covered with blood. Shrapnel had sliced open my windpipe. I sank back on the ground knowing that I was dying fast.[10]

Like many critically wounded American soldiers in Vietnam, Captain Cleland did not die. Speedy evacuation by a medivac helicopter, expert emergency care at a nearby field hospital, and timely movement to a highly specialized military hospital in Japan and then to Walter Reed Army Hospital in Washington, D.C., saved the day. Cleland lost both legs and his right arm, but he lived. By December, 1968, his physical wounds had healed. He was discharged from active duty and entered the Washington, D.C. Veterans Hospital for rehabilitation. Cleland writes of his first day in the VA Hospital:

> It was quickly impressed upon me that in the . . . VA a patient is known by his "claim" number, not his rank or branch of service. The word, I discovered, came from the fact that a veteran has to "claim" a wound or injury. . . . If the injury is the result of military service, a veteran supposedly gets priority treatment. My priority treatment this day resulted in a two-hour wait after which an attendant handed me a pair of light green pajamas.
>
> "You're going up to your ward now," he said. "You are to take no clothes, no personal effects, no food, no TV and no radio up there. Understand?" I nodded, wondering if I had been dropped off at a federal prison by mistake.
>
> An elevator carried me to a higher floor where I was wheeled into a large ward and pushed up next to an empty bed. I was stunned. Most of the men in the ward were 20 or more years older than I.
>
> Some stared at me like I was a man from Mars. Others blinked a couple of times and rolled over on their beds. It was obvious that these men had not the slightest inkling of what service in Vietnam had been all about. Within two and a half hours of leaving Walter Reed, I had been stripped of rank, denied the amenities . . . allowed at another government hospital just up the street and given no identification except for a number.
>
> I was scared. I had come here to get rehabilitated, but felt as if I had been sentenced to an old elephant burial ground. I expected the VA to be different but not this different.[11]

Despite this shaky start, Cleland did rehabilitate successfully at the VA Hospital. He enjoyed physical therapy and learned to swim. He learned to dress and care for himself, and how to get around in a wheelchair and use artifical limbs—formidable tasks for a triple amputee. By February, 1969, he moved out of the hospital into his own nearby apartment where he could continue his rehabilitation on an outpatient basis. He learned to drive a car.

In December, 1969, Peter Lassen, executive director of Paralyzed Veterans of America (PVA), invited Cleland to accompany him as a witness before a subcommittee of the Senate Committee on Labor and Public Welfare. Senator Alan Cranston (D-Calif.) chaired the hearings. The purpose of the hearings, which had begun in November and continued through January of 1970, was to assess the quality of medical care afforded Vietnam veterans by VA hospitals. Cranston, a World War II veteran who nonetheless was critical of American policy in Vietnam, had toured VA hospitals in response to complaints he had received from Vietnam veteran constituents in Los Angeles. He felt that special legislation, not forthcoming from the House Committee on Veterans Affairs, was required in order to implement within the VA the programs necessary to address the needs of Vietnam veterans. The hearings provided a forum for documenting these needs.

More than forty witnesses appeared before the committee, including Donald Johnson, national administrator of the VA. Cleland testified on December 16. He speculated that, had he received the same wounds in World War II or the Korean War , he almost certainly would have died. He recounted the swift evacuation by helicopter and the expert medical care he received throughout the chain of military hospitals. He contrasted this care with the care he and other Vietnam veterans received in VA hospitals:

> What this has meant to the stateside hospitals and the Veterans Administration is that they have had delivered to them by the most fantastic processes known to modern science, 19- and 20-year-old men with severe and sometimes totally disabling injuries. . . . Unfortunately, I did not find that the up-to-date rapidly applied medical techniques used in saving men on the battlefield had their counterparts in my rehabilitation and administrative processes. . . . When the severely disabled return from Vietnam, they face a rehabilitation process that is often based on World War II and Korean experience.[12]

Cleland concluded his testimony with a description of the psychological aspects of readjustment as he himself had experienced them:

> To the devastating psychological effect of getting maimed, paralyzed, or in some way unable to reenter American life as you left it, is the added psychological weight that it may not have been worth it, that the war may have been a cruel hoax, an American tragedy, that left a small minority of American males holding the bag.
>
> . . . [T]here is an automatic reaction to believe that what you did was worth it. You have every reason to believe that your sacrifice was worth it. So there is not an automatic reaction to self-pity. There is an automatic reaction to a determination to buckle down to the fact and get going with the program.
>
> . . . The inevitable psychological depression after injury, coupled with doubts that it may not have been worth it, comes months later like a series of secondary explosions long after the excitement of the battlefield is behind, the reinforcement of your comrades in arms a thing of the past, and the individual is left alone with his injury and his doubts. Anyone who deals with a Vietnam returnee, wounded or not, must understand this delayed, severe psychological symptom. And, in my opinion, more effort has to be made, especially by the VA, to insure that the small but se-

lect minority of Vietnam returnees in VA hospitals have adequate . . .
help . . . in readjusting to American life.[13]

No one hearing the testimony that day could have guessed that seven
years later in January, 1977, Cleland would be the first official appointment of a newly elected President of the United States. The position?
National director of the VA.

Operation RAW

VVAW sought to capitalize on the increasingly heated debate over war
atrocities. Reflecting some measure of Lifton's influence, VVAW leaders
decided to emphasize that atrocities by American troops took place routinely. The focus on atrocities served several purposes. To begin with,
there was some genuine concern that the war victimized the Vietnamese
people. More to the point, however, it was becoming apparent that
many Vietnam veterans felt confused and ashamed about their combat
experience. Many had witnessed or participated in acts of killing that
did not jibe with the their own idealized notions of how American
soldiers should act in war. Further, protests against the war left many of
them wondering if their experiences as purveyors and recipients of violent death had served any purpose. Public discussion provided an opportunity to expose the issues and assuage the guilt. From a political
standpoint, VVAW hoped that a public focus on these unpleasant aspects of the war would erode support for it. Like Lifton, and sometimes
as a result of discussions with him, VVAW leaders reasoned that fellow
Americans who found atrocities repulsive should demand an end to
U.S. military involvement.
Bill Crandell was one of the VVAW leaders who pondered this strategy. A VVAW chapter of sorts formed in Columbus, Ohio, after the My
Lai story broke. Crandell recalls:

My [initial] response to My Lai was, "This is an apparition, this is shock-
ing, this didn't happen." You know, I mean, I believed the story but I
thought this was way out of line. Nothing like this happened in my war. It
didn't meet my experience. And a professor . . . had another Vietnam vet
in one of his classes who was profoundly disturbed by [the story]. . . .
This guy had gone to [the professor] and said, "I don't know whether you
can help me but I need to see if we can pull some Vietnam vets together
just to talk about this."
So . . . they got a room on campus at the union and put up a flyer. . . .
And what astounded me was that everybody in the room had a story like
that. The common thread was essentially that people were killed for what
didn't seem like a good enough reason. And, the one in particular I re-

member, the guy was saying it was his first day with his unit, and this old man was coming down the road, and [they] yelled at him in English to halt, and he didn't halt, and they blew him away. And he said, "Well, maybe he didn't speak English, why did you do that?" And they turned him over and he had a grenade on him. But they didn't know that [when they shot him]. And each of these guys had a story like that. I was really shocked by it.[14]

That summer, leaders from the New York City chapter hatched the idea of a protest march during the 1970 Labor Day weekend. The plan, designated Operation RAW (Rapid American Withdrawal), called for VVAW members and anyone else who would join them to march from Morristown, New Jersey, to Valley Forge, Pennsylvania. Dressed in jungle fatigues and carrying toy M-16 rifles, they would cover about twenty miles per day. En route they would stage "guerrilla theater" that depicted war atrocities. Crandell called the VVAW national office and announced that the Columbus VVAW chapter wished to participate as a platoon. Recalls Crandell:

> The two leaders of the group were me, a platoon leader, and Art Fleisch, who had been a platoon sergeant in Vietnam. And everybody [in the Columbus chapter] was eager for us to continue to play those roles. . . . I contacted the national office and I said, "[The] Ohio Buckeye Army of Liberation wants to send a platoon on this!" And they said, "Absolutely!" Because nobody else really came as organized chapters, there weren't that many chapters as such, and mostly people just heard about it and came individually. We ended up being the demonstration platoon, marching up front.[15]

Crandell, Fleisch, and a woman friend traveled to New York City that summer to help plan the operation. They prepared leaflets, reconnoitered the route, and rehearsed the guerrilla theater incidents.

About 100 Vietnam veterans and fellow travelers began the march on September 4. Crandell's "Buckeye Platoon" led the way. En route the marchers staged incidents to the surprise, amusement, and anger of townspeople and passers-by. The *New York Times* account of the first day's events stated:

> While passing through [Bernardsville, New Jersey], the marchers attempted to demonstrate what they said it was actually like when American soldiers passed through a South Vietnamese village. . . . The marchers seized a private home just north of here and in a mock combat operation, terrorized its occupants, all of whom had agreed earlier to participate in the demonstration. . . . Less than an hour later, a "search and destroy" platoon moved ahead of the main column into the downtown section here. . . . The patrol seized a young woman who had been planted there

earlier in the day by the marchers and dragged her away, shouting ob-
scenities and abuse at her.[16]

After a similar demonstration on the following day in Flemington, New
Jersey, the marchers handed out flyers which read: "A U.S. infantry
company has just passed through here. If you had been Vietnamese, we
might have burned your house, shot you and your dog, raped your wife
and daughter, burned the town, and tortured its citizens."[17]

The demonstrators encountered hostility, particularly in rural Somer-
set county. Ernest Cummings, a forty-eight-year-old former paratrooper
and a veteran of the Battle of the Bulge in the Second World War, held a
large American flag across his chest, blocked the marchers path there,
and shouted: "You men are a disgrace to your uniforms. You're a disgrace to everything we stand for. You ought to go back to Hanoi."[18] A
woman, drinking coffee across the street from a staged incident in
Flemington, summed up the feelings of many on-lookers by saying, "If
these are the kind of soldiers we have in Vietnam, then we'd better give
up now."[19] Not all reactions were hostile; passing motorists occasionally
waved and raised two fingers in a peace salute.

On September 7, the marchers reached Valley Forge, Pennsylvania.
About 1,500 persons, mostly young people, gathered there to greet them
sympathetically and hear speeches by Representative Allard Lowenstein
(D-Pa.), movie stars Donald Sutherland and Jane Fonda, antiwar activist
Mark Lane, and black leader Charles Bevel. In Valley Forge, the
marchers also encountered a group of Vietnam veterans supporting
American military policy in Vietnam, and the two groups of veterans
traded curses and insults. The march ended at the Valley Forge VA
Hospital, where the marchers mingled with veterans who were patients
there. Crandell summed up the importance of this encounter:

> There were a lot of [Vietnam] vets [at the VA Hospital] there, mostly
> amputees who were terribly unhappy with the place. It was essentially set
> up as a place for World War II guys to die from alcoholism. And they could
> not get listened to, they could not get programs. At that time, it was totally
> inadequate. . . . That was one of the first places we got a focus, that the
> VA was part of the problem. . . . As far as they were concerned, we were
> expended brass and not even worth picking up.[20]

The New York City Rap Groups

Fresh from this venture, Jan Crumb of the New York City VVAW
chapter and national president of the few existing chapters wrote Robert

Lifton in November of 1970 seeking his advice and help on two related concerns. One was the desire to address "the severe psychological problems of many Vietnam veterans because of their experiences." The other desire was to oppose "the military policy of the war which results in war crimes and veterans' nightmares."[21] Lifton and fellow psychiatrist Chaim Shatan subsequently met with VVAW members in the New York City office. The veterans told them that they spent much of their time "rapping" with each other about the war and their lives since returning from it. They thought that they should formalize the rap sessions, and they invited Lifton and Shatan to join them, not as group therapists, but as coequals. The common thread between them would be their opposition to the war. They reasoned that the veterans and the psychiatrists could each bring special knowledge and experience to the process. Shatan recalls: "They said shrinks could join provided that we joined as peers. They knew more about the war than we did, and we knew more about what makes people tick."[22]

Shatan already had been involved in veterans' issues for many years. His father had fought in three wars—the Russo-Japanese War, the Balkan Wars, and the First World War—before moving his family from Poland to Canada. His father wrote short stories about his war experiences, and the younger Shatan translated some of them from Yiddish to English. Shatan attended medical school during the Second World War at McGill University and received thorough training in combat-related disorders. Shatan recalls of his work then:

> [In those days] we always took a military history. It was in working with World War II Canadian veterans that I first heard about a flashback. The vet called it a hallucination. He was a pilot who bombed a German submarine from the air. He saw a man who escaped from the submarine swimming in the water, but his orders were to keep circling the area to prevent rescue craft from reaching the scene. The German sailor eventually drowned before his eyes. That was his flashback. He saw the man swimming in the ocean, saw him drowning.[23]

In 1963, he accepted a faculty position in the postdoctoral psychoanalytic training program at New York University (NYU). In 1970, troubled by the war, Shatan considered moving his family back to Canada and traveled to Vancouver, British Columbia, to assess the feasibility. Participating in the rap group changed his mind. Shatan viewed this participation as a valuable way to oppose the war and to "help guys who were hurting." Within a month or so after the rap group's first meeting, Shatan circulated a memo to psychiatrists and psychoanalysts in the New York City area, soliciting help from other professionals who might wish to participate. The director of the NYU training program sympathized with Shatan's efforts and authorized his use of the program's letterhead stationary, staff, and copy equipment to aid rap-group activities.

The psychiatrists and veterans initially planned to meet on Saturday afternoons for two hours. The participants referred to each other by their first names, and they encouraged each other to describe the experiences and motivations that brought them to the group. This often was uncomfortable for both parties. The veterans often found it difficult and upsetting to express their feelings, and the psychiatrists were accustomed to analyzing the motivations of others without themselves being subjected to scrutiny. The first meetings, Lifton later wrote, were so emotionally charged by an "explosion of feeling" about the war that sessions usually lasted three or four hours.[24]

Jack Smith was one of those veterans who appeared at the first formal rap session. He served in Vietnam as a Marine in 1968 and 1969 and had been a firm believer in the policy of American military involvement. Unlike most American soldiers who served in Vietnam, he had studied Vietnamese history and the Vietnamese language before arriving in Vietnam. However, his experiences as a Marine led him to conclude that "whatever our intentions were, our policies had gone awry."[25] For Smith the final straw was a bizarre incident in which South Vietnamese troops fired Russian-made rockets into a Marine base camp in order to convince American commanders that the area was "too hot" and thereby get the Marines relocated somewhere else. In retaliation, the Marines rigged a fire direction plan to shoot a few artillery rounds back at the South Vietnamese compound. Smith recalls:

> As soon as I started firing on my allies, I said, "Fuck this shit, this is crazy . . . !" I really insisted that my troops do their job. I said, "Other people's lives depend on you." And all of the meaning kind of came apart for me. . . . I said, "We're playing some kind of game and we're just pawns in this thing. And whatever its good intention initially, I mean, the other side aren't the good guys, but this is crazy business here and I don't want any God damn part of it any more."[26]

After returning home, Smith put the war out of his mind. He enrolled at the University of Connecticut but had trouble settling down. In particular, he had frequent flare-ups with his boss at a construction firm where he worked. Shortly after the invasion of Cambodia by U.S. and South Vietnamese troops in April 1970, he again started thinking about the war. He put together a slide show from pictures he had taken in Vietnam, prepared a rock music soundtrack to accompany the slides, and presented the show to interested church and veterans' groups as a

way of telling them about the war. "[I was] not against the war, necessarily," he explains; "I was talking about being for what we stood for but
against how it was turning out." In December 1970, he saw a VVAW ad
in *Playboy* magazine and decided to join the organization. (*Playboy* had
donated the space for the one-page ad as a show of support for VVAW.)

Smith's initial trip to VVAW's New York City office coincided with the
first formal rap session. Almost immediately, he moved from Storrs,
Connecticut, to New Haven so he could commute weekly to the rap
sessions in New York City. Smith explains what participation in the rap
group meant to him at the time:

> When I started in the rap groups, I began to understand why I felt [out of
> sorts], okay . . . ? We had these shrinks, but we weren't really in therapy.
> We were trying to explore what we were feeling about the war. . . . What
> was important for me at that period was . . . that it was a safe place for me
> to talk, okay, with other people where we could sort it out. . . . We weren't
> thinking of ourselves as victims, but rather thinking, "How are we going
> to get our act together so we're not undone by our feelings about what's
> going on, and how are we going to convey what's going on to the general
> public?"[27]

Similarly, Vietnam veteran Arthur Egendorf, who had served in Saigon
in 1968 and 1969 as an intelligence officer and who had joined the rap
group in December 1970, later wrote about what drew him and other
veterans to the rap groups:

> The rap groups became known as a place where you could tell your sto-
> ry. . . . Over and over . . . the stories . . . reveal [the] discovery of some
> crucial ingredient, hard to name, that was missing on our side of the war.
> And because it wasn't there, no amount of good intention, American
> spirit, and material and military support to the people of South Vietnam
> could keep us from doing evil, and ultimately defeating ourselves. . . .
> Not all veterans talk this way, of course. . . . But the vets who came to the
> early rap groups brought with them, as an overwhelming residue from the
> war, a deep demoralization and loss of trust in their leaders, in the cause,
> and in the person they were before going in. Years before the humiliating
> retreat from Saigon in April 1975 . . . , and before the full exposure of
> offical deceit and confusion in the Pentagon Papers, released in 1971,
> many guys just knew.[28]

Hence, the rap groups differed both from conventional group therapy
and from various forms of "street corner" psychiatry.[29] Conventional
therapy assumed that psychiatrists had privileged knowledge and status, that the group members were patients in need of treatment, and
that patients achieved healing by projecting onto the psychiatrist the

conflicts originally experienced as infants with parents. In the rap
groups, the psychiatrists adopted with some difficulty a style of participation that avoided this conventional "transference" approach to treatment. Further, unlike most other varieties of street-corner psychiatry,
the rap group regulars—veteran and psychiatrist alike—intended to go
public with their experiences and conclusions as a means of protesting
the war. For many of them, the personal healing and political functions
were flip sides of the same coin.

The Winter Soldier Investigation

In January 1971, VVAW staged the "Winter Soldier Investigation" in a
Howard Johnson's motel in Detroit.[30] Originally, Mark Lane and Jane
Fonda had put up money to establish an undertaking called the Concerned Citizens Inquiry, and they hired Jeremy Rifkin and Todd Ensign
as organizers. They sought to film testimony about atrocities by U.S.
military personnel in Vietnam and to distribute it for use in protesting
the war. The purpose was to show that the killing of civilians at My Lai
was not an aberration but a direct result of conduct fostered by American
military policy in Vietnam. Rifkin and Ensign asked VVAW for help in
locating witnesses, especially veterans willing to testify that they themselves had committed "war crimes" or had seen them committed by
others.

During preparations for the inquiry, a split developed between Rifkin
and VVAW. Antiwar activists such as Rifkin and Ensign generally had a
much broader political agenda than did antiwar veterans, including a
structural critique of capitalism and a blanket condemnation of American foreign policy. With some exceptions, VVAW's position focused
more narrowly on ending American involvement in Vietnam. Jack Smith
recalls:

> We had these battles between people who . . . had fixed left-wing posi-
> tions and the group of veterans who were opposed to policy in Vietnam
> but were not . . . on the left. I mean, we weren't going to be part of any
> organization with boiler-plate rhetoric, okay?[31]

Because of the strife, VVAW, with backing from Lane and Fonda, became
the sole sponsor of the event and provided all the witnesses. VVAW
redesignated it the Winter Soldier Investigation. One hundred fifteen
Vietnam veterans and thirteen others, including Robert Lifton, provided
testimony. They described the killing of civilians, the mutilation of enemy dead, and the destruction of crops and villages. Lane and Fonda

filmed the testimony and arranged for its distribution. With a notable exception or two (such as a *Life* magazine article), the event received very limited coverage by the national media.

The highest ranking officer to testify was Lieutenant Colonel Anthony Herbert, a twenty-three year veteran of the U.S. Army and the army's most highly decorated enlisted man in Korea. Herbert had served in Vietnam as a battalion commander and had brought charges against his superior officers for covering up atrocities. He believed that incidents of the sort described in the Detroit testimony occurred in Vietnam because senior commanders tacitly condoned them by failing to aggressively condemn and reprimand such behavior. In an interview for *Life* magazine several months later, Herbert explained:

> It's easy to get soldiers to do what's right. You just have to tell them. When I first joined my battalion in Vietnam, in February 1969, they were getting R & R (rest and recuperation) leaves for kills. I changed that. I gave them R & R for live prisoners. They're worth information. . . . When . . . I saw the torture that went on in my battalion . . . I talked with other officers about it. They all told me, "That's the way it is. You can't antagonize the big dragons . . . or you're gone. . . ." [I say] this stuff would stop if we'd hang a couple of senior commanders. If it's no longer condoned, then it will cease.[32]

The VVAW strategy of emphasizing atrocities to disparage American military policy in Vietnam—an increasingly favored way to protest the war—aroused more than feelings about the war itself. It also stirred the sentiment that many Vietnam veterans themselves were worthy of contempt. Even those in sympathy with what VVAW was trying to accomplish sometimes found it difficult to accept and make sense of the stories without despising those who reported them. Bill Crandell, a participant in both Operation RAW and the Investigation, describes the turmoil that the testimony created within himself:

> There were things that were very hard. I really loved these [Vietnam veterans], and some of them had really done as well as seen some horrible things. . . . And then I shuddered. I had this sort of conflict between loving these guys and hating what they had been involved in. And I either had to put myself superior to them or share the guilt with them. And I chose the latter. And that was very hard. In a lot of ways, I took on some guilt that wasn't mine and became very depressed.[33]

Not all people resolved the dilemma as Crandell did. The subtleties of Lifton's explanation for atrocities—and the logic of his plea that those who supported or condoned the war should share the guilt for these

activities—probably were lost on most people. Repulsed by these stories, many people directed their discomfort and blame squarely at the
veterans themselves. For example, Sarah Haley recalls:

> Again, this attitude surfaced among clinicians. One therapist told me that
> you have to "love" a patient to treat him. Not love in any sexual sense, but
> in terms of caring and compassion. He said to me, "How can you love
> these murderers? How can you possibly care about them . . . ?" With such
> a negative reaction, the feelings of the therapist make treatment impossi-
> ble. You have interaction between one degraded worm and one perfect
> person.
>
> I would love to think I would have held onto my moral undershorts and
> not done many of the things our soldiers have done in combat. But I don't
> know for a fact that I would have been able to do that. That realization
> makes me humble. . . . They have been tested . . . , they know the best
> and the worst about themselves. They have no illusions. Our perfect ther-
> apist still has the illusion that he couldn't possibly do anything they did.
> Now that is an illusion![34]

During the week of the investigation, the United States and South
Vietnamese military launched Operation Dewey Canyon II, described
by policymakers as "a limited search and destroy incursion into Cambodia and Laos." Since many VVAW leaders from cities across the country already were together in Detroit, the organization was nicely situated
to plan its response. They turned their attention from the investigation
to the question of how to protest the invasion, which they saw as an
expansion of the war. They proposed a march on Washington, D.C. that
would attract as many Vietnam veterans as they could muster. But turning out in numbers called for planning, organization, and logistics. To
provide time for these concerns, they set a date three months later in
April and designated the march, Operation Dewey Canyon III, "a limited incursion into the country of Congress."[35]

Operation Dewey Canyon III

During the week of April 19, 1971, more than a thousand Vietnam
veterans arrived in Washington, D.C. as part of VVAW's protest. One of
the first issues was a practical one: where would the protesting veterans
sleep? An initial ruling by District Court Judge George Hart prohibited
them from camping overnight on the Mall near the Capital. VVAW, with
former U.S. attorney general Ramsey Clark serving as their legal counsel, filed an appeal. Clark argued that the camping ban curtailed the

opportunity for free speech. President Nixon's attorney general, Patrick Grey, countered that the government had no obligation to provide sleeping accomodations for citizens who come to Washington, D.C. to exercise their right of free speech. On April 19, Judge Harold Leventhal ruled in favor of the veterans, citing as precedent an earlier Boy Scout Jamboree encampment on the Mall.[36] The following day, Chief Justice Warren Burger reversed Leventhal's decision, thereby allowing the District Court Judge Hart's initial ruling to stand. Officials and police informed veterans that they could not camp or sleep on the Mall.

While these deliberations were underway, veterans carried out one phase of their planned protest by reenacting mock search-and-destroy missions at the Old Senate Office Building. Their "guerrilla theater" received considerable coverage by newspaper and television reporters. For example, a front-page account in the *Washington Post* stated:

> [W]hile scores of tourists looked on in astonishment . . . three girls wearing coolie hats attempted to run away from a squad of "infantrymen" armed with toy M-16 rifles. With a burst of simulated automatic firing of the weapons, the girls clutched their stomachs and burst plastic bags of red paint that splattered grotesquely over the Capital steps. "It's disgusting. It's horrible," said one middle-aged woman as she turned away. "Waste 'em! Waste 'em! Get the body count!" cried some of the mock raiders as their toy rifles cracked and the "victims" screamed. At the same time, the squad leader admonished spectators to stay out of the way of the enactment for the benefit of television cameramen.[37]

The more pressing problem, however, was what to do about Justice Burger's decision. The veterans assembled in state delegations on the Mall and voted 480 to 400 to defy the ban. The police informally put out word that the veterans could remain but asked them not to pitch tents or burn campfires. "We are not going in there at one in the morning and pick up some wounded veteran and throw him into the street," Police Lieutenant William Kinsey explained to a reporter.[38] Nevertheless, many veterans expected to be arrested, and many had their girlfriends, wives, and children leave the Mall to sleep elsewhere that night. Despite a steady rainfall, about 600 veterans stayed on the Mall in sleeping bags and ponchos. The following day, the Justice Department opened negotiations with the veterans about possible alternative campsites. The veterans rejected parkland space at Bolling Air Force Base and near RFK Stadium, saying they considered both sites too remote. Later in the evening, District Court Judge George Hart reversed his own initial ban against camping and criticized the Nixon administration for "degrading the federal judiciary" by taking the case to the U.S. Supreme Court.[39]

Another controversy concerned the numbers of protestors who were
Vietnam veterans. Rumor had it that officials, including President Richard Nixon, doubted that more than a third of them were Vietnam veterans. (To which one veteran retorted, "Only 30 percent of us believe
Richard Nixon is President!") Anticipating this problem, VVAW organizers had asked veterans to bring photocopies of their discharge papers
or other such evidence of Vietnam service. Disabled veterans, missing
arms or legs, were present in visible numbers. Many wore service ribbons, decorations for valor, and Purple Hearts on their fatigues. However, there were some demonstrators, similary dressed, who admitted
to never having served in Vietnam or to never having been in the military. Also, organizers from the antiwar movement who were not veterans huddled with VVAW leaders to talk strategy. However, the
protestors successfully established cordial relations with the police because so many could convince policemen that they were Vietnam veterans. Bill Crandell recalls:

> [The] D.C. police had a very high proportion of . . . Vietnam vets who
> had taken advantage of the early-out program to become cops. . . . We
> leafleted them on the basis of, we're not coming here to call anybody a pig,
> we're coming out to demonstrate about the war. They were still very
> suspicious but all week long there were cops stopping by our camp and
> seeing some guy with their own unit patch. You know, "4th Division!
> What battalion? Oh, really, then did you know so-and-so?" And it was
> clear in a couple of days that we were who we said we were and not just
> Marxist students claiming to be veterans. That had a major impact on the
> successes. The police treated us well.[40]

A second strategy consisted of meeting with members of Congress
and urging them to pass legislation requiring an immediate withdrawal
of all American troops from Vietnam. VVAW leader John Kerry—the son
of a former State Department lawyer, graduate of Yale University, and
former Navy lieutenant (j.g.) in Vietnam (and now Senator from
Massachusetts)—attracted the most attention from the media. Senator
William Fullbright, chairman of the Senate Committee on Foreign Relations, invited Kerry to appear before the committee on April 24 and
present his views. Kerry told the Committee that American troops had
been sent to die in Vietnam "for the biggest nothing in history."[41] Veterans, he said, were now protesting the war because their own experiences told them that it was a civil war in which "the average
[Vietnamese] didn't know the difference between communism and democracy," and that the tactics used by the United States involved "incredible brutality against civilians and soldiers alike." He concluded by
saying, "Each day someone has to give up his life so that the U.S.

doesn't have to admit what the world already knows, that we made a mistake." In response, several Republican senators defended President Nixon's refusal to withdraw unilaterally. Senator William Saxbe (R-Ohio) stated:

> I think that by the end of 1972 practially all American military personnel will be out of there [Vietnam]. I hope sooner, in fact. I reject, however, the contention that the President should set a definite date for removal of all American troops. To so telegraph our punches to the other side is both unrealistic and, I submit, ridiculous.[42]

The climax of the week occurred Friday, April 23, when VVAW staged the "medal turn-in" ceremony. On the last day, veterans gathered at the Capital Building to return their medals awarded for wounds, valor, and meritorious service as a poignant symbol of protest. The original plan was to return the medals in body bags. However, when the veterans discovered that the authorities had built a fence on the Capital steps, they decided instead to throw their medals back. Jack Smith, who participated as a VVAW organizer from Connecticut, states:

> I gave the opening talk for the medal turn-in ceremony. Just organizing that and running it, I mean, it was probably the most powerful moment of my life. Because we knew how much those medals meant to us. And yet we were so upset with the policies that (pause)—You know, I can still hear the dings of those medals, the Bronze Stars and the Silver Stars bouncing off the statue of [fourth chief justice of the Supreme Court] John Marshall, [and] the Purple Hearts, behind the barricades. And R.S. throwing away an Air Medal saying, "This is for lieutenant so-and-so, and this is for captain so-and-so who died." Ohh, it was incredible![43]

And Bill Crandell remembers:

> In psychological terms, it was enormously cathartic. All of us who did, it was if we had a device for throwing our sins away. You felt it, it was very powerful. . . . [A]n enormous sense of freedom went with that week. Wherever we went, we were free. That last day, standing there waiting for our turn to throw our medals back . . . it was a sort of sense of, all you have to do is do what you want to do. You know, we fought for our country and our country failed to recognize it.[44]

The Nixon Administration had begun withdrawing American combat troops from Vietnam in 1970. American involvement in Vietnam officially ended eight months after Dewey Canyon III on January 27, 1973. With the withdrawal of the last American combat troops, VVAW disintegrated rapidly. Once the troops were home, many VVAW members saw no need for further protest. Some however remained active; Americans were no longer being killed, but the war was still going on. Many of those who remained active gravitated toward more radical politics, and the organization splintered into warring regional and ideological factions. Some turned their attention, individually or through later collective initiatives, to the considerable readjustment problems that lay ahead for Vietnam veterans.

Acknowledgments

Much of the material in this chapter was published earlier in Wilbur Scott, "Vietnam Veterans Against the War: the Politics of Antiwar Protest," in *Perspectives on Social Problems*, vol. 4, ed. James Holstein and Gale Miller (Greenwich, Conn.: JAI Press, 1992), 229–252.

Notes

1. Douglas Robinson, "100,000 Rally at U.N. against Vietnam War," *New York Times*, 16 April 1967, A1.

2. Charles Moskos, Jr., *The American Enlisted Man* (New York: Russell Sage Foundation, 1970); Thomas Thayer, *War without Fronts: The American Experience in Vietnam* (Boulder, Colo.: Westview Press, 1985).

3. Within a week after the Tet Offensive, Bill Crandell saw an ad placed in the *New Republic* by VVAW. He wrote the New York City office for information. The reply informed him that "there were two guys in the entire Midwest that were members" and that he was one of them. The New York City chapter designated the two of them "Midwest Coordinators." Over the next several months, the two of them, and a handful of others who joined them on and off, participated in campus antiwar demonstrations as interested persons rather than an organization. William Crandell, telephone interview with author, 16 January 1989, Albany, New York.

4. Carl Bernstein, "Viet Vets Camped on Mall Resemble Basic Training Outfit," *Washington Post*, 22 April 1971, A-14.

5. Sarah Haley, personal interview with author, 25 October 1988, Dallas, Texas.

6. Sarah Haley, telephone interview with author, 9 November 1988, Somerville, Mass.

7. Robert Jay Lifton, "Why Civilians Are War Victims," *U.S. News and World Report*, 15 December 1969, 25; Robert Jay Lifton, "Guilt of the Survivor, A Profile of the Vietnam Veteran," testimony before the Subcommittee on Veterans' Affairs of the Committee on Labor and Public Welfare, United States Senate, Vol. 6, 27 January 1970.

8. Gilbert Steiner, *The State of Welfare* (Washington, D.C.: The Brookings Institution, 1971), 254; also cited in David Bonior, Stephen Champlin, and Timothy Kolly, *The Vietnam Veteran: A History of Neglect* (New York: Praeger, 1984), 135.

9. Frank Kuramoto, "Federal Mental Health Programs for the Vietnam Veter-

an," in *Strangers At Home: Vietnam Veterans Since the War*, ed. Charles Figley and Seymour Leventman (New York: Praeger, 1980), 293–304.

10.   Max Cleland, *Strong Broken at the Places* (Atlanta: Cherokee, 1986), 39.

11.   Ibid, 97–98.

12.   Max Cleland, testimony before the Subcommittee on Veterans' Affairs, Senate Committee on Labor and Public Welfare, Vol. 6, 27 January 1970, 270.

13.   Ibid.

14.   Crandell, telephone interview, 16 January 1989.

15.   Ibid.

16.   Ronald Sullivan, "Veterans for Peace Simulate the War," *New York Times*, 5 September 1970, A6.

17.   Ronald Sullivan, "War Protestors Meet Opposition," *New York Times*, 6 September 1970, A8.

18.   Sullivan, "Veterans for Peace, A6.

19.   Sullivan, "War Protesters," A8.

20.   Crandell, telephone interview, 16 January 1989.

21.   Quoted in Robert Jay Lifton, *Home from the War: Neither Victims nor Executioners* (New York: Basic Books, 1973), 75.

22.   Chaim Shatan, personal interview with author, 24 October 1988, Dallas, Texas.

23.   Ibid.

24.   Lifton, *Home from the War*, 75.

25.   Jack Smith, telephone interview with author, 22 December 1988, Cleveland Ohio.

26.   Ibid.

27.   Ibid.

28.   Arthur Egendorf, *Healing from the War: Trauma and Transformation after Vietnam* (Boston: Houghton Mifflin, 1985), 91, 104–105.

29.   Lifton, *Home from the War*, 80–81.

30.   The designation, "Winter Soldier Investigation," is drawn from Tom Paine's description of the winter of 1776 at Valley Forge: "The summer soldier and the sunshine patriot will in this crisis, shrink from the service of his country; but he that stands it now, deserves the love and thanks of man and woman."

31.   Smith, telephone interview, 22 December 1988.

32.   Quoted in Donald Jackson, "Confessions of 'Winter Soldiers,'" *Life*, 9 July 1971, 22–27.

33.   Crandell, telephone interview, 16 January 1989.

34.   Haley, personal interview, 25 October, 1988.

35.   "Protest: A Week against the War," *Time*, 3 May 1971, 11.

36.   Sanford Unger, "Vets Can Use Mall, Court Quickly Rules," *Washington Post*, 20 April 1971, A-12.

37.   Sanford Unger and William Claiborne, "Vets Camp on Mall Banned by Burger," *Washington Post*, 21 April 1971, A1, A8.

38.   "Vets Disobey Court Order, Sleep on Mall," *Washington Post*, 22 April 1971, A1.

39.   William Claiborne and Sanford Unger, "Judge Lifts Ban on Vets, Scolds U.S.," *Washington Post*, 23 April 1971, A1.

40.   Crandell, telephone interview, 16 January 1989.

41.   "Fullbright Panel Hears Antiwar Vet," *Washington Post*, 23 April 1971, A4.

42.   Ibid.

43.   Smith, telephone interview, 22 December 1988.

44.   Crandell, telephone interview, 16 January 1989.

POST-VIETNAM SYNDROME

"The so-called Post-Vietnam Syndrome confronts us with the unconsum-
mated grief of soldiers—impacted grief, in which an encapsulated, never-
ending past deprives the present of meaning."

Chaim Shatan, psychoanalyst

Post-traumatic stress disorder (PTSD) appeared as a diagnosis in the
American Psychiatric Association's (APA) third edition of its *Diagnostic
and Statistical Manual of Mental Disorders, DSM-III*, in 1980. Used largely
by practicing psychiatrists as a classification scheme for keeping records
and processing diverse administrative work (e.g., insurance claims)
both within psychiatry and in its dealings with outsiders, the manual
also stands as an official map of mental illness and disorder in the
society. It contains, in effect, what it is possible to suffer in the way of
problems psychiatrists recognize and treat. The description of PTSD in
DSM-III reads as follows:

> The essential feature is the development of characteristic symptoms
> following a psychologically traumatic event. . . . The characteristic symp-
> toms involve reexperiencing the traumatic event; numbing of responsive-
> ness to, or reduced involvement with, the external world; and a variety of
> autonomic, dysphoric, or cognitive symptoms.

> The stressor producing this syndrome would evoke significant symptoms
> of distress in most people, and is generally outside the range of such
> common experiences as simple bereavement, chronic illness, business
> losses, or marital conflict. The trauma may be experienced alone (rape or
> assault) or in the company of groups of people (military combat). Stressors
> producing this disorder include natural disasters (floods, earthquakes),
> accidental man-made disasters (car accidents with serious physical injury,
> airplane crashes, large fires), or deliberate man-made disasters (bombing,
> torture, death camps). . . .

> The traumatic event may be experienced in a variety of ways. Commonly
> the individual has recurrent painful, intrusive recollections of the event or
> recurrent dreams or nightmares during which the event is reex-

perienced. . . . Diminished responsiveness to the external world, referred
to as "psychic numbing" or "emotional anesthesia," usually begins soon
after the traumatic event. . . . After experiencing the stressor, many develop symptoms of excessive autonomic arousal, such as hyperalertness, ex-
aggerated startle response, and difficulty falling asleep.[1]

Chapters 2 and 3 describe how PTSD came to be an official psychiatric
disorder and examine the work done by diverse people that culminated
in its appearance in *DSM-III*. This story raises and examines questions
about the normal experience and response of soldiers to warfare. The
controversy over what is normal focused typically on what is abnormal.
I use the term "war neurosis" to refer to the general category of mental
disorders associated with warfare. However, observers have used many
labels to refer to war neurosis: shell shock, combat fatigue, gross stress
reaction, post-Vietnam syndrome, post-combat disorder, catastrophic
stress disorder, and post-traumatic stress disorder. With the PTSD diagnosis, psychiatrists now say it is "normal" for the horrors of war to
traumatize people; war neurosis, or PTSD, occurs when this trauma is
not recognized and is left untreated. Diverse champions of this new
diagnosis—among them Vietnam veterans and psychiatrists sympathetic to them—brought it to light as a discovery of what was present but
had previously been unseen.

This process occurred in reverse for homosexuality, which had previously been labeled a psychiatric disorder but then ceased to exist as
an official diagnosis.[2] Like the disappearance of homosexuality from
DSM-II, the story of how PTSD appeared in *DSM-III* is one that belies
the cool, clinical language describing the manual's diagnoses and syndromes. Psychiatrist Robert Spitzer, director of the APA Task Force on
Nomenclature that prepared the new volume and a central figure in the
homosexuality controversy in the APA, notes in *DSM-III*'s introduction
that each successive draft aroused "alarm, despair, excitement, [and]
joy" in the psychiatric community.[3] Similarly, the struggle for recognition of PTSD by its champions was profoundly political, and displays
the full range of negotiation, coalition formation, strategizing, and
struggle.

The Early History of War Neurosis

Observers of warfare have commented throughout the centuries on
emotional problems stemming from combat. However, the first documentation of war neurosis as a medical condition occurred during the
Civil War. Military leaders and the soldiers themselves sometimes re-

ferred to the depression and listlessness that afflicted many troops in that war as "soldier's heart." William Hammond, Surgeon General of the Union Army, formally diagnosed the condition as "nostalgia" and reported an incidence of about 3 per 1,000 troops. Civil War military records also show an incidence of about 20 per 1,000 of "paralysis" and 6 per 1,000 of "insanity."[4]

Military physicians reported similar disorders and rates for the Franco-Prussian, Spanish-American, Russo-Japanese, and Boer Wars. Also, several psychiatrists in noncombat settings who treated victims from European industrial accidents advanced a distinction between traumatic neurosis and organic syndromes. Charcot, for instance, argued that otherwise unharmed victims of railway accidents often suffered disorders as a result of "psychonervous commotion."

During World War I, armies inflicted massive casualities on each other with sophisticated weaponry, especially machine guns and artillery. Observers coined the term "shell shock" to denote the dazed, disoriented state many soldiers experienced on the battlefield. Physicians commonly attributed the condition to unseen physiological damage caused by exploding artillery shells. This position was intuitively satisfying and gained further acceptance after physicians found blood in the spinal fluid of some patients. British physician, Sir Arthur Hurst, for example, observed:

> In such cases, there is an organic basis, which consists of the more or less evanescent changes in the central nervous system, resulting from the concussion caused by aerial compression, to which is often added concussion of the head or spine caused by the sandbags of a falling parapet or by the patient being blown into the air and falling heavily on to his head or back.[5]

However, physicians often found the same symptoms among soldiers who had not experienced artillery barrages. This contributed to the suspicion, especially in military quarters, that shell shock was a variety of cowardice and malingering. Many military physicians and leaders also believed that those who "cracked" on the battlefield were weaklings and riffraff who had been marginally adjusted before the war experience. Conversely, the argument went, men who perservered in combat were made of sterner stuff. Officials of this mind used strategies ranging from hypnosis to torture to deal with the problem. One method in a French detention center consisted of galvanic currents administered from an overhead trolley with long connecting wires running the length of the room, "thus making the patient unable to run away from the current that is destined to cure him."[6]

In 1917, the United States entered the war and Thomas Salmon was appointed the senior psychiatric consultant for American forces in France.[7] Following the French example, he assigned a psychiatrist to each U.S. division and established procedures for treating war neurosis as quickly and as close to the front lines as possible. Treatment consisted of several days of creature comforts and the firm expectation that the soldier return to duty. The program directors considered it an immediate success: 65 percent of those treated returned to duty on the front lines. However, the program was fully in operation only a few months when the war ended.

Shortly after World War I, Sigmund Freud appeared as an expert witness in Vienna for a government inquiry into the mistreatment of wounded soldiers by Austrian military physicians. He argued that shell shock was psychological rather than physical in origin. War neurosis, he believed, occurred when catastrophic, incomprehensible events overwhelmed the psyche. Significantly, he distinguished the traumatic neurosis of war from the more common neuroses which have their origins in childhood. His recommended treatment for both was psychoanalysis. He also wrote of a more general ethical dilemma, war melancholy, produced by conflicting impulses within the personality between the "war ego" and the "peace ego." As other well-known psychiatrists emphasized the psychological origins of breakdown in the combat zone, physiological explanations of shell shock fell into disfavor.

However, the contention that war neurosis afflicted weaklings persisted, especially in military quarters. During the Second World War, the military sought to screen out marginally adjusted inductees. Draft boards in the United States declared more than one million men psychologically unfit to fight. However, the screening program did not eliminate war neurosis. For example, the U.S. First Army in Europe reported about 102 psychiatric casualties per 1,000 troops, and during one period in 1942, the number of soldiers discharged from the Army on psychiatric grounds exceeded the number of new inductees reporting for duty.[8] These developments produced a new round of speculation. Observers noted that soldiers who became psychiatric casualties were those who had passed screening standards, and some were seasoned troops who heretofore had fought bravely. Medical personnel, and the troops themselves, therefore called the condition "combat fatigue" and posited that "every man had his breaking point." Still, some military men saw it as cowardice. Major General Paul Hawley, Chief Surgeon of the U.S. Army in 1944, declared, "If every soldier knew that he would be executed for cowardice, for malingering, or for a self-inflicted wound, the vast majority of the weaklings would choose the more favorable odds offered in facing the enemy."[9]

In the effort to prevent war neurosis by culling out the unfit, the Salmon program for treating psychiatric casualties had been forgotten. In 1944, the military began the Salmon program anew. Each division received a psychiatrist and provided an aid station to treat psychiatric casualties as close to the front lines as possible. Besides providing rest and recuperation, the psychiatric teams made clear the expectation that those with combat fatigue would return quickly to front-line duty. They also used sodium pentothal and hypnosis to encourage soldiers to talk about their experiences and, if necessary, group therapy sessions to reinstill the will to fight. As in the First World War, official casualty figures declined, suggesting that the procedures reduced the loss of combat troops to psychiatric breakdown.

In 1945, psychiatrist William Menninger, a special consultant to the Surgeon General, appointed a commission of civilian psychiatrists to study more closely the nature of psychiatric casualties in combat. After an extensive tour of the Eurpean theater, the commission offered its tentative assessment:

> [T]his picture of psychological disorganization does not correspond, either in its moderate or its extreme form, to any recognized or established psychiatric syndrome . . . it certainly is not merely a state of exhaustion . . . it certainly is not a neurosis in the ordinary sense . . . it certainly cannot be adquately described as anxiety or fear. . . . It comes closer to a situational psychosis than anything else but its subsequent clinical course is quite different.[10]

The commission also concluded that several factors—lack of effective leadership, loss of comrades, killing of enemy soldiers, poor morale, miserable living conditions—may work cumulatively to produce emotional breakdown in combat troops.

Other studies conducted by sociologists and psychologists for the military during World War II addressed the other side of the issue: what makes soldiers fight effectively? Much of this research emphasized that personal attributes, such as a strong sense of patriotism and duty, produce an effective fighting man. However, Shils and Janowitz's study of German prisoners of war concluded that small group dynamics, not personality processes, held the key to understanding combat effectiveness:

> It appears that a soldier's ability to resist is a function of the capacity of his . . . squad or section to avoid social disintegration. When the indiviudal's immediate group . . . met his basic organic needs, offered him affection and esteem from both comrades and officers, supplied him with a sense of power and adequately regulated his relations with authority, the

element of self-concern in battle, which would lead to the disruption of the
effective functioning of his primary group, was minimized.[11]

Within five years after the end of the Second World War, the Korean
War broke out. Most psychiatrists who served in the Second World War
by then had returned to civilian life, and the military again was ill prepared to deal with war neurosis. Early in the Korean War, the military
laid plans for a large psychiatric facility in Japan to provide the first line
of treatment. The rate of psychiatric casualities was about 50 per 1,000
troops and accounted for nearly one-fourth of all evacuations from the
battlefield in Korea. To reduce this figure, Albert Glass, a consultant to
the Surgeon General and a psychiatrist who had served in the Second
World War, persuaded the military to establish psychiatric centers in
Korea within each division and to reintroduce the Salmon treatment
procedures that had worked effectively in the previous wars. With these
changes, official rates of psychiatric casualties declined to about 30 per
1,000 troops.

War Neurosis in *DSM-I* and *DSM-II*

In 1952, the APA published the first edition of its physician's desk
reference for psychiatrists, *DSM-I*. Drawing on the work of Abram Kardiner[12] and other psychiatrists who served in the military during the
Second World War, *DSM-I* contained the entry "gross stress reaction."
The editors said the reaction could occur among soldiers in combat, even
among those who showed no previous history of mental problems.
They distinguished it from a neurosis or psychosis and described it as a
temporary condition produced by extreme environmental stress. The
reaction, they concluded, should disappear after removing the individual from combat.

This diagnosis departed from relevant research on two points.
Grinker and Spiegel, who studied the reactions to combat by soldiers in
the Second World War, had noted that many reactions did not occur on
the battlefield but erupted afterwards.[13] Their study, and Kardiner's,
also revealed that symptoms could persist for months or even years.
These observations suggested a need to recognize "delayed" and
"chronic" components of gross stress reaction.

The United States sent combat troops to Vietnam in 1965. In contrast
to previous wars, an updated Salmon program was firmly in place from
the very start of Vietnam War. The military command provided each
battalion with medical personnel trained to treat psychiatric disorders,
and assigned a psychiatrist and staff to each infantry and marine divi-

sion. These personnel dealt with troops experiencing psychiatric diffi-culties as close to combat areas as possible with the firm expectation that the troops would return quickly to duty. The rate of breakdown was about 5 per 1,000 troops between 1965 and 1967. Military leaders and psychiatrists lauded the results. Military psychiatry appeared to have licked the problem.

Coincidentally, the APA had begun work on the second edition of the *Diagnostic and Statistical Manual* (*DSM-II*). Psychiatrists Paul Wilson and Robert Spitzer were responsible for assembling the materials and for writing the final draft under the direction of Ernest Gruenberg. *DSM-II* was to modernize the American psychiatric nomenclature and to bring it into line with the international system of classification. Psychiatrist Peter Bourne's writings expressed the dominant, though not unchallenged, view of war neurosis within the APA, culminating in his 1970 book, *Men, Stress, and Vietnam*. Bourne had served in Vietnam during 1965 and 1966 as a team member from the Walter Reed Army Institute of Research. The Institute directed him to study psychiatric casualties among United States troops. In Vietnam, business was so slow that Bourne "elected to spend part of [his] time investigating areas quite removed from combat itself."[14]

When the APA published *DSM-II* in 1968, it included previously un-specified disorders and omitted several that had appeared in *DSM-I*. One of the dropouts was gross stress reaction. Hence, *DSM-II* contained no specific listing for a psychiatric disorder produced by combat. The editors suggested that psychiatrists might code symptoms previously associated with gross stress reaction under "adjustment reaction to adult life." A likely explanation is that those writing *DSM-II* had no firsthand experience with war neurosis from World War II or the Korean War, and initial indications from respected psychiatrists in Vietnam were that the standard nomenclature covered the range of disorders they encoun-tered there.[15]

Some psychiatrists thought otherwise. For example, Archibald and Tuddenham conducted fifteen- and twenty-year follow-up studies of veterans.[16] They reaffirmed the significance of a diagnosis for war neu-rosis and documented the persistence of symptoms among those who had experienced combat stress during World War II and the Korean War. They also noted reports of similar findings in parallel studies of concentration camp survivors. Finally, they also suggested a treatment strategy tailored to the diagnosis:

[C]ombat was experienced in a group setting and can best be abreacted in one. Verbal reports of these men emphasize the intense, symbolic relation-ships of the combat unit, which when dissolved leave a feeling of pur-

poselessness and and estrangement from those who have not shared the
overwhelming emotions of combat. For these men, we deliberately recre-
ate a "band of brothers," and foster the abreaction which they have hither-
to assiduously avoided.[17]

However, Archibald and Tuddenham, and other psychiatrists who
shared their views, did not realize the status of gross stress reaction in
DSM-II was in doubt until after the manual's publication and had not
made their concerns known to the editors.

DSM-II and the Practice of Psychiatry

Mental health professionals across the country, therefore, assessed
disturbed Vietnam veterans using a diagnostic nomenclature that contained no specific entries for war-related trauma. In hospitals, insurance
companies and the courts, the *DSM-II* nomenclature was important because it provided the official diagnoses for categorizing sicknesses. Despite the absence of a listing in *DSM-II*, many psychiatrists still
considered war neurosis, and the specific listing of it in *DSM-I*, gross
stress reaction, diagnostically valid and useful. In 1969, psychiatrist John
Talbott, in a critique of *DSM-II* published in the *International Journal of
Psychiatry*, recommended that the future editors of *DSM-III* reintroduce
the gross stress reaction listing. Talbott, who had served in Vietnam as a
psychiatrist, recalled an incident that occurred in 1970 or 1971:

> I was asked to evaluate a disability case for the VA by Ed Koch, who then
> was a representative to Congress, now the Mayor of New York. . . . I
> looked at this kid . . . [and] videotaped him. He was such a classic
> case . . . [of] mental disability related to combat experience, that I pre-
> sented it to my class at Columbia [University Medical School] on stress
> disorders.
> [Psychiatrist] Larry Kolb was the senior person in that class and [he] came
> up to me afterward and said, "How on earth did you find this person? This
> person has everything imaginable!" . . . He had sleep disturbances, he
> had startle reaction, he had everything. Flashbacks. Had everything. And
> I had it all on videotape. And Larry said to me, "How did you find this
> guy?" I said, "This is a guy who has been disallowed benefits by the VA
> because he doesn't have a combat-related disorder!"[18]

VA psychiatrist Arthur Blank, who eventually would become the VA's
Chief of Psychiatric Services, years later described the procedure in
which "most American psychiatrists . . . based their encounters with
Viet Nam veterans on the offical view that no such thing as [war neuro-

sis] existed," as "dysfunctional and bizarre."[19] Even within the VA, however, adherence to the nomenclature for purposes of treating patients varied according to therapists' personal and clinical experiences. Sarah Haley recalls some psychiatrists on the Boston VA medical staff who informally collected military histories from patients they privately considered to be cases of war neurosis. These staff altered the treatment plan accordingly:

> The three or four people in my clinic who were listing traumatic war neurosis . . . , they would see as their job, their task, to talk with the person about what had happened in Vietnam. . . . "Oh, you lost this buddy, you lost that buddy, and that happened. Well, do you think about it now? Oh, I see, you blame yourself. You think if you had only [acted differently], this wouldn't have happened. I see. No wonder you feel so terrible. . . ." The people who thought that these fantastic stories were, you know, just indications of psychotic thought processes would give them antipsychotic medication. . . . [Or] they were seen as . . . character disorders. . . . This person must still be having these symptoms because— it's not that combat is so bad—it's just that they're weak sisters.[20]

In 1971, Haley provided a rating scheme for the local VVAW chapter to use in sending veterans to the Boston VA facility for treatment:

> I drew up a schedule of our intake meetings. There was a different team for each half-day. I highlighted in red the people who it was worthwhile for the vets to see, those people who would be empathetic. I marked others in black, skull and crossbones—don't send anyone to this team![21]

Vietnam veterans had a low and quiet profile, but, in the words of Vietnam veteran William Mahedy, " . . . [we were] not willing to sneak back into [our] homeland and resume life as if Vietnam had never happened."[22] In virtually every large city there were clusters of Vietnam veterans who met informally with each other to talk about their experiences. These groups often had political agendas as well. In the case of VVAW, some sought to remove American troops from Vietnam. However, others worked to improve and change services available from the local VA or sought remedies for personal or employment problems outside the VA. Such were the activities of Vietnam veterans at the Brentwood VA Hospital in Los Angeles. They sought healing and in so doing sought to change the system. They became the model for a national program adopted by the VA in 1979.

Dr. Phillip May, an expert in schizophrenia, was the director of psychological services at the Brentwood VA in 1971. He and some other staff members felt uneasy about the lack of fit between the services they provided and the growing number of Vietnam veteran patients. Noting that there was no Vietnam veteran on the staff, May hired Shad Meshad and instructed him to prepare a report about Vietnam veteran patients. Meshad, a clinical social worker, knew the problems of Vietnam veterans firsthand. He had served in Vietnam as a medical service officer and had received extensive wounds to his head and back in a helicopter crash. He later described the incident to reporter Myra MacPherson:

> "I split my head. I was scalped. I could feel my whole face slipping. Like an old basset hound, my face just kinda fell down. I tied a bandanna around it to hold it up."[23]

Following his return from Vietnam, he endured several painful operations and had "terrible" problems coming to terms with what happened to him as a soldier and a veteran. These experiences led him to champion the needs of Vietnam veterans and criticize the adequacy of VA services.

Meshad approached May's directive with the ardor of a zealot and submitted a blunt, unflattering report. He noted that "the veterans were hostile, the staff was afraid, and . . . the traditional VA services . . . useless."[24] Things were going badly at Brentwood. William Mahedy served with the 173rd Airborne Brigade as a chaplain and joined the Brentwood staff as a social worker in 1973. He later wrote:

> Most Brentwood psychiatrists I met during this period had not the slightest clue how to deal with Vietnam veterans. . . . One lesson we learned in Los Angeles was not to take traditional mental health services too seriously. Psychiatrists and clincial psychologists could function within their well-defined parameters, but they didn't know how to treat combat-related stress. Nor could they provide any guidance to the kind of total reintegration into society that we knew was necessary.[25]

May pressed for some means to address the problem. After consultation, Brentwood director John Valance authorized Meshad to do something about it. With the blessing of Social Work Chief John Fulton, they formed the Vietnam Veteran Resocialization Unit. Meshad's philosophy, drawn from his own experience rather than orthodox psychiatry, was simple and pragmatic. He felt that Vietnam veterans needed the opportunity to articulate and make sense of their combat experiences and, as they came to terms with their service in Vietnam, needed meaningful employment. This was not easy to achieve for veterans who were down and out, confused, and demoralized. More to the point, in 1971, many regarded Meshad's ideas as more radical than practical. Mahedy wrote of those days:

In every hospital situation I have encountered, the "doctor" calls the shots, but this was not the case in the Brentwood Viet-vet ward. Individual therapy and rap sessions were geared toward dealing specifically with the psychological issues resulting from combat. Psychiatrists and clinical psychologists who could not adjust to this . . . approach were simply thrown off the ward by Meshad. Many on the psychiatry and psychology staffs were not happy with the arrangement, but Valance and Fulton continued to back Meshad.[26]

Despite the numbers of Vietnam veterans on the Resocialization Unit, Meshad was convinced that most Vietnam veterans who needed help would not approach a VA hospital. Hence, he set up an extensive "storefront" operation in communities throughout Los Angeles. Here he held rap groups where veterans could talk about their war experiences at a neutral site. He would steer them to sympathetic workers within the VA to address their other needs. From this informal arrangement emerged a plan that Meshad eventually called "the circle of treatment," through which a Vietnam veteran could work through his problems and become reintegrated into the community. This work consumed his life, and Meshad freely admits that he was more than a bit unorthodox: "I was a madman, a maverick. Had long hair, a beard, wore a field jacket. But they referred vets from all over the country to me."[27]

Flanking Maneuvers

On October 26, 1970, the Legislative Reorganization Act established a separate Senate Committee on Veterans Affairs, chaired by Senator Vance Hartke (D-Ind.). The formation of the new committee signaled that change was afoot in the way Congress produced legislation pertaining to veterans. For starters, not all significant legislation would originate from the House Committee. There also were political differences between the two committees which inevitably would affect their working relationship. The Senate Committee had several members who were outspoken critics of American policy in Southeast Asia. House Committee members, though not sensitive to the needs of Vietnam veterans, were staunch supporters of the war effort.

As we have seen, Vietnam Veterans Against the War (VVAW) staged its last hurrah, the Dewey Canyon III protest march in Washington, D.C., in April of 1971. This small, loosely organized group comprised the most visible political initiative among Vietnam veterans during the early 1970s. Rusty Lindley, who served one tour in Vietnam as an advisor to a South Vietnamese airborne division and another with the U.S.

Special Forces, was a last-minute participant. He had been attending
college without much interest in Colorado Springs, Colorado. Following
Dewey Canyon III, he remained in Washington, D.C. in the hastily
created and ill-financed position of "legislative director" for VVAW.
Lindley recalls:

> Well, the whole New York office [of VVAW] was going through left-wing
> "post-traumatic stress," existential crisis, that you get into with politics, as
> well as the Red Brigade trying to infiltrate them. They were kind of losing
> their relevance and effectiveness.
>
> I sort of created the position of legislative director of VVAW, so that we
> would have an office and facilities to lobby on the Hill on behalf of Viet-
> nam veterans and also against the war. . . . John Kerry and the leadership
> helped out with funds. . . . [The office] was located on 47 Ivy Street . . . ,
> a nice location on Capital Hill, probably one of the closest buildings to
> Capital Hill. We had the student vote and Hughes for President in town-
> houses next to us. Also, the Concerned Officers Movement and POW
> Families Against the War. It was kind of a nice nest of credible antiwar
> activists and advocates.[28]

Reaction to VVAW's antiwar activities made it difficult, Lindley ac-
knowledges, to lobby successfully for VA programs needed by Vietnam
veterans:

> Having been associated with prisoner of war families, I knew there was a
> very comprehensive counseling . . . program prepared for returning
> POWs and their wives. Yet there was no corollary thing for [Vietnam
> vets]. . . . [Charles] Stenger [with the VA's Psychological Services] and VA
> administrator Donald Johnson . . . realized there was something seriously
> wrong among Vietnam veterans from [their] visits to VA hospitals. . . .
> And [Johnson] sent a memo to the White House in March [of 1971] saying,
> "We need to do more about this. Let's try and affirm the validity of Viet-
> nam veterans' service and provide whatever counseling might be
> necessary."
>
> But, about three weeks later, Vietnam Veterans against the War showed up
> [in Dewey Canyon III]. There was a radical change in attitude in the White
> House. . . . Chuck Colson and Richard Nixon had some strong views that
> they decided . . . to impose on the VA and on Donald Johnson. . . . [T]he
> basic theme was that the Vietnam veteran is too busy in school and on the
> job to have readjustment problems, and that Vietnam veterans will have
> no problems that will adversely affect public support for the war in
> Vietnam.[29]

In 1971, Alan Cranston of the Senate Committee on Veterans Affairs
introduced legislation to provide a new program for alcohol and drug

abuse treatment and readjustment counseling specifically for Vietnam veterans. Cranston had become convinced that Vietnam veterans had special needs that the VA was not equipped to meet. Some of these needs could be met by updating programs, such as the G.I. Bill, that had made it possible for large numbers of World War II and Korean War veterans to obtain a college education. Some needs required new programs and staffing to contend with the war-related injuries and trauma coming out of Vietnam. Cranston also believed that the one-year statute of limitations in defining service connection needed to be extended for psychological problems. Further, he and others worried about reports of widespread drug use among troops in Vietnam and the problems this might pose for readjustment. The cost of Cranston's bill for the recommended five-year period amounted to less than one percent of the VA budget for those years.

Cranston's measure passed in the Senate but died in the House Committee. House Committee members disagreed that Vietnam veterans needed special counseling programs. They observed that the VA had programs and treatments in place for dealing with these problems. Likewise, the American Legion and VFW lobbied against the measure. For example, the VFW testified before Cranston's Subcommittee on Health and Hospitals that it would favor the measure only if money for it "shall not be taken from existing funds," and the American Legion stated in the same hearing that the measure "should not be allowed to have an impact on any other health services."[30] Max Cleland recalls:

> [The American Legion and VFW] gave great lip service to Vietnam veterans, mostly because they wanted them to join the organizations and boost their ranks. But when it came time to funding programs for 'em, boy, they thought it was going to take away from them. And they, I found, the major veterans organizations fought tooth and nail, mostly quietly behind the scenes, to gut a lot of this [legislation for Vietnam veterans].[31]

Hence, the traditional veterans organizations feared that if Congress approved the measure, those who balanced the budget might include the service-connected program for Vietnam veterans at the expense of some program for older veterans that was not service connected. The older veterans were their constituents; Vietnam veterans were not.

Turmoil within the APA

Whereas dissatisfaction with the deletion of gross stress reaction from *DSM-II* was quiet and fragmented, discontent with the listing of homosexuality in *DSM-II* exploded into loud and disruptive protest. Traditionally, Freudian psychoanalytic theory and later schools of thought in American psychiatry all considered homosexuality as pathological. *DSM-I* included homosexuality as a mental disorder under "sociopathic disturbances," a category designating serious disorders in which afflicted persons showed no concern or remorse. According to this definition, *DSM-I* recognized homosexuals as "ill in terms of society and of conformity with the prevailing cultural milieu." *DSM-II* strongly reasserted the view that homosexuality is inherently pathological. It reclassified homosexuality, listing it with other "sexual deviations" such as fetishism, transvestism, and sadism under the heading "other nonpsychotic mental disorders."[32]

At first, the entry aroused little interest. Homosexual activist Frank Kameny of the Mettachine Society of Washington, D.C. already had articulated the position in 1965 that "homosexuality is not a sickness, disturbance or pathology but merely a preference, orientation or propensity on par with, and not different in kind from, heterosexuality."[33] However, homosexual activism became more strident and burst into full-scale rioting in June of 1969. That month New York City police conducted a raid on the Stonewall Bar in Greenwich Village. In the process they clubbed several gay patrons, and the gay community fought back violently in the streets. The riot marked the emergence of the Gay Liberation Front (GLF), a radical organization that selected a name to parallel in spirit the communist National Liberation Front's fight against the American military in Vietnam.

GLF held in contempt less radical homosexual groups who were unwilling to advance damning critiques of American society and cries for its literal destruction. Thus it was unable to attract the allegiance of large numbers of homosexuals. In this context, the Gay Activist Alliance (GAA) emerged as an organization focused solely on gay rights, although not necessarily less confrontational in the use of tactics to achieve this goal. "Zaps," disruptions of events sponsored by groups and organizations who publicly denounced gay rights, evolved as a favored GAA tactic.

GAA staged one of its earliest and most successful zaps at the 1970 annual meeting of the APA in San Francisco on May 11th through the 15th. Policy analyst Ronald Bayer recounts the height of the confrontation:

> In a room filled with several hundred psychiatrists, homosexuals . . . expressed their strongest outrage during the presentation of a paper . . . discussing the use of aversive conditioning techniques in the treatment of sexual deviation. Shouts of "vicious," "torture," and "where did you take your residency, Auschwitz?" greeted the speaker. . . . [The] demon-

strators exploded with the demand that they be heard. . . . At that, the meeting was adjourned and pandemonium ensued. As one protester attempted to read a list of gay demands, he was denounced as a "maniac." A feminist ally was called "a paranoid fool" and "a bitch." Some psychiatrists, enraged by the intrusion and the . . . inability . . . to protect their discussions from chaos, demanded that their airfares to San Francisco be refunded. One physician called for the police to shoot the demonstrators. While most of those who had assembled for the panel left the room, some did not, staying to hear their profession denounced as an instrument of oppression and torture.[34]

It would be misleading, however, to assume that gay activists disrupted an otherwise tranquil convention. By coincidence, the APA convened its meeting only days after the Cambodian invasion and the Kent State killings. Antiwar ferment also was brewing, both within the community and within the ranks of the conventioneers. In answer to my question about GAA's role in shutting down the convention, psychiatrist John Talbott, who later became national president of the APA, recalls:

JT: Since I'm one of the ones who helped shut [it] down—in fairness, the group at the microphone when the microphone was cut off and we were all sent packing, half of us were [protesting about] Vietnam. This was [the week of] Cambodia and Kent State . . . we were working with a crowd from Berkeley putting out newsletters every day, and so it was very involved with the [antiwar] protest movement. Half of them were . . . gay liberation-type people, so it was a combination.

WS: I see. That must have been a very interesting convention.

JT: It was a marvelous convention![35]

Wishing to avoid a similar debacle during the 1971 APA meetings in Washington, D.C., the APA Program Committee made arrangements beforehand with gay activists, including Frank Kameny, to hold a panel on homosexuality as a life style. Fearing that this would deprive the movement of its headway toward change, Kameny secretly enlisted the help of a local GLF collective in Washington to ensure the disruption of the APA meeting. The planned disruption occurred on May 3, the first day of the planned one-week meeting. During the disruption, Kameny grabbed the microphone and declared to shocked psychiatrists: "Psychiatry is the enemy incarnate. Psychiatry has waged a relentless war of extermination against us. You may take this as a declaration of war against you."[36]

Meanwhile, outside the convention hotel, demonstrators waged the largest antiwar protest to date in the streets. Ten days after VVAW's Dewey Canyon III, hundreds of thousands of protesters converged on

Washington according to plan. The police arrested roughly 12,000 of them. Back inside the convention, psychiatrist Jonathan Borus chaired a panel entitled "The Vietnam Veteran." Robert Lifton served as one of the panelists.

Shatan: The Grief of Soldiers

On April 30, 1971, a Detroit liquor store clerk shot and killed a young black man named Dwight Johnson as he attempted to rob the store at gunpoint. Ordinarily, a death such as this probably would have attracted little attention. Instead Johnson's story later appeared in the pages of the *New York Times*, the *Journal of American Orthopyschiatry*, and other publications, and a play about his life would appear off Broadway and on television. That is because about two and a half years earlier, President Lyndon Johnson had placed around Dwight Johnson's neck the Congressional Medal of Honor, the nation's highest award for heroism in combat. As Medal of Honor historian Edward Murphy later observed, his "was a tragic story that shocked America, rocked the Pentagon, and proved how difficult it can be to be a hero in an unpopular war."[37]

Johnson's combat heroics occurred about one week before his scheduled date of return to the States. He arrived in-country in February of 1967 and served with the same crew for eleven months in B Company, 1st Battalion, 69th Armor, 4th Infantry Division. On January 14, 1968, his commander reassigned him to another tank to cover for a sick driver. That day North Vietnamese soldiers ambushed the convoy on a road near Dak To, and the tank containing his customary crew caught fire. Leaving the safety of the tank he was driving, Johnson rushed to pull his buddies from the burning tank. He was able to extract only one of them before the tank exploded, killing the rest of the crew. For the next forty-five minutes, Johnson went on a rampage, almost singlehandedly breaking the ambush and subduing the enemy. Afterwards, he had to be restrained and anesthetized. A few days later, he returned to the States.

Upon his discharge from the Army, he sought work in the Detroit area without success. His employment drought ended only after he received the Medal of Honor. Suddenly, companies sought his services, including the Army, who lured him back as a recruiter and public relations person. Johnson had trouble with his new role, muffed assignments, and complained of stomach pains. The Army sent him to Selfridge Air Force Base near Detroit for treatment during the summer of 1970, and then reassigned him to the Valley Forge VA medical center in Pennsylvania. There doctors diagnosed him as suffering from "depression caused by post-Vietnam adjustment problems." In March of 1971, Johnson left the hospital on a three-day pass. He never returned. Chaim Shatan later wrote of Johnson's death:

> More than once [Johnson] asked his psychiatrist how society would respond if he were to react to the black dilemma in Detroit with the same uncontrolled ferocity that had won him the highest recognition in battle. He found his ultimate answer not in a distant jungle, but on the floor of a hometown grocery store. There he finally lived out his haunting fantasies and nightmares of being killed at point-blank range.[38]

Shatan had read Jon Nordheimer's May 26, 1971, front-page story in the *New York Times* and was deeply moved. He prepared a paper on the rap groups for the Op-Ed page of the *New York Times* in February of 1971, but the article did not appear immediately. In the spring of 1972, he drafted a longer, scholarly version to present at the AOA meetings in Detroit. While in Detroit, he met with and consoled Johnson's family.

In both papers, Shatan wrote of a "post-Vietnam syndrome" that, according to his observations, often set in nine to thirty months after return from Vietnam. He described the syndrome as "delayed massive trauma" and identified its themes: guilt, rage, the feeling of being scapegoated, psychic numbing, and alienation. He emphasized that these were not an accidental grab bag of symptoms, but rather stemmed from the inability of soldiers to grieve in the combat zone:

> Before World War I, Freud elucidated the role grief plays in helping the mourner let go of a missing part of life and acknowledging that it exists only in the memory. The so-called Post-Vietnam Syndrome confronts us with the unconsummated grief of soldiers—impacted grief, in which an encapsulated, never-ending past deprives the present of meaning. Their sorrow is unspent, the grief of their wounds is untold, their guilt unexpiated. Much of what passes for cynicism is really the veterans' numbed apathy from a surfeit of bereavement and death.[39]

After the AOA meetings, Shatan called the editor of the *New York Times* and suggested that this was an opportune time to publish the Op-Ed article he had prepared for them the year before. The editor agreed and, on May 6, 1972, the *Times* published it. Shatan recalls, "After that, the telephone was jumping off the wall."[40] He kept track of the phone calls. Shatan and, by extension, the VVAW rap group became an informal clearinghouse for putting interested parties, heretofore unaware of each other, in touch. Summarizing the impact of the article, Shatan says: "After the Op-Ed article, things started mushrooming."

The St. Louis Watershed

In November 1972, Robert Lifton put the finishing touches on his book, *Home from the War*. (The book appeared in print in 1973.) As in earlier Senate testimony, he argued that atrocities were endemic to all wars, and that the United States' lack of moral purpose and integrity in Vietnam accentuated this trait. He devoted part of the book to the My Lai massacre and the personal story of a "My Lai survivor," the veteran seen by Sarah Haley on her first morning at work. (Lifton and Haley had met through the New York City and Boston VVAW chapters.) Lifton encouraged Americans to shed their romanticized notions about war and to place a portion of the blame for atrocities in Vietnam on the war itself, and on themselves for allowing it, rather than exclusively on the Vietnam veterans who fought it.

Lifton also roundly criticized American psychiatry, particularly military psychiatry. He singled out two articles in the *American Journal of Psychiatry*, a 1969 article by H. Spencer Bloch and a 1971 article by Douglas Bey and Walter Smith, for special criticism.[41] Both articles boasted of psychiatry's success in containing war neurosis and returning troubled soldiers quickly to the battlefield. Especially contemptable, Lifton argued, was the stance of military psychiatry as an advocate of the military's interests rather than those of the soldier-patient. "The aim of [military psychiatry]," Bloch had written, was "admittedly a very pragmatic one—to conserve the fighting strength."[42] In Lifton's view, this "unholy alliance" between psychiatrists, chaplains, and the military command created a "counterfeit universe, in which all-pervasive, spiritually reenforced inner corruption becomes the price of survival," and is the central roadblock to reintegration after combat.[43]

By now Lifton and Shatan had established connections to the AOA, professional publication outlets, and prestigious universities. They next sought to formalize the VVAW's clearinghouse. They knew that small groups of veterans and others across the country were informally addressing the problem. This suggested a strategy: strengthen this grassroots movement and carry on the work through it. Among their many contacts outside the professional community was the National Council of Churches (NCC). Shatan and Lifton urged the NCC and anyone else who would listen to sponsor a conference in order to bring these people together face to face.

In 1970, NCC had established an office under Rev. Rich Kilmer, an ordained Presbyterian minister, to help "those [Americans] who had been hurt by the war in Vietnam." Initially, the office devoted most of its attention to draft resisters and antiwar protesters. However, in early 1973 Kilmer sought to expand the scope of his organization's ministry, and his assistant, Rev. Mark Hansen, laid plans for a meeting called the First National Conference on the Emotional Needs of Vietnam-Era Veterans. According to Jack Smith:

> Rich . . . was a minister in one of the churches [that] had worked with all the groups in Canada, . . . in all these draft-evasion offices. . . . And [we] had begun talking to them about the fact that they were not doing anything for veterans. They were only dealing with antiwar stuff. And that . . . if they were ministers, they had an obligation to minister to people who were in the war as well as out of it, okay? And so they began setting [it] up.[44]

The Missouri Synod of the Lutheran Church put up $80,000 for expenses and agreed to host the meeting in April at its seminary in St. Louis, a site all the more agreeable because of its central location in the country. Hansen worked with Vietnam veteran Arthur Egendorf of the original New York City rap group to come up with a list of veterans, psychiatrists, and others across the country who were actively involved in rap groups or organizations that helped Vietnam veterans. They also invited a delegation from the VA Central Office to attend.

Shatan recalls: "There were 130 attendees—60 vets, 30 shrinks, 30 chaplains, and 10 central office VA people who came on at the last minute."[45] The conference marked the first time that such a diverse collection of people working on readjustment issues among Vietnam veterans met and exchanged ideas. They discovered that their isolated groupings had several characteristics in common. Theirs were self-generated, self-help groups that "met on the vets' own turf." There were, however, many differences. For instance, Twice-Born Men, founded in San Francisco by Jack McCloskey and Chester Adams, brought together Vietnam veterans who were coming out of prison. Their rap groups were run solely by the veterans themselves and eschewed the presence of any mental health professionals. Joe Garcia's Seattle-Area Veterans Action Center (SeaVAC), on the other hand, focused on practical advice—benefits counseling, help in finding housing or buying a home, help in finding a job. Shad Meshad, though employed by the VA, operated the unorthodox and renegade unit at Brentwood.

The participants spent much of the time describing to each other the different approaches and discussing which offered the right model.

They concluded that circumstances had produced many variations and that there was no one right model, though they could learn from each other. The discussions were intense, boisterous, but usually friendly, except for some of the exchanges between veterans and representatives from the VA. Further, Shatan and Lifton spoke with reporters of extensive problems among Vietnam veterans in adjusting to civilian life. The VA personnel disputed their claim that the problems were widespread. Further, the animosity many veterans felt toward the VA itself spilled over into conversations with its representatives. Smith recalls:

> There were many friendships that were formed that exist to this day which came out of that conference for me. [But] . . . it was a knockdown, dragout battle at that. I remember very vividly . . . Charlie Stenger [of VA Central Office] . . . getting up and saying, you know, "I'm a World War II POW and I really understand what's going on and I'm one of your brothers." And I got up and launched into a tirade about how . . . everything he had written indicated he didn't have the foggiest notion of what was going on with us and how the hell could he call himself a brother? It was the beginning of a long and hostile relationship.[46]

The conference lasted three days. As it drew to a close, the participants created an organizational framework for carrying on the initiative. They named the it the National Veterans Resource Project (NVRP) and elected twelve participants to serve as a board of directors. In the weeks that followed, the board drew up a list of candidates from which to select a director. The consensus at the conference had been that the board should find a black or Hispanic to head the clearinghouse, but as board members reviewed the options, they agreed upon Jack Smith.

Smith was a hard person to overlook. Passionate, outspoken, and a tireless worker for the cause, he had been a participant in the New York City rap groups and Dewey Canyon III. In 1972, through Lifton's connections at the Drug Dependency Unit at Yale University, Smith had obtained a position teaching drug and alcohol education courses for the U.S. Army. His unconventional message—that Vietnam veterans in the military who abused drugs and alcohol did so to forget about their war experiences—conflicted with the Army's stand that abusers simply were "bad apples." After an undiplomatic verbal exchange over this with the then Chief of Staff General William Westmoreland, the Army brought Smith's teaching career to an abrupt halt. Though the selection of Smith as director of NVRP was popular, the news did not cause a stir one way or the other. The participants were back home, each "doing his own thing."

Growing Pains

One of Smith's first tasks at NVRP was to raise money for the Project itself. Raising money for this end proved especially difficult. Smith explains the dilemma:

> What we kept running into was, the foundations were saying, "Well, this is really a government problem. Why are you coming to us?" And we were saying, "Because the government denies there is a problem. . . ." And so finally we said, "Look, if we're going to anything, we're going to have to prove that we're not talking about something that's an illusion."[47]

NVRP initially had intended to provide grants to groups across the country such as Twice-Born Men and SeaVAC. It now added to the top of its priority list the conduct of an empirical study of the consequences of Vietnam service and the needs of Vietnam veterans.

For a while, however, efforts in behalf of NVRP were scattered and seemingly unsuccessful. To begin with, the participants were beset with unforeseen problems. Shatan, for instance, returned from a meeting at the Pentagon in June of 1973 to discover that his phone had been tapped. He and several other psychiatrists had journeyed to Washington to offer assistance in the readjustment of American prisoners of war returning from Hanoi. In July of the same year, he noted that some of his mail had been tampered with. That month, Shatan had been contacted by William Kunstler's Center for Constitutional Rights (CCR). CCR sought his advice in preparing a "post-Vietnam syndrome" defense for the so-called "Gainesville 8," eight veterans who had been charged with planning to blow up the 1972 Democratic and Republican conventions. Shatan states:

> Interesting things began happening. I started getting mail which had been opened. Only mail from three sources was opened—mail from veterans' organizations, from people who worked with Vietnam vets, and from [Robert] Lifton. The letter would be stamped, "damaged in handling" or "opened by mistake," and would have the official seal of the U.S. Post Office. Ironically, that seal contained the figure of liberty, the Statue of Liberty. All this just revved me up.[48]

In response, Shatan stepped up his appearances at conferences and other settings which he thought would bring visibility to the readjustment issue. He also traveled to Israel and met there with Israeli military psychiatrists, themselves well versed in the study of combat disorders.

Meanwhile, Smith sought ideas and funding for an empirical study of Vietnam veterans. Kilmer's office at NCC, in keeping with its evolving

mission statement, had changed its name to "Special Ministries, Vietnam Generation." Chuck Noel, Jansen's replacement and a draft resister
himself, wished to conduct a study of draft resisters; Smith, of course,
was interested in a study of Vietnam veterans. Their discussions led to
the position that both groups could be studied as the alternative responses and experiences of young men of the same generation. "One
group was the control group for the other," Smith explains. They proposed a study called the "Vietnam Generation Study." NVRP received
initial support from NCC. The Russell Sage Foundation then provided
$5,000 for a review of the literature, and the Edward F. Hazen Founda-
tion added $42,000 to begin a pilot study.

A parallel event within the APA that spring introduced a new sense of
urgency. In April of 1974, ten thousand APA psychiatrists voted on a
referendum regarding the status of homosexuality in *DSM-II*. In an effort to resolve the crisis, Robert Spitzer had proposed the substitution
of "sexual orientation disturbance" for "homosexuality" in *DSM-II*. He
initially defined sexual orientation disturbance as "a category for individuals whose sexual interests are directed primarily toward people of
the same sex and who are either bothered by, in conflict with, or wish to
change their sexual orientation."[49] In other words, only homosexuals
troubled by their sexual orientation would be regarded as "sick." Heated
debate ensued. Some psychiatrists were outraged that homosexuality
might be deleted from *DSM-II*, and others that the new diagnostic category was restricted to homosexuals. This latter group noted that heterosexuals too could be in conflict over their sexual orientations and hence
in need of professional help. Still others suggested that the APA consider separately the issues of deleting homosexuality from *DSM-II* and of
substituting an alternative diagnosis.

Spitzer's preference of handling both issues simultaneously prevailed.
With the tacit understanding that both homosexuals and heterosexuals
could suffer from sexual orientation disturbance, the change was approved in December, 1973, by the APA's Nomenclature Committee.
However, dissenting factions within the APA requested a vote of the full
membership on the change the following spring. This provoked more
controversy: were psychiatrists actually going to vote on the matter of
whether a medical condition really existed? The answer was, "yes, they
were." In a rancorous and divisive atmosphere, Spitzer's suggestion
passed, with 58 percent favoring the change.

Acknowledgments

Certain material in Chapters 2 and 3 were published earlier in Wilbur Scott,
"PTSD in DSM-III: A Case in the Politics of Diagnosis and Disease," *Social*

Problems 37 (1990):294–310; and Wilbur Scott, "PTSD and Agent Orange: Implications for a Sociology of Veterans' Issues," *Armed Forces and Society* 18 (1992):592–612.

Notes

1. American Psychiatric Association (APA), *Diagnostic and Statistical Manual of Mental Disorders*, 3rd ed. (Washington, D.C.: APA, 1980), 236.
2. See Ronald Bayer, *Homosexuality and American Psychiatry: The Politics of Diagnosis* (New York: Basic Books, 1984); and Peter Conrad and Joseph Schneider, *Deviance and Medicalization: From Badness to Sickness* (St. Louis: C.V. Mosby, 1980).
3. Robert Spitzer, Introduction to *Diagnostic and Statistical Manual of Mental Disorders*, 3rd ed. (Washington, D.C.: APA, 1980), 1.
4. Peter Bourne, *Men, Stress, and Vietnam* (Boston: Little, Brown, 1970), 10.
5. Quoted in D. Wilfred Abse, "Brief Historical Overview of the Concept of War Neurosis and of Associated Treatment Methods,"in *Psychotherapy of the Combat Veteran*, ed. Harvey Schwartz (New York: Specturm, 1984), 16.
6. Quoted in Myra MacPherson, *Long Time Passing: Vietnam and the Haunted Generation* (New York: Signet, 1984), 235.
7. Bourne, *Men, Stress, and Vietnam*, 13–14.
8. Ibid, 15.
9. Quoted in MacPherson, *Long Time Passing*, 235.
10. Quoted in Harry Kormos, "The Nature of Combat Stress," in *Stress Disorders among Vietnam Veterans: Theory, Research and Treatment*, ed. Charles Figley (New York: Brunner/Mazel, 1978), 5.
11. Edward Shils and Morris Janowitz, "Cohesion and Disintegration in the Wehrmacht in World War II," *Public Opinion Quarterly* 12 (1948):280–315.
12. See Abram Kardiner, *War, Stress, and Neurotic Illness* (New York: Paul B. Hoeber, 1947).
13. Roy Grinker and John Spiegel, *Men under Stress* (Philadelphia: Blakiston, 1945).
14. Bourne, *Men, Stress, and Vietnam*, vii-viii.
15. I could find no substantiating records in the official APA Archives. Psychiatrist Chaim Shatan suspected that gross stress reaction was omitted to reduce the financial liability of the VA following the Vietnam War. Shatan, personal interview with author, 24 October 1988, Dallas, Texas.
16. Herbert Archibald, D.M. Long, and Read Tuddenham, "Gross Stress Reaction in Combat—a 15-Year Follow-up," *American Journal of Psychiatry* 119 (1962):317–322; Herbert Archibald and Read Tuddenham, "Persistent Stress Reaction Following Combat: A 20-Year Follow-up," *Archives of General Psychiatry* 12 (1965):474–481.
17. Archibald and Tuddenham, "Persistant Stress Reaction," 480–481.
18. John Talbott, telephone interview with author, 24 February 1989, Baltimore, Maryland.
19. Arthur Blank, Jr., "Irrational Responses to Post-Traumatic Stress Disorder and Viet Nam Veterans," in *The Trauma of War: Stress and Recovery in Viet Nam Veterans*, ed. Steven Sonnenberg, Arthur Blank, Jr., and John Talbott (Washington, D.C.: APA), 73–74.

20. Sarah Haley, telephone interview with author, 9 November 1988, Somerville, Mass.
21. Sarah Haley, personal interview with author, 25 October 1988, Dallas, Texas.
22. William Mahedy, *Out of the Night: The Spiritual Journey of Vietnam Vets* (New York: Ballentine, 1986), 55.
23. Quoted in MacPherson, *Long Time Passing*, 273.
24. Shad Meshad, personal interview with author, 24 October 1988, Dallas, Texas.
25. Mahedy, *Out of the Night*, 56.
26. Ibid, 56.
27. Meshad, personal interview, 24 October 1988.
28. Rusty Lindley, telephone interview with author, 17 April 1989, Washington, D.C.
29. Ibid.
30. David Bonior, Steven Champlin, Timothy Kolly, *The Vietnam Veteran: A History of Neglect* (New York: Praeger, 1984), 131–133.
31. Max Cleland, telephone interview with author, 27 January 1989, Atlanta, Georgia.
32. American Psychiatric Association (APA), *Diagnostic and Statistical Manual, Mental Disorders*, 1st ed. (Washington, D.C.: APA, 1952), 34; APA, *Diagnostic and Statistical Manual of Mental Disorders*, 2nd ed. (Washington, D.C.: APA, 1968), 44.
33. Bayer, *Homosexuality*, 88.
34. Bayer, *Homosexuality*, 103.
35. Talbott, telephone interview, 24 February 1989.
36. Bayer, *Homosexuality*, 105.
37. Edward Murphy, *Vietnam Medal of Honor Heroes* (New York: Ballantine, 1987), 233.
38. Chaim Shatan, "The Grief of Soldiers in Mourning: Vietnam Combat Veterans' Self Help Movement," *American Journal of Ortho-psychiatry* 45 (1973): 644.
39. Shatan, "The Grief of Soldiers," 648.
40. Shatan, personal interview, 24 October 1988.
41. H. Spencer Bloch, "Army Psychiatry in the Combat Zone—1967–1968," *American Journal of Psychiatry* 126 (1969):289–298; Douglas Bey and Walter Smith, "Organizational Consultation in a Combat Unit," *American Journal of Psychiatry* 126 (1971):401–406.
42. Bloch, "Army Psychiatry," 292.
43. Robert Jay Lifton, *Home from the War: Neither Victims nor Executioners* (New York: Basic Books, 1973), p. 167.
44. Jack Smith, telephone interview with author, 22 December 1988, Cleveland, Ohio.
45. Shatan, personal interview, 24 October 1988.
46. Smith, telephone interview, 22 December, 1988.
47. Ibid.
48. Shatan, personal interview, 24 October 1988.
49. Bayer, *Homosexuality*, 128.

$$3$$

HORSE TRADING

"And so it's interesting that the final deal was a standard political trade. . . . Horse trading! It was just unbelievable! But it happened."

Max Cleland, former national director of the VA

American troops rotated home from Vietnam throughout the war, and the last combat troops came home in 1973. The American military presence ended when the North Vietnamese army captured Saigon in 1975. The return of troops from the combat zone adds another chapter to the costs of going to war. Soldiers cannot be easily compensated for losses, injuries, and disabilities they incur in time of war. Their setbacks cannot be calculated in terms of the marketplace and set straight in dollars and cents. The costs simply would be prohibitive. Hence, medical care, compensation, and other benefits—funded by Congress and executed by the Veterans Administration (VA)—stem first from a recognition of the veterans' altruistic service and then stand as visible symbols of collective gratitude. In general, the greater the gratitude, the more visible and the more generous the symbols.

As we have seen, conflicts over and frustration with the Vietnam War itself shaped attitudes towards those who fought it. Significant numbers of Vietnam veterans experienced problems of readjustment. Psychologist Jim Goodwin, himself a Vietnam veteran, draws an explanation from his experience as a counselor for Disabled American Veterans in 1979 and 1980, and from the writings of other observers.[1] The lack of societal gratitude and support, combined with the military's DEROS (date of expected return from overseas) system in Vietnam, he believes, are to blame.

Unlike previous wars (except for the Korean War), troops arrived in Vietnam knowing they would serve a specifed length of time, thirteen months for those in the Marine Corps and twelve months for all other branches. This arrangement had several consequences. It undermined the factors which ordinarily buffer the ill-effects of combat—unit morale, cohesion, and identification—by tying each person's war experi-

51

ence to an individual timetable.[2] On the other hand, the "DEROS fantasy" did offset losses in group support. The low rate of psychiatric casualties in the combat zone occurred, Goodwin contends, because troops knew exactly how long they had to endure and struggled successfully to prevail until their time came to go home.

However, these problems caught up with veterans once they returned from Vietnam. Since the war lacked popular support after 1968, soldiers not only re-entered singly but also returned to a divisive, sometimes hostile, atmosphere. Veterans seldom corresponded with those still in Vietnam. When the war ended, there was no triumphant return en masse and there were no victory parades. Units rarely held reunions. As a result, large numbers of Vietnam veterans experienced difficulties once home. Goodwin concludes:

> The usual pattern has been that of a combat veteran . . . who held on until his DEROS date. He was largely asymptomatic at the point of rotation back to the U.S.; on his return home, the joy of surviving continued to suppress any problematic symptoms. However, after a year or more, the veteran would begin to notice some changes in his outlook. . . . [He] began to feel depressed, mistrustful, cynical, and restless. He experienced problems with sleep and with his temper. Strangely, he became somewhat obsessed with his combat experiences in Vietnam. He would also begin to question why he survived when others did not. . . . [T]his problematic outlook [became] a chronic lifestyle affecting not only the veterans but countless millions of persons . . . in contact with them.[3]

The veterans that Goodwin describes had difficulty getting the treatment they needed from the VA for two reasons. First, as we saw in the previous chapter, *DSM-II* had no entry for combat stress. Nor did the *DSM-I* entry, gross stress reaction, contain a provision for delayed or chronic reactions. Second, if the first symptoms appeared more than a year after discharge from active duty—as Goodwin and others say they typically did—the VA did not consider the problem service connected. The stage was set.

Counseling As a Political Issue

The politics of readjustment counseling aroused strong emotions among participants in the debate and would not be fully resolved until 1979. The issue dredged up conflicts between generations of veterans and laid bare differences among groups divided over the conduct of the war in Vietnam. The House and Senate Committees generally cooperated in passing bills related to education and job programs for Vietnam veterans. However, House Committee members repeatedly balked at the notion that Vietnam veterans required special counseling programs to help them readjust. In 1971 the Cranston bill providing for the treatment of alcohol and drug abuse specifically for Vietnam veterans passed in the Senate but died in the House Committee on Veterans Affairs.

Guy McMichael, who served as legal counsel for the Senate Commmitee from 1971 to 1976, recalls:

> At that time there was no definable deal known as "post-traumatic stress syndrome." [So] . . . it was somewhat ill-defined. And the provisions in the bill for readjustment and medical counseling . . . were equally vague. Now, I have to tell you . . . there was a great deal of controversy about all of this. A part of it relates to the drug issue, and part of it relates to whether people were viewing returning Vietnam veterans as victims. . . . Societal . . . attitudes were intermixed with whatever medical values that these might have, and it became very contentious and was contentious during most of the 70's.
>
> . . . [T]he House Committee was dominated . . . by World War II veterans with very distinguished careers both in the military and in Congress. Olin "Tiger" Teague . . . was a highly decorated . . . veteran who lost half of his foot, so he was combat disabled as well. And I think there is a generational thing here . . . . Teague certainly had the attitude, well, you know, this is tough but we sucked it up, and we didn't need to go into . . . counseling and I am not sure that Vietnam veterans need this kind of counseling.[4]

Rusty Lindley, though having reservations about Cranston's bill, nevertheless lobbied for it, asking American Legion and VFW representatives, if they could not support the bill, to "at least not oppose it."

> . . . [T]he initial bill was predicated on the premise that drugs and alcohol were the principal problem, and that psychological problems were ancillary to drug and alcohol problems. . . . Just the converse is true for most veterans. . . . It was a nice liberal bill that had a nice antiwar tint to it. You know, look, the war is making a bunch of junkies out of our veterans so we should help the junkies but also end the war.
>
> . . . Teague was highly supportive of the war effort in Vietnam. He had two sons that served over there, one in Vietnam and one in Laos. And he did not like McGovern or this liberal attitude. So he was attuned to White House, you know, suggestions that Vietnam veterans were too busy in school and on the job, and we don't need a separate unique program for Vietnam veterans that World War II and Korean veterans didn't have.[5]

The VA had had programs for treating alcohol-related problems for some time. Alcohol abuse was the largest single diagnosis in VA facilities. However, in 1971 reports circulated in Congress and the VA of widespread abuse of drugs by troops in Vietnam. Particularly worrisome were reports of heroin use. However, as the troops returned home, hard drug use among veterans never materialized as an extensive problem. McMichael comments:

> Once it became obvious that, although a lot of people may have been using opium derivatives in Vietnam, that when they came back to the United States they weren't continuing to use. . . . It was simply not a major problem for them. So the readjustment portion was really riding along . . . with the drug and alcohol treatment portion. So once that did not seem to be some major epidemic, it lost a lot of impetus and push behind it.[6]

The Cranston bill passed the Senate again in 1973 and 1975, but both times suffered the same fate in the House Committee on Veterans Affairs that it had in 1971. Cranston remained convinced that the psychological needs of Vietnam veterans were different than those of the older veterans. However, there was no visible, organized constituency of Vietnam veterans advocating programs for readjustment counseling or, for that matter, any other kinds of benefits. Without political pressure from constituents, the Senate Committee had difficulty mustering support for special programs. It was especially difficult to convince Olin Teague, already suspicious about Vietnam veterans' needs, to support the Cranston bill when the major veterans' organizations opposed it. It made no sense to him to pass the bill over the objections of those organizations. David Bonior (D-Mich.), a Vietnam-era veteran elected to Congress in 1976, later wrote of the stalemate:

> Tiger Teague was prepared to fight against the major [veterans] organizations. . . . The veterans organizations constantly sought more. Members of Congress advanced their proposals, earning the organizations' praise and support. . . . The role of responsible leadership was to sort out the legitimate requestions from the budget boondoggles. Under these conditions, the chairman's job was to learn to say "No." . . . The veterans organizations . . . would not fail to advance needed programs. No chairman need to argue for programs against hesitant veterans groups.
>
> Abandoned by the major veterans organizations, Vietnam veterans needed an ally among the barons, one who would stand with them against the major veterans groups. The role was almost unintelligible to Chairman Teague.[7]

It was only a matter of time before the improvisation headed by Shad Meshad at the Brentwood VA Hospital would come to the Cranston's attention. Cranston's oft-defeated bill had called for readjustment counseling without specifying the form this might take. But here was a VA hospital in the senator's home state carrying out a treatment plan tailor-made for Vietnam veterans and wreaking havoc with VA regulations.

In 1974, Cranston ran for re-election. Max Cleland, who had successfully run for the Georgia State Legislature in 1971, had been defeated in a 1974 race for the lieutenant governor of that state. Cleland joined Cranston in California, campaigning in his behalf. After successfully retaining his seat, Cranston offered Cleland a position on his staff to conduct on-site studies of VA Hospitals. Both Cleland and Meshad testified in 1975 before Cranston's Subcommittee on Health and Hospitals. Meshad states:

> Senator Cranston visited the Brentwood VA [in 1975]. I took him around, showed him our storefronts, showed him around the ghetto. I took him places VA administrators don't usually go. [Afterwards] they gave me a phone number through to Cranston's office to his main man. I could call any time if there were any problems.[8]

Also in 1975, Ray Roberts (D-Tex.) became chairman of the House Committee on Veterans Affairs. Cranston was not about to give up on the his readjustment counseling bill.

Parallel Developments

John Wilson completed his Ph.D. in clinical and social psychology at Michigan State University in 1973. A conscientious objector during American involvement in Vietnam, Wilson performed three years of alternative service in a crisis and suicide intervention center instead of going into the military. Two of his best friends from his hometown, Columbus, Ohio, had gone to Vietnam in 1965 with the Marines. They returned changed people. Wilson states:

> I asked them, "What was it like?" One of them said, "Fuck it, it sucked." We never did talk about it. Something had changed. They had been fun-loving friends filled with the joy of life. Now they were sullen, bitter, and hostile. Before the war, we had no secrets. We had a codeword, "Buds." If we had something really personal to say, we used the word "Buds" before or after the secret. That meant it was to be shared only among us three buddies. They seemed to resent that I was in college. I had sent them letters when they were in 'Nam. Sent them booze in packages with their Moms' names on them to help disguise it. All that was gone. This planted a seed in my mind.[9]

Wilson's first academic position was at Cleveland State University, Cleveland, Ohio. An urban campus located in the heart of Cleveland, the university had a large number of Vietnam veterans enrolled as students. One of Wilson's undergraduate students, Chris Doyle, interviewed and reported the war stories of several Vietnam veterans for his class project in psychology. The project intrigued Wilson and he decided to expand it. He sent out letters to Vietnam veterans enrolled in school asking them to come in and talk about their war experiences. More than 100 veterans responded. Wilson and Doyle tape-recorded their life histories "covering life prior to Vietnam, into the military, a walk through of experiences in Vietnam, and what happened after Vietnam." Wilson recalls:

> I was shocked. The sessions were incredibly intense. There was a great deal of crying, anger, rage. There was something really big going on here. . . . I then discovered Department of Defense statistics which showed that the average [American combat] fatality [in Vietnam] was nineteen years old. I saw the identity diffusion discussed by [developmental psychologist Erik] Erickson. I could see how war stress impacted on personality development and ruined identity, produced identity confusion. I could see how they lost choice, direction.
>
> I had a sense of fear. I felt that I was looking down on an enormous phenomenon. What was happening to the vets was huge, immense. I had a sense that their stories and struggles had to be universal.[10]

The interview sessions consumed Wilson's work. His departmental chairman informed Wilson that he was wasting his time and threatened to block his tenure and promotion if Wilson did not establish a "more appropriate" research agenda. Instead of giving up the project, Wilson set up rap groups at the university for Vietnam veterans. "I didn't know what I was doing," he admits, "but I sensed that it was needed. There is much more to adaptation, adjustment than psychologists thought." Realizing however that he needed to publish in order to retain his academic position, he requested funding from the Cleveland Foundation and local veterans organizations to complete a preliminary study of Vietnam veterans. He found no takers. In 1976, a 100 percent disabled veteran whom Wilson had interviewed called the national office of Disabled American Veterans (DAV) in his behalf. In 1976, DAV provided $45,000 to complete the study.

Wilson and Doyle completed over 450 interviews and wrote the preliminary report entitled, *The Forgotten Warrior Project*.[11] Wilson noted that those who served in Vietnam were on the average nineteen years of age compared to an average age of twenty-six among soldiers in World War II. The effects of combat are intensified among the younger group of veterans, he explained, because this age encompasses an important phase in the transition from adolescent to adult identity. He detailed unique aspects of the Vietnam experience which produce problems for its veterans. Boyle, with Wilson paying for the airfare out of his own pocket, presented the preliminary findings at the 1976 meeting of the American Psychological Association in San Francisco.

At about the same time Wilson initiated his work, Charles Figley assumed the position of Assistant Professor of Family Studies at Purdue University.[12] Figley served in Vietnam in 1965 with the Marine Corps and so was among the first Vietnam veterans to return home. He completed his undergraduate degree and then attended graduate school in human development and family studies at Pennsylvania State University. He took part in Dewey Canyon III, his "first and last peace demonstration." There and at Bowling Green State University, where he held a temporary position, he met other Vietnam veterans and became aware of their widespread difficulties readjusting after Vietnam.

Figley was given free rein at Purdue University to investigate the pscyhological and social aspects of the recovery process. He compiled a bibliography on readjustment from combat and was struck by the lack of up-to-date research on the topic. He shared the bibliography with Vance Hartke of the Senate Committee on Veterans' Affairs. Hartke entered the bibliography in the *Congressional Record*. As a result, Figley soon was corresponding with fifty or sixty persons interested in exchanging information and scientific reprints. He organized panels in 1975 at the American Sociological Association and the 1976 American Orthopsychiatric Association. He met and began exchanges with Chaim Shatan, Robert Lifton, and others. Drawing on these contacts, he solicited articles and case histories from researchers and clinicians concerning their work with Vietnam veterans. To fill the void in the professional literature, he began work on an edited volume entitled *Stress Disorders among Vietnam Veterans*.[13]

Meanwhile, the VA itself had no formal research of its own to assess the needs of Vietnam veterans. In 1975, the Senate Committee initiated a bill, which Congress approved, mandating the VA to conduct such a study. As a result, the VA provided funds to Arthur Egendorf and the National Veterans Resource Project (NVRP) to complete the Vietnam Generation Study originally begun by Jack Smith, Chaim Shatan, and Robert Lifton.

DSM-III in Progress: "No Change Is Planned."

John Talbott, then director of Manhattan State Hospital, conducted some of the initial interviews for the Vietnam Generation Study. One of

Talbott's first interviews had a startling impact upon him and revealed a dimension of the problem he heretofore had not seen:

> I've just [now] done a book where we took letters to "Dear Abby" about family members who had schizophrenic kids living at home. Those letters reveal a side of living with schizophrenia that I as a therapist, as an administrator, as a teacher, had never seen. . . . And in some ways [this] interview was the same way.
>
> Here I'd been to Vietnam, I'd interviewed guys in Vietnam . . . , and here a guy comes and sits down and tells me about things that happened to him that he hadn't told his analyst, . . . his friends, his lovers. . . . He hadn't told 'em, any of them, that he'd been there, [that he'd been to Vietnam]! Incredible! Like it was a closed subject. . . . It was a conspiracy of silence between himself and everyone he knew.
>
> And for me to realize, "Holy shit! How many of these people are out there? How many in my own hospital?" And then I did a survey in my own hospital and found that most Vietnam veterans did not put down on their admission that they were Vietnam veterans. And I realized that we had a large problem—with the recognition of the syndrome, with the recognition of people, with the identification of self, and so forth.[14]

The successful challenge to the homosexuality entry in *DSM-II* opened a floodgate of inquiries about additional changes in the list of diagnoses. Robert Spitzer felt that his handling of the homosexuality issue provided a model for evaluating these requests. His position also implied that *DSM-II* should be completely redone. The news that *DSM-III* was in the works appeared in the June 1974 edition of *Psychiatric News*. About that time, a public defender in Asbury Park, New York, attempted to use a "traumatic war neurosis" defense in a case in which his client, a Vietnam veteran, was charged with destruction of property. The judge denied the strategy, saying that there was no such listing in *DSM-II*. The defender telephoned Spitzer and asked him if *DSM-III* would reinstate stress reactions associated with combat. Spitzer reputedly told him, "No change is planned."

Word of this conversation filtered back to Shatan through a reporter for the *Village Voice*. The news caught Shatan by surprise. He recalls: "I was startled. I got together with Lifton and said, we must do something about this."[15] The significance of the developments within the APA had not been lost on Lifton and Shatan. They felt that they had sufficient empirical evidence for a diagnostic category devoted to combat-related stress. They had assumed that the battle was mostly won. It was clear now that the reverse was true: without concerted and effective effort on their part, *DSM-III* would contain no listing for combat-related disorders. They would have to prepare a description and justification specifically for this purpose. They also knew that they still would have to drum up support for the change.

That month, Shatan and Smith met with Marion Langer, the executive director of the American Orthopyschiatric Association (AOA). They requested, and received, a grant to write a diagnosis for combat-related stress. The Vietnam Generation Study was proceeding very slowly. The initial interviewing had just begun. Smith expanded his staff. He hired Arthur Egendorf, a Vietnam veteran from the early New York City rap groups and then a graduate student in psychology at Yeshiva University. Later, Amitai Etzioni provided office space for the project at his Center for Policy Research at Columbia University. However, Shatan, Lifton, and Smith would have to push on, leaving NVRP and the Generation Study to fend for themselves.[16]

Vietnam Veterans Working Group

The strategy now, according to Jack Smith was very simple: "We realized that we needed to create some kind of public questioning. We needed to move from the arena of what did Spitzer think into the public arena, okay?"[17] To take their message to the public, Shatan, Lifton, and Smith first arranged with WBAI radio station in New York City for an all-day marathon broadcast on Vietnam veterans. They encouraged listeners in the New England area to call in with comments and questions. Vietnam veterans camped out in the lobby of the station. The broadcast won a local award for the best radio broadcast of 1974.

John Talbott could play a key role in this effort. To begin with, he could approach Robert Spitzer easily. They had been colleagues at Columbia University Medical School and were friends. Further, he was head of the New York City chapter of the New York Psychiatric Association and held prominence within the APA itself. (In 1984, Talbott would become national president of the APA.) Though participants at annual meetings of the APA, Shatan and Lifton were outsiders. Talbott sponsored monthly meetings within the New York City chapter. He invited Shatan, Sarah Haley, Arthur Egendorf, and others to give presentations on "Post-Vietnam Syndrome" in order to raise the issue's visibility within the APA. This group then arranged for a meeting with Spitzer at the 1975 APA convention.

Shatan and the others were especially excited by Sarah Haley's participation. The rest of them worked outside the VA with veterans who mostly avoided the VA. Haley had years of experience treating Vietnam veterans within the VA. In June of 1974, her article, "When the Patient

Reports Atrocities," had appeared in the *Archives of General Psychiatry*.[18]
The article detailed how a therapist's own feelings about war might
interfere with the ability to treat patients traumatized by war experiences. Haley recalls her difficulties in getting it published:

> The VA fought it tooth and nail. Papers must be cleared for publication by
> a VA board. They were not about to let the paper go out for publication.
> Finally, I went to see a guy, someone who was a good administrative
> person, and said, "C'mon, this is what happens in Russia. This is the U.S.
> of A.! Let me get it published!" He said, "Okay."[19]

Several high-profile appearances at professional meetings followed in
rapid succession. Shatan organized a roundtable discussion, "War
Babies," for the 1975 American Orthopsychiatric Association annual
meeting that March in Washington, D.C. The panel addressed the intergenerational transmission of stress and introduced Haley's work with
the children of Vietnam veterans. Psychiatrist Leonard Neff put together
a panel, "The Vietnam Veteran: Continuing Problems of Readjustment,"
for the APA annual meeting two months later in Anaheim, California.
The panel featured presentations by Lifton and Shatan. Neff, who previously had worked at the Los Angeles Brentwood VA, reported an incident which dramatized the dynamics of combat-related stress. Shatan
states:

> A vet escaped from the Brentwood VA and laid siege to some police cars.
> The vet was armed and took over a patrol car. Neff rushed to the scene and
> determined that [the vet] was having a flashback. So Neff called out to
> him, "Attention! This is Captain Neff. The mission is accomplished. You
> don't have to fight any more. Lay down your arms." The vet surrendered
> peacefully. The event showed that you could deal with the violence if it
> were understood and approached properly.[20]

Shatan, Lifton, and others met briefly with Spitzer in Anaheim. Spitzer reminded them that other psychiatrists and researchers also studied
Vietnam veterans, notably John Helzer and Lee Robins of Washington
University, St. Louis. Helzer and Robins argued, in their writings and in
their own meetings with Spitzer, that no separate classification was
necessary in diagnosing the problems of Vietnam veterans.[21] Spitzer
challenged Shatan's group to disprove that. Shatan recalls:

> [After the meeting with Spitzer], we all sat down. Neff, Haley, Lifton, and
> I—we formed the Vietnam Veterans Working Group. I said, "Who is going
> to do all this work [to disprove the claims of the St. Louis group]? The
> others said, "Well, you are, of course. We'll help!"[22]

Back in New York, Shatan took charge. He rounded up finanicial support and hired Jack Smith to work full time on the project. The Working Group designated the diagnostic category "post-combat disorder," and set about gathering evidence systematically. William Niederland, a long-time acquaintance of Shatan's, and Henry Krystal organized a conference on victimization at Yeshiva University. Krystal and Niederland's research focused on concentration camp survivors.[23] Shatan, Archibald and Tuddenham, and others earlier had noted similarities in the readjustment process between these survivors and combat veterans. The Working Group now began to think of the diagnostic category as a more generalized phenomenon of which post-combat disorder was but a single example. Niederland and Krystal joined the Working Group.

Committee on Reactive Disorders

That summer, the Working Group invited Spitzer to lunch at Columbia Presbyterian Hospital in New York City. They brought him up to date on their thinking and data-collection efforts. Spitzer listened but stressed that the burden of proof still rested with the Group. However, he now appointed a formal committee, the Committee on Reactive Disorders, to proceed with the inquiry and report to the *DSM-III* task force. The Committee consisted of three representatives from the *DSM-III* task force—Spitzer himself and psychiatrists Lyman Wynne and Nancy Andreasen. He instructed Andreasen, the committee chair, to work with Shatan, Lifton, and Smith in justifying and developing a diagnosis. Talbott explains:

> [Spitzer] started out being a very data-driven person. . . . If the data aren't there, the thing doesn't exist. . . . The pressure groups began to rise and say, "Look, this should be in and this should be out. . . ." And he would say, "There aren't data!" . . . I think he started out saying, we're going to throw *DSM-II* out the window, we're going to have zero-based budgeting, as it were. . . . And what he ended up doing was a two-part process, one, setting up task groups who were experts in the field, and two, subjecting it to a political process in the American Psychiatric [Association] that ensured that it would be adopted by them.[24]

The APA committee provided the Working Group with formal entry into the writing of *DSM-III* and was Spitzer's way of giving the issue a genuine opportunity to find its way into the manual. The appointment of Jack Smith to the Committee on Reactive Disorders was highly unusual. Of the roughly 125 experts serving on the various advisory committees who were to write and justify descriptions of mental disorders, only 6 were not M.D.s. Of the 6, only 2 were not Ph.D.s, and of the 2, only Smith did not have a graduate degree. In fact, as Smith states, "I didn't even have a bachelor's degree [at the time]. So, talk about irregular!"[25] Spitzer clearly was being accomodating.

The appointments, however, did not obscure the political hardball that lay ahead. The division of labor called for Shatan, Lifton, and Smith—the "Working Group three"—to convince the other three committee members with hard evidence that they should include some combat-induced disorder in the revised manual. Smith thought that Andreasen, a specialist in treating severely burned patients, would be the key vote.[26] He reasoned that problems arising out of the production of *DSM-III* would distract Spitzer himself and noted that Andreasen shared Spitzer's point of view as a hard-bitten empiricist. Though she also had other assignments, she could devote attention to the details of this committee's work. Smith expected Spitzer to accept Andreasen's verdict, thumbs up or down.

The original Working Group—which had continued as the organizational vehicle through which Shatan, Lifton, and Smith carried out their work for the Reactive Disorders Committee—steadily widened. Smith met with Harley Shands, the chief of psychiatry at Roosevelt Hospital in New York, who worked extensively with people who had been injured severely on the job. They concluded that the symptoms of these compensation victims were very similar to those of concentration camp survivors and combat veterans. Likewise, the Group corresponded with Mardi Horowitz of the University of California, San Franciso, who was in the final stages of his research on the physiology of stress.[27] Shands and Horowitz joined the Working Group. The Group then reviewed the literature on victims of catastrophes of other sorts. They solicited the help of specialists in each of these areas. This strategy put them in touch with a wide range of researchers and clinicians, many of whom fed them additional evidence, encouragement, and support.

In March 1976, the AOA held its annual meeting in Atlanta. The Working Group set up a workshop on combat disorders. They invited Andreasen to attend the session and marshalled their data for the new diagnostic category. They drew these data primarily from the case histories of Vietnam veterans who had attended the New York City rap groups. The Group also brought other evidence with which to persuade Andreasen. Haley recalls:

> What I did was stay after work at the VA and, without anybody knowing it, I went through the records of all the Vietnam veterans we had seen in a

year. I looked at what their diagnoses were. What I looked at was the official, the *DSM-II* diagnosis, the official one that you had to put down coded in the record. But then in parentheses [for some] was a working diagnosis. The working diagnosis was ususally "traumatic war neurosis." And so what I said was, "Look it, Nancy, we had to give these guys . . . diagnoses [consistent with DSM-II], but if you look at what [some] clincians are actually doing, . . . they're basing their treatment on the fact that they recognize in these fellows similar traumatic war neurosis as they saw in World War II and Korean war veterans. . . ." That really turned her around.[28]

They also spoke with Andreasen about her experiences in treating burn victims. She confided that she had observed stress reactions of the sort the Group described among her burn patients as well. By the end of the workshop, the Group felt that they had won Andreasen over. They now regarded her as an ally rather than an obstacle.

The Balance of Power Shifts

In 1976, Governor Jimmy Carter of Georgia received the Democratic nomination for President of the United States and defeated Republican incumbent Gerald Ford. President Carter appointed Max Cleland, who in 1972 had headed a commission on veterans' affairs for him in Georgia, as director of the Veterans Administration. Congress confirmed Cleland without a hitch. He was sworn in on March 2, 1977, and, by coincidence, Alan Cranston assumed the chairmanship of the Senate Committee on Veterans Affairs. Not coincidentally, Guy McMichael accepted the position of chief legal counsel for the VA.

In his confirmation hearings, Cleland asserted that readjustment counseling would be his top priority as chief of the VA. To accomplish this, someone would have to breathe new life into the Cranston bill, which already had gone down to defeat three times. Cleland sought out Shad Meshad. Cleland states:

> I first met Shad Meshad [in 1975], you can imagine, here I am a guy from Georgia and . . . I think Shad Meshad out in southern California is some Muslim, hippie, wierdo freak that is terrorizing the local bureaucracy in the VA with his incessant demands. I . . . have lunch with Shad Meshad and find out he's a good old boy from Birmingham, Alabama. And that Meshad is Lebanese . . . and the Shad is kind of a nickname. And find out that he's a . . . psychology officer out of Vietnam, went down in a helicopter crash, himself experienced disability, has had several operations since then, and carried a real burden for the guys coming back. [I wanted to go]

nationwide with the program. . . . See, . . . this was a good marriage. I
had the political clout, and he had the understanding of what it took to
make the program work. And so Meshad became the major consultant in
designing the program.[29]

Cleland himself was something of a maverick and, like President Carter, a outsider in the stream of Washington politics. Cleland's three pre-
decessors as chief adminstrator of the VA were all veterans of the Second
World War and former national commanders of either the American
Legion or the VFW. Recalling Cleland's appointment, Guy McMichael
chuckles:

[When Cleland was a consultant for the Senate Committee in 1975], he
was supposed to . . . go to some . . . VA hospitals, and take a look and
see what the situation was. He came back and wasn't back ten minutes and
I got all kinds of phone calls from people in the Veterans Administration.
Who is this man Cleland raising hell in this hospital? They wanted to
know who this wild man was. Max was not about to put up with any
nonsense and he wanted to get to the bottom of things, and find out the
problems. Impatient to get things done. And he scared the hell out 'em at
the VA, and he initially irritated them.

And when they found out that he was going to be [the national] administrator [of the VA], a sense of panic broke out among some people
[there]. . . . What is he going to do? [McMichael laughs] It was kind of
interesting, yeah.[30]

Meanwhile, the Working Group continued to collect and enrich the
case histories of Vietnam veterans until they had data on more than 700
subjects. In a position paper written by Shatan, Haley, and Smith, the
Group presented their specific recommendation and coding for *DSM-III*.
They called for an entry labelled "catastrophic stress disorder" and provided for acute, chronic, and delayed manifestations. They argued that
the only significant predisposition for catastrophic stress disorders was
the traumatic event itself, and stated that the symptoms, course, and
treatment differed by the cause and onset of the disorder. The paper also
included a section on a subcategory of the catastrophic stress disorder,
social catastrophe type—post-combat stress reaction. In May 1977, they
held a panel discussion at the APA annual meeting in Toronto to make
the proposal public.[31]

Opposition to the proposal continued to come from the researchers at
Washington University-St. Louis. Their basic position was that the standard diagnositic categories of depression, schizophrenia, and alcoholism adequately covered the symptoms manifested by Vietnam veterans
and the veterans of previous wars. By this time, however, the Working
Group was in good position to advance their case. They were members

of the APA Committee on Reactive Disorders. Their evidence was well prepared and well rehearsed. In short, they were well organized and politically active, and their opposition in St. Louis was neither of these.

Cleland in the meantime assembled a committee to provide a specific recommendation for a VA readjustment counseling program. The committee met in Washington, D.C. in October, 1977, and included Vietnam veterans Shad Meshad, William Mahedy, Charles Figley, and Dean Phillips, and VA representatives Guy McMichael and Tim Craig. Mahedy recalls of the meeting:

> That was the famous all-nighter. . . . Guy McMichael told us . . . they wanted a national program and needed a design for it. . . . And we talked about the ideas we'd had, the circle of treament and how that had to be, you had to get places outside away from VA hospitals, rap group counseling, and I included an employment component, . . . we needed an employment counselor right there, and so forth.[32]

Mahedy later wrote of the meeting:

> On Halloween night and into the morning hours of the next day, Shad and I put on paper the ideas that had evolved from the work in his Vietnam veterans unit, from Chuck Figley's research, and from anything else we knew of that seemed to work anywhere in the country. We finished our final draft about eight in the morning and immediately presented it to Guy McMichael. . . . He liked it and submitted it to Max Cleland and other officials within the agency.[33]

Cleland set up a subsequent committee headed by VA psychiatrist Jack Ewalt. Ewalt formerly was dean of the Harvard University Medical School and a specialist in community mental health services. Ewalt had credibility in the mental health field and expertise in setting up mental health centers. Ewalt and colleague Donald Crawford of the New Haven VA Hospital had already given the matter some thought. Anticipating that legislation for readjustment counseling might pass Congress in an upcoming session, Ewalt had put out a request in 1976 within the VA for proposals to implement a readjustment counseling program. Crawford had a modest prototype in place at the New Haven VA facility and had developed a detailed description it. However, now Cleland handed Ewalt the bare bones outline provided by the "Halloween night" committee and instructed him to expand it into a full-fledged proposal that could be implemented within the immense VA bureaucracy.

Ewalt and Crawford developed a comprehensive proposal. This was not an easy task, especially since the proposed program would operate outside traditional VA confines. McMichael explains:

I don't want to underestimate that there was a good deal of institutional reluctance within the VA medical community about how to proceed with this thing. I mean what Ewalt wanted to do wasn't necessarily what the chief medical director [wanted]. . . . I mean, hospital directors don't like this idea of funding going out to something which they can't see and don't have control over . . . . And certainly [the "Halloween night" committee] reinforced the need for something that wasn't so bureaucratically structured. It was important in terms of reinforcing Max's own instincts that this program had to be a little bit different than the run-of-the-mill program.[34]

Defeated Again

In January 1978, Spitzer called in the Working Group to present their findings to the Committee on Reactive Disorders. Lifton, Smith, and Shatan presented their evidence in a meeting with Spitzer, Andreasen, and Wynne. Lifton, Shatan, and Smith summarized their research and argued in favor of a listing entitled catastrophic stress disorder. They emphasized a wide circle of victims within the war zone, and the similarities between these victim groups and those traumatized in other "manmade" disasters and, to a lesser extent, naturally occurring disasters. The meeting went well. Later that month, Spitzer, Andreasen, and Wynne released the final draft of the committee's decision. They recommended a diagnosis under the label "post-traumatic stress disorder." Their description of PTSD de-emphasized the distinction between humanly produced and naturally occurring disasters, but otherwise appeared almost exactly as the Working Group had prepared it.

On March 5, 1978, Shatan wrote a letter to the members of the Vietnam Veterans Working Group. His letter provided good news:

This a letter of thanks to each and every member of the V.V.W.G., signaling the successful completion of our enterprise. . . . We are happy to say that the latest draft version of *DSM-III* (Jan. 1978) incorporates most of our formulations on stress disorders, not only for combat veterans but also for Holocaust survivors and victims of other disasters, both man-made and otherwise. . . . We are happy to have reached agreement on it.[35]

The APA completed and published *DSM-III* about two years later.

Cranston reintroduced his bill during the 1978 session. Despite its previous defeats by the House Committee, there was reason for optimism and concern about the bill's chances. As usual, the Senate Committee was fully behind it and, by now, Cranston had held hearings for seven years running to air publicly the need for some such program. The new president and a new chief adminstrator of the VA were both solidly behind the idea. The APA had just accepted the diagnosis for PTSD, and there was a specific plan outlining the form the program would take. Also in 1978, the eleven Vietnam-era veterans serving Congress had formed an official caucus, Vietnam Veterans in Congress (VVC). VVC included ten House members—Les Aspin (D-Wis.), David Bonior (D-Mich.), John Cavanaugh (D-Neb.), David Cornwell (D-Ind.), Albert Gore, Jr. (D-Tenn.), Thomas Harkin (D-Iowa), James Jones (D-Okla.), John LaFalce (D-N.Y.), and Leon Panetta (D-Calif.)—and Senator John Heinz (R-Penn.).

Chairman Ray Roberts of the House Committee on Veterans Affairs seemed annoyed by these developments. In a 1978 television interview concerning the needs of Vietnam veterans, Roberts stated in response to a reporters's statement that "the Vietnam veteran is really a minority with [the major] veterans organizations":

> Well, [the Vietnam veteran] is a minority, period. In five million veterans that were called during Vietnam, a million of them went over there and some, maybe in a combat zone, as against seventeen million in World War II. So, he is a minority."[36]

A dismayed VVC noted that the chairman of the House Committee on Veterans Affairs did not know how many Vietnam-era veterans there were (nine million), how many had served in the theater of combat (three million), or how many World War II veterans there were (twelve million), and, further, that Roberts seemed to imply that Vietnam veterans had not experienced much combat in Vietnam. In short, the House Committee was still hostile to the Cranston bill.

Meanwhile, VVC proposed its own bill, the Vietnam Veterans Act. It provided tuition grants and an extension of the statute of limitations on G.I. Bill education benefits, and expanded unemployment programs. It also included the Cranston bill on readjustment counseling and an earlier Cranston initiative for expanded drug and alcohol counseling. VVC requested, both verbally and in writing, a formal hearing with Roberts and the House Committee. Roberts rebuffed the requests, refusing to meet formally with VVC. His committee would not hold a single day of hearings on legislation introduced by VVC in the House. Without the backing of the House Committee, the VVC bill was doomed.

Nevertheless, a deal was in the works. In exchange for House Committee support of the Cranston bill, the Senate Committee offered to support House Committee legislation allowing the Committees on Veterans Affairs to have a say in choosing the location of future VA facilities. Having a say in the selection of these sites would provide members with a significant "pork barrel," that is, a way to enhance their own districts. Hence, the issues of readjustment counseling and VA site selection were tied to a larger package of VA health care programs. Backers of adjustment counseling lobbied the House vigorously. For instance, Shad Meshad recalls the loud clashes between himself and Olin Teague, now chair of a House Subcommittee on Aviation and Space Exploration:

> It was like pro wrestling, me against Olin Tiger Teague. When I came in [to his office] to talk with him, he wore his Medal of Honor [from World War II] around his neck. He'd say, "How can you little wimps be sick? Need counseling? A tour of duty only lasted twelve months! In World War II, soldiers fought in the war for years. How could you be traumatized?" He'd roar at me, and I'd roar right back at him. It was like pro wrestling.[37]

However, the proposed swap did not work out. The American Legion, VFW, and DAV continued to express the same budgetary concerns and opposed the bill. Roberts and House Committee member David Satterfield (D-Va.) remained adamantly opposed the provision for readjustment counseling. As Bonior later wrote:

> Vietnam veterans had many friends in Congress. They had friends on the Senate committee. They had friends in the House. But in veterans politics, the only friends who counted were the leaders of the House committee.[38]

Roberts allowed the entire package of veterans legislation die in the House Committee.

The Committees Strike a Deal

In 1979, proponents of the Cranston bill moved quickly to reintroduce it. The squabbling over readjustment counseling in 1978 had felled the entire legislative package, affecting older veterans as well as veterans of the Vietnam War. This debacle increased political pressure in both the House and Senate Committees on Veterans Affairs to do something. In short, they were motivated to pass significant veterans legislation during the 1979 session. It became increasingly clear that, in order to do this, the House Committee would have to give Vietnam veterans, as represented by interested persons and groups outside the House Committee and the major veterans organizations, a slice of the pie. Coincidentally, Olin Teague retired from Congress, leaving those opposed to the Cranston bill with one less influential voice.

Once again the major veterans organizations defined the problem as one pitting a service-connected program for Vietnam veterans against nonservice-connected programs for older veterans. The Disabled American Veterans (DAV) was the first organization to break ranks with this position. By definition, DAV's membership is made up only of veterans having service-connected disabilities, whereas only a minority of American Legion or VFW members have service-connected disabilities. DAV had become increasingly uneasy with the annual trashing of the Cranston bill. Though stopping short of publicly endorsing the bill, DAV muted its opposition and, by some accounts, provided covert support. The American Legion, and especially the VFW, remained adamantly opposed.

So, in 1979, the battle lines were familiar, but the bill's proponents had reason for optimism. Guy McMichael, chief legal counsel for the VA, recalls:

> Well, [the passage of the Cranston bill] was now in the cards. I mean now you had the adminstration backing you, and Senate backing it, and you had a changing attitude on the part of the veterans' organizations. You have a disabled Vietnam veteran heading the VA strongly urging its passage. At that point, it was on the track and no one was going to derail it.[39]

The same deal was on the table. The Senate Committee would swap site selection with the House Committee for readjustment counseling. The House Committee decided to accept the offer. Their acquiescence cleared the way, and on its fifth try in the decade of the 1970s, readjustment counseling for Vietnam veterans passed both the Senate and the House without incident. Max Cleland states: "And so, it's interesting that the final deal was a standard political trade. . . . Horse trading! It was just unbelievable. But it happened."[40]

On July 13, 1979, President Jimmy Carter signed Public Law 96–22 to establish the Vietnam Veterans' Outreach Program. The bill's enactment occurred as President Jimmy Carter declared a week to honor Vietnam veterans, leading columnist *Washington Post* David Broder to observe:

> What has happened is this: As their price for approving the special treatment for the psychologically damaged Vietnam vets, members of the House Veterans' Affairs Committee have demanded from the president and the Veterans Administration veto power over all significant future VA hospital and medical facility construction. . . .
>
> Next to tipping over a wheelchair, it is hard to imagine a shabbier way for Congress to mark Vietnam Veterans Week.[41]

Vet Centers

Whether the results were shabby or not, Cleland was pleased with them and moved to open the first VA facilities for readjustment counseling, dubbed "Vet Centers," as quickly as possible. The program called for a nationwide network of Vet Centers, each modeled after the storefront operations devised by Shad Meshad for the the Brentwood VA Hospital. The Vet Centers were to be located in the community away from other VA facilities. Each was to be manned by three or four specially trained paraprofessionals rather than psychiatrists or psychologists, and would provide individual counseling, rap groups, and benefits counseling. William Mahedy recalls the first meetings to get the program off the ground:

> And the first meeting was very informative. . . . Art [Blank, of the VA] was the only psychiatrist. And there were a couple of clinical psychologists and social workers. And then, an interesting collection of people from the streets, . . . people who were doing veterans' work informally and from little storefront centers around the country. The idea was to use their models. . . . [A]nd I remember talking to Art Blank. I said, "Art, for a national program, this is a real thin residue of experts." He said, "We know more about it than anybody else."
>
> The original norm as I remember it was, . . . the team leader should, where possible, have a master's degree level of training—social work, counseling, psychology, whatever. Nursing, even. . . . And the rest of the team should be skilled in dealing with vets off the street. Should be vets themsevles whenever possible. . . . Then you would refer serious cases to the VA hospital for in-patient or out-patient treatment.[42]

Cleland personally opened and dedicated the first Vet Center in a shopping center in Van Nuys, California in November, 1979. He then sent his team of "experts" from the VA around the country to set up other Vet Centers. Sometimes the road was very rocky. Cleland's intuition had been that the VA should have a treatment program for Vietnam veterans that departed substantially from the traditional services it provided. The form that it took evolved as idealism clashed with organizational realities. In the end, the Brentwood model on which the Vet Centers were based had to be ramrodded through the system. Cleland explains:

> [The VA] was bogged down in bureaucracy, especially to the non-service-connected veteran backed up by veterans' organizations that have non-service-connected members by the millions. They always outnumber the

service-connected guys. And so, the tail begins to wag the dog, and your priorities get out of joint.

So Vietnam veterans didn't fit the profile, they didn't fit the veterans organizations, they didn't fit the attitude of the country, didn't fit the existing bureaucracy. And the class of '46, as [World War II veterans] are affectionately known, thought [we] were a bunch of cry babies, wierdos, and barn burners. . . . And when I got there in '77, the class of '46 was running the agency and every major department. You understand what I'm saying? . . . [Y]ou had to bypass the whole bureaucracy to set the thing up."[43]

Mahedy describes the rough-and-tumble action at the level of the committee sent out to implement the program:

. . . [T]he conflict within the institution came from the very beginning. . . . I remember a meeting in Long Island. [The VA] brought in a guy from Central Office [in Washington, D.C.] who was going to give us the statistical requirements and what we needed in terms of bureaucracy. And there was open rebellion. We simply said, "We're not going to do it! [The Vet Centers] gotta be outside [the VA]! . . . Tell 'em to stick it! Go back home and do it again!" And he did. We ran him right out!

The VA, the Department of Medicine and Surgery, . . . wanted to run a medical model situation and we wanted to run a street-based model. Now the compromise was that . . . the Vet Centers were placed under DM&S . . . and the hospital had authority over logistic aspects of it. They would pay the bills. But they had no program control. Program control was exerted through what they . . . now call regional managers. There were six regions. . . . The program control, it went from the team leader to the regional manager to the Central Office program director. That's the way it worked.[44]

By 1981 the VA had established 137 Vet Centers across the country. Those who had sought and established readjustment counseling within the VA considered the Vet Centers an enormous success. Max Cleland, reflecting later on his days as national administrator of the VA, states:

"The thing that I'm proudest of, I guess, is the whole Vet Center program. And so, as I look back, I know that we healed, we helped heal a lot of minds and a lot of souls. . . ."[45]

In 1982, the commemorative Olin Teague Award for Outstanding Service and Innovation by a Federal Employee was announced. (Teague had died in 1980.) The first recipient of this award was Shad Meshad.

Notes

1. Jim Goodwin, "The Etiology of Combat-Related Post-Traumatic Stress Disorders," in *Post-Traumatic Stress Disorder: A Handbook for Clinicians*, ed. Tom Williams (Cincinnati, Oh.: Disabled American Veterans, 1987), 1–18.

2. See, for instance, Charles Moskos, Jr., "The Military," in *Annual Review of Sociology*, ed. Alex Inkeles, James Coleman, and Neil Smelser (Palo Alto, Calif.: Annual Reviews, Inc., 1976), 55–77.

3. Goodwin, "The Etiology," 7–8.

4. Guy McMichael, personal interview with author, 9 March 1989, Washington, D.C.

5. Rusty Lindley, telephone interview with author, 17 April 1989, Washington, D.C.

6. McMichael, personal interview, 9 March 1989.

7. David Bonior, Stephen Champlin, and Timothy Kolly, *The Vietnam Veteran: A History of Neglect* (New York: Praeger, 1984), 137.

8. Shad Meshad, personal interview with author, 24 October 1988, Dallas, Texas.

9. John Wilson, personal interview with author, 24 October 1988, Dallas, Texas.

10. Ibid.

11. John Wilson, *Identity, Ideology and Crises: The Vietnam Veteran in Transition: A Preliminary Report on the Forgotten Warrior Project* (Cincinnati, Oh.: Disabled American Veterans, 1977).

12. Charles Figley, telephone interview with author, 10 November 1988, Lafayette, Indiana.

13. Charles Figley, ed., *Stress Disorders among Vietnam Veterans: Theory, Research and Treatment* (New York: Brunner/Mazel, 1978).

14. John Talbott, telephone interview with author, 24 February 1989, Baltimore, Maryland.

15. Chaim Shatan, personal interview with author, 24 October 1988, Dallas, Texas.

16. Dozens of researchers, mostly on a part-time basis, participated in the Vietnam Generation Study at various times over the next few years. The plan was that each researcher would bring his or her own expertise and agenda, and that it would all fit together at the end. The research was completed and published in 1981. See Arthur Egendorf, Charles Kadushin, Robert Laufer, George Rothbart, and Lee Sloan, *Legacies of Vietnam: Comparative Adjustment of Veterans and their Peers* (Washington, D.C.: U.S. Government Printing Office, 1981).

17. Jack Smith, telephone interview with author, 22 December 1988, Cleveland, Ohio.

18. Sarah Haley, "When the Patient Reports Atrocities: Specific Treatment Considerations of the Vietnam Veteran," *Archives of General Psychiatry* 30 (1974):191–196.

19. Sarah Haley, personal interview with author, 25 October 1988, Dallas, Texas.

20. Shatan, personal interview, 24 October 1988.

21. John Helzer, Lee Robins, and D.H. Davis, "Antecedents of Narcotic Use and Addiction: A Study of 898 Vietnam Veterans," *Drug and Alcohol Dependence* 1

(1976):83–90, and "Depressive Disorders in Vietnam Returnees," *Journal of Nervous and Mental Disease* 168 (1976):177–185.

22. Shatan, personal interview, 24 October 1988.

23. Henry Krystal and William Niederland, eds., *Psychic Traumatization* (Boston: Little, Brown, 1971).

24. Talbott, telephone interview, 24 February 1989.

25. Jack Smith, telephone interview with author, 29 December 1988, Cleveland, Ohio. Smith later obtained a B.A. degree in psychology from Columbia University and entered the doctoral program in psychology at Duke University.

26. Smith, telephone interviews with author, 22 December 1988 and 12 September 1989, Cleveland, Ohio.

27. Mardi Horowitz and George Solomon, "A Prediction of Delayed Stress Syndromes in Vietnam Veterans," *Journal of Social Issues* 31 (1975):67–80; Horowitz, *Stress Response Syndromes* (New York: Aronson, 1976).

28. Sarah Haley, telephone interview with author, 9 November 1988, Somerville, Mass.

29. Max Cleland, telephone interview with author, 27 January 1989, Atlanta, Georgia.

30. McMichael, personal interview, 9 March 1989.

31. Chaim Shatan, John Smith, and Sarah Haley, "Proposal for the Inclusion of Combat Stress Reactions in DSM-III," paper for the DSM-III Task Force of the American Psychiatric Association, June 1976; Chaim Shatan, Sarah Haley, and John Smith, "When Johnny Comes Marching Home: Combat Stress and DSM-III," paper presented at the annual meeting of the American Psychiatric Association, Toronto, May 1977.

32. William Mahedy, telephone interview with author, 22 November 1988, San Diego, California.

33. William Mahedy, *Out of the Night: The Spriritual Journey of Vietnam Vets* (New York: Ballentine, 1986), p. 63.

34. MacMichael, personal interview, 9 March 1989.

35. Chaim Shatan, "Stress Disorders and *DSM-III*," letter to members of the Vietnam Veterans Working Group, 5 March 1978.

36. Quoted in Bonior, Champlin, and Kolly, *The Vietnam Veteran*, 139.

37. Meshad, personal interview, 24 October 1988.

38. Bonior, Champlin, and Kolly, *The Vietnam Veteran*, 136.

39. MacMichael, personal interview, 9 March 1989.

40. Cleland, telephone interview, 27 January 1989.

41. Bonior, Champlin, Kolly, The Vietnam Veteran, 134.

42. Mahedy, telephone interview, 22 November 1988.

43. Cleland, telephone interview, 27 January 1989.

44. Mahedy, telephone interview, 22 November 1988.

45. Cleland, telephone interview, 27 January 1989.

4

"ONLY WE CAN PREVENT
FORESTS"

Motto, Operation Ranch Hand, 12th Air Commando Squadron, U.S. Air
Force, Republic of Vietnam

By 1979 Vietnam veterans and their friends had achieved some significant victories. The third volume of the American Psychiatric Association's
Diagnostic and Statistical Manual (*DSM-III*) contained an entry for combat-
related difficulties in readjusting to civilian life, Post-Traumatic Stress
Disorder (PTSD). A disabled Vietnam veteran headed up the Veterans
Administration (VA). Significant alterations in the political lay of the land
were underway, and Congress finally had overcome its paralysis and
passed legislation for addressing readjustment issues among Vietnam
veterans. These changes would prove to be the calm before the storm.

A small number of disability claims filed by Vietnam veterans in 1978
produced a ruckus within the VA. Between 1965 and 1971, United States
armed forces in Vietnam had sprayed approximately eleven million gallons of an herbicide called Agent Orange. By the end of 1978, about 500
Vietnam veterans had claimed that exposure to this herbicide while they
had been in Vietnam some seven to thirteen years earlier had now produced health abnormalities among themselves or their children. Since
they attributed the cause to an event occurring while in the military, they
contended that the problems were service connected. The scenario
seemed unlikely to VA medical officials. Furthermore, it did not conform
to the VA's one-year statute of limitations in defining service connection.
VA administrators adopted a defensive posture and suggested that op-
portunistic veterans were pushing the issue to qualify undeservedly for
disability ratings and compensation payments. Several angry Vietnam
veterans filed what eventually would become a $4 billion class action
lawsuit against the manufacturers of Agent Orange.

Also in 1978, Vietnam veteran Bobby Muller founded what was to
become the largest and the most successful organization devoted solely
to Vietnam veterans, Vietnam Veterans of America (VVA). VVA began

simply enough in Washington, D.C. with Muller and three four or other veterans acting as a small but vocal advocacy group for Vietnam veterans. It had two aims: first, to lobby for congressional legislation on behalf of Vietnam veterans, and second, to address the larger meaning of the Vietnam experience. Out of financial necessity, VVA eventually cultivated dues-paying members, and by 1985 it had established itself as a organization with almost 250 local chapters across the country. In 1986, it received formal recognition from congress as an official veterans' organization.

The rise of Agent Orange as an issue and VVA as an organization are closely related. Significant numbers of Vietnam veterans were angered by their inability to receive answers to and treatment for troubling and serious health problems. When the congress and the VA reacted slowly and reluctantly to their inquiries—and, in some instances, openly opposed them—veterans interpreted the hesitancy and conflict as a flagrant violation of the pact between the government and its warriors, and as part of an overall pattern of indifference to them in American society. Hence, the Agent Orange controversy and the growth of VVA mark the politicization and emergence of Vietnam veterans in the postwar era.

This environment also sparked a third initiative. In 1979, Vietnam veteran Jan Scruggs announced to the world his dream of building a memorial listing the names of all Americans killed in Vietnam. This chapter recounts the early days of the Agent Orange controversy, VVA, and the Vietnam Veterans Memorial Foundation (VVMF).

Temporary Duty

Ideally suited for guerilla warfare, the dense jungles and forests of South Vietnam allowed communist troops to fight when they had the advantage and hide when they did not. Therefore, as early as 1961, the American military toyed with the idea of defoliating combat areas. In that year, then Vice-President Lyndon Johnson traveled to Saigon to discuss the types of assistance desired by the South Vietnamese government. The United States/Vietnamese Combat Development and Test Center (CDTC) was formed as a result of these talks. The CDTC examined an array of new counterinsurgency tactics and weapons, including the use of herbicides to deprive communist troops of cover and food supplies.[1] Dr. James Brown, Deputy Chief of the Crops Division at the Army's Chemical Warfare Center at Fort Detrick, Maryland, was directed to develop a defoliation program.

The initial plan called for Brown and his team to train Vietnamese pilots to carry out the spraying operations. South Vietnamese officials, excited about the program's possibilities, would be responsible for the testing of procedures and equipment and the execution of the program. Available aircraft, defoliants, and spraying equipment quickly proved insufficient for the task. However, Brown recalled that the Air Force had tested various aerial spraying systems during the 1950s at Ft. Detrick. These tests had established the effectiveness of an herbicide mixture containing the compounds 2,4,5-T (n-butyl-2,4,5-trichlorophenoxy-acetate) and 2,4-D (n-butyl-2,4-dicholorophenoxy-acetate) when sprayed from special 1,000-gallon tanks installed in the bomb bays of B-29 and B-50 heavy bombers or the cargo compartments of C-119 transports. The Air Force placed the special defoliant and its delivery systems in storage after the Korean War without using them. Although the U.S. Army originally developed 2,4,5-T during the Second World War for chemical and biological warfare, the military apparently considered it safe to use as an herbicide. Later, an Army training manual distributed in Vietnam described Agent Orange, a 50–50 mix of 2,4-D and 2,4,5-T, as "relatively nontoxic" to humans and animals.[2] Further, farmers and ranchers, the forestry industry, and government agencies had used phenoxy herbicides containing 2,4,5-T in the United States since the 1950s.

Brown now recommended that the military again purchase this herbicide mixture and requested C-119s for dispensing it. The Air Force informed him that C-119s were no longer in the inventory but that C-123s could perform the same mission. On July 13, 1961, the Air Force ordered the preparation of six C-123s for spraying missions "in the Far East" under the designation "Operation Ranch Hand."[3] Ambassador Frederick Nolting, Jr., suggested that the planes carry civilian markings and that the crews wear civilian clothes. This idea was rejected. However, the State Department asked that the South Vietnamese government formally request the spraying program and place it under its operation since the C-123s obviously were American aircraft and would be flown by U.S. Air Force pilots. Nevertheless, U.S. military officials adopted an extremely tight-lipped stance regarding the program and gave it a "Secret" classification.

The six planes arrived in Saigon on January 7, 1962, and were stored in a specially guarded Vietnamese Air Force compound at Tan Son Nhut airfield. Assignment to Ranch Hand represented "temporary duty" rather than a regular station or job rotation. As the spraying program commenced, the U.S. military purchased herbicides from American chemical companies, who mixed the ingredients according to military specifications and packaged them in color-coded fifty-five gallon drums that gave them their names: Agents White, Blue, Purple, Pink, Green and Orange.[4] The first spray missions, designed to train the pilots and test the equipment, dispensed a mixture of 2,4,5-T and 2,4-D known as Agent Purple.

At first, the spraying program was not readily accepted. Especially during 1962 and 1963, there was frequent discussion about the effectiveness and advisability of the use of herbicides. Many officials who visited the initial test sites in Vietnam were unimpressed. The results from these early efforts simply were not as dramatic as expected. Further, some officials feared that the program opened the U.S. to criticism. For example, Roger Hilsman, a short time later the Assistant Secretary of State for Far Eastern Affairs, opposed the program:

> Defoliation is just too reminiscent of gas warfare. . . . It [could] cost us international political support, and the Viet Cong [could] use it to good propaganda advantage as an example of Americans making war on the peasants.[5]

Hilsman also objected to the destruction of crops when "food denial" became an explicit mission in addition to that of depriving the enemy of cover, stating: " . . . the underfed people of South East Asia would never understand this act by a country with surplus food."[6]

Despite these concerns, in August of 1962 President John Kennedy approved the implementation of the spraying program in selected areas. By the summer of 1963, Ranch Hand personnel had developed the procedures and equipment to defoliate effectively. Changes in the pumps and spray booms allowed the C-123 to dispense 430 gallons of Agent Purple per minute, enough to cover a 240-foot swath with three gallons per acre. The Air Force conducted ongoing tests at Eglin Air Force Base, Florida, between 1962 and 1970 to continually assess and upgrade spraying techniques. Colonel Alvin Young, who holds a Ph.D. in herbicide physiology, and then was a newly commissioned lieutenant, participated in many of these tests. He states:

> I worked with an awful lot of pilots who flew in Vietnam. I was involved in . . . developing the spray equipment at Eglin. . . . In the spraying of malathion, we used "Teejet" nozzles that . . . were racketed . . . on the spray boom every few inches. . . . And this meant that the particle size was . . . about a 30 micron particle-size, [the size] you needed to be effective against the vective-carrying insects, particularly the mosquito.
>
> So that was very different than the case of the herbicide, where . . . you were looking for large particles, because you wanted them to come straight down. And so, we removed most of the nozzles, but we flared the pipes coming out of the boom. . . . [B]ecause of the altitude and speed, that gave us a particle size of about 250 to 260 microns . . . , which meant

that spray drift was still possible, but only marginal. We're talking about yards, you're not talking quarters or half a mile.

I stood underneath many, many spray flights. And actually watched them, and had the stuff land on me as the aircraft was flying over. We were very concerned about particle size and how fast it came down.[7]

A Permanent Organization

In April of 1964, Ranch Hand became a permanent organization rather than a temporary duty assignment. Between 1963 and 1970, defoliation of enemy strongholds was considered a highly desirable asset by unit commanders, and their requests for spray missions typically exceeded the number that Ranch Hand could possibly deliver. The number of aircraft assigned to Ranch Hand increased steadily, reaching thirty-three during the height of the spraying program in 1969. In 1965, the Air Force replaced Agent Purple with Agent Orange, a less expensive mixture but easier to use mixture of 2,4,5-T and 2,4-D. Over the next five years, U.S. armed forces sprayed approximately eleven million gallons of Agent Orange.[8] About 90 percent of the spraying took place in jungle and forest regions, about 8 percent was devoted to destroying croplands under their control, and the remaining was used to clear U.S. basecamp perimeters and communication lines. The 12th Air Commando Squadron (ACS)—Operation Ranch Hand—did most of the spraying. However, other military units sprayed the herbicide using helicopters, trucks, and backpacks to transport it.

In the course of the war, the 12th ACS was destined to become the most decorated squadron in the Air Force. The C-123s were an anomaly in the new "high tech" Air Force and required special skills and experience to fly. The pilots initially were apologetic about spending time in the cockpit of an aircraft that flew more by "feel" than by instrumentation. Paul Cecil, a Ranch Hand veteran, writes:

A C-123 instructor pilot best described the the special qualities of the relationship between the ungainly assault transport and modern Air Force pilots . . . : "Flying the one-twenty-three is a lot like playing with yourself—it's a hell of a lot of fun, but you're ashamed to admit that you do." Their missions required a close match of man and machine; performance had to be sensed, not judged by reference to complex instruments. The aircraft, however, matched the exact needs of . . . Ranch Hand. . . . Herbicide sorties . . . were a throwback to the . . . days of barnstorming and "seat of the pants" flying.[9]

The daily reality, however, was that the lumbering, low-flying C-123s made inviting targets. Some of the aircraft absorbed hundreds of "hits" from small arms and automatic weapons fire during the years of Operation Ranch Hand. Some hits were absorbed from the cluster bomb units of fighter jets that occasionally accompanied them, and Ranch Hand pilots sometimes encountered "friendly" artillery rounds impacting the target area during spraying missions. Patching up bullet holes and replacing shot-through parts was literally a routine part of daily maintenance on the aircraft. Pilots learned or developed for themselves various innovative flying techniques to reduce their vulnerability. For example, in the table-top flat Delta region, where the enemy had relatively clear lines of sight to track and fire on aircraft, pilots approached the area in which the chemical would be sprayed at 130 knots and an altitude of 20 feet, and then suddenly climbed to an altitude of 150 feet just before spraying the target zone. In the hilly and mountainous areas to the north of the Delta, aircraft approached downhill target areas at a higher altitude from the backside of the hilltop and then followed the contour of the slope to accomplish the spraying, or else negotiated entire valleys as close to the ground as possible. Another technique, advisable only when no enemy fire was encountered, called for one plane to circle the target area while giving directions and instructions to planes spraying at a lower altitude. Twenty-eight of the 1,200 men who served in Operation Ranch Hand at one time or another died in the line of duty.

These flying conditions fostered a great deal of camaraderie. The pilots had discussions as to which position in a formation was likely to take the most hits, and individual flyers lobbied the scheduling officers to be placed in the "hottest" spot in the up-coming day's formation. Likewise, the squadron maintained a tote board that tallied the number of times the aircraft in which each man was riding had been hit. Ranch Handers also took to wearing unauthorized black berets with Vietnamese insignia, a distinctive unit patch, and purple scarfs in "honor" of the first herbicide sprayed by them, Agent Purple. Cecil reports that Air Vice-Marshall Nguyen Cao Ky, at one time the Prime Minister of South Vietnam, began the latter tradition by giving his own violet-colored scarf to the aircraft commander after accompanying a Ranch Hand sortie:

> The violet scarf thus became one of the symbols of the spray organization, and was retained in spite of several later attempts to prohibit its being worn. In one instance, after General William C. Westmoreland's MACV Headquarters decreed a ban on the wearing of unauthorized uniform items by U.S. personnel in Vietnam, a special dispensation was granted for Ranch Hand scarves after a phone call to Ky, who then called the American ambassador, who in turn called the MACV commander. Report-

edly Ky threatened to close the gates of Tan Son Nhut Air Base if the spray crews were forced to remove their scarves.[10]

A Troubling Finale

In 1969 the Department of Defense received disturbing news. A a scientific study sponsored by the National Cancer Institute reported that laboratory animals exposed to trace amounts of dioxin, an unintended byproduct incurred during the manufacture of 2,4,5-T, developed cancer and had offspring with birth defects.[11] This coincided with reports to South Vietnamese officials of birth defects and other health problems in rural areas sprayed with Agent Orange. Complaints of this sort, dismissed as Viet Cong propaganda, had circulated since the start of the spraying program.

However, criticism was building. In 1966, Jean Mayer of the School of Public Health at Harvard University had assessed the impact of the food denial aspects of the spray program. He concluded that crop destruction affected children, women, and the elderly the most and fighting men the least. Summarizing Mayer's study and a subsequent investigation by the RAND Corporation, Paul Cecil concludes:

> Through interviews with VC prisoners and civilians from VC-controlled areas, . . . researchers determined that . . . the Viet Cong transferred the burden of the deprivation to local peasants [and] . . . , because most crops destroyed were civilian owned and cultivated, the indigenous population blamed the United States and the Saigon government for their economic hardships. . . . An indemnification program to compensate innocent and friendly victims of chemical attacks often failed to provide relief where intended, and thus failed to counter the propaganda advantage the program gave the VC.[12]

The American Association for the Advancement of Science (AAAS) sent an inspection team to Vietnam during 1969. The report, citing permanent soil contamination and a vast destruction of timberlands, called for a rigorous study of the long-term effects of herbicide use on human populations and the environment.

Apparently in response to such criticism and the concern that dioxin might pose a significant hazard to human health, the military in 1969 restricted the spraying program in Vietnam to "remote" areas. Without much explanation, Secretary of Defense Melvin Laird then reduced the budget for the purchase of herbicides that year from $27 million to $3 million. Within weeks after that, another Department of Defense direc-

tive announced a temporary ban on all spraying of Agent Orange in
Vietnam. Operation Ranch Hand in the meantime flew a reduced number of spray missions using Agents White and Blue. The ban on Agent
Orange became permanent in January 1971. Operation Ranch Hand flew
its last spraying mission on January 7, but some Army units failed to
receive word of the ban and continued spraying small doses of it
throughout 1971. On the homefront, the U.S. Department of Agriculture
placed restrictions on the use of 2,4,5-T in products or areas where direct
human contact was likely.

Questions about the consequences of herbicide use in Vietnam continued. In 1973, Dr. Matthew Meselson of Harvard University, an outspoken critic of herbicide use in Vietnam, developed a technique for
detecting dioxin at extremely low levels. His discovery allowed scientists
to requestion a large body of research that had failed to find evidence of
2,4,5-T's harmfulness. The scientific community soon was in agreement
that dioxin was very toxic; doses of three or four parts per billion killed
some laboratory animals.[13] Disagreement occurred over the issue, hotly
debated, of whether environmental exposure to herbicides containing
trace amounts of dioxin could produce cancer and birth defects among
humans. This remained a central bone of contention in the controversy
that would follow.

Nonscientific considerations were interwoven with this debate from
the start. Political divisions in the scientific community—for example,
between those who supported the war and those who opposed it, and
between "independent" researchers and those who worked for chemical
companies—were much in evidence. Colonel Alvin Young states:

> The agenda [of the 1969 AAAS inspection team] was not an agenda that
> talked about the health of the Vietnamese people. Their agenda
> was . . . they were wanting the military of the United States out of Viet-
> nam. . . . I think the fair assumption would be [that] most of the people
> who have ever had any experience with the herbicide—the agricultural
> community, the section to the public community who had experience with
> herbicides—probably lined up more with the military and the [position]
> that it was unlikely that there were health problems.[14]

The end of the spraying program left the question of what to do with
more than two million leftover gallons of Agent Orange, 860,000 gallons
of which were in open storage in Gulfport, Mississippi. In April of 1972,
all herbicides remaining in Vietnam were moved to Johnston Island in
the Pacific.[15] The manufacturers of the herbicides declined an offer to
buy them back, and a plan to sell them in diluted form to firms in South
America was rejected by the Environmental Protection Agency (EPA)

and the Department of State. The Air Force selected a high-temperature incineration process for ridding itself of the herbicides. The last of them were burned at sea on an incinerator ship on September 3, 1977.

Two Guys and a Mimeograph Machine

The Vietnam Veterans Coalition was founded in Washington, D.C. by Bobby Muller and Stuart Feldman in January of 1978 to serve as an advocate for Vietnam veterans. Almost immediately they changed its name to the Council of Vietnam Veterans (CVV). Their original position paper stated that "when the . . . war ended on April 30, 1975 . . . the American public ended its collective interest in the problem. In seeking to forget the war, they forgot the veteran as well."[16] The purpose of CVV was to bring the problems of Vietnam veterans to light. Muller, a former Marine Corps lieutenant paralyzed from the waist down by bullet wounds in Vietnam, was the spokesman; Feldman, a self-described "impolite civil servant" and lobbyist, was the strategist. Together they began what evolved into the largest membership organization comprised solely of Vietnam veterans.

Feldman had been an advocate for years of reforms in the G.I. Bill—a VA program begun after the Second World War that provides money for veterans to attend college—while holding various posts in the federal government. While working at the Department of Transportation in 1967, he had advanced a G.I. Bill "uplift program" to send a generation of Vietnam veterans to college just as the Bill had done for veterans of World War II.[17] The G.I. Bill, he felt, was doubly important for Vietnam veterans. Universal conscription during World War II had produced a veteran population drawn from the mainstream of American life. In contrast, those who served in Vietnam were drawn disproportionately from "the ragged fringes of the Great American Dream."[18] They were on the average nineteen years of age (compared to an average age of twenty-six among the Second World War soldiers), and they were poorer and had completed less formal education than their peers who avoided active duty.

Feldman's idea was to provide special provisions to help low-income veterans to make it through college. In late 1969, now employed at the Department of Health, Education, and Welfare, he proposed to tie the G.I. Bill to the first 25,000 troops to be withdrawn from Vietnam—an idea derailed because of discharge technicalities. In 1970, he hatched and orchestrated "Hope for Education." The project linked comedian Bob Hope's annual Christmas visit to Vietnam with the G.I. Bill by distributing thousands of enrollment forms while Hope entertained the troops. Fifty thousand soldiers signed up on applications provided by the Hope for Education tour.

However, the funding of the G.I. Bill for Vietnam veterans was hamstrung. After the Second World War, the bill paid a veteran's tuition directly to the university and provided books and a living allowance of $75 per month directly to the veteran. This allowed veterans to choose any university for which they qualified, including expensive private ones. Indeed, fully 59 percent of the students enrolled at Harvard University during the 1947–1948 academic year were veterans of the Second World War on the G.I. Bill. The figure for the same year for Notre Dame University was 85 percent; for Holy Cross College, 87 percent; for New York University, 54 percent; for Stanford University, 44 percent; and for the University of San Francisco, 66 percent—to name just a few.[19]

The House Committee on Veterans' Affairs changed the bill's payment plan for the veterans of Korea and Vietnam. For these veterans, the program offered a single payment for room, board, books, and tuition directly to the veteran. The amount for Korean War veterans was $110 a month and, for Vietnam veterans, $100 a month in 1966. A series of hard-fought amendments increased this latter figure to $310 a month by 1977. Though an improvement over the 1966 amount, all these allocations purchased much less education than the World War II plan. To begin with, the more expensive private schools were out of reach for those Vietnam veterans with limited budgets. For the year 1971–1972, 1.5 percent of Harvard's students were Vietnam veterans on G.I. Bill; the percentage was 1.7 percent for Notre Dame, .5 percent for Holy Cross, 4.2 percent for New York University, 1.6 percent for Stanford, and 8.0 percent for the University of San Francisco.[20]

Although the lower percentages for Vietnam veterans were somewhat attributable to differences in socioeconomic background between World War II and Vietnam veterans, and a smaller mobilization effort for the Vietnam War, Feldman believed that they also reflected the reduced purchasing power of their G.I. Bill. He showed, for example, that utilization of the G.I. Bill by Vietnam veterans was significantly greater in the Southwest and West, regions with state universities having relatively low tuition rates, than in the Midwest and especially the Northeast, which had higher state tuition rates and numerous private universities.[21] Since a return to the World War II plan was not in the cards, he lobbied for a number of novel, partial solutions. A *Fortune* magazine article later cited his role in increasing educational benefits as an inspiring example of "what one lobbyist can accomplish."[22]

However, the basic rub, Feldman felt, was that Vietnam veterans lacked an effective advocate. In 1973 he saw a television interview featuring the passionate and articulate Muller, then living in New York City. Born in Switzerland and raised in New York, Muller was commissioned in the Marine Corps upon graduation from Hofstra University in January of 1968. He served as a platoon leader with the 2nd Battalion, 3rd Marine Division for four months before becoming a Military Assistance Command (MACV) advisor with a South Vietnamese army unit. It was while serving as an MACV advisor that he received his paralyzing wounds. In 1970, *Life* magazine published an expose of deplorable conditions in a ward containing nine disabled veterans at the Kingsbridge VA Hospital in the Bronx. Bobby Muller was one of the nine. The report documented with photographs the dirty and degrading conditions on the ward and quoted its head doctor, who bemoaned the lack of staffing and facilities. One photograph depicted a dead rat caught in a trap that one of the "amputees not totally disabled [had] set . . . to protect the other [veterans]."[23]

The exposure in *Life* led to the first of Muller's five appearances over the next few years on the Phil Donahue Show. A member of the Eastern Chapter of Paralyzed Veterans of America (PVA), he soon served as the chapter's legislative director. He returned to Hofstra and received a law degree. Feldman urged Muller to move to Washington, D.C. to form an advocacy group. Muller initially remained with PVA but in 1977 decided to move. He recalls:

> I went to the guys that I had worked with for years and said, "Look, if there's even at this late date any chance of there being something done for Vietnam veterans, it's not going to be done from the vantage point of . . . this organization." Because the paralyzed vets, their needs were met more through a cooperative and sympathetic relationship with Congress than an adversarial, advocacy . . . kick-you-in-the-teeth kind of thing.[24]

The work with PVA had taught Muller a great deal about the world of veterans' politics. In particular, he noted, the bulk of the expenditures within the VA were directed now toward care for ailments that were not associated with military service. He intended to challenge this system in order to secure care for the needs of Vietnam veterans that were service connected. Hence, though PVA provided him with seed money to begin his venture in Washington, the relationship between Muller and the organization was a bit uneasy. Muller explains:

> I said, "If you guys would help me out, it would be appreciated." So they gave me a start-up grant of 42 thousand bucks. . . . It was nice . . . [but] the truth of the matter is, it was like, okay, Muller, take your radicalism, take your challenge to upset our applecart, and go play in another ball-

park. [Muller laughs] Very seldom is something really done on the merits.[25]

Upon arrival in Washington, Muller had a meeting with Phil Geyelin, then an editor of the *Washington Post*. Geyelin was very sympathetic to Muller's version of the issues concerning Vietnam veterans. During the course of 1978, Geyelin and columnist Coleman McCarthy placed more than thirty pieces on the Op-Ed page of the *Post* concerning Muller and the plight of Vietnam veterans. Within a day after the first editorial in February, Michigan Democratic congressman David Bonior, himself a Vietnam-era veteran who had served in the Air Force, called Muller and offered his help.

Bonior, however, had another pressing matter to confront first. Opposed by the American Legion and Veterans of Foreign Wars, he was in the midst of a fight for re-election. Muller traveled with Bonior throughout his district on a successful whistle-stop tour. They returned from the trip with ideas for a comprehensive "Vietnam Veterans Act" to present to Congress. On September 25, 1978, the newly formed Vietnam Veterans in Congress (VVC) introduced the bill. It would have granted tax credits to businesses who hired Vietnam veterans, expanded programs for readjustment counseling and the treatment of drug and alcohol abuse, provided a system of vouchers for veterans wishing to choose a physician or program outside the VA, extended the benefit period for G.I. Bill, added tuition assistance in states where education was more expensive, and provided low-interest home loans. It was an ambitious package. However, without the support of the House Committee on Veterans Affairs, who resented the upstart VVC, it was doomed. The bill failed without serious consideration.

At the end of the year, Muller and Geyelin had dinner together to assess the results of the first year's work. They agreed they had little to show for the effort. Muller states:

Geyelin said that he had never gone to bat editorially on behalf of a cause as he had with us on the Vietnam veterans' issues. . . . And he said, what's most remarkable is that he had literally no response to the campaign! He said, "Usually when we do a piece . . . , the White House calls us, [the] agency [involved] calls us, they demand the opportunity to rebut our allegations. . . . [Here] nobody called!" He said it was amazing.

So . . . we recognized that, you know, political science 101, you don't make costly programs by arguing for them simply in terms of morality and justice or some sense of equity. You make costly benefit programs a reality by bringing pressure on the representatives [in Congress].[26]

Geyelin had two suggestions. First, he urged Muller to address the overall "Vietnam experience" rather than simply focusing on veterans' benefit issues, as a way of "raising the level of discussion" and "creating a more sympathetic environment." Secondly, he advised Muller to convert CVV into a membership organization to generate political clout.[27] Some change was definitely needed. As Feldman quips: "You see, [the VA and Committees on Veterans' Affairs] dismissed us as two guys with a mimeograph machine, even though the 'mimeograph machine' was the *Washington Post.*"[28]

Agent Orange Gets White Hot

The VA received the first claims contending illness and disability due to herbicides in 1977. By then a scattering of Vietnam veterans had collected circumstantial evidence linking their health problems to exposure to Agent Orange in Vietnam. Among them was Air Force veteran Charlie Owens. Shortly after his retirement in 1977, his doctors diagnosed him as having lung cancer. Owens attributed his cancer to the Agent Orange sprayed by his unit in Vietnam. He expressed this concern to his wife Ethel, contending that the spray often was "so thick it looked just like Los Angeles smog."[29] Within a month after the diagnosis, Owens died. His wife relayed these concerns to Maude deVictor, a sympathetic caseworker for the VA. The VA rejected the notion that Owen's cancer was related to herbicide use in Vietnam, but did award Mrs. Owens death benefits since it found evidence that her husband had had difficulties with his lungs in Vietnam.[30]

DeVictor had not heard of Agent Orange; she asked other veterans if they recalled having been exposed to Agent Orange and requested information from the Department of Defense (DOD) about its possible harmful consequences. She called Dow Chemical Company, the VA Central Office in Washington, and scientists who might know something about Agent Orange, making 387 telephone calls in the month of October alone.[31] She spoke with Alvin Young, then a captain in the Air Force. The DOD sent her reprints of scientific studies that stated that there was no evidence of the herbicide's harmfulness to humans. Nevertheless she compiled files on about two dozen veterans who reported exposure to the herbicide. When her boss at the VA asked her to stop her informal investigation of Agent Orange, deVictor promptly turned over the files to Bill Kurtis, a reporter for WBBM-TV, Chicago's CBS affiliate.

Sensing a big story, Kurtis began work on a documentary about Agent

Orange.[32] He interviewed veterans who were themselves sick or who had children with birth defects. He also taped interviews with researchers. Dr. Matthew Meselson told of dioxin's potent toxicity and potential as a substance capable of producing cancer (a carcinogen) and birth defects (a teratogen). Environmentalist Dr. Barry Commoner told of how the process might work: the dioxin contained in Agent Orange could be stored in the body's fatty tissue and at a later date cause cancer or other diseases. Since the documentary would be broadcast to a local audience late at night, Kurtis sought to increase its exposure. In the week before its airing, he provided each senator and representative from Illinois with a transcript and videotape of the documentary and, on the day before the showing, held a private viewing for reporters from local newspapers.

WBBM aired the documentary, "Agent Orange: Vietnam's Deadly Fog," at 10:30 P.M. on March 23, 1978. The story attracted national attention. Hundreds of inquiries from veterans flooded into the VA office in Chicago. Representative Abner Mikva of Chicago (D-Ill.) arranged for a subsequent screening of the documentary before the House Committee on Veterans' Affairs. He invited other interested parties, including administrators from the VA, the Environmental Protection Agency (EPA), and the chemical companies who manufacturered Agent Orange. In one dramatic swoop, Agent Orange went from the private rumblings of a handful of veterans to the center of national attention.

In April of 1978, Representative Ralph Metcalfe (D-Ill.) asked the General Accounting Office (GAO), the official research arm of Congress, to elicit from DOD a review of herbicide use in Vietnam. DOD took the position that only the approximately 1,200 participants of Operation Ranch Hand were at risk, but nonetheless started compiling a computerized record of the spraying missions (called the HERBS tapes). Simultaneously, the EPA announced it would revoke the registration of (and hence preclude the further domestic use of) products containing 2,4,5-T unless manufacturers could document its safety for humans. The EPA cited studies of laboratory animals and of workers exposed to dioxin in industrial settings and accidents. The agency encouraged interested parties, including the general public, to submit information concerning exposure to dioxin and health problems. Residents of Alsea, Oregon reported a curious increase in miscarriages after a nearby forest was sprayed with Silvex, an herbicide containing 2,4,5-T. The EPA ordered an epidemiological study.[33]

The WBBM documentary touched off much concern within the VA about what to do. However, the initial reaction was more a scramble to defuse the issue rather than an effort to discover if there was something to it. The VA selected one of its medical specialists, Dr. Gerrit Schepers, to become the head of its first Agent Orange Policy Group. Schepers had previously been a researcher for Monsanto Chemical Company, one of the manufacturers of Agent Orange, and for DuPont Corporation. Joining him, among others, was VA physician Dr. Lawrence Hobson, who previously had been medical research director for a division of Olin Mathieson Chemical Corporation and, during World War II, the chief of the Medical Research Laboratory of the Government's Chemical Warfare Service.[34] In May of 1978, the VA circulated a memorandum describing procedures for dealing with Agent Orange-related inquiries. The memorandum stated that the effects of exposure to Agent Orange were short term and fully reversible. It urged the staff to reassure worried veterans but to make no statement that might support the notion that Agent Orange had harmed them.[35]

Richard Severo, an award-winning journalist for the *New York Times*, became interested in the Agent Orange story, and in early 1979 he interviewed VA officials about the matter. Using these data and memos later obtained under the Freedom of Information Act, he and attorney Lewis Milford devoted several chapters of their 1989 book to the Agent Orange story. In it, Severo and Milford describe an early meeting that set the tone of the VA response throughout much of the controversy:

> . . . [T]he VA concluded that it needed consultants to help evaluate what the veterans were claiming. It invited an unlikely pair of advisors to attend a meeting . . . on July 7, 1978: Dr. Ben B. Holder and Dr. Walter Melvin. Holder was the Medical Director of Dow Chemical Company, the major manufacturer of Agent Orange. . . . Melvin . . . was a former scientific director for the Air Force. . . . No other outside consultants came to the meeting. . . .
>
> . . . [At] the closed meeting, Holder said that the phenoxy herbicides were safe and that a "consensus of world experts" agreed that there would be no later health problems from Agent Orange unless the claimant first contracted chloracne. He did not . . . [report] that . . . a goodly number of scientists . . . were worried about the long-term effects of herbicides . . . in general, and Agent Orange in particular. . . . In the give and take of the meeting, the EPA representative said that studies suggested dioxin was a health hazard. But Melvin interrupted him right there, saying that just as many people said that dioxin was not a major problem.[36]

Paul Reutershan, a Vietnam veteran dying of abdominal cancer, filed a claim with the VA at about this time. The claim contended that the cause of his cancer was his exposure to Agent Orange while serving as a crew chief in a helicopter company for the 20th Engineering Brigade in Vietnam. Reutershan did not drink or smoke and considered himself somewhat of a health nut. He had agonized over the cause of his cancer until reading in the New York *Daily News* about Maude deVictor and the circumstantial evidence collected by her at the Chicago VA Hospital. He recalled his helicopter flying on many occasions through mists of Agent Orange. His doctors also had diagnosed him as having a skin condition known as chloracne, commonly considered by medical researchers as a reliable indicator of exposure to chlorinated compounds such as dioxin. Reutershan therefore felt that he had especially strong evidence for a claim with the VA. But although the VA acknowledged that he had cancer, it stated that Agent Orange was not its cause and denied him benefits despite the presence of chloracne.[37]

Angered by the decision, Reutershan explored the possibility of legal action. Judicial relief, however, is not easy for veterans to obtain. The doctrine of sovereign immunity and its related principle of intramilitary immunity, the Feres Doctrine, prohibit veterans from suing the government for damages incurred during military service.[38] Further, congressional legislation prohibits veterans from suing the VA over the disposition of a case.[39] Reutershan therefore filed a $10 million personal injury suit in a New York state court, naming Dow Chemical and two other manufacturers of Agent Orange as defendants.[40] Shortly before his death on December 14, 1978, Reutershan founded Agent Orange Victims International (AOVI) and pledged its handful of members to carry on the lawsuit after his death. "I died in Vietnam, but I didn't even know it," he said.[41]

The Issue Broadens

In December of 1978, the VA organized the Steering Committee on Health Related Effects of Herbicides. One of the committee's first tasks was to elaborate the VA's policy. Earlier directives instructed VA personnel to handle all Agent Orange inquires courteously but to make no statements in sympathy with the contention that Agent Orange might cause health problems. The committee noted that the VA considered an injury or illness as service connected only if it arose during military service or within a year after discharge from active duty. Since the symptoms reported by many Vietnam veterans did not appear during this time frame, they ruled that the ailments were not service connected and not the VA's responsibility. Lawrence Hobson of the Steering Committee explains the decision:

> . . . [I]f you lost a leg because of combat, nobody is going to quarrel with the fact that it was due to the exposure in combat. Or if you come back from the South Pacific with a tropical disease, nobody is going to quarrel

with what happened. When you have a long latent period, however, there is always room for doubt as to the causal relationship. That is what has created the problem for the VA in this connection.[42]

The committee also insisted on scientific evidence of Agent Orange's harmfulness, based on studies using human subjects, before it would treat or compensate those veterans whose initial symptoms did meet the criterion of temporary coincidence: that is, symptoms that occurred during military service or within a year after discharge from active duty. Dr. Paul Haber, the VA assistant chief medical director, explained the rationale to Richard Severo by stating that "all the studies you read about concern rats, mice, baboons, but nothing about men."[43] These rulings meant that veterans could not receive medical treatment from the VA for Agent-Orange related conditions or qualify for compensation.

In January of 1979, AOVI hired Victor Yannacone, an accomplished attorney in workman's compensation disputes and a passionate foe of the chemical industry, as their "legal field commander." Yannacone refiled Reutershan's complaint as a class action suit in federal court on behalf of all Vietnam veterans and their children who might have been damaged by the herbicide.[44] The suit named all six manufacturers of Agent Orange—Dow Chemical, Hercules, Northwest Industries, Diamond Shamrock, Monsanto, and North American Phillips—as defendants. Yannacone estimated the damages at $4 billion.

Agent Orange quickly proved to be no ordinary product liability case.[45] From the moment it was filed, the Reutershan suit attracted attention and notoriety in the media. Attorneys on both sides felt that this worked in favor of the veterans. Even after the WBBM documentary and its coverage, very few veterans—indeed, very few Americans—knew about Agent Orange. Press coverage of the suit developed awareness and encouraged veterans who thought they might be afflicted to initiate claims and join the suit. In also created sympathy for the veterans and suspicion about the chemical companies.

Peter Schuck, professor of law at Yale University, would follow the trial closely and later write a detailed account of it and its place in legal history. By 1979, he notes, the toxicity of dioxin was well known though the controversy over its impact on human health continued. Fellow professor at Yale, biologist Arthur Galston who specializes in herbicide research, described dioxin to Schuck as "perhaps the most toxic molecule ever synthesized by man." Schuck writes:

One cannot fully appreciate the significance of the Agent Orange case without understanding just how toxic TCDD (dioxin) is. . . . Galston reported that dioxin concentrations as low as 5 parts per trillion (ppt)—an amount roughly equivalent to one drop in 4 million gallons of water—

"can, when supplied on a daily basis, induce a cancerous condition in rats. Concentrations about 1 ppb (part per billion) result in premature death from more acute causes, and concentrations of 50 ppb produce rapid signs of acute toxicity and early death. . . . [Researchers] have found that lower concentrations of TCDD produce the same effects as higher concentrations, but merely take longer to do so. . . ."[46]

Researchers such as Galston, however, clearly did not have the ear of VA officials. In March of 1979, Severo interviewed J. C. Pecharsky of the VA's Compensation and Pension Service in March of 1979. He writes of the interview:

By that time . . . hundreds of veterans of Vietnam had inquired, complained, and even filed papers describing strange and ugly things that they said were wrong with them. Pecharsky's desk contained hillocks of their missives. They complained of cancer and deformed children or children born dead. They complained of miscarriages, loss of sex drive and low sperm counts. They complained of strange aches and weaknesses . . . , weird lumps . . . , festering sores . . . , things that doctors would tell them were precancerous, but with no explanation of where they came from.

. . . In [Pecharsky's] view, the veterans filing claims had either been misled about Agent Orange or were deliberately lying about it in order to get something for nothing. "Absolutely nobody had an Agent Orange claim," [he] declared. . . . "Its only natural," Pecharsky remarked, "for them to look for something to hang their ailments on."[47]

New Initiatives

The conversion from the Council of Vietnam Veterans to Vietnam Veterans of America (VVA) began quietly in January of 1979. The purpose was to develop a national organization solely for Vietnam veterans. The prospects were not promising. There were scatterings of small, autonomous groupings of Vietnam veterans in cities across the nation. However, no one had been even remotely successful in uniting them into a single organization or in building a national organization alongside them. VVA faced the same vicious circle that confronts most budding organizations. It needed a substantial membership in order to generate the funds necessary to build a successful organization. To attract that membership would require planning, expertise, good luck, and, of course, funds. Stuart Feldman had suggested the idea of soliciting support and donations from the politicans who ran the war and the firms who profited from it. There were, however, few takers.

Ken Berez began working for VVA as a volunteer in 1979 and in January of 1980 joined the organization as a full-time employee. Severely wounded in Vietnam while an infantryman with the 82nd Airborne in 1969, Berez had no particular training that prepared him for the task. However, he was a self-described "quick learner" and he believed deeply in the cause. He had spent four years in military and VA hospitals recovering and rehabilitating from gunshot wounds to the spinal column and stomach. His only prior contact with veterans' organizations had taken place at the Philadelphia VA Hospital. He states:

> . . . [I]n 1971, the hospital . . . allowed groups to come in [for] social evenings, the VFW (Veterans of Foreign Wars), the DAV (Disabled American Veterans). And we petitioned to have someone from VVAW (Vietnam Veterans Against the War). . . . And the social director . . . finally said, "Okay . . . you can have your night."
>
> And the auditorium was really packed. Must have been a couple of hundred Vietnam vet patients who gathered that night. And two guys came [from VVAW], . . . wearing berets, you know, . . . and fatigues, and they gave very political, very heated speeches. . . . [T]hey paid absolutely no attention, no time was spent on . . . who was in the hospital, or of advocacy for Vietnam veterans. . . . And to tell the truth, it left me and others cold. . . . End the war, fine! But they were speaking before . . . [wounded, disabled] Vietnam veterans and they showed absolutely no sensitivity to the audience. It was if we weren't even there.[48]

Berez remained apolitical until seeing Bobby Muller on a television talk show. He began his volunteer work as part of a class project for a political science course at American University. At first the organization struggled simply to stay in existence. He says of those early days with VVA:

> The VVA office . . . in [those days] was a beat-up townhouse in the inner city in northeast Washington. You know, rat-infested, too hot during the summer, too cold in the winter. There was nobody that got paid [regularly] . . . , so there were 4 or 5 people at any given time. . . . I remember times when we literally were going to have to shut down and we'd get a donation of a thousand dollars. . . . [W]e were six, ten months behind on rent, . . . we owed IRS . . . in payroll taxes, things like that. We had to borrow xerox paper from people that we knew, staffers up on the Hill. They'd give us, you know, a few reams at a time. When I say it was bad, I'm not engaging in any hyperbole.[49]

1979 was to become a year of confrontation. Though President Carter had expressed an interest in addressing the problems of Vietnam veterans after his inauguration in 1976, and had appointed Max Cleland as

director of the VA, Muller and others at VVA saw little of the kind of
progress they sought. The solution, they felt, lay in mobilizing Vietnam
veterans into a political force and, simultaneously, in challenging the
system in the world of veterans' politics. To begin the first task, VVA
and VVC initiated a bill that set aside an official week to honor Vietnam
veterans. Public Law 95–313 designated the week of May 28 through
June 3 as Vietnam Veterans Week. The law urged cities to hold celebra-
tions to honor those who served in Vietnam.

The announcements about Vietnam Veterans Week caught the attention of Jan Scruggs. An infantryman with the 199th Light Infantry Brigade and recipient of the Purple Heart for wounds incurred during a
mortar attack, Scruggs was in search of a forum to advance an idea. In
March of 1979 he had seen the film *The Deerhunter*. The movie had left
him uneasy and upset. What bothered him most were the film's images
of simple, blue-collar folk who groped to find some meaning for the
deaths of family members and friends in Vietnam. Their quandry
echoed his own emotions about the war. As he mulled over the film, he
hit upon the idea of building a monument to commemorate those
deaths. He wished to build a memorial that listed the names of the more
than 57,000 Americans killed in the war.

Scruggs presented his idea at a meeting of forty or so Vietnam veterans sponsored by VVA to plan activities for Vietnam Veterans Week. The
name of "every G.I. killed in Vietnam" would be inscribed on the memorial, Scruggs stated. The money would be raised by seeking donations
from the American people. No government money would be used. He
said that he envisioned a small, half-acre park with a black marble ob-
elisk thirty feet high containing all the names. To his surprise, his idea
encountered opposition rather than a warm reception. Some thought
the idea simply naive. Others, including Bobby Muller, feared a fund-
raising drive to build the monument would detract from efforts to gain
support for the legislative programs needed by Vietnam veterans.
Scruggs, however, did find one Vietnam veteran willing to work with
him: Bob Doubek, a former Air Force officer and now an attorney. His
first words of advice: "You ought to form a nonprofit corporation."[50]

An Unconventional Proclamation

VVA's confrontation of the system, the second part of the equation,
began during Vietnam Veterans Week. In the spirit of P.L. 95–313, New
York City planned a ceremony to honor Vietnam veterans on May 29,
1979. Mayor Ed Koch headed a list of dignitaries and local veterans'

organizations, including the American Legion and Veterans of Foreign Wars, announced that they would send representatives. Bobby Muller was asked to speak. He variously presented himself as head of the Council of Vietnam Veterans and as the founder of Vietnam Veterans of America.

The *New York Times* and the *Washington Post* both ran feature stories about Vietnam veterans during the week preceding the ceremony. The *Times* presented biographical accounts of Muller and two other veterans who now were associated with VVA: Joseph Zengerle, a West Point graduate who had served in Vietnam as a special assistant to General William Westmoreland, and David Christian, who, as a the recipient of the Distinguished Service Cross, two Silver Stars, two Bronze Stars, and seven Purple Hearts, is one of the most highly decorated of Vietnam veterans. All three described their disillusionment. Muller stated:

> Going to war is a landmark experience in the life of an individual, an episode of tremendous importance, but in the case of Vietnam vets, you learned quickly to repress it, keep it a secret, shut up about it, because people either considered you a sucker or some kind of psychopath who killed women and children.[51]

Christian, who grew up in a blue-collar neighborhood in Levittown, Pennsylvania, said of his experience:

> All my friends—we were kids together, we grew up together, we went to Vietnam together. They don't know what happened. They can't figure it out. These are confused and broken guys. . . . It breaks my heart.[52]

And Zengerle, also a graduate of the University of Michigan School of Law and an attorney in Washington, D.C., added: "In the first job interview of my life, with a large Washington law firm, I was asked whether I committed any war crimes in Vietnam. It blew my mind."[53]

Muller also described articulately his wounds and the experience of recovery. He was wounded in April of 1969 as he led a charge of South Vietnamese troops up a hill near the refugee village of Cam Lo:

> I caught a bullet through the chest, through both lungs, severed the spinal cord, and right out the back. I saw suddenly a kaleidoscope. Fragmented colors. Somebody was hitting me with a sledgehammer—that's what it felt like. Totally numbing. Then I'm looking at the sky and it's getting dark and I say, "I'm dying." I didn't believe it. "I'm going to die on this ground." And I felt myself recede from consciousness, and that was it.
>
> I should have died on the hill. The kind of wound. Where I got it. I was incredibly lucky. And when I woke up on a hospital ship, it was unbeliev-

able. When they came around and told me I was going to be a paraplegic, my response, really, was, "So what?" Man, was I lucky.

. . . From the time I got shot, I never cried. The hospital ship, the naval hospital—the doctors and nurses and attendants cared. When I got to Kingsbridge [VA] Hospital and saw that this was going to be the place where I was going to be staying, it so overwhelmed me that I broke down and cried. My mother broke down and cried. It was overcrowded. It was smelly. It was filthy. It was disgusting.

. . . On my first day at the hospital, I asked for a wheelchair, and they said, "We can't get you one," and I went crazy. "What do you mean you can't get me a wheelchair?" I was a quiet guy, always, but when they put me in a corner like that, I began to scream.[54]

The celebrants gathered in Central Park on May 29 for the ceremony to honor Vietnam veterans, complete with a band, speeches, and awards. A sparse crowd of about 100 persons attended. The ceremony proceeded routinely until Muller rolled forward to speak. His speech was an indictment, and as he spoke, his voice rose in anger and he pounded his fist on his knee repeatedly for emphasis. He said that five of his eight ward mates from Kingsbridge VA Hospital had since committed suicide. He spoke of the pain of being stereotyped as "junkies, crazed psychos or dummies that couldn't find their way to Canada." He concluded by saying:

You people really ran a number on us. Your guilt, your hang-ups, your uneasiness, made it socially unacceptable to mention the fact that we were Vietnam veterans. Whenever we brought it up, you walked away from the conversation. . . . That really hurts the pride we had. We fought hard and we fought well. . . . If you turn your back now on the Vietnam veteran, you turn your back on the principles of this country.[55]

The front page *Times* story of the event reported the following day that, as Muller spoke, a shocked silence fell over the crowd so that the only sounds besides his voice came from a landscaping crew at the far end of the park. At the end of the speech, Muller received a standing ovation from the veterans on the speakers platform, including those of World War II and the Korean War. A shaken Mayor Koch then rose to read the proclamation for the week. A man rarely at a loss for something to say, he groped for words before saying that Muller's remarks were the "most stirring" he had ever heard. Rising to the occasion, he then said:

[Vietnam veterans] are not required to carry this battle on by themselves. They were sent to fight a battle and they fought it well and we have to thank them. If the United States did a number on Vietnam veterans, we have to correct it, and forthwith.[56]

"It Can Be Done"

The day before, Jan Scruggs, who had never been to a press conference before, much less conducted one, held a press conference at the National Press Club to announce the formation of the Vietnam Veterans Memorial Foundation (VVMF). He presented his plans for the building a Vietnam memorial and the goal of raising one million dollars. He optimistically, maybe foolishly, told the dozen or so reporters that "the only thing we're worried about is raising too much money."[57]

Scruggs took a temporary leave of absence from his job at the Department of Labor and secured a mail box at the post office for receiving the donations. The donations were small, typically $5 or $10. Usually a note accompanied the donation, giving the name of someone—a son, a father, a friend, a husband, a buddy—and imploring Scruggs: "Help him be remembered. Keep his death from being meaningless."[58] One letter stated: "Don't waste time and money writing us back. Just keep working." Watching television a few evenings later, Scruggs saw an amused Roger Mudd announce at the tail end of the CBS Evening News that the organization seeking to build a national monument honoring Vietnam veterans had thus far collected a "grand sum" of $144.50.[59] Later the same evening, he by chance saw a network program in which the comedian delivered a few jokes about Scruggs and the organization's efforts.

However, one person watching television that evening was moved rather than amused. John Wheeler, Vietnam veteran and graduate of West Point, Yale Law School, and Harvard Business School, had previously led the successful effort to build a Southeast Asia Memorial at the United States Military Academy. He now called Scruggs and volunteered his services to VVMF. "It can be done," he said. "Let me call some people."[60]

Notes

1. See Paul Frederick Cecil, *Herbicidal Warfare: The RANCH HAND Project in Vietnam* (New York: Praeger, 1986), Chapter 3, for a detailed description of these early days.
2. Department of the Army (DA), *Employment of Riot Control Agents, Flame,*

Smoke, Antiplant Agents, and Personnel Detectors in Counterguerilla Operations.
Training Circular TC3–16 (Washington, D.C.: DA, 1969).
   3.   Cecil, *Herbicidal Warfare*, 26.
   4.   See American Council on Science and Health (ACSH), *The Health Effects of Herbicide 2,4,5-T* (New York:ACSH, 1981); Council on Scientific Affairs, *The Health Effects of "Agent Orange" and Polychlorinated Dioxin Contaminants* (Chicago: American Medical Association, 1981); and Pamela Lacey and Vincent Lacey, "Agent Orange: Government Responsibility for the Military Use of Phenoxy Herbicides," *Journal of Legal Medicine* 3 (1982):137–178.
   5.   Cecil, *Herbicidal Warfare*, 34.
   6.   Ibid., 38.
   7.   Colonel Alvin Young, personal interview with author, 6 March 1989, Washington, D.C.
   8.   See Council on Scientific Affairs, *Health Effects*; Miriam Davis and Michael Simpson, *Agent Orange: Veterans' Complaints and Studies of Health Effects.* Issue Brief Number IB83043 (Washington, D.C.: Library of Congress, 1983); and Arthur Galston, "Herbicides: A Mixed Blessing," *BioScience* 29 (1979):85–90.
   9.   Cecil, *Herbicidal Warfare*, 49.
   10.   Ibid, 65.
   11.   Colin MacLeod et al., *Report of 2,4,5-T: A Report of the Panel on Herbicides of the President's Science Advisory Panel* (Washington, D.C.: U.S. Office of Science and Technology, 1971).
   12.   Cecil, *Herbicidal Warfare*, 154–155.
   13.   See American Council on Science and Health, *Health Effects*; Council on Scientific Affairs, *Health Effects*; and Fred Tshirley, "Dioxin," *Scientific American* 254 (1986):29–35.
   14.   Young, personal interview, 6 March 1989.
   15.   Cecil, *Herbicidal Warfare*, p. 165.
   16.   Stuart Feldman, telephone interview with author, 7 May 1991, Washington, D.C.
   17.   Ibid.
   18.   The quoted phrase is drawn from Philip Caputo, *A Rumor of War* (New York: Ballantine, 1977), 26.
   19.   Stuart Feldman, *Sunbelt States Reap G.I. Bill Bonanza: Eastern and Midwestern Vietnam Veterans Lose Scholarship Opportunities.* Report prepared for the National League of Cities, United States Conference of Mayors, Washington, D.C., 1977, 12.
   20.   Ibid.
   21.   For example, by fiscal year 1976, more than 50 percent of the Vietnam veterans in California and Arizona had enrolled in college under the G.I. Bill. Corresponding figures for Pennsylvania and Ohio were about 20 percent. See, Feldman, *Sunbelt States*, 10–12, for the percentages in 1976 for all states.
   22.   See Juan Cameron, "Carter Takes on the Budget Monster," *Fortune* January, 1977, 83–84. The article states: "The special-interest groups involved in federal spending range from the platoons of lobbyists representing General Motors and the American Medical Association down to the highly effective one-man efforts of little-known operators like Stuart Feldman. A thirty-nine-year-old attorney . . . , Feldman became interested in the late 1960s in expanding the World War II package of G.I. educational benefits for Vietnam veterans. . . . Without Feldman, the $23-billion assortment of veterans' educational programs would be much smaller than it is" (p. 84).

23.   Charles Childs, "From Vietnam to a VA Hospital: Assignment to Neglect," *Life*, 22 May 1970, 28.
24.   Robert Muller, personal interview with author, 27 March 1991, Washington, D.C.
25.   Ibid.
26.   Ibid.
27.   Ibid.
28.   Feldman, telephone interview, 7 May 1991.
29.   Bill Kurtis, *Bill Kurtis on Assignment* (Chicago: Rand-McNally, 1983), 43.
30.   Richard Severo and Lewis Milford, *The Wages of War: When America's Soldiers Came Home—From Valley Forge to Vietnam* (New York: Simon and Schuster, 1989), 364.
31.   Ibid, 365.
32.   Kurtis, *Bill Kurtis on Assignment*, 42–46.
33.   See Environmental Protection Agency, "Rebuttable Presumption against Registration and Continued Registration of Pesticide Products Containing 2,4,5-T." *Federal Register* 43 (21 April 1978).
34.   Severo and Milford, *Wages of War*, 369.
35.   VA internal memo, circulated May 18, 1978. See Fred A. Wilcox, *Waiting for an Army to Die: The Tragedy of Agent Orange* (New York: Random House, 1983), Appendix A, for a full text of the memo.
36.   Severo and Milford, *Wages of War*, 368–369.
37.   Wilcox, *Waiting for an Army*, 99–100; Severo and Milford, *Wages of War*, 369–370.
38.   See Feres v. The United States of America, 340 U.S. 135, 1950; Peter Schuck, *Agent Orange on Trial: Mass Toxic Torts Disasters in the Courts* (Cambridge, Mass.: Harvard University Press, 1986), 58–69; and Lacey and Lacey, "Agent Orange," 153–180.
39.   See Dean Phillips, "Subjecting the Veterans Administration to Court Review," *Strangers at Home: Vientam Veterans Since the War*, eds. Charles Figley and Seymour Leventman (New York: Praeger, 1980), 325–341.
40.   Reutershan v. The Dow Chemical Company, No. 78-CV-14365, (N.Y. Sup. Ct., N.Y. County), filed July 20, 1978.
41.   Wilcox, *Waiting for an Army*, ix.
42.   Lawrence Hobson, telephone interview with author, 22 March 1989, Washington, D.C.
43.   Severo and Milford, *Wages of War*, 363.
44.   Reutershan et al. v. The Dow Chemical Company et al. and The United States of America, No. 78-CV-4253, (S.D.N.Y.), filed January 9, 1979. Memorandum Supporting Plaintiffs' Amended Verified Complaint, filed July 15, 1979.
45.   Legal references for the trial are: In re "Agent Orange" Product Liability Litigation (MDL No. 381), 475 F. Supp. 928 (E.D.N.Y.) 1979; 635 F. 2d 987, (2d cir.) 1980; 454 U.S. 1128, 1981; and 597 F. Supp. 740 (E.D.N.Y.) 1984 (Weinstein, C.J.).
46.   Schuck, *Agent Orange on Trial*, 18. For the Galston report, see Galston, "Herbicides."
47.   Severo and Milford, *Wages of War*, 360–362.
48.   Ken Berez, personal interview with author, March 27, 1991, Washington, D.C.
49.   Ibid.

50.   Jan Scruggs and Joel Swerdlow, *To Heal a Nation: The Vietnam Veterans Memorial* (New York: Harper and Row, 1985), 8.

51.   Bernard Weintraub, "Now, Vietnam Veterans Demand Their Rights," *New York Times*, May 27, 1979, sec. 6, p. 30.

52.   Ibid.

53.   Ibid.

54.   Ibid., 32.

55.   Ann Quindlen, "A Vietnam Veteran Stills Audience with Rebuke," *New York Times*, May 30, 1979, A1, B3.

56.   Ibid., B3.

57.   Scruggs and Swerdlow, *To Heal a Nation*, 8.

58.   Ibid., 9.

59.   Ibid.

60.   Ibid., 10. In an interview with author and *Washington Post* staff writer, Rick Atkinson, Wheeler recalled reading about Scruggs and the $144.50 in a newspaper rather than seeing a report about them on television. See Atkinson, *The Long Grey Line* (New York: Pocket Books, 1989), 564–566, for Wheeler's recollections.

POLITICS 101

"If you at least begin . . . to open the door a little bit, and . . . show . . . some . . . policies . . . instead of . . . complete denial . . . , you're going to win the hearts and minds of the Vietnam veteran . . . . To me, it's Politics 101."

John Terzano, legislative liaison, Vietnam Veterans of America

During the last days of 1979 and during the 1980s, the Agent Orange controversy and Vietnam Veterans of America both grew by leaps and bounds. VVA seized the opportunity presented by the squabble over the legitimacy of Agent Orange claims before the VA to establish itself as a membership organization. However, as we shall see, VVA, or at least its leadership, devoted itself passionately to many causes besides Agent Orange. The organization therefore followed a course of development unrelated in many ways to Agent Orange. Likewise, Agent Orange had many champions other than VVA. It became a powerful and controversial issue with an identity and course of events far exceeding its connection with VVA. In particular, the class action lawsuit became the center of activity and media attention.

The story of the lawsuit, and of developments within other arenas where confrontations took place, shows that as the Agent Orange controversy peaked and waned it was championed by a changing array of interested persons and groups. The battle over Agent Orange allows us to see the politics of how facts are created and substantiated in an especially clear light. Several trends within the legal system boosted the significance of the Agent Orange suit.[1] To begin with, a series of decisions had gradually extended a manufacturer's liability to all individuals who used or were exposed to a product. Previously, the obligation to produce and market nondefective goods—the duty of care—had extended only to the purchaser of the product. In addition, strict liability without fault became the standard for assessing a manufacturer's culpability, whereas, in the past, the plaintiff had been required to show that the manufacturer failed to exercise reasonable precaution. The courts no longer required the plaintiff to prove that a specific defendant made the product that caused the damage so long as some reasonable method existed for allocating damages.[2] Finally, the amounts that courts and juries awarded in compensation for damages skyrocketed. Awards in excess of one million dollars became commonplace.

The growth, success, and eventual fragmentation of VVA over this same period provides insight into the history of an organization whose goal was to change social conditions. From the beginning there were serious rifts between VVA and the Iron Triangle—the House Committee on Veterans Affairs, the VA, and the traditional veterans organizations—and between the leaders of VVA and the membership they attracted. The former divisions, as we shall see, occurred by design. The latter necessarily developed as part of the process of building an organization.

Finally, the Vietnam Veterans Memorial Foundation (VVMF) quickly developed during the early 1980s into a major success story. VVMF faced many obstacles, but it struck a responsive chord and resourcefully devised strategy after strategy for clearing each hurdle in its path. The memorial, completed in 1982, would become the most visited of all the monuments and attractions in Washington, D.C. More significantly, it would indeed serve, as Jan Scruggs had hoped, as a beloved tribute to those who died in the war.

A Brand New Lawsuit

Victor Yannacone came very close to not being part of the class action suit that would make legal history. He had declined an offer to participate before the suit ever got off the ground. In July of 1978, Paul Reutershan had convinced Edward Gorman, a Long Island attorney, to file a $10 million personal injury suit against three of Agent Orange's manufacturers. Gorman soon realized he was in over his head and sought advice from other attorneys. Yannacone was one of those he approached for help.

Yannacone was an excellent choice. A highly competent, charismatic, and creative attorney, he also had the kind of driving and dominating personality that would be required for this case. Fred Wilcox, who interviewed Yannacone in preparation for his 1983 book, *Waiting for an Army to Die*, writes:

> Victor Yannacone has been called flamboyant, arrogant, a genius, and, I'm
> sure, many less complimentary things by those whose vested interests he
> challenges in the name of what he calls the "public good." Certainly, he is
> not modest. . . . Nor is he always gracious or polite, thundering like an

evangelist, occasionally answering questions with the clipped irritability of a man who has little time for fools, because he knows only too well that they can be depended on to lose; and Yannacone doesn't intend to lose when he goes to court on behalf of 2.5 million Vietnam veterans and their families.[3]

Of equal importance, Yannacone was a passionate foe of the chemical industry who took great delight in having led the legal charge that resulted in the banning of the pesticide DDT. However, when Gorman urged him to get involved in the Reutershan suit, he declined. He doubted that a link between Agent Orange and disease could be successfully established in a single case. Peter Schuck writes of Yannacone's initial reaction:

> A toxic tort is like being hit by a chemical bullet. The difference is that, unlike being hit by a car, you have to negate other possible causes. . . . I had already paid my dues to society in the DDT litigation, and I recognized that to take on another case of that magnitude without any resources, with a much more difficult scientific problem, and with much more well-entrenched chemical companies than in the DDT cases was basically a hopeless task.[4]

Agent Orange Victims International (AOVI), however, had pledged to carry on the suit after Reutershan's death. One of those who had made that pledge was Frank McCarthy. McCarthy himself was not an Agent Orange claimant. He had served in Vietnam as an infantryman with the "Big Red One," the First Infantry Division. He had been part of the unit when it trained at Ft. Riley, Kansas, and then redeployed in Vietnam in 1965. Booby traps and needless casualties—due, McCarthy believed, to restrictive rules of engagement that gave the advantage to the enemy—depleted the ranks of the division. McCarthy returned disillusioned, and his disillusionment turned to bitterness when protesters assailed veterans as well as the war. In 1975, he formed the Vietnam Veterans Unifying Group, initially to challenge limitations in the G.I. Bill and later to provide more general benefits counseling.

A friend had given McCarthy a newspaper clipping about Reutershan, and it was as head of the Unifying Group that McCarthy offered his help. Skeptical at first, he became a believer after fielding hundreds of telephone calls at the Reutershan household from veterans who were ill or had children with deformities. Schuck writes of McCarthy's conversion experience:

> McCarthy began to see Agent Orange as a metaphor for Vietnam veterans' helplessness and suffering, a symbol that could exert a far more powerful

galvanizing effect than the elusive bureaucratic enemy at the VA. As he had done in the early 1960s, [he] decided to join an army and a war, enlisting his remaining energy and ideals in a struggle against Agent Orange.

In late 1978 . . . [the] army was still only a tiny contingent, confined largely to his VFW post in Stamford, Connecticut. That post . . . was not typical. . . . [I]t was one of the "toughest" in the country, perhaps the first to be completely run by Vietnam veterans, most of whom were hardened combat soldiers harboring lots of painful and angry memories. . . . [T]he post [became] the core of the fledgling AOVI organization.[5]

This zealousness had its costs. Tensions between AOVI and Gorman escalated rapidly after Reutershan's death. The feeling was mutual: the case needed revitalization and AOVI needed a new attorney to direct it. After being rejected by more than a dozen attorneys, McCarthy called Yannacone at Gorman's suggestion. At first Yannacone refused to become involved, but several days later he relented. He had decided that a class action suit might work.

Yannacone's strategy consisted of four parts.[6] He would file a class action in federal court in New York on behalf of all Vietnam veterans who might have been harmed. Vietnam veterans and their families would then be encouraged to join the suit by having their own lawyers file related suits within their own jurisdictions. Yannacone would consolidate these suits into a single class action. Finally, he would be responsible for raising funds necessary to accomplish the task. Wilcox provides a description by Yannacone of the case:

> . . . [B]ecause of the size of the litigation . . . [we] would make an agreement with each attorney to divide the case into two parts: liability and damages. We here in New York would handle liability and what we call "Cause in Fact" or Generic Causation. In other words, how toxic is dioxin? And just what can it do? . . . Then each individual attorney . . . would handle his own client as a personal injury case as far as proximate cause and damages . . . , meaning: "Did this particular veteran manifest the kind of symptoms that would be attributed to . . . herbicides used in Vietnam? And if so, how much damage is he suffering?"
>
> . . . [W]e agreed from the very beginning—and this is unique—that we should subject our fee ratings to the court for supervision. We then agreed that we would limit our fees, which are contingent of course only upon winning, to no more than one-third of recovery, even though some states still allow 50 percent.[7]

The talk of damages indicated the staggering scope of the trial. After the initial calculations, damages were estimated to lie between $4 billion and $40 billion, sums that obviously would bankrupt the defendants without a full recovery of damages. Yannacone therefore advanced the notion of paying damages through a trust fund established out of the defendant's earnings. This novel solution would provide a reserve for paying damages now and in the future without driving the defendants into bankruptcy. Further, once a court had established the effects of Agent Orange, Yannacone hoped that affected veterans might also receive benefits and compensation from the VA. Finally, the fund would stand as an ongoing symbol of the "nondelegable fiduciary duty on the part of the chemical manufacturers to be the trustees of the public health."[8]

The suit was instantly a hit. Yannacone recounted to Schuck with obvious relish: "The phones rang off the hooks all day—150 calls, with the last coming at 3 A.M. from soldiers in Australia."[9]

Mixed Signals

As Vietnam Veterans Week—May 27 to June 2, 1979—drew to a close, Max Cleland, national director of the VA, was able to take satisfaction in two events. First, Congress had at last approved Senator Alan Cranston's long-suffering bill (described in Chapters 2 and 3) to establish a program of readjustment counseling for Vietnam veterans within the VA. Also, President Jimmy Carter held a reception for a select group of Vietnam veterans at the White House. Cleland, however, had little time to savor the victories. In response to the pressing Agent Orange question, he announced that the VA, the Air Force, and the Department of Health, Education, and Welfare had all embarked upon studies into the long-term effects of exposure to Agent Orange. The VA also prepared a pamphlet bearing Cleland's picture that encouraged concerned veterans contact their nearest VA medical center for information about Agent Orange.

However, the government was sending out mixed signals. Mrs. Richard Lutz earlier had written President Carter himself to tell of her concerns about the exposure of her son to Agent Orange in Vietnam. In a letter dated April 4, 1979, Deputy Assistant Secretary of Defense, George Marianthel, informed her that "we do not believe that a study of the health of our Vietnam veterans would add to the knowledge of the long-term health effects" of Agent Orange. The veterans' symptoms, he explained, "are almost certainly due" to something other than Agent Orange.[10] Further, a VA memo dated April 19, 1979, later obtained by Lewis Milford under the Freedom of Information Act, declared:

It is to be emphasized that . . . the VA Medical Centers will refrain from efforts to induce veterans who are not currently part of their patient population to undergo an examination for the possible health-related effects of herbicides.[11]

Meanwhile, the VA held firm to its position that it was not responsible for treating ailments suspected by veterans to be associated with Agent Orange with the exception of chloracne. On May 31, the National Veterans Law Center, a team of lawyers formed to advance the interests of veterans, asked the federal district court in Washington, D.C. to declare illegal the VA's refusal to consider disability claims of Vietnam veterans who said they were exposed to Agent Orange. If the VA appeared beleaguered, its officials in fact were groping to get a handle on the situation. Guy McMichael, who by this time had moved from the Senate Committee to the VA as Cleland's chief legal counsel, explains:

. . . I don't mean to cast the media [in a bad light] or anything, but there were elements of this which sold newspapers. . . . [Y]ou can show a Vietnam veteran, from a war that was highly unpopular . . . , [who] had not been accorded the same kind of reception coming back that other veterans had. When you get that with somebody who has cancer, whose child has a birth defect, throw in the war profiteers, Dow Chemical and those who made the stuff, and now an uncaring bureaucracy that won't provide them benefits. I mean, you've got a first-rate story here.

And this then began to cause people within the VA to become defensive. I mean, suddenly, it was very hard to say you are out there trying to find out what the information is when people are accusing you of ignoring hundreds of thousands [of] Vietnam veterans who are in suffering agony out there, who have children with birth defects, and you guys are being technical, you guys are being bureaucratic. So I mean that was the kind of situation in which [our] people were [working].[12]

In late May, the *New York Times* published a three-part series about Agent Orange written by Richard Severo. Part three addressed, among other things, what the policy should be concerning Agent Orange claimants, given the controversy over the herbicide's harmfulness. Dr. Charles Wurster, visiting scientist at the National Cancer Institute, criticized the position of waiting until scientific proof became available before acting on the claims. He explained to Severo:

The fallacy in the argument is that these are chemicals, not humans. Chemicals are not innocent until proven guilty, because if you consider the chemical innocent until proven guilty, people are going to have to get tumors to prove it guilty. . . . In other words, if you confer human rights on chemicals, you can only do so by taking them away from humans.[13]

However, a frustrated Gary Jones, public affairs manager of the Dow Chemical plant in Midland, Michigan, responded generally to this sort of criticism, telling Severo:

> How much proof do you think it's going to take to take the heat off 2,4,5-T? There are 40,000 technical reports. We know more about 2,4,5-T than we know about aspirin. How long do you want the chemical industry to continue to prove that nothing has happened?[14]

Dow Chemical was in fact quite concerned about how the controversy in general, and the lawsuit in particular, would unfold. An interoffice memorandum between Dow and its insurance company, Fireman's Fund—not intended for public consumption but somehow nonetheless ending up in Severo's hands—stated that "the complexities of chemistry, coupled with our country's post-Vietnam guilt and the emotional issues of cancer and birth defects, make these cases potentially very difficult to defend."[15]

Enter the Atomic Vets

On June 8, 1979, two veterans, James McDaniel and Harry Coppola, held a news conference sponsored by Rep. Pat Schroeder (D-Colo.).[16] The two stated that they had bone marrow cancer that they thought was caused by their exposure to residual radiation when they had been in the military. However, McDaniel and Coppola were not Vietnam veterans: they had served in a Marine unit dispatched in 1945 to gather and dispose of rubble in Nagasaki, Japan, within a month after the United States had dropped an atomic bomb on that city. Both had filed claims with the VA in 1974 but had been denied. Now an article in *Progressive* magazine reported a higher incidence than normal of bone marrow cancer among Marines who had been stationed near the blast area.

The VA had about 200 such cases on its hands. The list included veterans who had served in and around blast areas in Japan at the end of the Second World War, and those who participated in training exercises at atomic test sites in Nevada and in the Pacific Ocean during the 1950s. The most common complaints were bone marrow cancer, leukemia, and malignant lymphoma. One claimant was Orville Kelly of Davenport, Iowa, who in 1978 had founded the National Association of Atomic Veterans. Kelly had been stationed at the Enewatak Atoll test site in the Pacific from November 1957 through November 1958. He said that he observed during that period the explosion of twenty-two 450-megaton atomic bombs—bombs about nine times the size of that dropped on Hiroshima. His unit wore no special protective clothing other than tinted goggles. He now had malignant lymphoma and had been denied benefits by the VA.

The problem again lay in the latent period between the purported cause and the onset of disease. The VA simply ruled that the diseases were "not service connected" since the cancers had not emerged during active duty or within a year after discharge from the service. However, Vice Admiral Robert Monroe also suggested that the claims were groundless. He told New York Times reporter Jo Thomas:

> The common concern that huge numbers of people are dropping like flies is just wrong. There was immense concern to avoid radiation exposure. . . . A second idea is that there were massive exposures. That's wrong. Wrong as hell. The average exposure was half a rem.[17,18]

Monroe further elaborated on the problem of numbers. Of 250,000 Americans the age of participants at the test sites, he stated, 16 percent—the incidence of cancer in the general population—or 40,000 of them would die of cancer. Exposure to one rem of radiation among 10,000 people will produce 1 fatal cancer; hence, among 250,000 people exposed to half a rem, 12 fatal cancers will occur. "Of 250,000 people, you would get 40,012 cancers, of which 40,000 are not related to radiation and 12 which are," Monroe concluded. "How do you find that 12?" the VA's J.C. Pecharsky asked Thomas.[19] To assist in answering that question, the Senate Committee on Veterans Affairs conducted hearings on the atomic cases the week of June 20.

However, an informal solution was already in play. In 1978, the VA appeals board heard sixty-three cases from cancer patients. One was Paul Cooper, a participant in the Smokey Shot atomic test in Nevada during 1958. Cooper now was dying of leukemia. After being denied benefits by the VA, Cooper asked Dr. Glyn Caldwell of the Centers for Disease control for help in preparing an appeal. Dr. Caldwell calculated that given on the incidence of leukemia in the general population, one would expect to find four cases of leukemia among the 3,000 Smokey Shot participants. He managed to locate half of the participants and found eight cases of leukemia—twice the expected number had he located them all. Irving Kleinfeld explained the developing logic in the atomic cases:

> I don't think, frankly, anybody knows what radiation does to people. If [veterans] come down with the type of cancer generally associated with

radiation, and if the evidence is in balance, I'll resolve it in favor of the veteran.[20]

Cooper won his appeal but died before he could collect benefits.

Congressional Action

In June the House Subcommittee on Oversight and Investigation of the Committee on Interstate and Foreign Commerce held the first congressional hearings on Agent Orange and its effects on Vietnam veterans. Heretofore the attention had focused on the complaints of the veterans themselves. The hearings raised and highlighted another issue: the possibility of birth defects among the children of exposed veterans. Vietnam veterans Michael Ryan and John Woods both testified at the hearings that they feared Agent Orange exposure had produced the birth defects suffered by their children.

Ryan, a police sergeant in Long Island, New York, and his wife, Maureen, had called Victor Yannacone with their story.[21] Ryan had served in Vietnam in 1966 where, by his account, he had lost weight, and suffered migraine headaches and a series of mysterious maladies. Four months after his discharge from the military in 1971, his wife gave birth to a baby girl with severe birth defects: she had missing bones, a hole in her heart, twisted limbs, deformed intestines, a partial spine, shrunken fingers, and no rectum. The Ryans spent much of the next seven years seeking and obtaining treatment for Kerry. The Ryans had no history of birth defects in either of their families, and the doctors had no explanation for Kerry's condition.

While in a waiting room at the Johns Hopkins University Hospital, Maureen by chance spotted a magazine article on the effects of herbicides on human health. The symptoms listed in the article seemed remarkably similar to those Michael had experienced in Vietnam. She had read of Reutershan's death and Yannacone's class action suit. The Ryans discussed the possibility that they had stumbled onto the cause of Kerry's birth defects and decided to give Yannacone a call. Yannacone and the Ryans hit it off immediately, forming a relationship that would last long after the trial. Schuck writes of them:

> In the Ryan family, Yannacone had the articulate, photogenic, all-American parents and the lovable but tragically damaged child that he needed as the lead named plaintiffs in the case. In Yannacone, the Ryans

had a champion, a lawyer whose unflagging fidelity to their cause continues to inspire their devotion [even] today.[22]

The congressional hearings were undeniably emotional. The *Washington Post* coverage of the hearings contained a photo of Kerry Ryan and
Bobby Muller sitting side by side in their wheelchairs at the witness
table.[23] After describing his family's ordeal, Michael Ryan stated: "We
were told the enemy was in the bush and he wore black sandals. We
never suspected the enemy could be in the air around us." And John
Woods, a member of the Green Berets in Vietnam and the father of two
normal sons before going to Vietnam and two with congenital health
problems after his return, concluded: "We are not the veterans. Our kids
are the veterans."

Upon hearing the testimony, Rep. Bob Eckhart (D-Tex.) called the VA's
failure to conduct a study of veterans claiming exposure "a national
disgrace," and he called upon the National Institutes of Health and the
Centers for Disease Control to conduct studies in the manner of the
Atom Bomb Casualty Commission that had studied Hiroshima victims.
Rep. Martin Russo (D-Ill.) asserted that "the government is ducking the
Agent Orange problem," and he added:

> I would like to send the generals and the Veterans Administration [offi-
> cials] and the chemical company [executives] to fly the helicopter and
> spray [Agent Orange]. I'd like them to be the guinea pigs. I wonder how
> many of them would volunteer.

In response to the hearing and the mounting public pressure, Congress
enacted Public Law 96–151 directing the VA to provide medical treatment for Vietnam veterans claiming exposure to Agent Orange and to
conduct an epidemiological study of veterans exposed to Agent Orange.
Dow Chemical's worst fears concerning the case were becoming a
reality.

Disrupting the Applecart

VVA still resembled the Council of Vietnam Veterans in 1979. By this
time Bobby Muller had dissolved his relationship with Stuart Feldman
and was in the process of assembling a board of directors and hiring a
full-time staff member or two for the new organization. On the plus
side, Muller was repeatedly successful in keeping his name, and that of
the organization, in the media. In addition to his high-visibility activities
during Vietnam Veterans Week and the subsequent Senate hearings on

Agent Orange, he appeared on a number of television talk shows. However, the necessity of attracting a dues-paying membership remained, a problem that would take several years to resolve fully.

Steve Champlin, who would join Rep. David Bonior's congressional staff in 1980, was the first director. During the summer of 1979, John Terzano became the legislative liaison. A Vietnam veteran who had served in the Navy, Terzano had just completed his studies at George Washington University. Like Ken Berez, he had done volunteer work for the Council of Vietnam Veterans. Though VAA's financial resources ranged from shaky to nonexistent, its idealism ran high. Berez states: "We had lots of energy. And we felt righteous about the issues. . . . We had energy, a sense that we could accomplish things. That's what drove us."[24] For a while, that would have to suffice.

Muller's high-profile appearances began to attract letters to the organization. Berez's initial job was to answer the mail. He recalls:

> [My] assignment was to answer the bundles of mail . . . , the letters which resulted from these shows. . . . And I'd type out a response letter to each of them. Preparing, basically, form letters, coming up with types of responses to the letters.
>
> The typical letter, if you can generalize, was a hand-written, four or five page letter about my son, or my husband, or my dad, my brother, is a Vietnam veteran who's in a shell, who's very angry, who doesn't want to talk about it. What can I do to reach him? Where can I go to get help? . . . Very little cash, checks. . . . It was a great learning experience for me because I literally read hundreds, thousands of these letters. And it gave me an appreciation of, an understanding of, the void out there. Of the need! . . . And I got more out of that . . . than from all the analysis that was being done at that time about Vietnam veterans.[25]

VVA's developing philosophy was unconventional for a veterans' organization. Combined with its confrontational style, its posture put it in conflict with all three sides of the Iron Triangle: the House Committee on Veterans' Affairs, the VA, and the traditional veterans organizations. And, very shortly, one could add to that list Senator Cranston's Senate Committee on Veterans' Affairs. Terzano explains:

> . . . [E]ven early on, we [had], let's say, a progressive agenda when it comes to working on justice issues and war and peace issues, and foreign policy issues. When it comes to the area of veterans' benefits, however, we are the most conservative, at least our philosophy was always the most conservative philosophy around, and we're even to the right basically of the Heritage Foundation on some of this stuff.[26]

By comparison, the traditional veterans organizations were boldly conservative on domestic and foreign policy issues, but unashamedly "liberal" in stance when it came to entitlements for the veteran. Likewise,
VVA's liberal positions on most issues clashed with those of the House
Committee, and its conservative philosophy on veterans' issues left VVA
at loggerheads with both the House and Senate Committees. All this
made for an uphill struggle.

VVA drew its philosophy from a report prepared in 1956 for President
Dwight Eisenhower by General Omar Bradley. In an era of increasingly
numerous programs lavished upon veterans of the Second World War,
the Bradley Commission Report addressed the issue of what a society
owes its veterans. It proposed a set of principles for deciding which
programs veterans ought to have as a matter of fairness and which ones
simply were excessive. According to the report, two principles should
serve as guidelines for compensating veterans for their service.[27] First,
the highest priority should go to programs that extend medical care for
service-connected injuries or illnesses, ease re-entry into civilian life,
and provide adjustments for career advantages lost while in the service.
Second, when there is doubt about a claim, the veteran should be given
the benefit of the doubt.

Terzano explains VVA's interpretation of the Bradley Commission
Report:

> Bradley's philosophy was . . . that, first and foremost [the government
> had responsibility] to those wounded on the field of battle, and . . . to
> provide them health care second to none. Now, interestingly enough, that
> doesn't necessarily mean the VA hospital health care system. . . . It's al-
> ways been our view that war-wounded veterans should be given the op-
> portunity to go to the doctor of their choice where they think that they're
> going to get the best care. . . . Like, give them a credit card, wherever they
> go, . . . the government will pay for it. That was number one.
>
> The other main thing that Bradley talked about, which got us into trouble
> with (Sen.) Cranston and the House Committee after 1978, was . . . that
> the government needs to provide those . . . programs that are necessary
> for those who sacrificed . . . to bring them . . . parity with those who did
> not serve. Once you achieve parity with your nonveteran peers, then the
> government's responsiblity, as far as we were concerned, and as Bradley
> argued, is over. . . .
>
> That's where we really parted company with the rest of the veteran com-
> munity, because what we were arguing was hey, just because you're a
> veteran . . . doesn't necessarily entitle you to lifelong services coming out
> of the VA.[28]

In 1979, VVA worked with Veteran Veterans in Congress—led by Rep.
Bonier in the House and Senator John Heinz (R-Penn.) in the Senate—to

present an updated version of the the Vietnam Veterans Act. The 1979 version of the act contained most of the provisions it had listed in 1978, but also earmarked funds for the treatment and compensation of Agent Orange claimants. At the same time, the Committees on Veteran's Affairs had under consideration a pension bill for older veterans. The Congressional Budget Office estimated the cost of the pension bill for the first year at $900 million and the cost of the Vietnam Veterans Bill at $200 million.

Cost aside, the two bills made for a showdown between the differing philosophies of the parties involved. According to Muller, the non-service-connected benefits, such as pensions, medical care for ailments not associated with military service, and the like, were prompted because the country lacked—and still does not have—adequate social welfare and medical care plans for all Americans. Hence, these needs among veterans have been met by passing special legislation under the rubric of veterans' benefits. He states:

> This is where we ran into . . . [Guy] McMichael [of the VA] and [Jon] Steinberg [of the Senate Committee]. . . . As McMichael said . . . directly [to us] . . . , I can go to Strom Thurmond (D-S.Car.), and I can say, . . . we've got people . . . , they're impoverished, they're devastated, their lives are completely overwhelmed. We need to give these people some minimum level of assistance. And Thurmond's going to throw me out of his office. I can go to Strom Thurmond and say, we have veterans that fought for this country that aren't even being afforded a minimum measure of dignity to be able to subsist without some token of appreciation. And I'll get Strom Thurmond to back me.
>
> . . . I said, look, nobody's . . . more sympathetic than I am to having minimum social welfare policy for all Americans . . . than me. All right? That's my political orientation. I want to see people have access to medical care. . . . I want to see people have minimum levels of assistance so they're not beggars and outcasts in the street. But the way you argue for that, I said, is honestly. By . . . discussing, do we as a nation provide for these essential rights for everyone in this country. Straight out.
>
> . . . Okay? I came back to a medical care system that, less that 15 percent of the patient care was going for service-related disabilities. The overwhelming majority of guys on my ward in the VA hospital were not service-related guys. They were there because they were derelicts, they were there because they were crazy, they were there because the VA is the provider of last resort. . . .[29]

Not surprisingly, this kind of talk won VVA few friends among the major players in the world of veterans' politics. Using these arguments, VVA vocally opposed the pension bill while advocating their own legislation. The pensions, they said, constituted a nonservice connected wel-

fare handout in the guise of veterans benefits. They justified the inclusion of the Agent Orange provisions on the basis of both the "field of
battle" and the "benefit of the doubt" clauses in the Bradley Report.
Amidst angry retorts, Muller also received some fatherly advice from the
traditional veterans organizations:

> . . . [T]hey said, look, long after your need for readjustment programs,
> with all of its high costs which puts all of our . . . programs of pensions
> and medical care at risk, you'll be very glad to fall back on our medical care
> system that we've put together. You know, don't break the fuckin' bank,
> guys! All right? Don't disrupt the applecart.[30]

Internal Strife

The slow and arduous process of moving the Agent Orange case to
trial had begun. A Multi-District Litigation Panel assigned the case in
May of 1979 to Federal Judge George Pratt. Dow officials were pleased
with the choice. In a second interoffice memorandum, which also ended
up in Richard Severo's hands,[31] Dow officials had fretted about Judge
Robert Lee Carter, to whom the case had first been given. Carter, whom
the memo described as "a very liberal black judge," might be overly
sympathetic to the veterans' claims, Dow feared. They felt much more
comfortable with "a very conservative judge named Pratt."

Though the team defending the chemical companies was well
financed—they would spend more than $100 million in legal expenses
before the case ended—money was an acute problem for the plaintiffs.[32]
During the spring of 1979, Victor Yannacone staged a presentation for a
large group of attorneys, most of whom were veterans of World War II
the and Korean War. He invited them to participate in the lawsuit and
asked them to put up seed money for the case. He promised to bring
the case to trial for $1 million. Though many were skeptical about the
scheme's realism, enough of them decided to give it a try to make the
meeting a success. On September 20, 1979, the consortium of Yannacone
and Associates was formed to direct the case for the veterans.

Tensions flared almost from the start. To begin with, Frank McCarthy,
and many veterans who participated, saw the case as only one part of a
broader strategy of vindication for Vietnam veterans as victims of the
war, not just Agent Orange. Others simply sought a fair resolution of
the Agent Orange issue. Peter Schuck writes of Michael Ryan's version
of the schism:

> "Frank," Ryan [said], "was the kind of veteran who refers to Vietnam as
> 'Nam, who cannot stop living the war. He wanted desperately to build a

veterans' organization around that nightmare. He was always looking back to Vietnam, saying 'We got fucked over in 'Nam and now it's happening again here.' " Ryan, in contrast, [thought] of himself as . . . a crusader not so much on behalf of veterans as against what he [saw] as the growing chemical contamination of the world.[33]

Yannacone appeared in sympathy with both impulses among the veterans. He gladly traveled around the country in what Schuck has called a "colorful, headline-grabbing" fashion,[34] holding meetings to entice veterans to join the suit and to raise the political consciousness of Vietnam veterans or any other sector of the public who would listen. Some of Yannacone's associates looked askance upon this barnstorming and, in particular, resented paying for it out of their limited budget. Critics among his associates thought these travels fell more in the category of ego-tripping than in sensible preparation for the trial.

Yannacone thought that the weakest point in their case was the lack of substantial scientific evidence linking Agent Orange exposure to ill health among humans. He sought to rectify this by conducting his own scientific study using the Vietnam veteran participants of the class action as subjects for the research. Schuck writes:

> With the assistance of his wife, Carol, he planned to take computer coded case histories on the individual veterans—including their pre-war medical condition, their exposure to Agent Orange in Vietnam, their postwar symptoms—and those of their families, and store these on computer tapes. Starting with this information base, he would then refine the data in an effort to develop patterns of exposure, symptomatology, etiology, and legal responsibility that could stand up in court. Although he had been warned that a creditable study would cost tens of millions of dollars, Yannacone insisted that a three-year study could be completed for less than a million.[35]

Though they humored him on many points, his partners refused to go along with Yannacone on this issue, saying it would be too expensive. Yannacone and his wife proceeded with the plan nonetheless, and Yannacone later claimed that 3,000 such medical histories were compiled. Several associates, however, claimed that no medical files were completed that had legal or epidemiological value. As wrangling continued over this and other issues, Yannacone occasionally threatened to inform Judge Pratt of the dissention in their ranks. This ploy, which could have resulted in the dismissal of Yannacone and his entire legal team from the case, bluffed his critics into submission more than once.

In an interview with Schuck, David Dean, who eventually became the plaintiffs' chief trial attorney, commented upon the difference between the "conservative, buttoned-up style of the Wall Street lawyers" who represented the chemical companies and the fire drill atmosphere that characterized Yannacone's team:

> The contrast to us could hardly have been greater. Their paper work was superb; we sometimes filed our briefs without staples, cutting and pasting on our way to the courthouse. The Wall Street boys would file errata sheets correcting an incorrect page cite; we made so many errors we didn't bother. We were almost all trial lawyers. . . .[36]

Meanwhile, the case itself was bogged down in a legal quagmire. Product liability cases ordinarily fall under state tort law. However, applying varied state laws in a federal court would be time consuming and burdensome. Nevertheless, the chemical companies argued that the product liability laws of each state in which individual plaintiffs resided should apply. Whether this would favor them was uncertain: some states had very restrictive laws and others not. What the motion would do, however, was to complicate the procedure enormously. The more complicated the procedures, they felt, the fewer the veterans who would stick out the suit. The chemical companies also moved to have the case dismissed outright. Yannacone and his associates, on the other hand, maintained that federal common law—principles derived from the decisional law of federal judges rather than from constitutional or federal statutes—should govern the case in order to simplify matters. Either way, Judge Pratt's decision would be controversial.[37]

At the same time, the chemical companies filed third party complaints against the government for indemnity as war contractors. They argued that the government had not simply purchased herbicides from them, but also had specified their content, supervised their production, and controlled their application in Vietnam. Further, they noted, government regulations forbade them from selling the same mixtures in civilian markets.

In November 1979, Judge Pratt reached his first decision in the case. He accepted the case as a federal question and refused to accept the chemical companies' motion to dismiss. The companies immediately filed an appeal. The plaintiffs had survived the first round.

Mau-Mauing the VA

Early in 1979, Senator Charles Percy (R-Ill.) had requested a second General Accounting Office (GAO) inquiry into herbicide use in Vietnam. GAO released its report in November 1979.[38] This investigation included an initial assessment of the HERBS tapes and acknowledged that the Air

Force, as well as other units, had often used herbicides without proper precautions. For example, spraying from the C-123s often took place close enough to troops, the report said, that wind drift may have exposed them to the herbicide, and ground troops frequently entered contaminated areas shortly after spraying. Further, it stated that troops sometimes used empty herbicide drums for constructing latrines and even home-made hibachis. The report concluded that as many as 40,000 Army, Marine, and Air Force personnel had experienced significant exposure to the herbicide. It also provided a listing of units whose personnel it considered officially at risk.

The GAO report legitimated the concerns of worried veterans. After publication of the report, it was difficult to contend that defoliation took place under carefully controlled conditions in areas remote from American troops, or that only the participants of Operation Ranch Hand had been exposed. The question now shifted to the consequences of exposure, an issue that has remained unresolved and a matter of intense controversy to the present time.

The second GAO report appeared about the same time that Max Cleland was proudly opening the first Vet Center in Van Nuys, California in November of 1979. Cleland and a team of dignitaries, including Senator Alan Cranston, were assailed on that trip by Vietnam veterans protesting the VA's handling of the Agent Orange issue. Cleland had worked long and hard to get the Vet Center program, and he clearly was disturbed by this turn of events. He states:

> I think part of the frustration for me was to go to . . . open up a Vet Center, you know, something that you know is absolutely demonstrable, and you've been working for four years to sell it to Congress, to sell it the media, to . . . the White House, to . . . the agency, to . . . the veterans' organizations, and finally you've got a tangible . . . product here that you're able to deliver for Vietnam veterans. And you get Mau-Maued by a bunch of guys dressed in orange shirts, screaming and hollering before the television camera, bitching and moaning at me, obscuring the whole opening of the Center. Taking that as an occasion to say I haven't solved all the problems on Agent Orange.
>
> . . . [I]t became guerilla war again. It became street tactics. . . . I almost got, I was out with [Sen.] Cranston in Los Angeles, and they had whipped the crowd to a frenzy so that some psyched-out Vietnam veteran took a swing at me![39]

Guy McMichael, who accompanied Cleland that day, recalls:

> The people [who] became active in Agent Orange were people we had not seen or had [not] been involved in veteran matters before. . . . I remember

showing up at the Center and being confronted by maybe forty or fifty people wearing orange shirts and carrying signs saying "Agent Orange Victim." . . . I mean, leaving aside the question of whatever validity they had, they were clearly in a highly . . . emotional state, to the point that the hearing which then took place . . . was one in which they threatened physical violence to Max. They were about ready to throw him out the window.[40]

Cleland believed passionately in the need for readjustment counseling. He could relate to it directly through his own experiences. Further, he found support and affirmation for his position among those around him. For him, the Agent Orange issue was just the reverse. He found it difficult to empathize with the Agent Orange claimants, and those who surrounded him in the VA reinforced his doubts. He states:

I mean, . . . it was kind of hard for me to believe, having been a Vietnam veteran and been out there on the ground two of the three peak spraying years, it's hard for me to believe that walking by and touching some jungle foliage, all of a sudden I had a better risk of coming down with cancer. I mean, I couldn't compute that. And we went through, you know, [VA] physicians didn't quite buy all that. They didn't buy the connection. They could buy the connection with chloracne, you know, but this leap from you're a Vietnam veteran, therefore your risks of cancer are greater, those kind of claims which were made from the beginning, boy, that was kind of tough to compute!

And so, sure, claims on Agent Orange were, you know, looked at askance. But we took the question seriously in terms of investigating the connection. . . . And, see, that could not be proven. But I think the VA owed the veterans the hot pursuit of the answer. . . . So that was the thin line you had to walk! You had to say, yes, we want to check this out and so forth, but while you were saying, yes, there may be a problem, there was a screamer over here saying, "I had a deformed kid, I was there, I know that there is a problem, Agent Orange did it to me, and it's doing it to hundreds of thousands of others out there, why don't you do something?"[41]

In December 1979, President Jimmy Carter formed the Agent Orange Working Group (AOWG) to report directly to the president the findings of the various agencies of the Executive Branch who were investigating the Agent Orange issue. Congress's Office of Technological Assessment (OTA) was invited to sit in on the group, first as observers and later on as participants. One of the members from OTA was Michael Gough, a biologist with a Ph.D. in genetics from Brown University. Gough helped prepare several reports on Agent Orange and later wrote a book of his own on the subject. His focus in these reports and in his book was on the the identification of who was exposed to the herbicide, and an assessment of the extent of exposure, for purposes of determining the effects of dioxin on human health.

Gough argued that those exposed to the herbicide fell into four categories: the "production workers" who manned the reaction vessels in which the herbicide compounds were made; the "formulators" who mixed and prepared Agent Orange at chemical company plants; the "applicators" who disseminated Agent Orange into the environment, especially the participants of Operation Ranch Hand; and those who were "environmentally exposed," including an "unknown fraction" of those who served in Vietnam.[42] A dispersal rate of three gallons per acre by Ranch Hand aircraft, he thought, would have resulted in extremely low levels of environmental exposure. He estimated therefore that production workers probably were the most highly exposed group, then formulators, then applicators, and, last, the least exposed of all, the people who encountered dioxin in the environment. However, "some Vietnam veterans claim," he noted in his book, "that they were drenched with Agent Orange from airplanes. Clearly, anyone who was soaked in the stuff was significantly exposed."[43]

Gough also calculated the expected frequencies of various cancers among Vietnam veterans if Agent Orange had no effect whatsoever on their health. He contended that if the incidence of cancers among Vietnam veterans were identical to the national incidence, 25 percent—700,000 of the 2.8 million who had served in Vietnam—would have cancer at some time during their lives, and about 20 percent—560,000—would die of cancer. He writes:

> Paul Reutershan died of a cancer in his pelvis that grew so wildly out of control that the pathologists could not decide what organ or tissue it had originated from. About 1000 men and about 800 women between the ages of 25 and 29 died from cancer the same year. Therefore, death from cancer at age 28 is uncommon but far from unknown. There has been no trend either upward or downward in death rates from cancers for men 25 to 29 years old since records began to be kept in 1933. . . . It is clear that young men died of cancer before Agent Orange was used. Whatever caused any one of the other nearly 2000 deaths among young men and women in 1977 could have caused Paul Reutershan's.[44]

The Question of Presumption

In November of 1979, Orville Kelly, founder of the National Association of Atomic Veterans, became the first veteran to receive service-connected benefits for illness associated with radiation.[45] The scientific evidence based on human subjects concerning the relationship between exposure to radiation and certain cancers was mixed. Some studies showed a relationship, while others did not. More conclusive experimental studies had used laboratory animals as research subjects. Nevertheless, the VA elected to grant a "presumption of service connection" to the atomic veterans: if a veteran had an illness that might be the result of radiation exposure—such as bone marrow cancer or leukemia—and if the veteran claimed to have been on a site in the line of duty where exposure to radiation took place, the VA would proceed as if the illness were the result of radiation exposure incurred during military service. Kelly announced his victory at a rally sponsored by an antinuclear protest group. His doctors gave him less than a year to live.

Agent Orange Victims International (AOVI) was the most visible veterans organization devoted to the issue of Agent Orange. However, a number of other Vietnam veteran organizations already in existence and oriented toward other issues had quickly adopted a stance on the issue. One of those organizations, of course, was VVA. It had already articulated a philosophy concerning veterans' legislation in the area of diseases and disabilities that restricted their interests to those which were service connected. The Agent Orange claims, if verified, would fall within that realm. Hence, the organization seized the issue and moved on it aggressively.

The Agent Orange claims before the VA, independent of their merits or validity, offered VVA and other veterans organizations an opportunity. Hence, as VVA undertook the transition toward becoming a membership organization, the Agent Orange issue played a key role. John Terzano explains:

> [Agent Orange] gave us something concrete that people could really . . . relate to as an issue. . . . It was and still is today a very important issue. . . . [W]hat it gave us as a vehicle was something visible for people. I mean, people don't want to . . . , they're not really into talking about head problems or job problems or school problems. . . .
>
> The pain isn't there. The suffering isn't there. But when you start talking about cancer, you start talking about birth defects, you start talking about a ravaged country, those are visible things that people can see. . . .[46]

VVA's position was that the VA should extend a presumption of service connection to Agent Orange claimants as it had to the atomic veterans. VVA, however, though interested in seeing scientific studies carried out and legal remedies pursued to the fullest, did not itself invest much effort as an advocate or supporter of these initiatives. Their position was that initiatives such as these took years to resolve and had a high potential for ending without clear-cut solutions. Since they saw Agent Orange as "a social, political problem," VVA leaders sought a political strategy to resolve it. Their preferred remedy lay in the passage of legislation by Congress that promptly cut through the ambiguities and provided an immediate solution.

At the time, Terzano claimed, there were more than forty diseases or conditions for which the VA extended a presumption of service connection. By definition, a presumption of service connection denoted that the evidence was spotty, but that the veteran was given the benefit of the doubt. The reasons behind the generosity varied, but typically included an effective advocate. Though usually mandated by Congress, the extension of such a presumption did not require an act of Congress. Under certain conditions it also could be made administratively by the national director of the VA. Terzano states:

> The classic point . . . has to do with amputations. . . . Max Cleland did it administratively. And DAV (Disabled American Veterans) was the principle backer of this, and what this presumptive legislation stated was that, if you have certain types of catastrophic amputations . . . and if you develop heart [and] circulatory problems later in life, they would compensate you for it. . . .
>
> That administrative act, that Max Cleland . . . with the stroke of a pen [put] . . . on the presumptive rolls, was based on . . . a National Academy of Science study which stated that certain types of amputations may, and they used the word "may," lead to circulatory problems later on in life. There was no [firm] conclusion. I mean, there wasn't even, you know . . . , this is a 50–50 shot.[47]

VVA's demands were that the VA treat and compensate those veterans with chloracne—probably the only point of agreement between the VA and VVA—and that the VA prepare a list of diseases and conditions for purposes of offering a presumption. If this could not be achieved legislatively, they hoped that Cleland would do it administratively. They would take it either way. However, neither scenario occurred. According to Terzano:

> You know, we used to argue with these people, if you at least begin the process to open up the door a little bit, and . . . show that you've got some type of responsive policies, show that you're at least being responsible about the issue instead of in a total, complete denial of what went down, you're going to win the hearts and minds of the Vietnam veteran. . . . [W]e used to say this in the VA and . . . to the people in the [House and Senate] committees. How can we come in and beat you over the head if you guys are doing something? You know. Don't you understand? To me, it's Politics 101. Give us something.

. . . Max was the only Vietnam veteran who headed up the VA, and you
know, we thought he would be our champion, and he was on some
issues. . . . [B]ut . . . what happens an awful lot, you quit being an advocate . . . when you get in positions like that.[48]

The Politics of Commemoration

The organizers of the Vietnam Veterans Memorial Fund (VVMF)—Jan
Scruggs, Bob Doubek, and John Wheeler—set an ambitious timetable
for completing the project.[49] They planned to purchase the land for it in
1980, complete the fundraising in 1981, and build the monument in
1982. For dedication of the memorial, they penciled in Veterans Day,
November 11, 1982.

Even people sympathetic to the project were doubtful that this schedule could be met. They told Scruggs, Doubek, and Wheeler that the
timetable was simply unrealistic, and some suggested that a goal of
dedicating the memorial by the end of the century was more tenable.
The Lincoln Memorial, for instance, initiated in 1867, had not been
completed until 1922. Others warned that, whatever its merits, the plan
would certainly fail. During the 1950s, an impressive blue-ribbon panel
sought to build a memorial for Franklin D. Roosevelt. The panel spent
several million dollars and several years before tossing in the towel
without even breaking ground. Pitfalls for projects such as this were
everywhere, even under the best of circumstances.[50]

The two biggest obstacles facing VVMF, they were told—beyond the
usual problems of organizational survival and fundraising—were the
lingering vestiges of the Vietnam antiwar movement and the Washington, D.C. bureaucracy. Both were formidable foes. Building a memorial
could spark the same antagonisms that had eventually forced the United
States to call it quits in Vietnam. Constructing it also would require the
approval of the Fine Arts and National Capital Planning Commission,
the National Park Service, and the National Capital Memorial Advisory
Committee—a political minefield, to be sure. Scruggs, however, was, as
he later admitted in his book, "naive" and "audacious." "We've got
something good here," he wrote to Wheeler. "Enclosed are envelopes
and stationery. Write anyone, ask for anything."[51]

One of the first members of Congress to respond to their requests for
help was Sen. Charles Mathias (R-Md.). An opponent of the war,
Mathias saw the project as a symbol of reconciliation. He immediately
swung into action. In September of 1979, Mathias called a meeting in his
office with Scruggs, Wheeler, and Doubek to select a site for the proposed memorial. A month earlier, a member of the Fine Arts Commis-

sion had directed their attention to a site across the Potomac River from Washington along the road leading to Arlington Cemetery. After an on-site visit, the three organizers rejected the idea outright. What they had in mind, they said, was something more centrally located with, in Wheeler's words, "a landscaped solution, a garden-type approach." As they pondered a map in Mathias' office, the senator picked out a choice spot in the Constitutional Gardens across from the Lincoln Memorial. Scruggs writes of that moment:

> Once the possibility of this site entered [our] consciousness, it seemed overwhelmingly logical. Right at the foot of the Lincoln Memorial—what a spot! No one could ignore it. Members of Congress would see it every morning as they drove to work. Presidents would see it whenever they ventured to set forth from the White House. Everyone in America, especially Vietnam vets themselves, would know that a special honor had been granted. The symbolism was perfect.[52]

Placing a memorial there would prove to be no easy task. Mathias suggested that the group reduce its perils by having Congress pass a law that specifically designated this site for the memorial. Mathias introduced a bill in the Senate to do just that. The bill had twenty-six co-sponsors that reflected the spirit of reconciliation. Vietnam veteran James Webb approached Rep. John Hammerschmidt (D-Ark.) to sponsor a corresponding bill on the House side. Webb had impressive credentials: he was a graduate of the Naval Academy, a highly decorated combat veteran, and the author of two novels about the Vietnam War. The conservative Hammerschmidt agreed to sponsor the bill, but nearly killed the bill's chances of passing by declaring that Vietnam veterans now would reclaim the site in Constitutional Gardens where thousands once protested against the war.

The tone of Hammerschmidt's remark contradicted an informal understanding that had evolved among VVMF's organizers and would now become its official policy.[53] The memorial would be nonpolitical. It would not address the rightness or wrongness of the war. It would not glorify the war or seek to establish its place in history. Rather, it would focus simply on those who served and died in it. This strategy, they believed, would short-circuit opposition from the antiwar movement, permit the participation of the broadest spectrum of supporters, and make possible a first step towards reconciliation. Consequently, VVMF proudly counted among their supporters people who had been on opposite sides of the fence during the war. It would be the first time that Sen. George McGovern (D-S.D.) or Rev. Theodore Hesburgh, President of Notre Dame University—vocal critics of the war—publicly agreed with hawks such as Sen. Barry Goldwater (R-Ariz.) or comedian Bob Hope on anything concerning Vietnam.

Meanwhile, money was a pressing problem. Bob Doubek was the only paid staff member at a salary about half that of the position he left to join VVMF. On the bright side, donations were increasing. The Veterans of Foreign Wars contributed $2,500. Endorsements from the Gold Star Mothers—an organization of mothers having a son who died in combat—the American Legion, the Marine Corps League, the Retired Officers Association, and the National Guard Association helped. A breakfast attended by representatives from major defense contractors, sponsored by Sen. John Warner (R-Va.) and featuring eggs and sausage cooked by his wife, Elizabeth Taylor, raised $40,000. H. Ross Perot donated $10,000. Tom Carhart, a graduate of West Point and a highly decorated Vietnam veteran, secured a $45,000 loan for the memorial using only his "honor" as collateral.[54] Mostly, however, donations remained in the $10 to $20 range. All this made possible the mass mailing of as many as a million letters to inform people about the project and to request their financial support.

VVMF drew the initial mailing list of 200,000 from the rolls of organizations associated with military service and from old "McGovern for President" campaign lists. The ideological mix of the memorial's sponsors evoked hundreds of letters of protest, especially about McGovern's presence among them. VVMF pondered the question of how to respond, and decided to stick with the posture of reconciliation. McGovern remained on their list of sponsors. After expenses, this first mailing netted about $6,000. Though people knowledgeable about such matters told Scruggs this was quite good for their first effort, the organizers worried privately that their schedule indeed was in jeopardy. After all, the projected cost of the memorial had by now risen to $2 million.

VVMF also began to seriously confront the issue of exactly what the memorial should look like. They received some free advice from art critic Wolf Van Eckert. In his *Washington Post* column, Van Eckert commented that VVMF also would have to reconcile "established notions of 'good art' and popular notions of meaningful art." Most war memorials glorify a particular war as well as service and patriotism. He also noted that the ill-fated Franklin Roosevelt committee had impaled itself on the issue of modern versus traditional art. Van Eckert offered his views of how to resolve the dilemma:

In other countries . . . our time has produced monuments that are neither modern nor not modern. They are simply emotionally moving. . . .

The simplest yet most haunting memorial I have seen, or rather "experienced," is nothing but a dark space built of rough boulders. It is the "Hall of Remembrance" on Har Hazikaron in Jerusalem. On its somber mosaic floor are inscribed the names of 21 of the largest Nazi death camps.

[Such monuments in other countries] are powerful ideas translated into a powerful emotional experience. And that is what I think the Vietnam Veterans Memorial needs. . . . The emphasis should be on simplicity.[55]

He further advised VVMF editorially on how to proceed: hold a competition for the design open to all American artists with professional credentials and, for picking the winning design, select a jury composed of both experts and ordinary people. His advice would prove invaluable.

As Congress approached the final days of its session in May, the House bill that would designate two acres of land in Constitutional Gardens for the memorial had yet to pass. The Senate had already approved the bill. By the time of the vote, all 100 Senators had listed themselves as the bill's cosponsors. Although it had only 177 cosponsors in the House, VVMF was confident that the House bill also would be enacted. As the vote neared, however, Rep. Phillip Burton (D-Calif.) raised an objection to the bill.[56] Burton could not be simply ignored as one dissenting vote. He sat on a House subcommittee that had jurisdiction over the use of public lands. With time running out, and at Burton's behest, the resolution was amended to read "two acres in the District of Columbia." The details concerning where in the District would be resolved later in a House-Senate conference committee.

VVMF organizers were stunned but maintained their composure. The location in Constitution Gardens had become their one nonnegotiable demand. Though expressing disappointment, they were not openly critical of Burton. A serious breakdown here with Burton could delay site selection indefinitely. They sought instead a private meeting to iron out their differences. Burton accepted and explained to them his opposition. Scruggs writes:

"It's just like the Gulf of Tonkin Resolution (which gave President Lyndon Johnson the authority to fight the war)," the congressman said. He opened a filing cabinet and pulled out a thick file. "It's all in here. LBJ talked me into supporting quick passage. It needed more study, and so does your bill. I won't make the same mistake twice."

[We] explained how [the] memorial was aimed at reconciliation, not reopening old wounds. [We] finally won Burton over with one simple sentence: "George McGovern is on our sponsoring committee."[57]

With Burton's blessing, the House-Senate conference committee adopted the Senate version of the bill, giving VVMF two acres of land in Constitutional Gardens.

Notes

1.   See Peter Schuck, *Agent Orange on Trial: Mass Toxic Torts Disasters in the Courts* (Cambridge, Mass.: Harvard University Press, 1986), 26–34.

2.   In a landmark case involving diethylstilbestrol (DES), the plaintiff could not show which company produced the actual pill that harmed her. However, the court required the manufacturers to pay damages in proportion to their individual shares of the DES market (Sindell v. Abbott Laboratories, 1980).

3.   Fred Wilcox, *Waiting for an Army to Die: The Tragedy of Agent Orange* (New York: Random House, 1983), 98.

4.   Schuck, *Agent Orange on Trial*, 43.

5.   Schuck, *Agent Orange on Trial*, 41–42. For a detailed biography of McCarthy, see 38–42.

6.   Ibid., 45.

7.   Wilcox, *Waiting for an Army*, 101–102.

8.   See Schuck, *Agent Orange on Trial*, 46, for the quote by Yannacone.

9.   Ibid., 45.

10.   Richard Severo and Lewis Milford, *The Wages of War: When America's Soldiers Came Home—From Valley Forge to Vietnam* (New York: Simon and Schuster, 1989), 377.

11.   Ibid., 377.

12.   Guy McMichael, personal interview with author, 9 March 1989, Washington, D.C.

13.   Richard Severo, "Herbicides Pose a Bitter Mystery in U.S. Decades after Discovery," *New York Times*, 29 May 1979, A1, A18. Quote appears on A18.

14.   Ibid., A18.

15.   Severo and Milford, *Wages of War*, 375.

16.   Jo Thomas, "Cancer Victims Seeking U.S. Aid, Say A-Bombs Caused Disease," *New York Times*, 9 June 1979, A12. Rep. Schroeder's general interest in the case was prompted by her concern about the presence of low levels of radiation in Denver, where several uranium dumps were found under the city.

17.   Jo Thomas, "Stakes High as Senate Examines Cancer in Troops at Atom Tests," *New York Times*, 20 June 1979, A1, A24. Quote begins on A1 and continues on A24.

18.   A rem is a unit that measures the effect on the body of one roentgen, a measure of radiation. The Atomic Energy Commission specified 1.3 rems per month as the maximum "safe" level of exposure. The military variously used maximum safe exposure levels as high as 5 and 10 rems.

19.   Thomas, "Stakes High," A24.

20.   Ibid.

21.   The background story of the Ryans is reconstructed from Schuck, *Agent Orange on Trial*, 47–48, and Margot Hornblower, "A Sinister Drama of Agent Orange Opens in Congress," *Washington Post*, 27 June 1979, A3.

22.   Schuck, *Agent Orange on Trial*, 48.

23.   See Hornblower, "Sinister Drama," A3. The quotes attributed to Ryan, Woods, Rep. Eckhart, and Rep. Russo which follow are from the Hornblower article, A3.

24.   Ken Berez, personal interview with author, 27 March 1991, Washington, D.C.

25.   Ibid.

26. John Terzano, telephone interview with author, 4 April 1991, Washington, D.C.

27. House Committee on Veterans Affairs, *Veterans' Benefits in the United States: A Report to the President by the President's Commission on Veterans' Pension*, House Commission Print No. 235, 84th Congress, 2nd sess., 1956.

28. Terzano, telephone interview, 4 April 1991.

29. Robert Muller, personal interview with author, 27 March 1991, Washington, D.C.

30. Ibid.

31. Severo and Milford, *Wages of War*, 375.

32. Schuck, *Agent Orange on Trial*, 51.

33. Ibid., 50.

34. Ibid., 58.

35. Ibid., 50–51.

36. Ibid., 73.

37. Ibid., 54–71.

38. U. S. General Accounting Office (USGAO), *U.S. Ground Troops Were in Areas Sprayed with Herbicide Orange*, FPCD-80–23 (Washington, D.C.: USGAO, 1979).

39. Max Cleland, telephone interview with author, 27 January 1989, Atlanta, Georgia.

40. McMichael, personal interview, 9 March 1989.

41. Cleland, telephone interview, 27 January 1989.

42. Michael Gough, *Dioxin, Agent Orange: The Facts* (New York: Plenum, 1986), 35–36.

43. Ibid., 37.

44. Ibid., 66–67.

45. See *New York Times*, "Veteran Exposed to Atomic Tests Given Benefits," 27 November 1979, A18.

46. Terzano, telephone interview, 4 April 1991.

47. Ibid.

48. Ibid.

49. See Jan Scruggs and Joel Swerdlow, *To Heal a Nation: The Vietnam Veterans Memorial* (New York: Harper and Row, 1985), 12–13.

50. See Wolf Van Eckert, "The Making of a Monument," *Washington Post*, 26 April 1980, C1, C7.

51. Scruggs and Swerdlow, *To Heal a Nation*, 13.

52. Ibid., 16.

53. Description of this policy, money, and mailing lists is drawn from Scruggs and Swerdlow, *To Heal a Nation*, pp. 16–35.

54. See Rick Atkinson, *The Long Grey Line* (New York: Pocket Books, 1989), 574–577, for a description of the Warners' breakfast and Carhart's loan.

55. Van Eckert, "The Making of a Monument," C7.

56. See Ward Sinclair, "Vietnam Memorial: Another Symbol of Frustration for Vets" *Washington Post*, 26 May 1980, A3.

57. Scruggs and Swerdlow, *To Heal a Nation*, 41.

6

OPENING UP THE EARTH

"When I looked at the site, . . . I wanted something horizontal that took you in, that made you feel safe within the park, yet at the same time reminding you of the dead. So I just imagined opening up the earth. . . ."

Maya Ying Lin, designer of the Vietnam Veterans Memorial

The Agent Orange lawsuit had begun with a bang. Now that the initial volleys had been fired, the two teams continued a series of pretrial maneuvers designed to wrest the advantage to one side or the other. As we have seen, Judge George C. Pratt had accepted the case as a federal question, and both sides understood that the Feres doctrine protected the government from liability. However, that did not mean that these were dead issues.

The plaintiffs under Victor Yannacone were satisfied to leave the federal government out of the suit, at least for the time being, and focus on the chemical companies. Part of their reasoning was strategic, and part of it was that veterans such as Frank McCarthy really did not wish to sue the government. As McCarthy explained to Peter Schuck, who interviewed him after the settlement:

For the veterans, it has always been a moral point. We think that it is wrong to charge the government—our government—with what amounts to criminal responsibility without far stronger evidence of culpability than we have seen. The chemical companies are the responsible parties. The government did no more than use stuff that my mother used to kill weeds in her garden.[1]

The strategic consideration reflected an untenable situation stemming from the chemical companies' plan of defense. The defense lawyers felt that they had much to gain by bringing the government into the suit. Theoretically, they could argue under the Stencel doctrine, an extension of the Feres principle, that the government's indemnity also covered them as government contractors. Since this argument was unlikely to hold up in this particular case, the defense team devised a second strategy: though they could not bring the government back into the suit directly, they would seek to escape their own culpability for Agent Orange by demonstrating that the government had been solely responsible for its production, its use, and, most important, its misuse. After all, the government had requested the herbicide, specified its contents, purchased it, and used it as it saw fit.

The "government contract" defense, according to law professor Schuck, was pure "genius."[2] It guaranteed that the federal government and questions about its culpability would be part of the suit, and that although the government would not play the role of defendant it would serve as a device for relieving the chemical companies of guilt. Yannacone's team quickly realized that if they vilified the government too strongly, they could inadvertently let the chemical companies off the hook. To win the case, they would have to prove that the chemical companies misled the federal government—in particular, the Department of Defense—who in turn had acted in good faith. The plaintiffs would have to soft-pedal the government's culpability.

This posture by the defense offered another potential advantage. Under it, the chemical companies could preclude a trial by seeking a summary judgment. A summary judgment simply entails a ruling from the court without a trial when the facts in the case are not in dispute. In this instance, Judge Pratt could decide that there was no need for a trial if he felt that the chemical companies and the veterans both agreed that the federal government had acted irresponsibly. Hence, in March of 1980, the chemical companies requested a summary judgment from the court. The federal government quickly moved to dismiss the chemical companies' claims on the basis of the Feres doctrine. If these motions were successful, Yannacone and the veterans would never see their day in court.

As Judge Pratt pondered issues, a three-judge panel of the Second Circuit Court reached a decision of its own in November of 1980. In a two-to-one vote, the panel overturned Judge Pratt's earlier endorsement of the suit as a federal case. The majority opinion stated that there was no "identifiable federal policy at stake in [the Agent Orange] litigation that warrants the creation of federal common law rules."[3] This ruling meant that state law, the specifics of which vary greatly from state to state, would apply to the case. This complicated the the scope and procedures of the Agent Orange suit tremendously. The harried plaintiffs immediately sought to have the Supreme Court reverse on the decision, but the Court declined to hear the case. The parties of the defense were pleased. The more complications, they felt, the better. The veterans and their attorneys were a fragile coalition and short on cash.

In December of 1980, Judge Pratt announced his decisions on several key issues. He ruled that he would not permit the federal government to be a part of the suit directly: the veterans could not sue the government and the chemical companies could not claim immunity as war contractors. However, he would allow the chemical companies to use a "government contract" defense. He then certified the case as a "section (b)(3) class action"[4] and authorized the discovery phase of the pretrial proceedings to begin in January of 1981. The two sides could now begin assembling and validating documents and interrogating witnesses for the trial. The case was moving forward, albeit slowly. At this rate, it would consume years and hundreds of millions of dollars in legal fees.

The Politics of Design, Round One

The Vietnam Veterans Memorial Steering Committee, headed by Jan Scruggs, John Wheeler, and Bob Doubek, still faced the tricky problem of what kind of memorial to build. In 1980, they had been approached by a young sculptor, Frederick Hart, who had been an apprentice under Felix de Weldon, sculptor of the Iwo Jima Memorial. Hart recommended to them "a pavilion structure, with design influenced by elements of a Buddhist pagoda, . . . containing two works of sculpture, one a realistic depiction of two soldiers and the second a more abstract form of plexiglass with internal images."[5] There were advantages to simply hiring a person to design the memorial. Tom Carhart suggested that they design it themselves and checked a book out of the public library, *Anyone Can Sculpt*. After some discussion and strife, the committee decided to hold an open competition. It was the democratic thing to do.

The central problem facing the committee through the last half of 1980 was how to select a jury who would in turn select the winner of the competition. One possibility was to impanel a jury of art professionals along with some Vietnam veterans, Gold Star mothers, and relatives of those still missing in action. However, the experts might feel compelled to defer to the veterans and relatives who, while long on the appropriate sentiments, might be short on the ability to correctly visualize the finished memorial from a drawing or model of it. Also, the veterans and relatives were a diverse grouping, both politically and socially. There were many headaches either in putting a representative sampling of them on the panel or in purposely representing only segments of them. On the other hand, a panel consisting only of professionals might pick an artistically correct design that veterans and their families nonetheless did not like. Some committee members thought this option would be easier to defend. If veterans picked the winner, it might be more open to attack from those with antiwar sentiments. But others countered that a choice by veterans might be more vulnerable to criticisms from the federal commissions that the design lacked artistic merit.

The issue proved divisive. Scruggs later wrote:

> . . . [B]oard members sometimes stood and screamed at each other during meetings. In one session, Wheeler pounded the table with his fist, insisting that women and blacks—groups deeply affected by the war—also be represented. Another time, Dick Radez argued, "We've got to have Vietnam veterans so we can get what we want."
>
> "What do we want?" Doubek asked.
>
> No one could answer.[6]

In September of 1980, the committee reached a compromise. They would select an jury comprised entirely of prominent professionals. However, they would screen them to ensure that each juror had "sufficient sensitivity to what service in Vietnam had meant."[7] How a potential juror felt about the war in Vietnam was not an issue as long as he or she clearly supported veterans. After consultation with experts and lengthy deliberations, they announced their selections. It was a very prestigious jury: Pietro Bellusci, Harry M. Weese, Garrett Eckbo, Hideo Sasaki, Richard H. Hunt, Constantino Nivola, James Rosati, and Grady Clay. The committee placed no restrictions on what the design would entail, other than to stipulate that the memorial "will recognize and honor those who served and died" but "will make no political statement regarding war and its conduct." It empowered the jury full say over the competition. The entry fee for the competition was set at $20, first prize at $20,000, second prize at $10,000, and third prize at $5,000. Any American citizen could enter. Designs were to be submitted by March 31, 1981. This, committee members hoped, would begin the healing process.

The response from all quarters was positive. No one questioned or quibbled with the credentials of the jury. But what kind of memorial would heal the bitter divide in America over the war? "What are you going to do," war correspondent Peter Braestrup asked them of the design, "Show a hippie hugging a Marine?"[8]

The Hostages Come Home

The nation was embroiled in another crisis. Ostensibly unrelated to Vietnam veterans, it nonetheless would draw them into its drama also.

On November 4, 1979, a group of militant Iranian students had stormed the United States embassy in Tehran and taken 100 of its personnel hostage, including 63 Americans. Foreign Minister Ibrahim Yazdi promised American representatives that he would be able secure their release within a day or so. However, Yazdi himself was ousted by what became a full-fledged revolution in Iran.

In the days that followed, the students released several black and women hostages. The remaining fifty-two American hostages were blindfolded and paraded through the streets of Tehran. They encountered angry, fist-shaking mobs who burned American flags and shouted for their execution. The students and the Iranian government decided to hold them for ransom, demanding of the United States the extradition of former Iranian ruler and close American ally, Shah Mohammed Rezi Pahlavi, and the return of several billion dollars that the Shah had deposited in U.S. bank accounts. The Shah had aroused the ire of his country's Moslem conservatives by imposing on them widespread changes aimed at modernization. His family's immense wealth and his harsh, sometimes brutal tactics had fueled the resentment. Having left Iran in June of 1979, he was in the United States for what he termed an "extended vacation."

The negotiations went poorly. At first, most Americans rallied behind President Jimmy Carter, whose declining popularity before then had already invited significant challenges for his re-election. As the months passed without a resolution, Carter's ratings fell. On April 25, 1979, an attempt to rescue the hostages by an American commando team ended in disaster. Carter cancelled it after a helicopter and a cargo plane involved in the rescue collided in the Iranian desert, killing eight American commandos. The exuberant Iranians displayed the wreckage and the charred bodies. During the succeeding months, the "hostage crisis" became a significant and highly symbolic issue in the presidential campaign. *Washington Post* columnist Haynes Johnson later wrote of the situation:

> Through the intense focus of television, hour after hour, day after day, month after month, the hostages assumed a critical role in national and world affairs. In time, the taking of the hostages symbolized a period of national soul-searching about the country's purpose and direction and its perceived departure from past days of glory. Coming after the bitterness of defeat in Vietnam, the failure to protect and then to free our embassy personnel in Iran made people wonder whether we had become the Gulliver of our age, an important giant incapable of exercising our power to meet the impudent challenge of a primitive society. . . . To Americans, Iran came to represent an unparalleled test of national will and pride.[9]

On November 4, 1980, coincidentally the one-year anniversary of the crisis, American voters went to the polls, and a majority of them voted for the Republican challenger, Ronald Reagan. The hostage crisis was not the only issue which spelled defeat for Jimmy Carter, but it was one of the principal ones. Following the election, Carter worked to secure the hostages' release in the final days of his administration. At 3:16 A.M., January 20, 1981, less than nine hours before President-elect Ronald Reagan was scheduled to assume office, Carter and the Iranians, negotiating through Algerian intermediaries, finalized a deal. The United States promised to release $4 billion in Iranian funds—the Shah had since died of a stroke in a New York City hospital—in return for the immediate release of the hostages.

The reaction was immediate and emotional as thousands of Americans took to the streets to celebrate. Seizing the moment, the Reagan administration planned an elaborate homecoming. The hostages were flown to Weisbaden, West Germany, for a few days of medical examinations and recuperation. Upon their return to the United States, they would spend two days privately with their families at the United States Military Academy in West Point, New York. The public celebration would begin later in Washington, D.C. There the hostages and their families would occupy all 340 rooms at the Crystal City Marriott Hotel. New York City asked to be the host city for the official ticker-tape homecoming parade.

The president's jet, Freedom One, touched down with the hostages on January 26, 1981. A solid wall of people lined the seventeen-mile route from the airport to the military academy. The country clearly was in the mood to celebrate. Reporter Bill Peterson of the *Washington Post* wrote:

> It was an extraordinary outpouring of emotion. It was if all the pent-up rage, frustration and all-but-forgotten American commodity, patriotism, had suddenly burst forth all over the Catskill Mountains. . . . At New Windsor Containment . . . , 60 large American flags fluttered from masts on either side of the roadway—one flag for each of the returned 52 hostages and eight others, at half staff, for the eight men killed in the futile attempt to rescue them. . . .
>
> "It simply feels good to be an American again," said Bob Hickson of Yorktown Heights, N.Y. "I think integrity has been restored to our nation." . . . The atmosphere was festive. Throughout the afternoon people sang "America the Beautiful" and chanted "U.S.A., U.S.A."
>
> "There's a warm feeling here," said Misty Arochas, 20, who wore a "Kiss Me—I'm an American" button on her coat. "This is how you can tell we have a nice country. Everyone cares so much."[10]

A few days later, more than 500,000 people turned out in Washington, D.C. for the public welcoming. Haynes Johnson described the reception:

> Washington, a ceremonial city accustomed to taking in stride everything from the return of victorious armies to astronauts from outer space, welcomed home 52 hostages from the isolation of captivity in Iran with an unabashed, unashamed outpouring of emotion. Their arrival touched off a display of feeling seldom equalled in the history of the nation's capital.[11]

The Crystal City Marriott provided an "open bar" for the hostages and their families during their stay, and Lorimer's Market prepared elaborate complimentary baskets containing Perrier Jouet Flower Bottle champagne, macadamia nuts, Godiva chocolates, French goose liver paté, fresh Mexican strawberries, and assorted other goodies. Later, in New York City, more than two million people took part in a ticker-tape parade featuring twenty-three of the hostages. Afterward, the city hosted a dinner for the returnees and their families atop the World Trade Center, where they ate chocolate truffles and viewed from the 100th floor a fireworks display put on in their honor.

More parades and adulation ensued as the hostages made their separate ways home. Hostages were given free cars, shopping sprees, and lifetime passes to major league sporting events. A Congressman introduced a bill to award each of them a gold medallion commemorating their service. The krewe of Bacchus selected Marine Sgt. John McKeel, Jr. to reign over their Mardi Gras parade in New Orleans. "Everyone," Bill Peterson wrote in the *Washington Post*, "wanted to get into the act."[12] It was quite a homecoming.

The Awakening

Many Vietnam veterans watched and participated in the festivities with mixed emotions. On the one hand, most of them felt that the hostages deserved a dramatic reception and an effusive, public thank you. However, the scope and intensity of the celebration stood in sharp contrast with their own homecoming experiences. Some also decried the lack of attention to prisoners of war and those missing in action from the Vietnam war. Many veterans began to express feelings of resentment, envy, and anguish. After the parade in New York City, Vietnam veteran Brian Sherwood wrote to the *New York Times*:

In August of 1969, after nearly 400 days in Vietnam, I stepped off a plane in Twentynine Palms, Calif., to be greeted by a welcoming committee made up of three 70-year-old retired men handing out four-ounce paper cups of orange juice.

After rude and mechanical paperwork processing by military clerks, a fellow Marine and I were charged twice the meter rate for a . . . cab ride to Los Angeles International Airport. We flew to New York in near anonymity. . . .

My family met me at the gate in New York, and we soon were all weeping, hugging and kissing in a joyous but deliberately quiet reunion. We certainly didn't want to draw attention to ourselves.

I have watched the hostages and the flood of joyous emotion which has greeted their every moment since their return. They deserve all the adulation we can give them. They are heroes.

But so were many of the hundreds of thousands of us. We laid it on the line for our country every day we spent in Southeast Asia. No one offered us, not one of us, a public gesture of thanks. No media coverage, no dental check-ups, no sprees at the PX, no isolated decompression, and certainly no ticker-tape parades.[13]

Similarly, Peter Tiffany, who had served in Vietnam for twelve months as a military policeman, told a reporter that the nation's gleeful reaction was a "slap in the face. It's rubbing salt in our wounds. The hostages deserved the free services being offered them," he continued, "but not once since I got home has anyone sought me out to find out how I'm doing."[14] In Indianapolis, Gregory Steele, a former infantryman in Vietnam, organized a march of about 400 Vietnam veterans from the Veterans Administration Hospital there to the Mexican-American War and World War I memorial. He told a reporter:

This isn't meant to take anything away from the hostages. We just want to remind people that there were guys without arms and legs lying in that hospital right now who never got a parade, and that there are still people missing in Vietnam who still may be alive. Where are the yellow ribbons [a symbol used during the hostage crisis] for them?[15]

And Sheila Waters of Baltimore and Director of P.O.W. International, whose letter to the *New York Times* appeared on the same page as Sherwood's, wrote that "it is time to focus some attention on the Americans who are still unaccounted for in Vietnam and seemingly have been forgotten."[16]

Vet Centers across the country reported sharp increases in the numbers of Vietnam veterans seeking assistance. Many added special sessions to allow veterans to discuss their feelings about the return of the hostages. "They're not angry at the hostages," reported psychologist William Weitz of the Vet Center in Miami. "They're glad they're free." Weitz went on to describe the significance of the "ritual of return," stating that a triumphal homecoming takes some of the burden off the shoulders of the returnee and disperses it on the nation as a whole. "It is a ritual that would have helped many of the Vietnam veterans . . . ," he concluded. "It would have helped them put their experiences in place."[17]

These pleas did not go unheeded. Vietnam veterans soon noted that the good will and good feelings unleashed by the hostages' return spilled over into an increase in support for their projects and organizations. Jan Scruggs, still struggling to raise funds to build the Vietnam Veterans Memorial, later wrote that "the hostages were heroes that unified America."[18] Following their return, he claimed, contributions to the Memorial Fund arrived at a faster pace, the size of the average contribution increased, and additional newspapers encouraged their readers to back the construction of the memorial. "The Ayatollah Khomeini [the staunchly anti-American leader of Iran's revolutionary government] was helping to solve the Fund's money problems," he concluded. And Bobby Muller of Vietnam Veterans of America (VVA) states emphatically:

. . . [T]he whole thing turned around for us, I mean, black and white, I can pinpoint it to the day. To the day. It was that dramatic. The whole game changed with the return of the hostages from Iran.

. . . I happened to be in the [VVA] office in New York when they had the ticker-tape parade for the returning hostages. . . . The phones really rang all day. And it was a first. We had never, ever gotten unsolicited calls in the office from people saying, "I'd like to do something for you. I'd like to help you out." . . . The contrast between what America was doing in going ga-ga for the returning hostages with what clearly we had never done for the returning Vietnam veteran was such a dramatic contrast in the minds of people that they recognized it. . . . And guys were coming forward for the first time. . . . Even veterans came forward. . . . [T]he contrast made it so clear that there had been an injustice and was a catalyst for the veterans themselves to come forward in large numbers.

. . . The most important part was . . . [that] people for the first time were talking about Vietnam. . . . [A]s you look to the issue of war and peace and concerns of the world community, what's the reference point, . . . the baseline from which discussion can progress? It was the Vietnam experience. . . . And you could talk about this experience, start to reflect and examine it and learn from it. . . . The experience of it for all of us . . . could finally be publicly engaged in for discussion. And that came at the same time that there was this response by the public to do justice for the Vietnam veteran.[19]

The Politics of Design, Round Two

On March 14, 1981, H. Ross Perot contributed $160,000 to underwrite the design competition. Though a contribution of this size was of course welcome, it did provoke some uneasiness. Some veterans did not want any contributor, and the outspoken Perot in particular, to have an undue say in the outcome of the competition. That decision should be left, the committee agreed, solely to the jury of professionals that had been already selected. By the deadline at the end of the month, 1,421 designs had been submitted.

The designs were trucked to an empty hangar at nearby Andrews Air Force Base, where they could be displayed for easy review by the judges.[20] The Air Force also provided twenty-four-hour-a-day security. The committee feared that an "antiwar or antimilitary group" might try to destroy the designs. The symbolic potential was great. Only one problem surfaced immediately. Resident pigeons promptly crapped on the designs. Though the damage was unintentional, it just would not do to leave the situation unchecked. The guards were given pellet guns and instructed to handle the problem informally.

The schedule called for the jury to deliberate from Monday, April 27 through Friday, May 1. Each juror had agreed to view each entry at least once. By Tuesday, the jurors had eliminated 1,189 of the designs. Only 232 now remained. By Thursday, they had distilled the number of 32. Of these, 15 would receive honorable mention. On Friday, the number was down to three. The unanimous winner was design number 1,026. The jurors were ready to present it to the committee. Jan Scruggs later described the scene:

> As [the committee] entered the hangar, they saw rows and rows of designs hung on metal braces. It was breathtaking. The competitors had obviously invested an extraordinary amount of time and talent. . . . Scruggs walked off by himself to calm down. . . . A flapping sound distracted him. Flopping along the floor was a wounded, bloody pigeon.
>
> . . . A juror went behind the curtain and brought out the number-three design. . . . Scruggs recognized the work of Frederick Hart. It was great. Beautiful. He could not wait to see the next one.
>
> The second place winner . . . looked weird to Scruggs. It was like a pile of twisted steel on two marble pillars.
>
> He pushed deeper into his chair. . . . The next one would be a winner, a great design.
>
> Then it came. A big bat. A weird-looking thing that could have been from Mars. Scruggs smiled. Maybe a third-grader had entered the competition and won. . . .
>
> Silence hit. One second. Two seconds. Three seconds.

[John] Wheeler felt the confusion around him. It was hard to envision the pastel sketches as finished stone. But he began to see it: massive, longer than a football field. Every name. Every name.

The moment was slipping away. It was time for commitment. "This is a work of genius," Wheeler said.

The group applauded.[21]

Despite that verbal vote of confidence, the committee knew that it had a public relations problem on its hands. They themselves found it difficult to visulize what the memorial would actually look like once built. The jurors had to explain it to them for several minutes before they felt they understood. Though they felt more at ease once they understood, they sensed that others would have the same problem. It was not a design that instantly would sweep the committed, the critics, or casual observers off their feet. They had quite a sales job ahead of them.

The winner of the competition was Maya Ying Lin, a twenty-one-year-old senior architecture major from Yale University. The committee met and talked with her. She had entered the competition after it was assigned as a class project. The professor of the class had also entered the competition but had not finished in the top fifteen. Lin was from Athens, Ohio, where she was born and raised ten years after her parents had fled mainland China during the late 1940s. Her father, Henry Huan Lin, was a well-known ceramist and the dean of Fine Arts at Ohio University. Her mother, Julia C. Lin, was a poet and professor of Oriental and English literature. The committee learned that she knew very little about Vietnam or war. She had never read a book or seen a television documentary about the war there, nor had she read any of the literature concerning other wars. Nevertheless, they were pleased. They found her to be bright and sincere.

At first glance, the design did resemble a bat. It consisted of two elongated, tapered walls that joined at the higher ends to form an open V. The backside of its black granite walls would be landscaped so as to be even with the ground. The open frontsides would gradually slope downward into the earth to a depth of ten feet where the two wings would meet. The names of all the more than 57,000 men and women who died in the war would be inscribed on the walls chronologically, beginning with the first to die and ending with the last. "The names will trace the war from beginning to end," she told a reporter of the walls that would appear to recede into the earth at each end. "Thus . . . the war is complete, coming full circle."[22]

Among the first to forcefully express his distaste for the design was Perot, who had gotten wind of the selection before the winner had been publicly announced. He urged Scruggs to get rid of it and pick another design. According to author Rick Atkinson, a disgruntled Jim Webb met with others at the Vietnam Inn in Arlington "to smoke cigars, swig Muoi Ba beer, and air their grievances."[23] Webb characterized the design as a "mass grave" and Tom Carhart called it "an open urinal." Carhart and Webb sharply resented the strong endorsement of the design by Wheeler, who had served in Vietnam as a noncombatant, and the selection of a design by an Asian woman. In response to a request for possible inscriptions for the memorial, Doubek told Atkinson that Carhart had suggested, "How about 'Designed by a gook'?"

Most of those who viewed the design, however, liked it. The committee plunged ahead with the fund-raising. During the summer of 1981, fund raising featured the design and the donations soared. In one weekend radiothon that the committee hoped would raise $35,000, they received more than $250,000. However, the sniping continued. One controversy arose when Lin, in response to the statement that some people thought the V-shape stood for the words "veterans," "victory," or "Vietnam," was quoted as saying that it did not stand for "veterans." Scruggs added to the problem by saying, "The Memorial says exactly what we wanted to say about Vietnam—absolutely nothing."[24] Lin meanwhile clarified her position about the V-shape in a letter to the *New York Times*:

> I never thought of these walls as being a letter "v" written into the earth. This labeling is a false simplification of my design; the memorial's two walls come together at a 130 [degree] angle, hardly a "v" at all in my opinion.
>
> For [the prior article in the *Times*] to say that my design for the Vietnam Veterans' Memorial has nothing to do with the Vietnam veteran is totally wrong.
>
> I feel that your article damages the meaning of the memorial; and that it is a great injustice to the veterans for whom the memorial is designed. The time sequence, which has the dates of the first and last deaths meeting at the intersection of these walls, is the essence of the design. It is a segment in time, meant to recognize all those who served during this war, and giving special recognition to those who will never return from it. In this sense, this v-shaped (if you insist on calling it that) memorial has everything to do with the veterans.[25]

The controversy would not end here.

Round Three

Many potential roadblocks lay ahead and the political landscape was rapidly changing following the election of Ronald Reagan. The VA would have no say in the construction of the Memorial, but, the steering committee noted, the turmoil there might be indicative of things to come among those who did have a say. In late February of 1981, the Reagan administration let out word that it intended to nominate John Behan to replace Max Cleland as head of the VA. Behan, who had lost both legs in combat while serving with the Marine Corps in Vietnam, was a representative in the New York Assembly. However, on March 21, the White House announced that President Reagan's advisors had decided that Behan lacked sufficient administrative experience to handle the agency.[26] The opposition to Behan's appointment came most forcefully from the Veterans of Foreign Wars (VFW). Behan's Achilles heel was that he had organized the Vietnam Veterans' Caucus in the New York Assembly to draw attention to the needs of Vietnam veterans, particularly those exposed to Agent Orange.

That same month David Stockman, President Reagan's budget director, signaled the closing of ninety-one Vet Centers across the country as part of an overall plan of cutbacks in the federal budget. These Centers had just been opened by Cleland in the last year of the Carter Administration. The plan aroused outcries from many organizations and hampered the search for a new director for the VA. In April, President Reagan made public his second choice to head the agency: Jim Webb. Webb withdrew his name before the confirmation procedure had begun, saying that the absence of "good signals" and the threat of "more budget cuts" prompted his decision.[27] The Reagan Administration ultimately settled on Robert Nimmo, a 59-year-old World War II bomber pilot, to head the VA. Nimmo stated in an televised interview during his first day on the job that Vietnam veterans had not been neglected or shortchanged by VA. "We do have some [veterans] who have particular problems primarily related to the so-called delayed stress syndrome," he said, "and we are addressing ourselves to that as rapidly as we can."[28] Ten days later he announced that the ninety-one Vet Centers would not be closed and that forty-two new ones would be added.[29] The traditional veterans organizations had one of their own back in the driver's seat, and the Vietnam veterans had their Vet Centers.

The political appointment by President Reagan most likely to affect the building of the Memorial was his selection of self-proclaimed superconservative James Watt to head the Department of the Interior. The outspoken Watt was the one who would have to issue the building permit allowing construction on the selected Mall site to actually begin. Controversy about the design—particularly if it tapped strong sentiments concerning traditional versus modern art or the rightness versus the wrongness of the war—could provide a ready excuse to kill the project. At first there were no snags. On July 20, 1981, the Fine Arts Commission unanimously approved the proposal to build the Memorial, and the National Capital Planning Commission unanimously approved the design on August 6.

Meanwhile, relations between Maya Lin and the steering committee had become strained. By virtue of having created the design, she was now a public figure and spokesperson for the memorial. In truth, she had become a celebrity in her own right. Lin preferred to dress casually and somewhat unconventionally—she was, after all, an undergraduate student and an artist—a trait that rubbed some conservatives the wrong way. The laid-back attire reminded them of the "hippie" look or of avant garde art, symbols that complicated things politically. Getting the memorial approved by the various commissions and Secretary Watt would be tricky enough without attracting additional flak. Lin also considered it her design, and members of the media sometimes referred to it as her memorial. As the veterans pressed their case on a number of issues, they struck her as "too militaristic."[30]

More importantly, the committee sought a resolution on three design issues. One concerned the listing of the names. Some veterans wanted the names listed in alphabetical rather than chronological order to ease the task visitors would have in locating the name of a loved one. Lin resisted, and the committee eventually agreed with her. An alphabetical listing would not only violate the spirit of her design, but would read too much like a granite telephone book. A second problem was the absence of an inscription. The committee won out on this question. They added a brief prologue and epilogue to the design. Finally, professionals would be needed oversee the building of the memorial from the proposed design. The task called for skills that Lin simply did not have. The committee hired architects Kent Cooper and William Lecky of Washington, D.C. to direct the work. They, in turn, hired Lin as a consultant.

Meanwhile, Tom Carhart broke ranks with the memorial's steering committee. He approached the others and told them that he could not live with Lin's design. He demanded a less abstract design that depicted heroism, such as the one he himself had submitted to the competition. Scruggs had recognized Carhart's entry and thought it amateurish—which it was. The steering committee listened but was not swayed. They had, each for their own reasons, come to like Lin's design. They also were nearing the final days of approval and the date for breaking ground. But the disgruntled Carhart was not to be consoled. Finding no solution within the committee, he decided to go public with his complaints.

On October 13, 1981, Carhart appeared to testify against the design at a routine meeting of the Fine Arts Commission. Wearing two Purple Hearts pinned to his suit, he stated:

> Unless something unexpected happens, ground will soon be broken for the Vietnam Veterans' Memorial. . . . Although I have long awaited this moment, as it now approaches I feel only pain.
>
> I believe that the design selected for the memorial in an open competition is pointedly insulting to the sacrifices made for their country by all Vietnam veterans. By this we will be remembered: a black gash of shame and sorrow, hacked into the national visage that is the Mall.[31]

Carhart went on to say that the jury had contained civilians whose only knowledge of the war was the political one that had occurred on the homefront. " . . . [B]lack walls sunk into a trench would be an appropriate statement of the political war in this country," he declared, "but it is not the war whose veterans the Fund has been authorized to memorialize."[32]

Despite Carhart's testimony, the Fine Arts Commission stuck by its earlier decision.[33] Not yet ready to throw in the towel, Carhart wrote letters to the White House and to the Department of the Interior, claiming that one of the jurors had had previous ties with the Communist Party. Jim Webb resigned from the National Sponsoring Committee in support of Carhart, as did Admiral James Stockdale, the senior prisoner of war (POW) in Hanoi during the war and a winner of the Congressional Medal of Honor. Webb wrote other members of the Sponsoring Committee—Gerald Ford, Rosalyn Carter, Bob Hope, Nancy Reagan, Jimmy Stewart, and William Westmoreland—asking them to resign in protest as well. None did. In December, 1981, Representative Henry Hyde (R-Ill.) drafted a letter to President Reagan asking that Interior Secretary Watt deny the construction permit for the Memorial. Twenty-seven other Republican congressmen signed the letter.

On December 22, the Veterans of Foreign Wars (VFW) decided that it was time to make a statement. The national commander, Arthur Fellwock, held a press conference at the the National Press Club in Washington, D.C. and personally delivered an oversize four-foot long check for $180,000 to the steering committee. The Vietnam Veterans Memorial was going to need every friend it could get. On January 4, 1982, Secretary Watt declined to issue the building permit until further notice.

A Trip to Hanoi

On December 13, 1981, the Vietnamese government extended an invitation to Vietnam Veterans of America (VVA): they would issue visas for Bobby Muller and three others to visit Hanoi. The purpose of the visit would be to talk about the effects of Agent Orange and the whereabouts of some 2,500 American servicemen still missing in action (MIA) from the war. The United States and Vietnam had had a number of informal exchanges concerning these servicemen. However, the two countries have not had any formal diplomatic relations since the end of the war, and there were no informal talks going on at the time. James Menard, a State Department Asian Affairs aide, approved of the trip, saying, "We support efforts by private citizens to join Government efforts in achieving full accounting for those missing in action."[34]

The trip was not a complete surprise. In October, Muller had met in London with the Vietnamese ambassador, Tran Hoan, and later with Vu Dung, a Vietnamese official at the United Nations. He had expressed to them the desire "to be the first delegation of former American troops to return to Vietnam" to discuss these issues. He told *New York Times* reporter Bernard Weinraub, who would accompany them on the trip, "We made it clear that we didn't expect to be statesmen or play politician but to be simply who we were—veterans who have concerns about veterans' issues."[35] He had heard nothing from them in two months. Now the call arrived: can you be here in six days?

Accompanying Muller on the trip—which *Penthouse* magazine paid for—were Tom Harbert, a New York business consultant and former Air Force sergeant in Vietnam; Tom Bird, a former infantryman with the 1st Cavalry Division, who had been briefly captured and tortured by the North Vietnamese; and John Terzano, who had served on the Navy destroyer *Robison* during the blockade of Haiphong harbor. The four were very nervous. Terzano recalls: "You gotta understand . . . , when we went over there on that first trip, we had no idea what to expect. . . . We didn't know if we were going to be asked to sign confessions when we reached there or what. . . ."[36] Harbert later told Weinraub: "I had fantasies that they were going to take me prisoner because I was in the Air Force and flew in bombing missions over the North."[37] Weinraub described the arrival in Hanoi for the *Times*:

> Four American veterans of the Indochina War, trembling with emotion, stepped off the plane at a bleak Hanoi airport late this afternoon to an enthusiastic welcome by Vietnamese officials.
>
> One of the veterans, Tom Bird . . . , started walking down the steps of the plane before noticing a group of Vietnamese soldiers waiting to greet him.
>
> Mr. Bird swiftly returned to the plane, trembling.
>
> "My first instinct was to call the whole thing off," Mr. Bird said several minutes later, returning outside. "It's just too strange. I feel a little out of control."
>
> Mr. Muller, who was crippled in the war, was carried down the plane steps and was promptly surrounded by Vietnamese officials and local

photographers. In his car, [he] said quietly, "I can't even sort out my emotions now. I can't believe it. I am in Hanoi."[38]

Their stay lasted six days. They met with a number of different committees and, on the third day, they met for ninety minutes with Foreign Minister Nguyen Co Thach.[39] Thach promised them that he would welcome specialists who wished to study areas of his country that had been heavily sprayed with Agent Orange. He denied that his government had withheld any information in the past about missing American servicemen and stated that no Americans were currently being held prisoner in Vietnam. Finally, he stated that he wished to continue communication with Americans through VVA, but would not issue visas to anyone formally connected with the Reagan Administration. The delegation asked for another meeting with the committee in charge of the American MIA issue. Terzano states:

> . . . [W]e worked hardest . . . just to get them to realize and understand that irrespective of how they view[ed the MIA issue], it was a real issue in the United States that needed to be addressed before there was going to be any type of better relations between the two countries. . . . [T]hey sat across the table from us and said, "You guys don't understand. We are veterans too." And they started showing us their scars from battles with the French, with the Americans. These guys had been fighting for twenty, thirty years. [They said], "We understand what [the issue] is." They talked about their own people that are still missing. [They said], "You got to understand what the Foreign Minister said to you. He said he will work with you. . . . [T]hat is a big turnaround in our government. That they are willing now to work [with Americans.][40]

The VVA delegation visited many parts of the city, including a home for veterans wounded during the war and the mausoleum where Ho Chi Minh is buried. The latter prompted discussion among them the night before the event about what to do. They wished to see the mausoleum but did not want their hosts to use their visit there as propaganda. Their one complaint about the trip had been the "posturing" and "propagandizing" by some of the Hanoi officials, particularly during the opening statements. "I could have done without all those words they used: 'aggression, evil, imperialist,' " Bird told Weinraub, "[But] I didn't take it personally. . . ."[41] Following the custom for VIPs visiting the mausoleum, they gave their guide money to buy a wreath to place at the tomb, but they asked the Vietnamese to take no pictures of their visit there.

The stay in Hanoi had had a profound effect on their feelings. Their memories about Vietnam as it had been during the war had been altered by their firsthand experiences of the country six years after the war had

ended. As they departed, Muller confided to Weinraub: "Objectively,
the trip was a success. But personally, emotionally, it's changed my view
of the Vietnamese people and the reality is I've got to temper this when I
get home." Bird stated, "The war finally stopped in my mind," and
Harbert added, "The war is over, really over for me. I went through
some anxiety when I came here. I was nervous as hell. . . . But now
we're dealing with issues, we're dealing with reality, not the past."[42]
The Vietnamese invited them to return in February, 1982, for a second
visit.

The VVA delegation returned to a storm of criticism. On December 28,
they held a news conference in New York City to announce their accom-
plishments. The press conference was, Terzano recalls, "horrendous." It
was attended by hostile representatives of other veterans' groups, and
the delegation spent most of the time defending themselves against the
charges that they had sold out and had served Vietnamese propaganda
purposes. Feelings ran high. "I feel you are a total disgrace," shouted
Vietnam veteran Albert Santoli, who said he represented the sentiments
of seven veterans' groups, including the VFW and American Legion.
"These gentlemen are a fraud," Agent Orange Victims International
(AOVI) president Frank McCarthy declared of them. And George
Brooks, president of the National League of Families of American Prisoners of War and Missing in Southeast Asia (NLF), characterized the
trip as a failure. The VVA delegation, he stated, had brought back no
concrete information about American POWs and MIAs.[43] Subsequent
letters to the *Washington Post* accused them, among other things, of being
traitors.[44]

Two months later, in February, a second delegation returned to Vietnam. This one included representatives of the United States government. Terzano states:

> [The February, 1982 trip] was the first [one] over there to deal officially
> with the [POW/MIA] issue. . . . Foreign Minister Thach told us in a meet-
> ing with him in 1982, he said, "The way you guys conducted yourself on
> your first trip . . . enabled me . . . to open a lot of doors that would have
> never been opened. . . ." What he meant by that was, as veterans who
> fought coming back on a mission of peace and reconciliation and paying
> some respect to their leader, Ho Chi Minh, enabled Thach . . . not only to
> move along the process on the MIAs, . . . to get [our two] governments
> talking again, but also to begin the process of opening up the doors to the
> people of Vietnam. . . .[45]

Round Four

The *Washington Post* published a feature story about Maya Lin on January 3, 1982. In it, Lin described her family, her art, the process by which

she had created the winning design of the Vietnam Veterans' Memorial, and her life in Washington, D.C. since winning the competition. Lin came from a long line of artists and poets, and the artistry in her family's heritage, she said, is steeped in the Oriental philosophy of Taoism. However, in creating the design for the Memorial she had not consciously drawn on her family's tradition, Taoist ideas, or anything else. She simply had made a design that reflected what she felt at the time. She recalled the moment for reporter Phil McCombs:

> It was while I was at the site that I designed it. It just popped into my head. Some people were playing Frisbee. It was a beautiful park. I didn't want to destroy a living park. . . .
>
> When I looked at the site, I just knew I wanted something horizontal that took you in, that made you feel safe within the park, yet at the same time reminding you of the dead. So I just imagined opening up the earth. (She put her hands together gently, as if in prayer, and then opened them slowly.)
>
> It's like opening up your hands. It's not so threatening that way. You're using the earth, asking people to come in, protecting people from sounds [of the city]. . . .
>
> [The polished black granite] is a mirror. . . . It makes two worlds, it doubles the size of the park. If it were white, it would blind you because of the southern exposure. Black subdues that and creates a very comforting area.[46]

Nonetheless, the influence of her family and Taoism is there, she admitted, in the simplicity and style of the design. She concluded:

> It's a memorial that does not force or dictate how you should feel. It asks and provokes you to think whatever you should think. In that sense, it's very Eastern—"This is what happened, these are the people." It wants you to . . . come to your own personal resolution.[47]

Black stone. Oriental influence. No explicit statement. These were the characteristics that the opponents of Lin's design said they did not want in a Vietnam Veterans' Memorial. This was the kind of story that riled the opposition, who by now had gotten through to Interior Secretary James Watt. Though few in number, they were a formidable bunch. They included billionaire H. Ross Perot, Tom Carhart, Jim Webb, ex-POWs Admiral James Stockdale and Sen. Jeremiah Denton (R-Ala.), and Rep. Harry Hyde (R-Ill.). Calling the design a "wailing wall" for antidraft demonstrators and the like, Webb had enticed Hyde into the fray. They demanded a new design that was white, above ground, and more traditional. They wanted it to state explicitly that there had been glory and honor in the war. In January, Nancy Reagan quietly resigned from the

National Sponsoring Committee. Perot approached Scruggs and offered to finance a Gallup Poll of all Vietnam veterans to gauge their opinions about the Memorial's design. Scruggs dismissed the idea.

Supporters of the design outnumbered the opposition and, sensing trouble, began to assert their views as well. General William Westmoreland wrote Carhart a letter, stating that the simplicity of the design "strikes me as beautiful."[48] Ellsworth Bunker, former U.S. Ambassador to South Vietnam, John McElwee, president of John Hancock Mutual Life Insurance Company, and Stanley Resor, former Secretary of the Army, wrote letters to Secretary Watt supporting the design and urging him to issue the construction permit. On January 26, 1982, the American Legion made the single largest donation to the Memorial Fund by pledging one million dollars. The same day, Scruggs and Bob Doubek met with Hyde, hoping to persuade him of the design's suitableness. Hyde was cordial. He politely viewed their slide show and stated that Lin's design was "impressive," but did not agree to call off his counterattacks.[49]

Meanwhile, Sen. John Warner (R-Va.) had scheduled a meeting for the following morning in the chambers of the Senate Committee on Veterans Affairs to seek a compromise. Scruggs later described the meeting in his book. The opponents showed up in force, outnumbering by four to one the memorial steering committee, representatives from the American Legion and VFW, and other friends of Lin's design. Perot alone brought ten people with him to testify. Reading from 3×5 cards, they made their demands. General George Price, one of the military's highest ranking black officers, then responded to their demand that the memorial be made of white stone, saying, "Black is not the color of shame. I am tired of hearing it called such by you. . . . We are all equal in combat. Color should mean nothing now."[50] The debate continued throughout the day without a break, sometimes calm and reasoned, at other times angry and chaotic. Author Rick Atkinson later described the action:

> . . . [T]he parties decanted their spleen in the smoky room. When someone objected to the esthetics of placing a "stringy" American flag next to the wall, Tom Carhart, who sat next to Ross Perot, leaped to his feet and howled, "Take that back, you motherfucker!" Scruggs, equally enraged at the opponents naysaying, jabbed his finger at Perot's crowd. "Where were you during the past three years?" he yelled. "Why didn't you help? Why are you trying to destroy this memorial now that it's ready to be built?"[51]

Finally, at 7:30 P.M., General Mike Davison, a supporter of Lin's design, made a proposal: " [T]his has gone on too long. . . . Why don't we just add a statue to the design, improve the inscription, and add a flag?"

Both sides wearily concurred by a voice vote, and the opponents of Lin's design agreed to call off the dogs.[52]

The matter, however, was far from over. First, the committee knew that Lin and other supporters of her design might not accept the changes. Scruggs told Lin the following day, "Aesthetically, the design does not need a statue, but politically it does."[53] Lin did not like it but, for the moment, accepted the change pragmatically. Further, any modifications would have to be approved by the National Capital Planning Commission, the Fine Arts Commission, and the Joint Committee on Landmarks. Also, Watt would have to issue the construction permit.

Scruggs met with Watt on February 4. Watt agreed with the modified design. An elated Scruggs told reporters after the meeting, "I met with Jim Watt and he says, 'Bring on the bulldozers!' "[54] An infuriated Watt immediately called Scruggs, demanding a retraction and threatening to freeze the project indefinitely. A contrite Scruggs met with reporters for the second time that day to say that he had erred in making Watt's views public: "That's what I said, but that's not what I should have said. The fact of the matter is that Secretary James Watt has not officially agreed to let us break ground . . . I didn't realize the meeting itself was a more private type meeting."[55] Watt indeed had approved the modification in principle, but planned to sit on the construction permit until the committee produced satisfactory, finalized plans for the flagpole, statue, and inscription. Otherwise, the opposition feared, the modifications might get lost in the shuffle once ground was broken.

Scruggs had hoped to break ground on March 1. Even with the compromise, that date was quickly doomed. On February 18, the National Planning Commission gave final approval for the construction of the Memorial. They announced, however, that they would have to meet again in March to consider the addition of a flagpole and statue. The clean simplicity of Lin's design, the Committee felt, would not detract from the Lincoln Memorial 600 feet away. They were not so sure about the proposed changes.[56] A week later Watt announced that he would not issue the construction permit until both the Planning Commission and Fine Arts Commission approved the modifications. On March 4, the National Capital Planning Commission voted to approve "the development of a concept" for placing a pole for the American flag "somewhere at the site in Constitutional Gardens" and a statue of a serviceman "within the area before the apex."[57] On March 9, the Commission on Fine Arts rendered its cautious approval of a statue and flagpole. "We believe it is possible," chairman J. Carter Brown wrote in a letter to Watts, "to find a solution for adding those elements in such a way as to obtain approval of the Commission."[58] Brown went on to suggest that the flag and statue serve as an "entry point" for the Memorial.

This would leave the original design intact while providing for the modifications.

Watt accepted these recommendations, but did not issue the construction permit. Nor would he return telephone calls about it. *Washington Post* columnist Benjamin Forgey, angrily editorialized:

> Opponents of Maya Lin's competition-winning design . . . , because a few of them are rich and a few are congressmen . . . , have managed to get the ear of a headstrong secretary of the interior [and] are busily . . . forcing through a "compromise" design that promises to muck up an extraordinary work of memorial art.
>
> In Lin's design those black walls, engraved with the names of our Vietnam dead, will emerge from the earth with a healing force and speak, as . . . James J. Kilpatraick observed . . . , "with a poignant, almost unbearable eloquence." To transform those noble walls into a backdrop for a lonely statue is an absurdity that ought not be countenanced.[59]

On March 11, Scruggs and Senator Warner again met with opponents of the design to select a statue. Scruggs brought to the meeting more than eighty slides of statues that had been submitted during the original design competition. Perhaps they could simply select one of them and be on their way. Ross Perot had other ideas. He quickly gained control of the meeting and, by a voice vote, changed the agenda to a discussion of where to place the flag and statue. The ensuing debate lasted several hours and became ugly. Suddenly, the motion was on the floor to chuck Lin's design and begin again back at square one. There were enough opponents present for the motion to pass. However, "Perot," Scruggs later wrote, "silently shook his head" to indicate his disapproval. The motion failed. Design opponent Milt Copulos wrote of the vote:

> Something remarkable happened. Veterans split over the issue realized that the project was in jeopardy, and chose to set aside their preconceptions and come together . . . to develop a consensus. . . . Some might argue that these changes are mere symbols, and hardly worth the pain and anguish they caused. But soldiers fight for symbols—symbols that embody the principles in which they believe.[60]

Watts still did not issue the permit. Warner put in a call to the White House. Apparently this one was going to be decided at the highest level. Four days later at 11 A.M., Bob Doubek called the steering committee's office. He had the construction permit. Scruggs wrote of the moment:

> Everyone . . . cheered. [John] Wheeler brought over a bottle of champagne. When it was empty, he reminded everyone that Watt still could be

persuaded to revoke the permit. "Get the construction crews on the site," he said. "Now!"

The construction foreman was a combat vet. He stood with Scruggs on the Mall.

"Do you know what it looks like after a B-52 raid?" Scruggs asked. . . . [He] nodded toward the beautifully manicured grass where the Memorial would stand. . . . "Can you give us a lot of holes all over the place that no one could ever fill?"

The foreman smiled. . . . If Watts ever tried to revoke the . . . permit, he would have a lot of explaining to do.[61]

Discovery Continues

The Agent Orange lawsuit meanwhile inched along laboriously. Attempts to secure any piece of information developed into a three-way tug of war among the lawyers representing the veterans, the chemical companies, and the government. Of course, each of the three had its own interest and stake in the suit, and cooperation was grudging at best. The usual two-way struggle found in most lawsuits was difficult enough; a three-cornered process of discovery was especially complicated and cumbersome.

However, things were to become even more complicated and more than a bit strange. As discovery progressed, fissures within the consortium representing the veterans had become wider and deeper. Three distinct groupings now existed.[62] At the center of the storm was Victor Yannacone & Associates, who had been allied from the beginning with Frank McCarthy and Agent Orange Victims International (AOVI). They represented a core of veterans numbering now about two thousand. A second contingent had developed around a Houston-based law firm headed by Benton Musselwhite and Newton Schwarz. These two lawyers represented more than a thousand veterans, most of whom were members of a Vietnam veterans organization called Citizen Soldier. Musselwhite and Schwarz now were joined by Rob Taylor of the law firm Ashcraft & Gerel, also representing more than a thousand veterans. These veterans mostly were affiliated with Vietnam Veterans of America (VVA). AOVI and VVA had clashed over the trip by the VVA delegation to Hanoi, and to say that bad blood existed between the two organizations was an understatement. In short, the plaintiffs were not a unified group, but rather comprised warring factions of attorneys and Vietnam veterans.

The wrangling and subterfuge among the three factions understandably magnified the discovery problems. In addition to the political strains among the veterans, the plaintiffs were not of a single mind concerning strategy. Musselwhite, Schwartz, and Taylor had threatened to draw out of the class action and pursue their cases individually. The sets of lawyers therefore did not trust each other. They were slow to share documents and information, and at times accused each other of spitefully withholding information. Peter Schuck wrote in his book of a typical exchange in which one attorney for the plaintiffs called Yannacone's office, saying, "Get me that paper from that prick bastard."[63] Yannacone responded in kind. The bickering attorneys eventually approached Judge Pratt and asked him to impose some order on their ranks. They suggested that the judge formally appoint a committee representing the three factions to direct the discovery process among them.

Schuck observed that there were two other issues brewing in this already bubbling mix of politics and personalities. The first revolved around benefits likely to befall the lead attorneys of the suit. The Agent Orange lawsuit was setting legal precedents and making legal history. The bulk of the recognition, standing in the profession, fame, and, should the veterans win, fees awarded by the court, would quite naturally go to the lead counsel. Hence, none of them wished to play second fiddle to the other. Further, in a class action suit, the court would play a more intrusive role in shaping the case than in other types of lawsuits. In doing so, the court would consult with the lead attorneys, thereby providing them with a great deal of potential for defining the case. These matters were difficult to accept by attorneys who did not share a consensus about what to do, had competing interests, and, frankly, had come to detest each other.

On February 24, 1982, Judge Pratt declined to name a steering committee for the plaintiffs. Yannacone & Associates remained in charge of the suit. A month later, Pratt made a significant decision: he appointed Sol Schreiber as a special master to speed up the process of discovery. Schreiber's appointment helped solve the principal problem of discovery apart from the plaintiffs' internal feud.[64] The chemical companies needed documents to prove complicity on the part of the government. But what documents to look for? The government was not about to allow a fishing expedition through its files. Further, many of the documents still were classified as secret. Judge Pratt recommended that the government extend Schreiber a security clearance and allow him to examine the Pentagon's files. From the mountain of documents Schreiber could choose those that he considered relevant to the lawsuit for the defense to examine. The government approved the plan. After several weeks of reviewing the files, Schreiber singled out 154 documents, only one of which the Pentagon refused to release on security grounds. One logjam was broken.

Meanwhile, a fissure was developing among the chemical companies as well. Through a circuitous, secondhand process, the consortium for the veterans learned early in 1982 that Dow Chemical had held a meeting in March of 1965 with representatives of several other chemical manufacturers to discuss the problem of dioxin. The consortium assigned attorney David Dean to search in chemical company files, under the provisions of the discovery process, for a document detailing the minutes of the meeting. He found it in the files of Diamond Shamrock. Dean described the moment and the memo's contents to Schuck, who wrote:

> "As soon as I read it," Dean recalls, "I shouted 'Holy Christ!' We had found the smoking gun."
>
> . . . Dow had called the meeting to discuss the health hazards involved in the production of 2,4,5-T. . . . Dow had not yet contracted to produce Agent Orange for the government, and the government was not present. Dow . . . had learned about the dioxin contamination problem in 1964, had developed a method of detecting it at concentration levels as low as 1 ppm (part per million), had concluded that dioxin at that level was "safe," and had succeeded in reducing dioxin levels in its 2,4,5-T below 1 ppm. . . . At the meeting, Dow explained that repeated exposure to 1 ppm of dioxin could be dangerous, that precautions were necessary, and that it had examined herbicides sold by other companies and found some to contain "surprisingly high levels" of dioxin.[65]

Taken at face value, the memo could provide evidence which would let the government off the hook. Dow, at least, knew of the dangers before entering into contracts with the government, and all of them had failed to warn others after the meeting. The government could say that it had used the stuff in good faith. The memo also established a new angle: Agent Orange was not a generic product, but one whose toxicity had varied considerably from manufacturer to manufacturer. Dow prided itself in having made "clean" Agent Orange, and resented other manufacturers—Monsanto, for instance—who had made "dirty" batches of the herbicide, that is, Agent Orange containing much more than 1 ppm of dioxin. However, if the suit ended in a verdict favoring the plaintiffs, the manufacturers would share equally in the blame and would pay in proportion to their market shares of Agent Orange. Dow and Monsanto were the two largest manufacturers of the herbicide, each having made about 30 percent of the total produced. Though Dow had made clean Agent Orange and Monsanto dirty Agent Orange, each would pay the same amount: 30 percent of the settlement apiece.

The consortium decided to try to split Dow away from the other manufacturers. Badly in need of money and shamelessly shopping again for "investors," they hoped the strategy would allow them to kill two birds with one stone. In July 1982, they authorized attorney Edward Gorman, who had a long-standing professional relationship with Leonard Rivkin, Dow's lead attorney, to explore the possibility of an out-of-court settlement with Dow. If Dow took the bait, they then could use the money from the settlement to proceed with the suit against the manufacturers of the dirty Agent Orange. In December 1982, Gorman had a series of secret meetings with Rivkin, who had agreed to listen to their proposal. In January 1983, Gorman reported to the consortium that Rivkin would recommend to Dow that they settle out of court with the veterans for a deal that was worth $100 million (but would actually cost Dow only $40 million).

As the consortium considered and bickered about the amount, Rivkin suddenly withdrew the offer in February, 1983. Several consortium lawyers later heard that Yannacone, unknown to the others, had initiated his own talks with another of Dow's attorneys. Dow had withdrawn its offer, Yannacone's colleagues claimed angrily, because corporate leaders were confused about who actually represented the consortium. Dow, they said, also feared further bad press that might result from being denounced by one faction for accepting the offer of another faction. Finally, the defense could hardly help but think that the consortium representing the veterans would self-destruct at any minute.[66]

Round Five

Ground had been broken for the Vietnam Veterans Memorial on March 26, 1982. A Memorial based upon Maya Lin's design apparently would be built. However, the fight over the statue and flagpole was not yet over. Two days prior to groundbreaking, Jan Scruggs and Sen. John Warner had announced a compromise.[67] They said that the flagpole would be placed at the top of the Memorial at the point where the two walls met. The statue, which they said would depict "a strong, commanding figure symbolizing all who served in Vietnam," would be placed in front of the two walls. They also agreed to add two inscriptions. One would contain the words spoken by Jeremiah Denton— himself held captive for seven and a half years—upon the return to the United States of American prisoners of war from North Vietnam: "We are honored to have had the opportunity to serve our country under difficult circumstances. . . . God bless America!" The other would read: "For those who fought for it, freedom has a flavor the protected will never know."

That same week, John Wheeler organized a subcommittee to oversee the planning for the proposed statue.[68] He placed on it two opponents of Lin's design—Jim Webb and Milt Copulos—and two supporters of the design—Art Mosley and Bill Jayne. The subcommittee selected Frederick Hart, whose bronze statuary had won third prize in the design competition, to create the statue to be added to Lin's design. He suggested that the statue facing the V-shaped walls might have three figures, rather than one, and depict soldiers as they typically looked in Vietnam. The subcommittee agreed and Hart began work on a model of it for their approval.

Meanwhile, the purchase and preparation of the granite had begun. No quarries in the United States produced granite with a solid black color, so the 315 tons of black granite for the Memorial was purchased from a quarry near Bangalore, India. Natavi & Sons Granite Industries of Vermont carefully cut it into 150 panels, each measuring three inches thick and forty inches wide. The height of the panels ranged from ten feet eight inches to eight inches, depending upon where along the wall the panel would be placed. The firm then polished the granite to a glossy shine and packed it into special shipping crates. From Vermont the panels went to Binswanger Glass Company in Memphis, Tennessee, whose job it would be to sandblast onto them the more than 57,000 names.[69]

On July 7, Maya Lin, who to this point had kept quiet about the proposed changes, broke her silence. In an article which appeared in the *Washington Post*, she angrily claimed that the steering committee had kept her in the dark about the changes. As for how she felt about the changes, she stated: "This farce has gone on too long. . . . I have to clear my own conscience. . . . Past a certain point it's not worth compromising." She dismissed the idea of placing a flagpole on a two-acre park, observing: "It's going to look pretty much like a golf green." "It's crucial what you come across first," she said of the proposed statues, "I don't want it to appear [the statues are] going to shoot you as you start walking down toward the walls. . . . The sculpture is going to make you feel watched." She also singled out Hart for criticism, accusing him of "drawing mustaches on other people's portraits."[70] Lin had not been present for the groundbreaking ceremony. She had purposely been out of the country (in Taiwan) on the day of the groundbreaking in order to avoid answering questions about the proposed changes. She continued:

I would have loved to have been there under any other circumstances. The design was one of the best things I've ever done. I waited all year for the groundbreaking—then I couldn't show my face there. . . . I can just picture myself sneaking up at the the dedication: a voyeur at my own work.[71]

She concluded the interview by saying that she had been quiet to this point as part of "a gentlemen's agreement not to speak out for several months. . . . [T]he whole idea was to let them have their groundbreaking."[72]

Scruggs had long since adopted a pragmatic posture concerning the controversy over the flagpole and statue. At the groundbreaking ceremony, he dismissed charges he had sold out to his critics by accepting the compromise, saying: "I'm here to build a monument, not put a Rembrandt on the Mall." Informed of Lin's charges, he said he saw no problem with two artists contributing to the final configuration of the Memorial: "[It's not a problem] . . . as far as I can see. . . . It's just a reality—that's what's happening. [As for Lin] . . . , [w]e fought like hell for her design. . . . Her job's really kind of done."[73] And Hart responded carefully the next day to a reporter's questions: "It's not Maya Lin's memorial or Frederick Hart's memorial. It's a memorial to, for and about the Vietnam veterans to be erected by the American people—in spite of art wars that occur."[74] *Washington Post* columnist, Benjamin Forgey, who had followed the controversy closely and contributed a number of articles about it, commented philosophically:

> What is really fascinating about monument building in this city is that in almost every case, whether the final product resulted from a competition or a commission, certain clear divisions occur: professional standards versus popular taste, modernity versus tradition, abstract symbolism versus realist representation. The results have been mixed. . . .
>
> . . . If the debate over Lin's earth-hugging design . . . reflects a time-honored pattern it is, if anything, more intense because the subject itself is so difficult and so close in time. The politically inspired compromise . . . obviously is not with precedent. . . .[75]

In the meantime the slow and tedius task of inscribing the names onto the granite panels had begun. Bob Doubek had directed months of effort to compile the list of the names. They had to be sure that no one had been left out, and that the names were spelled correctly and in the proper chronological order. Architect Kenneth Cooper traveled to Memphis to experiment with varying textures, methods, depths of engraving, and the like in order to come up with the combination which presented the best effect. Scruggs later described the process in his book:

> As he tested the . . . engraving, Cooper . . . asked the workmen to move the 400–500 pound test panels out onto the parking lot surface. . . . [H]e noticed something strange as . . . the workmen stepped back. The sky

was on the ground. Clouds were moving. Color, texture, shading, and depth . . . all . . . were mirrored on the black granite.

Maya Lin had insisted on black granite in part because it was "reflective." Neither the jurors nor anyone who worked on the wall had considered this attribute to be especially important. Now, as he stared down at clouds, Cooper felt his heart pounding.

. . . Sandblasting was done by humans rather than machines, because even a few seconds of a malfunctioning or jammed machine could ruin an entire panel. . . . Concentration was essential. If they moved faster to the left than to the right, the panel would be streaked. . . . Different parts of the granite had different hardness, so it was often necessary to stop and use a micrometer to check the depth of the letters. If a letter was too deep, . . . a panel would be ruined, and there were only three spare panels.

One particularly emotional moment came when a woman whose brother had died in Vietnam engraved his name.[76]

Back in Washington, the fight was on again. Lin retained an attorney who threatened a lawsuit to halt construction of the Memorial if plans for a statue and flagpole remained. Ross Perot also was back in the picture. He likewise threatened to sue to stop the construction until after the flagpole and statue were actually built and in place. Scruggs' strategy was simply to keep the project moving. Each day of construction, he believed, made it politically more difficult for anyone to halt the progress toward completion and dedication. Fearing that the salvos being fired by Lin and Perot might prompt Watt to step back into the picture, the steering committee called Memphis and requested that a fully engraved panel be delivered to the Mall as quickly as possible.

Six panels had already been completed. One was selected, and the 665 names on it were sent to the steering committee so that they could invite family members to the ceremony. The names were of those of killed between January 2, 1970, and July 8, 1970. A number of tricky problems had to be solved to move a 3,000-pound panel from Tennessee to Washington, D.C. without breaking it. However, within days it was at the Mall. It arrived during the night, and within hours after daybreak, engineers had carefully put it in place with a crane. On July 21, Emogene Cupp, whose son was killed in Vietnam and was buried on his twentieth birthday, drew aside the blue curtain covering the ten-foot high panel, and Scruggs declared: "Until today, only two [American heroes] have had their names on the Mall: George Washington and Abraham Lincoln. Now those two have been joined by these 665."[77] Scruggs introduced those parents of the slain soldiers who were able to attend, and each family placed a long-stemmed rose next to the panel. Scruggs then noticed family members doing something he had not anticipated: they touched the stone and traced the names lovingly with their fingers. "Nobody can stop the dream now," he later wrote of the moment.[78] His optimism was a bit premature.

On September 20, Frederick Hart unveiled his rendition of the statue to be added to the Memorial. Its style stood in marked contrast to the abstract modernism of Lin's design. His sculpture depicted three young soldiers, two of them white and one black, in startlingly realistic detail down to their open flak jackets and dog tags. Most who saw it were pleased. Columnist Benjamin Forgey wrote of the showing in the following day's *Washington Post*:

> In gesture and facial expression, especially, it is an impressive ensemble: The soldiers are portrayed at the telling moment, all the more intense because of its expectant ambiguity.
>
> . . . Hart said the contrast in styles between his group of soldiers and Lin's wall is intended to "effect an interplay between image and metaphor. . . . I see the wall as a kind of ocean, a sea of sacrifice that is overwhelming and nearly incomprehensible in its sweep of names. I place these figures on a shore of that, gazing upon it, standing vigil before it, reflecting the human face of it, the human heart."[79]

The infighting, however, was not over. The target date for the dedication of the Memorial was Veterans' Day, November 11. But the steering committee could not announce plans for a dedication without approval from James Watt, and his office indicated that no approval was forthcoming until the issue of the statue and flagpole was completely resolved. This matter would be taken up by a meeting of the Commission on Fine Arts in early October. To keep the pressure on, Perot paid for a polling of former POWs to assess their opinions about the Memorial. Days before the Commission's meeting, Carhart called a news conference to announce that a majority of the POW's "disliked" and "were unhappy" with the design.[80] A day later, the *Washington Post* published a lengthy, thundering critique by writer Tom Wolfe of the drive to build the Memorial. Wolfe attributed the dream of building a memorial to many Vietnam veterans, principally Tom Carhart. Referring repeatedly to the Memorial as "the Tribute to Jane Fonda," he detailed a history of modern art in the United States and blasted the jury of the design competition as "the mullahs of modernism" whose definition of good art is "art that is offensive to the American people."[81]

The Commission convened on October 13. Donald Paul Hodel, undersecretary of the Interior, testified that Secretary Watt would allow a date for the dedication only if the Commission approved the compromise design. A "parade" of witnesses passionately praised or condemned Lin's design. The Commission called a recess near sundown to hurriedly view a mock-up of Hart's statue on the Memorial's construction site. Now it was decision time. Chairman J.C. Brown announced that the Commission approved of the flagpole and the statue prepared by Hart. However, he continued, the Commission also recommended that the pole and statue be placed together with a third element, the directories that visitors would use to locate the names on the panels, apart from the proposed center location. He suggested instead one of the sides in order to "help enhance the entrance experience of the memorial." Undersecretary Hodel declared, " . . . [I]t looks good for the dedication." Hart praised the "Solomon-like" decision of the Commission and Lin expressed "relief in a small sense." On October 19, Watt gave permission to dedicate the Memorial on November 11. The last obstacle had been removed.[82]

About a month before the commission's meeting, Scruggs had telephoned conservative columnist James Kilpatrick and invited him to visit the nearly finished Memorial. Kilpatrick took him up on the offer, and a few days later shared in his column what he felt during that visit. He wrote:

> [Scruggs and I] met by the temporary board fence that surrounds the site. . . . We walked through the usual litter of a construction site, and gradually the long walls of the memorial came into view. Nothing I had heard or written had prepared me for that moment. I could not speak. I wept.
>
> There are the names. The names! The names are etched in white on polished black marble. The names are arranged chronologically by the date of death, running from July 1959 to May 1975.
>
> . . . This memorial has a pile driver's impact. No politics. No recriminations. Nothing of vainglory or of glory either. For 20 years I have contended that these men died in a cause as noble as any cause for which a war was ever waged. Others have contended . . . that these dead were uselessly sacrificed in a no-win war. . . . Never mind. The memorial carries a message for all ages: this is what war is all about.
>
> . . . On this sunny Friday morning, the black walls mirrored the clouds of summer's ending and reflected the leaves of an autumn beginning, and the names—the names!—were etched enduringly upon the sky.[83]

Notes

1.   Peter Schuck, *Agent Orange on Trial: Mass Toxic Torts Disasters in the Courts* (Cambridge, Mass.: Harvard University Press, 1986), 60.
2.   Ibid., 60–61.
3.   Ibid., 66.

4. See Ibid., 65, for a discussion of a (b)(3) class action. Schuck writes that this is appropriate for cases in which "the questions of law or fact common to the members of he class predominate over any questions affecting only individual members. . . ."

5. Jan Scruggs and Joel Swerdlow, *To Heal a Nation: The Vietnam Veterans Memorial* (New York: Harper and Row, 1985), 49–50.

6. Ibid., 51.

7. Ibid., 52.

8. Ibid., 54.

9. Haynes Johnson, "America Has Been Liberated Too—Freed of its Pent-Up Emotions," *Washington Post*, 21 January 1981, A27.

10. Bill Peterson, "The Welcome," *Washington Post*, 26 January 1981, A1, A12.

11. Haynes Johnson, "A Capital Welcomes Its Heroes, With Emotion," *Washington Post*, 28 January 1981, A1, A25.

12. Peterson, "The Welcome," A12.

13. Brian Sherwood, "Time to Remember our Vietnam Heroes," *New York Times*, 3 February 1981, A18.

14. John Burgess and Eugene Robinson, "Overflowing Joy over Ex-Hostages' Return Not Shared by All Americans," *Washington Post*, 28 January 1981, A29.

15. Iver Peterson, "Vietnam Veterans Parade in Shadow of 52 Hostages," *New York Times*, 1 February 1981, A22.

16. Sheila Waters, "Time to Remember our Vietnam Heroes, *New York Times*, 3 February 1981, A18.

17. Peterson, "Vietnam Veterans," A22.

18. Scruggs and Swerdlow, *To Heal a Nation*, 57–58.

19. Robert Muller, personal interview with author, 27 March 1991, Washington, D.C.

20. Scruggs and Swerdlow, *To Heal a Nation*, 59–61.

21. Ibid., 64–65.

22. "Student Wins War Memorial Contest," *New York Times*, 7 May 1981, A20. The quote, "Thus . . . the war," attributed in the article to Maya Lin was not said to the reporter but written by her for the design competition.

23. Rick Atkinson, *The Long Grey Line* (New York: Pocket Books, 1989), 587–588.

24. Scruggs and Swerdlow, *To Heal a Nation*, 69.

25. Maya Ying Lin, "The Vietnam Memorial," *New York Times*, 14 July 1981, A24.

26. Irvin Molotsky, "White House Withdraws Support of Long Islander to be V.A. Head," *New York Times*, 21 March 1981), A-10.

27. "Prospective V.A. Chief Withdraws over Cutbacks," *New York Times*, 29 April 1981, A25.

28. "New V.A. Chief Says Veterans of Vietnam Not Neglected," *New York Times*, 16 July 1981, A13.

29. Peter Kihss, "U.S. Adding 42 Centers for Veterans of Vietnam," *New York Times*, 26 July 1981, A6.

30. Summarized from Scruggs and Swerdlow, *To Heal a Nation*, 67, 76–79.

31. The *New York Times* published an excerpt of his testimony, from which this quote is taken. Tom Carhart, "Insulting Vietnam Veterans," *New York Times*, 24 October 1981, A23.

32. Ibid.

33. Summarized from Scruggs and Swerdlow, *To Heal a Nation*, 84–88.

34. Bernard Weinraub, "Vietnam Invites 4 U.S. Veterans to Visit Hanoi," *New York Times*, 13 December 1981, A1.
35. Ibid., A24.
36. John Terzano, telephone interview with author, 9 April 1991, Washington, D.C.
37. Bernard Weinraub, "4 Veterans End Vietnam Trip Nervous about Return to U.S.," *New York Times* 25 December 1981, A:2.
38. Bernard Weinraub, "Vietnam Veterans Take an Emotional Journey to Hanoi," *New York Times*, 19 December 1981, A3.
39. Bernard Weinraub, "Hanoi Aide Welcomes Study of Herbicide Impact," *New York Times*, 23 December 1981, A10.
40. Terzano, telephone interview, 9 April 1991.
41. Weinraub, "4 Veterans End Trip," A2.
42. Ibid.
43. Terzano quote from telephone interview, 9 April 1991. Other quotes from "Four Veterans Defend Visit to Vietnam," *New York Times*, 29 December 1981, A3.
44. "Shadows of Vietnam: The Trip to Hanoi . . . ," *Washington Post* 9 January 1982, A22.
45. Terzano, telephone interview, 9 April 1991.
46. Phil McCombs, "Maya Lin and the Great Wall of China: the Fascinating Heritage of the Student Who Designed the Vietnam Memorial," *Washington Post*, 3 January 1982, F9-F12.
47. Ibid.
48. Information about the Westmoreland letter appeared in Phil McCombs, "Reconciliation: Ground Broken for Shrine to Honor Vietnam Veterans," *Washington Post*, 27 March 1982, A1, A14.
49. Scruggs and Swerdlow, *To Heal a Nation*, 97.
50. All quotes in this paragraph from Scruggs and Swerdlow, *To Heal a Nation*, 99–101.
51. Atkinson, *Long Grey Line*, 594.
52. Scruggs and Swerdlow, *To Heal a Nation*, 101.
53. Ibid.
54. "Yesterday . . . ," *Washington Post*, 5 February 1982, A25.
55. "Personalities," *Washington Post*, 5 February 1982, B2. Scrugg's "bulldozer" statement and his retraction both appeared in the *Post* on the same day.
56. Paul Hodge, "Vietnam Vets' Memorial May Begin in Two Weeks," *Washington Post*, 19 February 1982, A18.
57. Benjamin Forgey, "Vietnam Vet Memorial Action," *Washington Post*, 5 March 1982, B9.
58. Benjamin Forgey, "Monumental 'Absurdity," *Washington Post*, 6 March 1982, C5.
59. Benjamin Forgey, "Commission Acts on Vets Memorial Design," *Washington Post*, 10 March 1982, B6.
60. Summary of meeting and quote from Milt Copulos from Scruggs and Swerdlow, *To Heal a Nation*, 106.
61. Ibid., 107.
62. See Schuck, *Agent Orange on Trial*, 74–75.
63. Quote appears in Schuck, *Agent Orange on Trial*, 74. See 75–77 for Schuck's assessment of the conflicts within the consortium.
64. Summary of the special master's role appears in Schuck, *Agent Orange on Trial*, 82-83 and 92-93.

65.   Quote appears in Schuck, *Agent Orange on Trial*, 85, and a discussion of the Dow memo's significance on 85–88.

66.   Summarized from Schuck, *Agent Orange on Trial*, 88–90.

67.   "Compromise on Vietnam Memorial," *Washington Post*, 25 March 1982, 83.

68.   Scruggs and Swerdlow, *To Heal a Nation*, 115.

69.   Ibid., 109–110.

70.   Rick Horowitz, "Maya Lin's Angry Objections," *Washington Post*, 7 July 1982, B1, B6.

71.   Ibid., B6.

72.   Ibid.

73.   Ibid.

74.   Isabel Wilkerson, "Art War" Erupts Over Vietnam Veterans' Memorial," *Washington Post*, 8 July 1982, D3.

75.   Benjamin Forgey, "Monumental Problems," *Washington Post*, 17 July 1982, C10.

76.   Scruggs and Swerdlow, *To Heal a Nation*, 118–119.

77.   Charles Fishman, "Memorial's First Names Unveiled," *Washington Post*, 22 July 1982, E3.

78.   Scruggs and Swerdlow, *To Heal a Nation*, 123.

79.   Benjamin Forgey, "Hart's Vietnam Statue Unveiled," *Washington Post*, 21 September 1982, B1, B4.

80.   "Most Ex-POW's Polled Dislike Vietnam War Memorial Design," *Washington Post*, 12 October 1982, C2.

81.   Tom Wolfe, "Art Disputes War: The Battle of the Vietnam Memorial," *Washington Post*, 13 October 1982, B1, B3, B4.

82.   Benjamin Forgey, "Vietnam Memorial Clears Last Major Hurdle," *Washington Post*, 14 October 1982, A1, A2.

83.   James J. Kilpatrick, "The Names," *Washington Post*, 21 September 1982, A19.

7

BETTER SETTLED THAN TRIED

". . . [T]his case would be better settled than tried. If it can be settled, let's. If I can help you, I will."

Judge Jack B. Weinstein, Eastern District Circuit Court, New York

The steering committee organized the dedication of the Vietnam Veterans Memorial as a "salute to Vietnam veterans."[1] The events began on Wednesday, November 10, 1982, and ran through Sunday. At 10 o'clock on Wednesday morning, a round-the-clock candlelight vigil in honor of those killed in Vietnam and still missing in action commenced in the National Cathedral. Over the next three days, their names were read in alphabetical order by volunteers, mostly veterans and family members. So that families and friends would know when to be present to hear the name of a loved one read aloud, newspapers carried a schedule of the reading times for alphabetized segments of names. President Ronald Reagan and his wife Nancy dropped by for one of the readings and lit a candle.

Thursday and Friday were days of receptions and getting acquainted or reacquainted. The American Legion, Veterans of Foreign Wars (VFW), Vietnam Veterans of America (VVA), Gold Star Mothers, Disabled American Veterans (DAV), Jewish War Veterans, and AMVETS all hosted open houses. A register was posted to facilitate reunions among veterans. The steering committee sponsored ceremonies placing flowers at the memorial by children of those killed or missing in action and laying wreaths at Arlington Cemetary. VVA and Vietnam Veterans in Congress convened a panel on Capitol Hill to discuss issues related to Agent Orange. Hollywood entertainers and the U.S. Army Band provided free concerts.

The celebration culminated on Saturday with the dedication ceremony. Reporter Phil McCombs described the scene for the *Washington Post*:

Thousands of Vietnam veterans from across America marched in a grand parade down Washington's Constitution Avenue yesterday, then gathered in a vast throng on the Mall to dedicate the National Vietnam Veterans

Memorial, on whose polished granite walls are etched the names of their 57,939 dead and missing comrades-in-arms.

It was a day of flags and tears and stirring music, of marching Green Berets in jungle fatigues and Gold Star Mothers in cream colored capes. There were military color guards and high school bands . . . ; and, at noon, an overflight of military aircraft, the roar of jet airplanes and the haunting thud of rotor blades.

"All of us can now say we are proud to be Vietnam veterans . . . and I know that our country appreciates our service," Jan C. Scruggs said at the dedication ceremony.

. . . Some 150,000 attended the parade and dedication despite gusty winds and temperatures in the 40's. . . . Many spectators said they had no direct involvement in the Vietnam War but came to pay tribute to those who fought an unpopular war. "I felt like I owe it to the people who served," said John Pebbles, a 26-year-old graduate student at George Washington University. . . .[2]

Vietnam veterans basked in the attention and graciously accepted the acclaim. Some veterans did complain that it all should have occurred ten years earlier, and reporter Lou Cannon noted that neither President Reagan nor the director of the Veterans Administration, Robert Nimmo, attended the dedication ceremony. ("I can't tell until [my staff] tells me. I never know where I'm going," the President responded earlier that week when asked whether he would attend.)[3] However, the negative sentiments largely were lost in a sea of emotion and reconciliation. The salute ended on Sunday with a prayer service calling for a healing of the divisions caused by the war.

Still No Protocol

The Agent Orange issue was still perking on several fronts. There was, of course, the lawsuit, and in December 1979, Congress had enacted Public Law 96–151 commissioning the VA to provide medical treatment for Agent Orange claimants on a "nonservice connected" (low) priority basis and to conduct an epidemiological study of Vietnam veterans who were exposed to "any of the class of chemicals known as dioxins" in order to determine any long-term effects. That same month, the Carter administration had formed the White House's Agent Orange Working Group (AOWG) to coordinate the federal government's policy concerning herbicides containing dioxin, especially Agent Orange. AOWG included representatives from the Departments of Agriculture, Defense, Health and Human Services, and Labor, as well as from the

VA, the Environmental Protection Agency, the Office of Management and the Budget, and the Office of Technology Assessment. Soon there were numerous proposals on the table for dioxin research.

The VA proceeded carefully with its mandate. In June 1980, Dr. Lawrence Hobson prepared the proposal that would solicit bids for writing the protocol for the VA Agent Orange study. In a deposition provided to attorney Lewis Milford of the National Veterans Law Center, who later sued the VA, Hobson described the proposal. Richard Severo and Milford later wrote of his internal memo: "[Hobson] said . . . the VA sought a scientist with 'political sensitivity' who could realize the 'political implications of the questions [and] . . . who is able to be objective in the face of political pressure.' [Hobson] added, 'We definitely don't want an investigator who is going to contribute to any kind of political strife or socio-economic strife either inadvertently or intentionally.'"[4]

The VA selected Dr. Gary Spivey, a professor of public health at the University of California, Los Angeles, to design a study. Spivey got himself in hot water almost immediately. In December 1980, he testified against a bill before the California assembly that would establish an outreach program for Vietnam veterans who thought they might have been affected by Agent Orange. Veterans' groups and other observers, including Senator Alan Cranston, felt that Spivey had compromised his integrity. His testimony led them to think that Spivey firmly believed Agent Orange was harmless though he had yet to write the protocol for the study. Nonetheless, in May 1981, the VA awarded Dr. Spivey a $114,288 contract to do just that. In November 1981, the VA returned to Spivey his first draft of a protocol after a panel of reviewers outside the VA rejected it as too vague. One problem was that Spivey had not specified what health effects would be studied. He feared, he said, that if that information were released, veterans might misrepresent their symptoms to match those being studied.[5]

By the time Dr. Spivey had readied a second draft of the protocol in November of 1982, the VA was under intense criticism for the long delay. In September 1982, Rep. Thomas Daschle (D-S.D.), leader of the Vietnam Veterans in Congress (VVIC), charged that "certain parties in the V.A. are deliberately trying to delay the Agent Orange study."[6] He threatened to introduce legislation stripping the VA of responsibility for the study unless the agency advanced a protocol within one week and began a pilot study within one month.

Dissatisfaction with the VA's handling of the study extended far beyond VVIC. A month later, Representatives G.V. "Sonny" Montgomery (D-Miss.) and John Paul Hammerschmidt (R-Ark.), chair of the Committee on Veterans' Affairs, wrote a letter signed by 100 members of Congress to VA director Robert Nimmo. The letter demanded that the VA relinquish control of the study. On October 16, Nimmo announced that he would allow the national Centers for Disease Control (CDC) in Atlanta take over the study. The VA could have done the study, he said, but " . . . the need for public acceptance of both the conduct of the study and the study results is recognized. . . . Therefore I am persuaded that it would be prudent to enter into an agreement with a non-V.A. scientific body to perform the Agent Orange epidemiological study."[7] Nearly three years after Congress's mandate, the protocol for the study was back to square one.

In November 1982, *New York Times* reporter Phillip Boffey published an assessment of the scientific research currently underway or in the planning stage concerning Agent Orange. He noted that the fifty-five studies under the sponsorship of the federal government had a projected cost of more than $100 million, but claimed that there was slim hope for firm answers. He wrote:

> Few scientists expect the studies to produce unequivocal results or provide a clear guide to public policy. . . . Few scientists doubt that Agent Orange can be toxic. And few doubt that at least some military personnel . . . were virtually swimming in the chemicals. But nobody knows whether the average soldier in a one-year tour of duty got enough of a dose from Agent Orange sprayed around him to produce an adverse health effect. And scientists warn that, even if there is an effect, it may not make a notable blip in epidemiological studies.
>
> "In most environmental studies, the people who urge the study are unhappy when the results become available," warns Lewis Kuller, an epidemiologist at the University of Pittsburgh . . . [and] an Agent Orange consultant for the Congressional Office of Technology Assessment. "The effects are very difficult to measure and are often small compared to whatever else happens in the world."
>
> [K]nowledgeable scientists cite several problems [with proposed studies] that may limit their ability to unravel the cause of veterans' ailments. The most significant is that an overemphasis on Agent Orange may actually divert attention from other toxic materals that may have harmed the veteran. . . . The Department of Defense estimates that most troops probably got heavier exposures to insecticides, antimalarial drugs, fuel vapors, diseases, parasites, narcotics, alcohol and many other toxic substances than they did to Agent Orange.[8]

Boffey's article would prove to be prophetic. Questions concerning who should be studied, what should be studied, how exposure should be measured, and how effects should be detected were already infused with both methodological and political considerations. The battle lines were shaping up in the research wars over Agent Orange.

A Pretrial Setback

In March of 1982, Judge George C. Pratt set the date for the trial in the Agent Orange lawsuit: July 13, 1983. The process of discovery, which had begun two months earlier and continued on into 1983, had been complicated enormously by the three-cornered tug of war among the attorneys representing the veterans, chemical companies, and federal government, and by internal conflicts within the plaintiff and defense teams.

Law professor Peter Schuck has described the scrambling that occurred on both sides as the trial date approached.[9] In February of 1983, the consortium representing the veterans, virtually paralyzed by the constant bickering, admitted privately that they could not be ready for trial by July. Having botched the opportunity to settle out of court with Dow in December of 1982, they remained in bad financial shape. The consortium pulled together long enough to add Chicago attorney Steven Schlegel to the team and to agree to a new financial arrangement that would allow them to limp along a little longer. Schlegel was a specialist in class action lawsuits. With Schlegel aboard, the thinking went, the consortium members perhaps could break their stalemate and develop a more fitting legal strategy. As for Schlegel, he hoped to gain fame by reconceptualizing and leading the case for the veterans.

The defense lawyers, meanwhile, also doubted that they could be ready by the scheduled trial date. In March they met to discuss the possibility of requesting a one-year delay. They also considered raising again the issue of a summary judgment. They could argue that the government contract defense did not require a trial but could be settled by the court purely as a matter of law. This option seemed especially appropriate since they now had a smoking gun of their own. Dr. Gordon MacDonald, who had been a member of President Lyndon Johnson's Science Advisory Committee, was prepared to testify that the committee had discussed the "potential toxicity" of 2,4,5-T and dioxin in a series of meetings between April and July of 1965.[10] Dow and the others may not have informed the government, but, if MacDonald's assertion held up, the government would seem to have been aware of the problem anyway. To some of the chemical companies, the government contract defense looked better than ever.

Sol Schreiber, the special master designated by Judge Pratt to moderate such pretrial manuvering, suggested a compromise. He advised that if the defendants would agree without protestation to accept the case as a (b)(3) class action and would pay for the costs of informing class members of the suit—a potentially expensive notification—then the plaintiffs might agree to allow the government contract defense issue to be decided by the court. The proposal's attractiveness to the defendants was strategic: they could avoid a trial by jury. To the plaintiffs, the lure was financial: though the consortium felt that their chances were better before a jury, the defendants would pay for notification. Further, those veterans and their lawyers who did not want the court to decide the issue had the option of checking out and pursuing their claims individually.

The consortium for once was in agreement. They did not care for the proposal. However, it was the defense who had the prerogative to initiate the request. Five of the chemical companies wanted to pursue the proposal, but two of them—Monsanto and Diamond Shamrock—balked. As the companies who had made the "dirtiest" Agent Orange, that is, batches containing much more than 1 part per million (ppm) of dioxin, they were the most vulnerable defendants. Schuck wrote of their dilemma:

> [Monsanto and Diamond Shamrock] were almost certain to lose the government contract defense; what judge or jury, after all, would believe that the government had known that their dioxin levels were so high? Monsanto . . . was especially nervous. As the largest marketer of Agent Orange, it might have punitive as well as compensatory damages to an enormous class assessed against it. And if their "cleaner" codefendants prevailed on the defense or settled out of the case, the two companies might later have to confront the plaintiffs and an unsympathetic jury alone. . . . Their best hope was to put off the trial, conduct more discovery, and hope that plaintiffs' lawyers would run out of money.[11]

The defendants reluctantly rejected Schreiber's proposal. However, in an effort to clear up the matter, Judge Pratt instructed the defendants to file for a summary judgment. Five of the companies complied; Monsanto and Diamond Shamrock refused.

Dow spearheaded the motion for summary judgment and dismissal of the case on May 4. Its attorneys argued that President Johnson's Science Advisory Committee was concerned enough about dioxin in 1965 "to provide the impetus for the National Cancer Institute study" that later showed that the chemical caused cancer in mice. Also, they said, Secretary of Defense Robert McNamara and the Joint Chiefs of Staff had in their possession in 1967 a report by the Rand Corporation that stated in a footnote that "it was possible that in some small areas the spray dumped from overlapping patterns from planes might provide a lethal dose for a 6-kilogram child. . . ." At the same time, they contended, Dow itself had no knowledge of any health hazards associated with using Agent Orange in the form Dow had concocted it—batches containing less than

1 part per million of dioxin. The government continued using Agent Orange despite these warnings because it regarded the spraying program as a military necessity; hence, Dow's attorneys argued, the government was the party who had acted irresponsibly.[12]

On May 20, 1983, Judge Pratt ruled on the motion for summary judgment.[13] His decision was sweeping and left the attorneys for both the plaintiffs and the defense reeling. The judge upheld part of the government contract defense advanced by the chemical companies. The government, he said, had indeed specified how Agent Orange should be produced, and the chemical companies had followed their instructions. However, concerning the issue of the government's knowledge of the herbicide's potential harm, he decided that there was ample evidence, apart from whatever the chemical companies might have said or not said, that the government was at least aware that use of an herbicide like Agent Orange involved some health risks. The government was still in the case.

Concerning the chemical companies' knowledge of the risks, Judge Pratt observed that some of the companies knew more than others. Dow, in particular, he felt, had known a great deal about the hazards. He therefore dismissed the cases against three of the companies— Riverdale, Hoffman-Taff, and Thompson Chemicals—stating that they had been unaware of the potential harm. No representatives of these companies had attended the 1965 meeting where Dow had discussed the hazards of dioxin and the toxicity of herbicide mixtures containing more than 1 ppm. Judge Pratt then granted summary judgment to Hercules because, he said, the company had produced clean Agent Orange and had had little knowledge of the risks of herbicide use. However, he continued, although Dow had also made clean Agent Orange, it had had extensive knowledge of the risks. Therefore, Dow would have to stand trial with the dirty manufacturers, Monsanto and Diamond Shamrock.

Judge Pratt did not stop there. He developed the implications of his decision for the subsequent course of the lawsuit. Schuck assessed the impact:

> The most momentous feature of Pratt's decision concerned the relationship between the factual question of what level . . . of dioxin could actually harm the plaintiffs, and the knowledge element of the government contract defense. "I have concluded," [Judge Pratt] wrote, "that a separate trial of the open issues on the government contract defense with respect to the remaining defendants is no longer appropriate. . . . [W]hen the 'knowledge' factor of the government contract defense is placed alongside a liability theory of negligent failure to warn, the issues . . . tend to merge. . . . [J]ustice would be served by combining what remains of the

government contract defense issues with . . . a trial . . . covering the issues of liability, general causation, and the government contract defense."

Pratt's bland language scarcely concealed the thunderbolt he had
hurled. . . . [T]he structure that [he] had imposed [on the case] and that
had guided its development for two and a half years . . . was suddenly
out the window. A litigation organized around a focused, relatively well-
defined set of issues to be tried only one month hence, was instantly
transformed into a completely open-ended free-for-all involving a diffuse,
highly interrelated tangle of issues that would be subject to discovery,
trial, and decision at some unspecified time in the . . . distant future.[14]

Dow's attorneys were very upset. They felt that they should have also
been excused from the case and were in no mood to cooperate with
Monsanto and Diamond Shamrock. Dow had made clean Agent Orange, and as for the knowledge issue, they noted that Hercules had had
representatives at their 1965 meeting. Now, Dow's attorneys felt, it was
every chemical company for itself. The rift among the makers of Agent
Orange was open and public. However, the consortium representing
the veterans felt little cause to celebrate. They had severe problems of
their own, and now, more than four years after Victor Yannacone had
filed the lawsuit, the case was back at square one in the pretrial phase.

Times Beach

In December of 1982, the Environmental Protection Agency (EPA)
announced that the town of Times Beach, Missouri, had dangerous
amounts of dioxin-contaminated soil and encouraged its 2,400 residents
to move elsewhere. The problem had begun some ten years earlier in
nearby Verona, where Northeastern Pharmaceutical and Chemical Company (NEPACCO) made hexachlorophene, an active ingredient in surgi-
cal soap, talcum powder, and other skin care products. NEPACCO had
leased a building there in 1969 from Hoffman-Taff, who at the time was
making Agent Orange on the Verona site. As with Agent Orange, hexachlorophene manufacture unavoidably produced dioxin. By filtering,
NEPACCO produced "clean" hexachlorophene containing less than
than 0.1 part per million (ppm) and three dioxin waste products: contaminated water, filter clay, and thick, gooey "still bottom."[15] The company buried most of the filter clay. It treated some of the contaminated
water, sold some to a nearby wastewater technical school, and leaked
some into the nearby Spring River. The contaminated water contained
about 2 ppm of dioxin, about the amount in the Agent Orange that had
been sprayed in Vietnam. The still bottom contained considerably

more—around 300 ppm. The Federal Drug Administration banned hexachlorophene in 1971 after reports from France that thirty-six infants had died after being powdered with talcum containing abnormal levels of the chemical.

The still bottom posed a serious disposal problem. Because it was expensive to incinerate—the preferred method of disposal—NEPACCO sold the still bottom to a St. Louis firm, Independent Petrochemical Corporation, who in turn subcontracted the responsibility for getting rid of it to a self-employed waste hauler, Russell Bliss. Bliss enjoyed a "we haul anything" reputation.[16] Independent's executives say NEPACCO did not tell them the still bottom contained dioxin, but Indpendent nevertheless warned Bliss that it probably was toxic and offered protective clothing; Bliss contends that he was never so advised. In any case, he did not dispose of the goo. Instead, he added used crankcase oil to it in a tank near his rural home and then tarred dirt roads and stable areas with the mixture. "It wouldn't have been worth it for me to drive some 250 miles . . . if it wasn't used oil that I could sell," Bliss explained to reporters years later.[17]

On May 25, 1971, Gary Lambarth, one of Bliss's drivers, delivered a truckload of "oil" to the Shenandoah Stables in nearby Moscow Mills, Missouri, owned by Judy Piatt and Frank Hampel. A *Post-Dispatch* investigation later reported:

> The material in Lambarth's tank truck that morning seemed unusually thick and heavy. [He] spent 10 to 15 minutes priming the pump. . . . Once the material began oozing out, Lambarth drove around repeatedly until he had saturated the floor inside the corrugated metal arena building. After [he] left . . . a foul, burning odor lingered.

> The next evening, a quarter horse in the arena became severely ill. Within five days, five more horses had fallen ill. In the following weeks . . . , many more horses [became ill]. . . . Some died. Cats and dogs died, too. Birds dropped from rafters. Over a period of weeks, hundreds of birds died—mostly sparrows, but also cardinals and woodpeckers. Hampel spent hours raking up dead birds. Eventually, Mrs. Piatt says, 62 registered horses at Shenandoah died or had to be destroyed.

> . . . Hampel, Mrs. Piatt and her daughters [also] suffered flu-like symptoms—diarrhea, headaches, aching joints and shoulders. . . . [On August 21], [Piatt's 6-year-old daughter] Andrea was rushed to St. Louis Children's Hospital with severe bleeding and inflammation of the bladder. . . . Doctors said that Andrea had been chemically intoxicated. They did not know by what.[18]

Piatt and Hampel suspected that something in Bliss's waste oil was the culprit. Though Bliss reassured them that the material was only "old crankcase oil," Piatt and Hampel removed the top layer of soil from the arena. Over the next fifteen months, they also shadowed Bliss's trucks and developed a log of pickups and deliveries. One of Bliss's customers was Times Beach, where his trucks sprayed 40,000 gallons of "oil" onto virtually every street in town. At the request of Piatt and Missouri officials, the Centers for Disease Control (CDC) took soil samples in 1971, 1972, and 1973 from Shenandoah Stables. On July 30, 1974, CDC identified the contaminant in the soil samples as dioxin.[19] They notified the Missouri State Department of Health and dispatched a team to discover where the dioxin came from. Using Piatt and Hampel's notes, CDC's investigation led to Russell Bliss and NEPACCO, which by now was out of business.

The CDC conferred with Missouri officials about what to do. Their impression was that two sites had received straight, undiluted still bottom: Shenandoah Stables and a farm owned by Bliss himself that one of his drivers had used once as a dump site. Piatt's list led them to two other contaminated home sites owned by Vernon Stout and Harold Minker. CDC's estimate, believed to be accurate at the time, was that the dioxin was naturally decomposing in the soil at a rate of about one-half of the total per year.[20] CDC recommended destroying the still bottom tank in Verona and digging up and reburying contaminated soil from the four sites. Syntex Corporation, who now owned the Verona site, agreed to destroy the tank using a new technique, photolysis. Missouri officials elected to leave the soil in place, noting that the sites would reach safe levels shortly, and to halt the search for other contaminated sites.

In 1979, a disgruntled former employee of NEPACCO provided an anonymous tip to the EPA that corroded drums containing more still bottom and filter clay were located near the old hexachlorophene plant. In April 1980, an EPA team led by Daniel Harris found the site and discovered that waste materials leaking from the drums contained 2,000 ppm of dioxin. Syntex agreed to clean it up. However, Harris's testing had produced a disturbing finding: the dioxin was not decomposing as quickly as expected. He decided to expand his investigation to the other forty-one sites listed in Piatt and Hampel's notes. Harris's superiors at the EPA, however, instructed him to "not spend any more resources" on the investigation.[21]

The EPA meanwhile was in turmoil. Reagan appointee Rita Lavelle was the EPA offical in charge of hazardous waste management after 1980. Lavelle brought a pro-business stance to the job, having previously been a public relations specialist for Aerojet General Corporation of Sacramento, Califormia. Her job there had been to deflect criticism that the company had contributed to waste problems in that state. In September 1981, Lavelle rejected the recommendation from the regional

office that the EPA use Superfund money—set aside by earlier legislation to clean up hazardous waste in the United States—for the Stout and
Minker home sites. Lavelle ruled that the situation in Missouri was "no
emergency."[22]

A feud, however, had developed between EPA director Anne Burford,
also a Reagan appointee, and Lavelle. Lavelle had close connections
with Edwin Meese and the White House and preferred to confer outside
of the chain of command. "She wouldn't go through the normal public
affairs office—and that bothered me," Burford acknowledged to a *Times-
Dispatch* reporter. Burford concerned herself with other issues, leaving
the Missouri dioxin controversy for her subordinate to handle. A high-
level EPA official told the *Times-Dispatch* that "[Burford] . . . allowed
[Lavelle] to go very far out on the limb" in hopes that Lavelle would do
herself in.[23]

That fall, Senator John Danforth (R-Mo.) faced a tight race against
Democratic challenger Harriett Woods. Danforth had been Missouri's
attorney general at the time of the decision to leave the contaminated
soil in place. The Environmental Defense Fund, a Washington-based
environmental group, made public a list of the forty-one suspected dioxin sites in Missouri. They charged that the EPA was downplaying the
problem to conceal Danforth's inaction while attorney general and senator. On the day before the election in November, the EPA at Lavelle's
suggestion issued a last-minute news release proclaming that a "promising" new technique had been discovered for decontaminating dioxin.
Several EPA officials later admitted that the release had been "cooked
up" to help the Danforth compaign.[24] (The technique referred to in the
release was still years away from use.) By the end of November, Representative Richard Gephardt (D-Mo.) had convinced the House Energy
and Commerce Committee to hold hearings on the dioxin problem in
Missouri.

Media coverage of these events sparked angry town meetings and
dozens of tips concerning the location of contamination sites. The EPA
decided to move on the issue. They started with Times Beach, the site
with the largest population. On December 2, 1982 EPA technicians,
wearing white plastic "moon suits," rubber gloves, and respirators, collected soil samples in the town. A day later, heavy rains and flood
waters swept over Times Beach, causing many residents to evacuate and
raising fears that whatever contamination was present had been further
spread about the town. On December 23, the CDC analyzed the samples
and found that some contained 300 ppm of dioxin.[25] The CDC urged the
town's residents who had left because of the flood not to return and
those who had remained to pack up and leave. Of the 2,400 residents,
only about 300 refused the advice.

On January 5, 1983, Lavelle met with the Missouri congressional delegation. The meeting started badly—Lavelle announced that the EPA
considered Times Beach to have only a flooding problem—and went
downhill from there. On January 9, sanitation workers, again wearing
respirators and moon suits, began removing 800 truckloads of contaminated silt. At a town meeting, angry residents, who had stood by and
watched the sampling and removal of soil, wondered why the government had not supplied them with moon suits. "This is the first time
anyone ever asked for them," an EPA official told them. "Under no
circumstances would I want to raise a family in Times Beach," CDC
epidemiologist Dr. Gary Stein said in response to a question about the
risks. Faron Powder, the town's burly bartender, expressed the frustra-
tions of many who remained in Times Beach: "Why, if it's so dangerous,
did the government wait 10 years to warn us? I figure anyone's who's
been contaminated done been contaminated. Why put your tail between
your legs and run now . . . ?" Chrysler assembly line worker Larry Col-
lier placed an American flag in his yard as a symbol of defiance: "You
win a battle, you stick up a flag. This is a war to stay on the land you
worked and paid for. . . . I'm staying. . . ."[26]

Vietnam veteran groups concerned about Agent Orange took an avid
interest in these developments. They pushed the link between themselves and civilian victims of chemical exposure. Veteran Edward Manear's letter to the *Washington Post* typified the stance:

> Please help me understand what has happened. . . . [The] government is
> keeping the residents of Times Beach . . . from their homes because high
> levels of dixoin have been discovered there.
>
> Since the government has never admitted that dioxin was hazardous to
> the lives of men and women who served in Vietnam, could it be that
> dioxin is poisonous only when it is used within the continental . . .
> United States? Perhaps dioxin is poisonous only when in proximity to
> civilians but harmless to men and women in uniform. Maybe dioxin is
> poisonous only when political mileage can be gained without regard to
> military or civilian status.
>
> Those of us exposed to dioxin in Southeast Asia are dying to know the
> answer.[27]

Chaos reigned. At the center of the problem was Lavelle, who opposed any plan for temporary or permanent relocation of Missouri residents. As EPA and CDC administrators bickered in open disagreement,
the White House appointed EPA administrator Lee Thomas to head a
task force to figure out a solution. On February 4, Burford fired Lavelle
and subsequently made it known that she would accept a "buyout" plan
if Thomas and the CDC both concurred. They did.

On February 22, speaking at the Eureka, Missouri, Holiday Inn, Burford concurred with the CDC's assessment that Times Beach was "too contaminated to be safe for human habitation" and should be abandoned.[28] All homes and businesses in the town would be purchased by the government, she said. The estimated cost was $33 million, 90 percent of which would be paid by the federal government and 10 percent by the state of Missouri. A loudspeaker carried Burford's announcement outside the motel to assembled Times Beach residents, who alternately cheered and jeered her remarks. Laine Jumper, a Times Beach resident who had campaigned for several months in behalf of a buyout, commented, "A lot of people think that Times Beach is full of backwater rubes, but we can smell a political deal as easily as anyone in Washington.[29]" And Evelyn Zuffalt, a school bus driver and mother of seven, said:

> You have to wonder if anybody in Washington really cares. This buyout answers our immediate problem, but I don't think we'll have the answers for generations. I think of my children. It will be a stigma all their lives . . . that they grew up here.[30]

Presumption Denied

Robert Nimmo had an excuse for failing to attend the dedication of the Vietnam Veterans Memorial. He was by then the lame duck director of the VA. On October 4, 1982, a month before the dedication, he had resigned under pressure as the agency's chief administrator. He had agreed to remain on as director until a replacement could be named. The precipitating event was a pending General Accounting Office (GAO) report containing charges that Nimmo had illegally used chartered military aircraft and first-class commercial air travel for his own purposes and had a personal chauffeur in violation of federal law.[31] Also, Nimmo had been under constant fire from Vietnam veterans' groups for comments and policy stands that they considered insensitive to their needs. Apparently the antagonisms were mutual. Shortly after turning in his resignation, Nimmo claimed that Vietnam veterans wanted "preferential coddling" and claimed that the scientific evidence on Agent Orange showed that the herbicide caused only a skin condition no worse than "teenage acne."[32]

The American Legion urged the Reagan administration to select a successor who was a Vietnam veteran rather than "another World War II vet such as Nimmo." "They [Vietnam veterans] are the generation," explained Mylio Kraja, director of the Legion's Washington, D.C. office, "which feels their problems are not being met."[33] The names initially circulated by the administration as possible replacements were of men who had served in Vietnam. However, President Reagan chose a political friend, Harry Walters, who at the time was Assistant Secretary of the Army.[34] A 1959 West Point graduate, Walters had left the Army in 1963 to enter private business and therefore had not served in Vietnam. The selection signaled that there would be no change in policy. Veterans organizations and the Senate Committee on Veterans Affairs—the full Senate would have to approve the nomination—were not enthusiastic about Reagan's choice. Even Senator Alan Simpson (R-Wyo.) and Senator Strom Thurmond (R-S.C.) were displeased. They felt that there were Vietnam veterans available for the job—Thomas Harvey, staff director of the Senate Committee, for example—who could better lend credibility to the administration's stance on veterans' issues. After some stall kicking, however, the Senate approved the Walters nomination.

Also in October of 1982, Rep. Thomas Daschle (D-S.D.) had introduced a bill to provide relief for Vietnam veterans suffering from certain diseases while the federal government conducted its time-consuming epidemiological studies. If passed, the bill would instruct the VA to presume that cancer of certain soft-tissue organs (lung, stomach, or muscles), porphyria cutanea tarda (a condition that affects the liver, blood, and skin), and chloracne originated during military service and to provide compensation for these diseases. To receive benefits, veterans with these diseases need only show that they had served during the war in an area sprayed with Agent Orange. Compensation would be terminated if the studies then underway eventually showed no correlation between Agent Orange and the ailments. Daschle estimated that about 2,500 veterans would qualify for compensation under the bill and that the cost would run about $3 million to $4 million annually.

One hundred and six Representatives signed on as coauthors of the bill. Similar compensation bills aimed at providing relief for seriously ill Agent Orange claimants had been introduced in the past, but the Veterans of Foreign Wars (VFW) and American Legion had opposed them. In November, the VFW broke ranks and endorsed the proposed bill.[35] James Currieo, the VFW commander in chief, explained that the decision had been reached after polling his membership. Their recommendation, he said, concurred with his own personal conclusion that the VA was "foot-dragging" on the Agent Orange issue. The American Legion the year before had passed a resolution at their national convention in support of Agent Orange claimants. In March 1983, two weeks after the EPA announced the Times Beach buyout, the Legion joined the VFW and endorsed the bill. They agreed with Daschle that it would be "irresponsible" to admit a problem and buy up the homes in Times Beach while refusing to compensate Agent Orange claimants. Further, national commander Al Keller, Jr. stated: "[The] scientific evidence is available pinpointing three medical disorders that may be caused or aggravated by exposure to the herbicide."[36]

Two trends paved the turnabout by the nation's two largest veterans' organizations. First, their hostility toward Vietnam veterans' issues during the 1970s had created an organizational dilemma. Only a tiny fraction of the 2.9 million Vietnam veterans had joined their ranks, and the average veteran of the Second World War was now more than sixty-five years of age. The American Legion and VFW needed many more members from the Vietnam generation of veterans if they were to survive. The building of the Vietnam Veterans Memorial had provided the first step toward reconciliation. Unlike other concerns previously raised by Vietnam veterans, the desire to commemorate those who died in battle struck a chord with the VFW and American Legion leadership. They staunchly backed the Memorial and had provided the two single largest donations at crucial times when the project was in doubt. In the process, the two organizations discovered Vietnam veterans and a surge of Vietnam veterans responded to them. They were now ready to address Agent Orange together.

Both Senator Alan Cranston (D-Calif.) and Representative Sonny Montgomery (D-Miss.) of the Senate and House committees were lukewarm to the idea of granting a presumption of service connection. A senior Senate Committee on Veterans' Affairs member admitted that "it isn't going to be easy for either committee to hold the line [against the presumption] now" that the American Legion and VFW had backed it.[37] However, useful ammunition was forthcoming that would reinforce the committee members' reluctance. On April 26, VA director Walters testified before a congressional panel that the VA opposed extending a presumption of service connection for the three diseases. There was insufficient evidence, Walters said, to justify such relief while the studies continued, and he argued that Daschle's bill, if enacted, would "jeopardize the viability of [the VA's] compensation program."[38] On June 22, Dorothy Starbuck, the VA benefits director, assured the Senate committee in a public hearing that the VA's opposition was not based on the potential cost of the bill.[39] Daschle's bill cleared the House but died in Senate.

A New Judge, A "New" Lawsuit

Judge George Pratt resigned from the Agent Orange lawsuit on October 13, 1983. His workload in the Circuit Court had been building, he explained, and he had found it increasingly difficult to give the Agent

Orange case the time it required. Selected as his replacement was Judge Jack Weinstein, described by Peter Schuck as a brilliant, highly respected professor of law at Columbia University and "perhaps the most unconventional jurist in the federal system."[40] Judge Weinstein assured the press that matters would proceed smoothly. "It'll be like a relay race," he told reporters, "[I'll] pick up the baton and run with it without missing a beat."[41]

Infighting within the consortium representing the veterans had been especially fierce in the weeks prior to Judge Pratt's resignation. Most of the plaintiff's lawyers doubted that Victor Yannacone's computer files contained useful information or that Yannacone was prepared to direct the attack in court. To manage the criticism, Yannacone approached Pittsburgh attorney Tom Henderson, who had successfully directed the plaintiff's case in the asbestos lawsuits against Johns Mansville. Henderson joined the group and worked with the others to develop a plan. However, "the hostility," he later told Schuck, "was so thick you could cut it with a knife."[42] Soon he too found Yannacone extraordinarily difficult to work with. In the ensuing power struggle, the other attorneys handed the initiative on the case to Henderson and relegated Yannacone to the role of Henderson's assistant.

Judge Weinstein called a meeting of all the attorneys connected with the case on October 21, 1983.[43] The attorneys representing the veterans were as optimistic as the legal teams from Dow, Monsanto, and Diamond Shamrock were grim: Weinstein was known as a liberal Democrat and humanitarian, and was a veteran of the Second World War. The lawyers from Hercules, Riverdale, and Hoffman-Taff were relaxed; Judge Pratt after all had dismissed them from the suit. They assumed they were there as observers. Though optimistic, the veterans' attorneys continued to squabble all the way into the judge's chambers. Maneuvering for advantage, Yannacone asked Henderson just before they went into session with Weinstein if he, Yannacone, could help run the suit when it went to court. "No fucking way," Henderson told him.[44]

Weinstein opened the meeting with a thunderbolt of his own. The legal solution, he declared, required the participation of all the concerned parties. There would be no summary judgment; no one, including the federal government, was out of the case. The case would be disposed of promptly and would be heard by a jury in Long Island, New York. Thumbing through his calendar, he selected May 7, 1983 as the first day for jury selection. Causation—the effect on American troops of exposure to Agent Orange—and not the government contract defense, he continued, would be the focus of the trial. He suggested that the veterans' attorneys select "six to ten of their best cases" to present at the trial "to see if there is anything to [them]."[45] If the plaintiffs prevailed

with these cases, he reasoned, the chemical companies would be motivated to settle out of court with the remaining claimants; if the plaintiffs
lost with these cases, the litigation would be over. Weinstein established
a cutoff date of January 1, 1984 for veterans and their children to join the
suit. Anyone not part of it by then could forget it.

The lawyers were stunned. For the second time in six months, the
presiding judge in the lawsuit had completely changed the substance
and ground rules in the case. Weinstein had seized the case, reconcep-
tualized it, and laid down a firm timetable for bringing it to trial. The
magnitude of the task and the time constraints imposed by him placed
an almost insurmountable burden on the attorneys. For example, the
discovery phase of the suit, which had already consumed almost three
years, had been invested solely in the government contract defense,
now out the window. The judge was well aware of this, and so closed by
raising the possibility of an out-of-court settlement. Schuck wrote of
Weinstein's closing remarks:

> . . . [T]his case [Weinstein said] would be "better settled than tried. If it
> can be settled, let's. If I can help you, I will." Settlement would be difficult,
> he stressed, unless "the other two pieces"—the VA and Congress—could
> be brought in the case; unfortunately, he added, "we can't do that because
> of limited jurisdiction. The intelligent way to handle it would be if there is
> any liability . . . [for] the VA to take over the whole thing, then to just
> have the manufacturers make a lump sum donation to help defray some of
> the costs of the [VA] paying the costs of the damages, if any, attributable to
> Agent Orange."

The meeting established Weinstein's strategy for dealing with the
case. The suit had already dragged on for nearly four years, and he was
determined to bring it to an end. The tight deadline and enormous
workload enhanced the prospects for an out of court settlement. Finally,
he sought to keep the government in the case, both to increase the
capacity for restitution should the plaintiffs win and to widen the options in finding a solution in a case he regarded as much a political
problem as a legal one.

The defense attorneys felt relieved. They were well financed and
ready to throw everything into the fray. However much the pressures
and constraints might pain them, they could always take solace in the
certainty that their squabbling and financally strapped counterparts representing the veterans were suffering twice as much. In fact, the veterans' lawyers were in near panic. They had neither the money nor a
consensus about strategy for the trial. Henderson and several others
quickly formed a new "plaintiffs management committee" (PMC). Five
of them put up $250,000 and Henderson himself $200,000. They re-

cruited other backers, including one lawyer who kicked in $500,000. David Dean, who would be the lead in-court counsel, and two others agreed to contribute time but no money. In the event of a victory, the PMC would pay its cash contributors "off the top" and the others under a formula based on hours worked and merit. The arrangement allowed them to carry on, but introduced another fissure among attorneys already split three ways over the groups of veterans they represented. The financiers among them, newcomers to the case and first in line to be paid, were more willing to consider an out-of-court settlement.

Frank McCarthy, who had initiated the suit in 1979, was thoroughly dejected by the developments. He later told Schuck:

> I was low as I could be. We . . . were now being represented by peo-ple . . . who we didn't know, . . . who didn't understand our cause. . . . I saw that as the final blow against Victor [Yannacone]. I had seen him lose power steadily within the consortium, seen the lawyers lose respect for each other. Victor and his group were our commander, battalion leaders, down to the squad leaders in each state. We would do whatever they thought necessary. After that, I had little hope in the lawsuit.[47]

Over the next three months, Judge Weinstein resolved one legal prob-lem after the next, steering the case surely toward trial. He defined the class to include all American, Australian, and New Zealand veterans who had served in Vietnam between 1961 and 1972 and who thought they may have been harmed by the herbicide program. He also certified all spouses, parents, and children of the veterans born before January 1, 1984 who might have been harmed as a result of the veterans' exposure. He ruled that notification of the class—the attempt to inform all possible claimants—could be handled by mailing flyers to those known to the court and all veterans listed in the VA's Agent Orange Registry. (The Registry turned out to have names but no addresses.) The word could be more widely spread through media advertisements. As to which state's law had jurisdiction, Weinstein reasoned that each major choice-of-law theory would lead a state judge to seek out federal or national consensus law rather than the laws of any one state.[48]

With these matters out of the way, Weinstein turned his attention to the issue of government immunity. He argued that if servicemen and civilians were both injured by the same event, the Feres doctrine prohib-ited servicemen, but not civilians, from suing the government. For in-stance, if a military aircraft crashed, killing military and civilian personnel on the ground, the soldiers' estates could not sue the govern-ment for damages but those of civilians could do so. Though on shaky legal ground, Weinstein proclaimed that Feres similarly did not bar the family members of servicemen from suing for direct, as distinct from derivative, injuries. For example, if a military herbicide harmed a serviceman, the serviceman could not sue for damages and his family members could not sue for derivative damages such as wages lost by the serviceman. Under Weinstein's reasoning, however, family members could sue for direct injuries, such as birth defects that were the direct result of the serviceman's having been harmed by the herbicide.[49]

The government, Weinstein concluded, must stand trial with the chemical companies. Arvin Maskin, the lead counsel for the government informed the judge that the government intended to appeal and was not preparing for trial. Weinstein instructed Maskin:

> I suggest that you inform your superiors that I consider that attitude very unusual in a case where the government has a potential liability of some billions, b-i-l-l-i-o-n-s, of dollars. . . . [Y]ou will be part of the trial.[50]

Preliminary Ranch Hand Reports

The U.S. Air Force reported its preliminary findings in July of 1983 from a study of Operation Ranch Hand pilots and crew members. The Ranch Hands had been selected for study because they were the ones who handled and sprayed Agent Orange from aircraft, presumably on a daily basis throughout their tours in Vietnam. The Air Force had instigated the study in 1978 as the Agent Orange story was gaining prominence in the news. If research on the Ranch Hands was to be done, the Air Force certainly wanted to be in control of it. The study, designed by Air Force scientists, would compare over time (until the year 2002) the mortality and morbidity rates among Ranch Hands with those of a sampling of Air Force personnel who had served in Vietnam in squadrons that flew planes like those in Operation Ranch Hand but did not spray Agent Orange.

The Ranch Hands proved to be a definable and cooperative study group. Colonel Alvin Young, a participant in the design of the study, recalls:

> I think the Ranch Handers have always been concerned about the effects of the herbicide, in the sense that they were the ones who were most heavily involved. And if there's going to be a health impact from Agent Orange, they are the ones who are going to show it. . . . The . . . Ranch Handers . . . felt that they, their contribution to the war effort in Vietnam was a real human sacrifice effort. They lost a lot of their men, many of them were wounded themselves. And so you're talking about men that

have a tremendous esprit de corps. You know, the government told them that this was safe, and that this mission was an important mission, and they went over [and] put their life on the line and flew it.

So when we went back to the Ranch Handers and said, "Look there's probably no other group in the world that will be able to be looked at and answer the question as you will be. Will you fly one last mission with us?" And that's when [they] stepped forward and said, "Yes, we'll do it on that basis. We'll put an end to the argument, is there a health problem or is there not?" Because they wanted the answers . . . , but they also recognized that they were one of the very few groups that could give the answer.[51]

Though it made sense to study the Ranch Hands, there also were some shortcomings. The main problem was that they were few in number. There were only about 1,200 of them, so if Agent Orange caused a cancer or other disease with an incidence of less than 1 in 1,200, the study probably would not detect the disease. However, Air Force scientists and scientists of the National Research Council who reviewed the protocol did not consider this an overwhelming problem. Michael Gough, then a researcher for Congress' Office of Technological Assessment, explained the situation later in a book that reviewed the Ranch Hand study:

The . . . [council] emphasized that the relatively small number of Ranch Hands would make it impossible to detect diseases that occur only rarely. If the council had expected Agent Orange to double the frequency of cancer or to double the number of deaths at early ages, it would not have included that reservation about the size of the population. The study is big enough to detect a doubling of those events. Nevertheless, the council scientists did not expect to see any such increase in cancer or early deaths because they considered the premise that Agent Orange had caused disease to be very unlikely. So, even before the Ranch Hand study was off the drawing board, there was a clear dichotomy between claims that Agent Orange was the cause of overwhelming disease burdens and the expectations of many scientists that there would be few, if any, detectable effects of exposure.[52]

On July 1, 1983, Major General Murphy Chesney, Deputy Air Force Surgeon General, announced the initial mortality findings at a press conference. He declared that the death rates and causes of death among the Ranch Hands did not vary significantly from those of the control group. He stated that there were some variations—such as a slightly lower incidence of cancer deaths among the Ranch Hands and a higher incidence due to liver disorders among them—but that the small numbers were "statistically insignificant." He indicated that enlisted men who had handled the herbicide showed a slightly higher death rate than officers, but that this was only of "mild concern." Both subgroups, he concluded, were experiencing "favorable mortality." In response to a question, he responded: "Do I worry as a physician because we used it? The answer is 'No.' I say war is hell. You've got to win it."[53]

On February 24, 1984, Major General Chesney held a second news conference to release the initial morbidity findings. The report indicated that the Ranch Hand fliers were in generally "good health" but had significantly higher rates of skin cancers, liver ailments, and circulatory problems in the legs than did the control group. The report also stated that Ranch Hand fliers and their spouses reported a higher incidence of birth defects—primarily rashes and birth marks—among their children than did the controls, and fourteen babies of Ranch Hand families had died within twenty-eight days after birth compared to four among families of the control group.[54]

General Chesney characterized the findings as "reassuring." "These men are not dying off like flies," he said. "They are healthy people. No early diseases, no big diseases are showing up." Colonel Royce Moser, commander of the Air Force school of aerospace medicine, provided further commentary. He said that it was still too early to tell why these "statistically significant" disorders were detected among the Rand Hand fliers. He suggested that the skin cancers might be attributable to excessive exposure to the sun, the liver dysfunctions to excessive smoking and drinking, and the circulatory problems to a hardening of the arteries. Colonel Moser also noted in passing that the small sample size did not allow the detection of rare diseases such as soft-tissue sarcoma and porphria cutanea tarda—the diseases for which Rep. Daschle had sought a presumption of service connection. As for the higher rate of birth defects, this might have occurred because of overreporting by worried Ranch Hand parents. The two officers promised a review and updated report on the birth defects as quickly as possible.[55]

Dr. Richard Albanese, an Air Force biomathematician and one of the authors of the study, agreed that the findings did not constitute evidence that the health abnormalities among the Ranch Hands were caused by exposure to Agent Orange. However, Dr. Albanese took exception to calling the findings "reassuring." "A degree of concern is warranted," he told reporters. "One can't have the sense that one should stop worrying about this. . . . I cannot account for such differences by chance; on the other hand, I cannot explain their cause."[56]

Two weeks later, the VA released to the press its own commentary on the Ranch Hand morbidity report. The VA called the findings "good news for Vietnam veterans."[57]

An End to the Lawsuit

The attorneys plunged ahead with the task of preparing for the Agent Orange trial, scheduled to begin on May 7, compacting—as one of them later told Schuck—"three years of normal discovery into three months." The pace was hectic and grueling. At one point, Monsanto requested a later trial date after its lead counsel suffered a nervous breakdown. "You have a large firm," Weinstein responded, "Get someone else." And PMC attorney Dean related to Schuck, "This case ruined my health, my marriage, and my practice."[58]

A major issue facing the plaintiff management committee (PMC) was that of selecting the "representative plaintiffs" from the thousands of claimants, a task that fell to Henderson. He concluded that there were five categories of harm to veterans and their families: chloracne, systemic dysfunctions, neurological disorders, cancers, and birth defects. His initial inclination was to select cases that represented more than one category: for example, Michael Ryan, whose daughter Kerry suffered from birth defects, had had chloracne and now had a neurological disorder. He also selected three veterans who had died from soft-tissue sarcomas, a rare form of cancer. When asked why he had included deceased representatives, he replied, "Because a lot are dead. They have a right to be represented too."[59] Weinstein, however, instructed Henderson to select cases to represent specific categories, so as not to confuse the causation issue for the jury, and to confine himself to living representatives who could actually appear in the courtroom.

As the date of the trial neared, Weinstein brought in two professional negotiators, Kenneth Feinberg and David Shapiro, in hopes of fashioning a settlement. Feinberg's job was to devise a plan for the settlement and the distribution of money; Shapiro was the one to meet with the attorneys and extract the cease-fire. Feinstein and Shapiro met with the attorneys from both sides on April 20, 1984, and Shapiro afterwards met separately with the plaintiff and defense teams. Government counsel Aravin Maskin refused to attend but said the government approved of the negotiations. The plaintiffs said they would settle for no less than $700 million; the defense told Shapiro they would pay no more than $100 million, and then only if the government matched the same amount. The two sides, though miles apart, were at least talking settlement.

On April 24, 1984, Weinstein met with PMC lawyers.[60] He told them that "my heart bleeds for deformed children" but that he personally considered the case they were about to make in court to be "very weak." He predicted they would lose and go bankrupt in the process. The PMC pondered the judge's words and lowered their settlement price to $250 million. Weinstein then called in the attorneys for the chemical companies. He reminded them that the Long Island jury who would decide the case probably would feel sympathy for veterans who had served valorously and now were sick with cancer. And what jury would not be moved by the sight of their children with birth defects? The companies held their ground at $100 million.

Weinstein called the defense team back in that same day and announced an allocation plan—should there be a settlement—based upon the percentage of Agent Orange each of them had produced and upon how "clean" their batches were. Monsanto and Diamond Shamrock had made the "dirtiest" Agent Orange and therefore, he reasoned, should pay in proportion greater than the volume of Agent Orange they had produced. He estimated that Monsanto had made 29.5 percent of the Agent Orange used in Vietnam, and so set their pay-out share of the settlement price at 45.5 percent. For Diamond Shamrock, he set the corresponding figures at 5.1 percent of volume and 12 percent of settlement pay-out. The judge figured pay-out percentages below the volumes produced for the "clean" makers of Agent Orange. The percentages were 28.6 percent of volume, 19.5 percent of pay-out for Dow; 19.7 percent of volume, 10 percent of pay-out for Hercules; 7.2 percent of volume, 6 percent of pay-out for T.H. Agriculture; 2.2 percent of volume, 2 percent of pay-out for Thompson Chemicals; and 6.5 percent of volume, 5 percent of pay-out for Uniroyal.

Dow's lawyers were pleased; they said they would settle immediately so long as the final total figure for all the companies did not exceed $150 million. That would mean each pay-out percentage point would cost a company about $1.8 million. With the exception of Monsanto's team, the others concurred. Faced with the prospect of going up against the veterans alone, Monsanto caved in and reluctantly agreed.

Shapiro then met with the PMC. He told them that chemical companies would not settle for $250 million but that he thought they would cough up $200. The veterans' attorneys reconsidered; after much heated discussion, they all, except for Dean, voted to settle for $200 million. Schuck wrote of the PMC meeting:

> Dean was the only dissenter. . . . [K]eyed up for trial and overcome by feelings of frustration and betrayal, [he] fled to an empty courtroom,

where he sobbed. "There had not been one day during the last two years when I had not thought about my opening to the jury," [Dean] recalls. "I was a lawyer with blue balls. I was physically exhausted, and I felt that we would not be able to go out and face our clients."[61]

Shapiro and Feinberg carried PMC's $200 million counteroffer to the defense lawyers. After securing several specific protections from Weinstein concerning any subsequent challenges to the settlement, the defense countered with $180 million. Shapiro and Feinberg conferred with Weinstein. The judge decided that $180 million was a fair amount for the defendants to pay and suggested to Shapiro the strategy of selling the PMC on a settlement of $180 million plus interest. If the chemical companies put the $180 million in an interest-bearing account, Weinstein noted, it would be worth more than $200 million by the time the first payments were doled out to the claimants. Shapiro relayed the judge's idea to the PMC. When PMC balked at accepting the offer, Weinstein called them into his chambers. He reminded them of the weakness of their case. He spoke hypothetically of rulings he could make that would make the case even more difficult for them.

PMC's attorneys by now had been part of settlement talks for days. Struggling with the an avalanche of last-minute preparations for trial, they had gotten little sleep and were exhausted. With Dean still the lone dissenter, they decided to settle. At one o'clock in the morning on May 7, 1984—nine years to the day after the last American troops were evacuated from Saigon and only eight hours before the trial was to begin—Weinstein informed the defense lawyers that the PMC had accepted their deal. The chemical companies would establish a fund from which to compensate the claimants. According to the agreement, establishing the fund did not represent an admission of guilt by the chemical companies or a conclusion that Agent Orange had harmed Vietnam veterans or their children. It simply represented the value of settling the suit.[62]

Reaction by veterans was swift and dramatic. Thousands called Frank McCarthy's office seeking clarification about what had happened. Some wanted information about applying for the settlement; others wondered if this meant they should be worried about getting cancer or having deformed children. Some called to condemn the settlement as a sellout. Particularly galling to these veterans was the lack of answers to questions about dioxin's harmfulness or the manufacturers' guilt or innocence. "How could $180 million be a sellout?" McCarthy asked a reporter rhetorically. "It's an incredible start. We wanted a trust fund and we got it without going through a trial and opening old wounds." And attorney Tom Henderson added, "Sure, there's something lost in a settlement because you never get at the issue of culpability. But now you've got money to deal with the problem that needs to be dealt with now."[63]

Angry veterans had their chance to address the court three months later in special hearings conducted by Judge Weinstein to discuss settlement procedures. David Martin, a former Marine infantryman, expressed the position of many veterans who wanted the case to go to trial:

> We wanted our day in court. I want the truth to come out. . . . We want the world to know how Dow Chemical poisoned Americans in Vietnam. No amount of blood money could ever repay what the bastards did to our children.[64]

Disabled veteran Bobby Sutton presented another point of view:

> We could prove our case in court but it would take too long. Too many guys are going to die, and I'd rather see them taken care of. We don't need more studies. We need h-e-l-p, so we can get our own doctors.[65]

Following the hearings, the court established a maximum payment from the settlement of $3,400 to survivors of those Vietnam veterans who had died from a disease arguably related to Agent Orange exposure, and a maximum of $12,800—$1,280 per year for 10 years—to those veterans exposed to the herbicide who were now 100 percent disabled. After almost five years of haggling to work out the legal and practical details, the fund established by the chemical companies mailed out its first checks to the families of Vietnam veterans in March of 1989.

Notes

1. "Events Listed in Salute to Viet Veterans," *Washington Post*, 10 November 1982, A20.
2. Phil McCombs, "Veterans Honor the Fallen, Mark Reconciliation," *Washington Post*, 14 November 1982, A1, A18.
3. Lou Cannon, "Reagan & Co.: White House No Longer Pulling Together in the Traces," *Washington Post*, 15 November 1982, A3.
4. Richard Severo and Lewis Milford, *The Wages of War: When America's Soldiers Came Home—From Valley Forge to Vietnam* (New York: Simon and Schuster, 1989), 383.
5. Ibid., 391.
6. Richard Severo, "V.A. Assailed on Delayed Agent Orange Study," *New York Times*, 16 September 1982, A25.
7. "Agency to Yield on Herbicide Issue," *New York Times*, 16 October 1982, A6.
8. Phillip Boffey, "Agent Orange: Despite Spate of Studies, Slim Hope of Answers," *New York Times*, 30 November 1982, C1, C7.

9.   Peter Schuck, *Agent Orange on Trial: Mass Toxic Disasters in the Courts* (Cambridge, Mass.: Harvard University Press, 1986), 94–96.

10.   Ibid., 98.

11.   Ibid., 96–97.

12.   David Burnham, "Dow Says U.S. Knew Dioxin Peril of Agent Orange," *New York Times*, 5 May 1983, A18.

13.   Schuck, *Agent Orange on Trial*, 98–100.

14.   Ibid., 100–101.

15.   Material for this summary is drawn from a special report, "Dioxin: Quandry for the '80's," *St. Louis Post-Dispatch*, 14 November 1983, 1–2. See also, Michael Gough, *Dioxin, Agent Orange: The Facts* (New York: Plenum, 1986), 121–126.

16.   Laszio Domjan, Marjorie Mandel, Jo Mannies, and Margaret Freivogel, "Dioxin in Missouri: How It Happened," *St. Louis-Post Dispatch*, 14 November 1983, sec., "The Poisoning: How It All Came About," 4.

17.   Ibid., sec. "How the Plant's Waste Was Spread," 8.

18.   Ibid., sec. "The Mystery of the Horse Arena," 5.

19.   Ibid., sec. "Closing in on the Killer Agent," 6.

20.   Ibid., sec. "Consequences of a Mistaken Theory," 9.

21.   Ibid., sec. "A Go-Getter Gone, An Inquiry Stalled," 12.

22.   Ibid., sec. "The Business and Style of Rita Lavelle," 14.

23.   Ibid., sec. "Behind the Scenes in the EPA."

24.   Dale Russakoff, "U.S. Offers to Buy Poisoned Homes of Times Beach," *Washington Post*, 23 February 1983, A2.

25.   Art Harris, "Town Struggles with Toxic Legacy," *Washington Post*, 10 January 1983, A3, A8.

26.   Ibid., A8.

27.   Edward Manear, "Poison or Not?" *Washington Post*, 14 January 1983, A14.

28.   Domjan et al., "Dioxin in Missouri," sec. "Byword for Times Beach: Buy-Out," 17.

29.   Russakoff, "U.S. to Buy Homes," A1.

30.   Ibid., A2.

31.   Lou Cannon and Pete Earley, "Embattled VA Chief Steps Down," *Washington Post*, 5 October 1982, A1, A7.

32.   Bill Prochnau, "VFW Lines Up with Viet Vets on Agent Orange," *Washington Post*, 23 November 1982, A1, A4.

33.   Pete Earley, "Many Are in Line to Take on a Tough Job," *Washington Post*, 22 October 1982, A19.

34.   Pete Earley and Lou Cannon, "Army Official in Line to be VA Chief," *Washington Post*, 5 November 1982, A1, A6.

35.   Prochnau, "VFW Lines Up," A1.

36.   Pete Earley, "Agent Orange Compensation Gains Favor," *Washington Post*, 9 March 1983, A3.

37.   Ibid., A3.

38.   "VA Opposes Agent Orange Bill," *Washington Post*, 27 April 1983, A21.

39.   "Veterans' Agency Opposing Measures on Toxic Chemical," *New York Times*, 23 June 1983, A21.

40.   Schuck, *Agent Orange on Trial*, 110.

41.   Ralph Blumenthal, "Judge Withdraws from Suit over Agent Orange," *New York Times*, 14 October 1983, B7.

42.   Schuck, *Agent Orange on Trial*, 107.

43. Schuck interviewed several of those present at the meeting and has provided a detailed reconstruction of it. See Schuck, *Agent Orange on Trial*, 112–116.

44. Ibid., 116.

45. Ralph Blumenthal, "Judge Speeds Up Agent Orange Suit," *New York Times*, 13 November 1983, A31.

46. Schuck, *Agent Orange on Trial*, 115.

47. Ibid., 116–117.

48. Ibid., 122–130.

49. Ibid., 131–136.

50. Ibid., 136.

51. Alvin Young, personal interview with author, 6 March 1989, Washington, D.C.

52. Michael Gough, *Dioxin, Agent Orange: The Facts* (New York: Plenum, 1986), 69

53. R. Drummond Ayres, Jr., "Air Force Reports No High Death Rates Among Defoliant Sprayers," *New York Times*, 2 July 1983, A9.

54. Pete Earley, "Study Panel Cautious on Viet Sprays," *Washington Post*, 25 February 1984, A1, A2; "No Major Diseases Cited in Agent Orange Sprayers," *New York Times*, 25 February 1984, A12.

55. Earley, "Study Panel," A2.

56. Ibid.

57. "Inside: the VA," *Washington Post*, 9 March 1984, A17.

58. Schuck, *Agent Orange on Trial*, 140, 118, 122.

59. Ralph Blumenthal, "Test Cases Chosen for Herbicide Trial," *New York Times*, 12 December 1983, B28.

60. Judge Weinstein's discussions with the PMC and lawyers representing the chemical companies are summarized from Schuck, *Agent Orange on Trial*, 155–161.

61. Ibid., 157.

62. The terms of the settlement are: (1) defendants agree to pay $180 million plus interest beginning from May 7, 1984; (2) initially, the settlement fund will pay class notice and settlement administration expenses; (3) no other payments may be made until appeals from a final settlement order are completed; (4) defendants may obtain reverse indemnification for veteran opt-out claims upheld by state courts up to $10 million until January 1, 1999; (5) the class definition will include veterans whose injuries had not yet been manifested; (6) plaintiffs may retain defendant's documents for one year; (7) all parties reserve all rights to sue the United States; (8) defendants deny all liability; (9) defendants have the right to reject the settlement if a "substantial" number of veterans opt-out of the class; (10) any class member who opts out retains the right to opt back in; (11) unclaimed funds will revert to the defendants after 25 years; (12) the settlement agreement is subject to a Rule 23(e) "fairness" hearing; (13) the distribution plan will make special arrangements to meet the needs of children with birth defects born to veterans after the lawsuit; (14) the court will retain jurisdiction until the settlement fund is exhausted. See Schuck, *Agent Orange on Trial*, 165.

63. David Bird, "Veterans Divided on Damages Pact," *New York Times*, 10 May 1984, A24. See also Pete Earley, "Agent Orange Settlement Divides Vietnam Veterans," *Washington Post*, 5 August 1984, A3.

64. Margot Hornblower, "Vietnam Veterans Divided Over Agent Orange Battle," *Washington Post*, 9 August 1984, A3.

65. Ibid.

8

BENEFIT OF THE DOUBT

"[The VA] both imposed an impermissibly demanding test for granting service connection . . . and refused to give veterans the benefit of the doubt. . . . [I] hereby invalidate . . . the . . . regulation which denies service connection for all other diseases but chloracne. . . ."

Judge Thelton E. Henderson, California Northern District Court

The Centers for Disease Control (CDC) in Atlanta had taken over the VA's Agent Orange epidemiology study in October of 1982. Congress had reassigned the study because, after three years of work, the VA still had not completed a satisfactory protocol for it. CDC officials appeared eager to assume control of the study and optimistic about the chances of completing it successfully. Prior to the transfer of responsibility, the CDC's Dr. Vernon Houk assured James Stockdale, head of the White House Agent Orange Working Group (AOWG)—the presidential task force established earlier by President Jimmy Carter to oversee all government research and policy concerning Agent Orange—that the CDC could handle the task. In a March 1982 memo to Stockdale, later obtained by attorney Lewis Milford under the Freedom of Information Act, Dr. Houk wrote to Stockdale:

We view as the only remaining factors that will prevent the successful completion of this study to be the degree of participation among the selected veterans and the nonavailability of the necessary resources.[1]

Likewise, the CDC did not assume that there was nothing to the claims by Vietnam veterans that their illnesses were caused by exposure to Agent Orange. Testifying in May of 1983 before a House subcommittee of the Committee on Veterans' Affairs, Dr. Houk stated that federal health agencies were of the opinion that an association did exist between exposure to dioxin and the cancer soft-tissue sarcoma. Milford, sitting directly behind Dr. Barclay Shepard of the VA at the hearing, overheard Shepard whisper to a VA colleague during Houk's testimony, "Somebody's gonna have to take him on."[2]

191

With an initial budget of $55 million, the CDC set about designing the study. The central problem was that of devising a measure of exposure to Agent Orange. For the study to be valid, the measure had to discriminate among levels of exposure with great precision. If a measure classified veterans as having been "highly exposed" when in fact they had not been, or as "less exposed" when in fact they had been, the study would underestimate or miss altogether the true effect of exposure. Several options were available. Researchers could rely upon self-reports—they could simply ask veterans if they had been exposed to Agent Orange— or upon "deep fat" tissue tests or blood tests to detect the presence of dioxin in veterans' bodies. CDC scientists considered the self-report technique to be unreliable: the veterans' subjective judgments about the extent of their own exposure, they felt, introduced unknown amounts of error into the measure. However, scientists knew very little about the ability of the "deep fat" tissue and blood tests to effectively detect dioxin levels in the body ten to fifteen years after exposure.

Consequently, the CDC team settled upon the "hits" method for measuring exposure and for selecting 18,000 Vietnam veterans to study. The method would rely upon computerized Ranch Hand records, the HERBS tapes, to determine first where the swaths of herbicides had been sprayed on a daily basis. Another set of records, those of troop movements, would then be used to identify combat units that had been in or close to the spray swaths within days after each spray mission. The more often a member of a combat unit was within a so-designated spray zone during his tour of duty, the more "hits" he accumulated. Depending on number of "hits," a veteran would be classifed as "likely" or "less likely" to have been highly exposed. Someone who had never been within these spray zones would be counted as "not likely" to have been exposed. Unit size would have to be tightly enough defined so that its members were truly within the spray zone. Defined too loosely, the unit would include too many veterans who actually were elsewhere simply because the entire unit was not situated on the ground together. Finally, unit "morning reports" would have to be used to determine exactly who was present in each unit each day. The more errors in the records and in the classifications, the more watered down and the less valid the proposed measure would be.

Research Wars

The "hits" method required an extensive knowledge of military records and an enormous amount of tedious labor. The person selected to oversee this job was Richard Christian, a retired career Army colonel who was a veteran of both Korea and Vietnam and a specialist in the compilation of such records. Christian was not employed directly by the CDC, but by the U.S. Army and Joint Services Environmental Support Group in Washington, D.C. Christian's mission was to assemble the necessary records and to copy the information so that company level operations—a unit size of about 200 men—could be tracked for spray zones of various widths and time frames.

Christian set about his task with zeal. Working with a staff of up to fifty-five employees, Christian in 1984 gathered 40,000 linear feet of records occupying more than 40,000 boxes and weighing more than 800 tons. The painstaking process of extracting and computerizing the data began. Christian states:

> I had the unit locations from the unit daily journals. And I had the HERBS tapes. So I had both locations. All I had to do was to program the computer to tell me how close that unit was to that spray mission. . . . I can say, well, this unit, this company, this battalion was within two kilometers of this spray mission within a three-day period, or six days. Whatever. You can set the dials. I can give you eight kilometers, ninety days if you want to. The further up you go, the more "hits" you're going to get. . . . So then I had to go to St. Louis to get the morning reports, so I could find out who was in that company.
>
> [The people at the CDC] thought it was great. Everybody did. . . . We briefed them all the time. We gave more briefings than Carter's got "Little Liver Pills." We gave them to anybody that would listen.[3]

In February of 1985, the CDC submitted an interim report to the Congressional Office of Technology Assessment. The report stated that about half of the HERBS tapes had been analyzed by Christian's shop. It indicated that trial runs had showed that the movements of company-sized units could be correlated with spray areas for purposes of establishing level of exposure. Everything appeared to be going smoothly.

In fact, however, disagreements, doubts, and political intrigue lay at every corner and were about to overwhelm the study. For starters, the CDC was experiencing significant turnover, both at its upper levels of management and within the research teams assigned to the Agent Orange study. These changes in personnel also ushered in changing ideas about the study. Some members of the CDC staff began to express doubts about the quality of the information collected by Christian. They noted, for example, that combat units were not always where they were supposed to have been according to the records, and that the records sometimes were incomplete. Further, spraying had taken place around base camps and the like, and these were not recorded in the HERBS tapes. Under the "hits" method, veterans so exposed would end up in the "not likely" to have been exposed group.

Christian was miffed by these charges. He freely admitted that the records were incomplete—"Combat records were never made for any epidemiological study and anyone who thought so was out of his mind," he later told Milford and *New York Times* reporter Richard Severo[4]—but he was convinced he had all the records that could be had, and that he had executed the original plan, which CDC had certified as sound, according to CDC's specifications. As for the other spraying, he felt that other strategies could be worked out for pursuing them within the records which did exist.

Shortly after the interim report in February, the CDC requested information on battalion-sized units of 1,000 men rather than on company-sized units as stipulated in the study's protocol. The rationale was to increase the number of "hits," thereby increasing the number of sample subjects in the "likely" to have been exposed group. The CDC also restricted those eligible for the study to those who were in grades E1 to E-5, i.e., privates through the lowest rank of sergeant, and to those who had served only one tour in Vietnam. They also widened the years examined—originally 1967 to 1968, the peak spraying years—by six months. Though an administrator, not a scientist, Christian opposed these changes on methodological grounds. He noted that the companies and command post which make up a battalion typically were spread out over a large area. If so, tracking battalions rather than companies, he argued, would load up the "likely" group with many subjects who, though in the battalion, were nowhere near the spray area. Also restricting the eligibles to the lower ranks and to one tour also made it more difficult to come up with the required number for the "likely" and "less likely" groups, and widening the time interval by six months extended it beyond the years of peak spraying. In the quarreling that ensued, the CDC requested the records so that they could conduct a pilot study themselves. Now suspicious, Christian supplied copies of records rather than turning over the originals. Unfamiliar with the records, the CDC at first mistakenly matched spray swaths with Viet Cong troop movements.[5]

In November 1985, the CDC published a second interim report. This report expressed doubts about the quality of data that could be obtained from the military records assembled by Christian. It also intimated that Christian was withholding key information from the CDC. Christian reacted angrily. He did not know exactly what was up, but by this time he suspected that the CDC was about to scrap the Agent Orange study and that he had been selected as the the scapegoat for its demise. He explains:

> . . . I was appalled [the CDC] would pull such a thing. I am used to "duty, honor, country." You know, if you as a lieutenant told me to do something, I would go do it. That is how the government is supposed to work. Especially everybody working on the side of the government is supposed to be on the same team. I was on a different team than everybody else. . . . The other team was the team that decided they didn't want to do this study. The only problem was, I was the only one that didn't get the word.[6]

On December 24, 1985, Alvin Young of the White House Agent Orange Working Group (AOWG) called Christian in for a meeting. Young informed Christian that his work was suspect and would be reviewed by two outside observers. In early 1986, AOWG selected retired Major General John Murray and John Hatcher, an Army archivist, to conduct the review. Among other things, Murray later told Severo and Milford, Young asked him to determine if Christian "was providing all he had to CDC."[7]

A thorough and professional military man, Murray embraced the task. Christian recalls:

> [Murray] was an expert, two tours in Vietnam. There wasn't anything he didn't know about Vietnam or troop movements and stuff like that. He put us through, quite frankly, the guy put us through hell for four and a half months. Sat right down there with my lowest researcher and sat there and watched them while [they were] going through the daily journal. That is a laborious chore. . . . [Murray was] extremely thorough. Like everything else in the military, you put these guys on there, they don't always stick to exactly what they are told. I mean, sometimes, if they find something, they are liable to go and uncover it. I had no problem with his report.[8]

General Murray filed his report in May of 1986. Murray praised Christian's efforts, saying they were "of inestimable worth" and "an excellent model of the careful performance of dull toil."[9] However, the "hits" method did not strike Murray as a strategy likely to produce findings that would resolve the controversy over Agent Orange. Rather than complete the study, Murray wrote, the federal government—who by now had already spent almost $60 million on the far-from-finalized CDC study—instead should use the money required to finish the research to compensate Vietnam veterans for "their loss of grievance." Murray forwarded copies of his report to AOWG, Secretary of Defense Casper Weinberger, the Chairman of the Joint Chiefs of Staff, and other high-ranking officials.

Reaction behind the scenes to Murray's report was swift and designed to keep it from ever seeing the light of day. Donald Newman, Under

Secretary of Health and Human Services, quickly alerted Secretary Weinberg about AOWG's concerns. Severo and Milford later obtained a copy of Newman's letter to Weinberger, written on White House stationery, and described its contents:

> Newman . . . [protested] to Weinberger . . . : "[The] release of General Murray's report . . . will seriously undercut the validity of our position." [Newman] did not say what that "position" was. It seemed clear, however, that he was referring to the Government's strongly held . . . opinion that Vietnam veterans claiming sickness from Agent Orange should not be paid. . . . Newman added that "the . . . premature release of [this report] could cause embarrassment to the Government" [and] . . . concluded, "[m]y purpose in writing you is to alert you to the situation and preclude a premature release or discussion of this sensitive report."[10]

Murray's report was never made public.

Calm before the Storm

AOWG suspended the CDC's Agent Orange study until its members could reach some consensus about what to do. Rumors about the study had been circulating behind the scenes for several months, but the news that the Agent Orange study had hit a snag broke on May 19, 1986. *New York Times* correspondent Iver Peterson reported in a front-page story that day that "the study has stalled . . . because of disputes over how to handle the work." He noted that a medical team had been assembled since February, 1986, at the Loveland Medical Clinic in Albuquerque, New Mexico, to begin the physical examinations of Vietnam veterans selected to participate in the study. "[E]xpensive equipment, technicians and doctors are standing idly by, waiting for orders," Peterson wrote. At least one CDC official, Robert Diefenbach, suggested that the agency go ahead with the Agent Orange interviews and examinations and resolve at a later time how the data might be effectively used.[11]

Dr. Carl Keller, an epidemiologist and head of AOWG's Science Panel, however, stuck to his guns. He defended the delay, saying, "We would desparately like to please the veterans, and at the same time we find it necessary to make a scientifically meaningful study or else we've wasted all our time and money. . . ." Helen Gelband, of the Congressional Office of Technological Assessment (OTA) backed Keller's decision. "Sometimes the CDC is just impossible to work with," she said, "but that is not the case here. The root of the problem is that not very many people were exposed to Agent Orange in Vietnam. And why should that be a problem? Because nobody will believe us."[12]

Biomedical researcher Michael Gough, who had worked for OTA and had been responsible for oversight of CDC's design protocol, fully agreed with Gelband's assessment. Gough had approved CDC's original design, which called not only for the Agent Orange study but also for a "Vietnam Experience" Study and a "Selected Cancers" study. The Vietnam Experience Study would compare the health and mortality rates of those who served in Vietnam with those of controls who served elsewhere in the military, and the Selected Cancers Study would be a retrospective study of veterans who had come down with cancer. Gough calculated how much dioxin a veteran might have been exposed to as a result of being under or within a half-mile of a Ranch Hand spraying mission. He later wrote:

> . . . [W]e do not know the exact amount that a veteran might have been exposed to, but . . . the exposure can be estimated. According to the calculations, no veteran directly under the most dioxin-contaminated spray was exposed to the minimum dose necessary to cause chloracne. That calculation appears to be correct because fewer than two dozen Vietnam veterans have diagnosed chloracne, and even those cases could have originated from exposure to other chemicals.
>
> It is tricky to estimate the amount of dioxin that would enter a soldier's body from chemicals deposited on his clothing. However, a soldier directly under some dioxin-contaminated Agent Orange spraying could receive a dose greater than the amount the Food and Drug Administration estimates to be a virtually safe dose if ingested daily for 70 years. Even 0.5 kilometers away fromt the spraying, exposure drops to 2% of the maximum; at 1 kilometer, it [is] 0.03%. . . . The calculated exposures are thus very low.[13]

In June of 1986, the Science Panel of AOWG, of which Dr. Houk was a member, decided that it was not possible to conduct a scientifically valid Agent Orange study using military records unless CDC scientists could develop some measure of exposure other than the "hits" method. The CDC pushed ahead with the Vietnam Experience Study and also began a pilot study on use of blood tests to determine the amounts of dioxin in Vietnam veterans who had experienced different levels of exposure. On September 17, 1986, the New Jersey Agent Orange Commission reported that its researchers had found that dioxin could be successfully detected in the blood of exposed veterans. In a $400,000 study funded by the New Jersey State Legislature, toxicologists examined ten veterans who claimed to have been "highly exposed" with a like number of matched controls. Toxicologists found an average of about forty-eight parts per trillion (ppt) of dioxin in the blood of the exposed veterans and about 5 ppt of dioxin for the controls. The study seemed to affirm both the "self-report" method of exposure and the use of a blood test for detecting dioxin.[14]

The appearance of another study at about the same time raised further concerns, not about dioxin, but about 2,4-D, an active ingredient in Agent Orange. (Agent Orange had been a 50–50 mix of two chemical compounds, 2,4,5-T and 2,4-D.) On August 20, 1986, a National Cancer Institute/University of Kansas research team headed by Dr. Sheila Hoar announced its findings from a study of farmers and farm laborers in Kansas. The NCI/Kansas researchers had examined 948 cancer victims and an equal number of matched controls without cancer. The study found that Kansas farmers who had been exposed twenty days or more per year to herbicides containing 2,4-D were 600 percent more likely to develop a form of lymphatic cancer—non-Hodgkin's lymphoma—than those who did not work with the herbicide. Also, farmers who mixed and applied the chemical were 40 percent more likely to develop cancer if they did not wear special protective clothing or gloves. Dr. Hoar noted that the study successfully ruled out other competing explanations such as smoking, radiation, and a family history of cancer. She concluded, "One can't base a regulatory program on one study alone, but if this finding is confirmed there would be serious regulatory implications such as restricting the use of herbicides."[15]

The NCI-Kansas study carried far-reaching implications. Not only had 2,4-D been used in Agent Orange, but it was also an ingredient in some 1,500 products that could be purchased over the counter in the United States. "What is of concern to the regulatory community," John Moore of the Environmental Protection Agency (EPA) told reporters, "is that the chemical enjoys such wide use—a lot people are exposed." Since the study was "a very good one," Moore continued, the EPA would re-examine its regulations covering the use of products containing 2,4-D. Companies making or using such products also took note of the study. "We will be interested in how the scientific community in and out of the industry judge the strength of their data," commented John McCarthy of the National Agricultural Chemicals Association. "The people at the National Cancer Institute are very good epidemiologists."[16]

Two months later, Chem-Lawn, the nation's largest professional lawn care company, elected to quit using all products containing 2,4-D. Stephen Hardyman, manager of legislative affairs for the company, explained the decision to reporters: "The study is inconclusive, but it's a good study and we don't want to take any chances." However, David Dietz, director of the Pesticide Public Policy Foundation, stated that his organization's stance remained the same—"2,4,-D is perfectly safe"—and Daniel Hogan, the vice-president of the Consumer Products Division of Chevron Chemical company, asserted, "We're not concerned about 2,4,-D at all."[17]

An End to the Agent Orange Study

The CDC released its preliminary mortality findings from the Vietnam Experience Study (VES) on February 10, 1987. The CDC had drawn a random sampling of 9,324 Army veterans who had served in Vietnam between 1965 and 1971, and 8,989 veterans who had served in the Army in Korea, Germany, and the United States during the same time frame. The study tracked the subjects from the date of discharge from the service through 1983. The findings showed that the mortality rate of Vietnam veterans was 45 percent higher during this period than for their controls. Researchers attributed most of the excess mortality to the higher incidence of death among Vietnam veterans due to suicide, murder, and motor vehicle accidents. For example, the suicide rate among Vietnam veterans was 72 percent higher than for the control group for the first five years after discharge from the service. The study contained no measure of exposure to combat; hence, researchers could not pinpoint what it was about the "Vietnam experience" that produced the findings. The CDC speculated that the higher mortality probably was due to "the unusual stress endured while in a hostile fire zone" and to "the unique environment and experience of serving in Vietnam and returning to an unsupportive and sometimes hostile climate in the U.S."[18]

Meanwhile, the CDC continued its pilot study using blood tests to match levels of dioxin in the body with the exposure groups from the "hits" method. A hint that a bomb was about to be dropped appeared in a *New York Times* story on July 24, 1987. The article stated that the CDC researchers were having difficulty finding any differences in the serum dioxin levels between "likely to have been exposed" veterans and their controls. The researchers had examined 646 Vietnam veterans who, according to the "hits" method, had been exposed. Their median dioxin level was 3.8 parts per trillion (ppt). The lowest concentration found among them was 1 ppt, and the highest was 45 ppt. The median dioxin level for the 97 controls was 3.9 ppt, with a range of 1 to 15 ppt. In a "self-report" of exposure, the Vietnam veteran with 45 ppt classified himself as "no exposure;" the other Vietnam veteran with more than 20 ppt of dioxin in his blood classified himself as having been exposed to Agent Orange.[19]

On August 31, 1987, the word was official: after almost eight years since it was mandated by Congress and after more than $65 million dollars expended on the effort, the Agent Orange Study was terminated midway through completion. Dr. Vernon Houk of the CDC announced that he had decided to cancel the study because the CDC could not locate enough soldiers who were exposed to significant levels of Agent Orange to do a valid study. Reaction was immediate and angry. John Terzano of Vietnam Veterans of America told reporters:

> CDC has only proved that the methods it employed for doing the study will not work, not that the study was impossible using other methods. If the study is abandoned now, there will be very, very real problems, political problems.[20]

And Dr. Peter Kahn of the New Jersey Agent Orange Commission remarked in disgust: "The federal effort has been pitiful in this whole business." He said that his commission would continue its work to link blood tests with an exposure criteria.[21]

As the CDC was airing its decision, the VA was sitting on a bomb of its own. Six months earlier, the VA had completed a mortality study of 24,235 Army and Marine Corps and 26,685 controls made up of veterans who served elsewhere. The VA study found that Army Vietnam veterans had a significantly higher proportionate mortality rates of accidents and poisonings, and that the Marine Corps Vietnam veterans had significantly higher proportionate mortality rates of non-Hodgkin's lymphoma and lung cancer. The VA had not yet made these findings public, but the findings were leaked to the press.[22] In light of the NCI/Kansas study, concern about the VA's findings ran high. Seeking to reassure worried veterans, Dr. Lawrence Hobson of the VA told reporters: "I wouldn't say it's terribly worrisome. If I were a Vietnam veteran, I wouldn't be the least bit disturbed by [these findings]." Hobson explains:

> Let me point out, first of all, that that has nothing to do with the incidence of either lung cancer or non-Hodgkins lymphoma. It gets a little complex to explain, but . . . [a] proportionate mortality study, basically, is a percentage study. That is, if you have a higher percentage of deaths, not the number of deaths, but the higher percentage of deaths, you have a higher proportionate mortality ratio. What that study showed, first of all, was not that there were more Marines dying of non-Hodgkin's lymphoma, but that there was a higher percentage of the deaths among the Marines ascribable to that. Obviously, if you have a higher percentage dying of lymphoma, you have a lower percentage dying from other things. It came out to 100 percent anyway.
>
> . . . The medical significance is at best, a suggestion that there be an attempt to determine what is the actual mortality rate in comparison to

others. . . . It would be only fair to conclude that among the deaths of Marines who served in Vietnam in that time period . . . there were a higher percentage of them who died of non-Hodgkin's lymphoma than of some other disease. As far as the lung cancer is concerned, there is a well-established link between lung cancer and cigarette smoking.[23]

Siding with Dr. Hobson, Alvin Young of the AOWG termed the findings, "a statistical fluke." However, Rep. Lane Evans (D-Ill.), a member of Vietnam Veterans in Congress, promised to look into the matter, saying that the study provided "evidence that something is wrong for Vietnam veterans."[24]

The CDC officially released the second stage of the VES concerning morbidity (illnesses) in the May 1988 issue of the *Journal of the American Medical Association*. For this phase of the research, the CDC located and interviewed by telephone about 90 percent of the almost 18,000 Vietnam and Vietnam-era veterans in the study. In a third stage, researchers arranged for about 42 percent of those interviewed by phone to go the Loveland Clinic in Albuquerque for comprehensive physical examinations. The CDC said that the Vietnam veterans reported having more physical and psychological symptoms than were actually found during the medical examinations and that, for the most part, virtually all of the examinations detected no significant differences between the Vietnam and the Vietnam-era veterans in the study. There were, however, some differences: a larger percentage of Vietnam veterans were found to have high frequency hearing loss (9.4 vs. 6.2%), stool occult blood (1.5 vs. .3%), evidence of part infection with hepatitis B (14.1 vs. 11.1%), lower sperm concentrations (15.9 vs. 8.1%), lower average proportions of morphologically normal sperm cells (15.9 vs. 11.4%). About 15 percent of the Vietnam veterans reported psychological distress meeting the criteria for post-traumatic stress disorder. With no specific measures of exposure to anything, the researchers could not say why these anomalies existed between the two groups.[25]

In March of 1988, Dr. Houk asked the VA to reallocate some $14 million dollars in funds—originally set aside for the Agent Orange study and now in danger of reverting to the Treasury Department unused—to allow him to keep his Agent Orange research team together for purposes of following up these differences between Vietnam veteran subjects and their controls. The VA denied Houk's request. In later written Congressional testimony, VA officials defended their decision:

CDC and VA financial groups believed that the money would have to be reappropriated, a process too slow to make funding available for Dr. Houk to save his team.

. . . Discussion of the CDC proposal extended over several months and involved Department of Medicine and Surgery personnel at several lev-

els from the Deputy Chief Medical Director down. Both scientific and fiscal issues were obviously involved; the outcome was justified in both
areas.[26]

The Air Force Ranch Hand Study also resurfaced as an issue in March,
1988. In late February, the Air Force approved for public release a revised
and updated version of the 1984 study. According to the updated report,
researchers had found that Ranch Hand personnel had toxicological
profiles that differed significantly from those of their controls in six of
the eleven areas investigated. It concluded that although dioxin could
"not be confidently identified as the causative agent" of these findings,
it could not be "exonerated" either. Commenting upon the significance
of the updated study, Barry Kasinitz of Vietnam Veterans of American
(VVA) told a New York Times reporter: "For the first time, the Air Force
is saying in a major way that they cannot rule out dioxin as a cause of
health effects."[27]

Senator Thomas Daschle (D-S.D.), who in 1987 had moved over from
the House to the Senate, had by this time received evidence that the
original 1984 report had been tampered with by the White House Agent
Orange Working Group (AOWG). The opening sentence in the conclusion of original draft of the 1984 Ranch Hand report stated, "It is incor-
rect to interpret this baseline study as 'negative'" (that is, the findings
should *not* be taken to mean that exposure to Agent Orange had not
harmed the Ranch Handers).[28] However, when the Air Force researchers submitted the report to the AOWG for clearance prior to release, someone at AOWG deleted that sentence from the report and
added in its stead a sentence describing the findings as "reassuring." In
June of 1988, Senator Daschle's staff obtained a copy of a memo written
by Donald Newman, chair of the AOWG's Domestic Council, to all
directors of federally funded research on Agent Orange ten days after
the release of the updated 1984 study. It read in part:

> The Domestic Policy Council Agent Orange Working Group . . . was cre-
> ated by President Reagan with the express mission of overseeing and
> coordinating Federal Government research activities relating to Agent Or-
> ange exposure and its possible health effects. The AOWG was given the
> responsibility for reporting to the public the results and implications of all
> research in the Agent Orange area.
>
> The release of any report, without the review mandated by the Agent
> Orange Working group procedures, could constitute a serious breach. . . .
> Because of the emotional and sensitive nature of Agent Orange research, it
> is essential that each principal insist that this procedure be observed with
> the utmost care.[29]

Senator Daschle took exception to this position. A memo circulated by Daschle's staff noted that the Ranch Hand Study's protocol stated that the Air Force researchers themselves were responsible "for the security of the data, for all data analysis, and all interpretation of analysis," subject only to monitoring by the Air Force Ranch Hand Advisory Committee "to obviate any appearance of Air Force management bias."[30]

The American Legion Study

The American Legion, meanwhile, had been conducting a study of its own since 1983 on the effects of combat and exposure to Agent Orange. On Veterans Day, November 11, 1988, Legion representatives announced the findings of the study, and in December their findings were published as a series of epidemiological studies in the scientific journal *Environmental Research.*[31] The purpose of the research was to assess the effects of combat and of exposure to Agent Orange on the physical and mental health of Vietnam veterans. The sample, drawn randomly on October 15, 1983, from the membership rolls of American Legion posts in Colorado, Indiana, Maryland, Minnesota, Ohio, and Pennsylvannia, contained 2,858 Vietnam veterans and a control group of 3,952 veterans who had served elsewhere during the Vietnam War. Legionnaires in the study filled out a lengthy questionnaire, reporting in the process the extent of their exposure to combat and to Agent Orange, and their personal and family health histories. The study's authors—Dr. Stephen Stellman of the American Cancer Society's Department of Epidemiology and Statistics, his wife, Dr. Jeanne Stellman of Columbia University's School of Public Health, and John Sommer, Jr. of the American Legion— also obtained copies of the HERBS tapes and troop movement records and analyzed them in conjunction with their survey data.

The American Legion researchers affirmed the usefulness of the HERBS tapes and military records in documenting exposure to Agent Orange. In their study, they had sought to validate the "self-report" method by linking self-reports of herbicide exposure with the "hits" method. Could veterans who claimed to have been exposed, they asked, be shown "likely" to have been exposed by the "hits" method, and would those who said they had not been exposed fall into the "not likely" category according to the "hits" method? Their answer was an unqualified "yes." Jeanne Stellman praised the quality of the military records at a later congressional hearing:

> So we obtained a copy of the tape and put together a methodology by which we could ask veterans where they were and do this kind of

computer linkage. . . . In the beginning, we didn't actually know whether we would find anybody exposed or whether the method would work. Two studies later . . . we became convinced that it would work. . . .

. . . In May 1988, thirty-nine reels of tape arrived at my husband's office. At first, we didn't know what they were. Two tapes were clear. One was a tape that had been assembled by the [Environmental Support Group]. . . . It had 75,000 bi-weekly entries of where troops were. A second tape contained a file called a "Command Post List," which has over 5,000 additional entries consisting of named places in Vietnam, their exact . . . co-ordinates, and dates of occupancy by specific military units. . . . We did not know what those other thirty-seven tapes were because Dick Christian was under a gag order from the Department of Justice, which I guess is the White House, to not speak to us, so we could not call him up and say, "What are these reels?"

We finally did find out but even before we knew what these other reels were, we submitted an enthusiastic report . . . , because we believed we were in epidemiologist heaven. We thought this is the most incredibly wonderful data that you could have and we reported very positively . . . that we could now, we felt, determine exposure versus nonexposure for some 300,000 men at least.[32]

The Stellmans and Sommer also criticized "previous government studies," especially the CDC's Vietnam Experience Study (VES). They stated that the CDC had committed the cardinal sin of epidemiological research by using as its explanatory variable the "generalized Vietnam experience." This diluted, they said, the effects both of combat and of herbicide exposure on health by placing in the same category all who had served in Vietnam. Since Vietnam veterans varied tremendously in terms of the amounts of combat and Agent Orange they had encountered, comparisons of them—all in the same category—with the control group had led the CDC investigators to obscure and therefore underestimate the effects of combat and herbicide exposure. Despite this flaw, they said, the CDC study still had detected some harmful effects similar to those found in their own study.[33]

The American Legion study showed, said the Stellmans and Sommer, that the experience of combat and exposure to Agent Orange were highly correlated with each other, largely because much spraying had been done in areas frequented by enemy troops and, hence, American combat units. They argued that combat and Agent Orange exposure had each had an impact on the health of Vietnam veterans. Veterans who had experienced combat, they reported, were more prone to depression, anxiety, excessive drinking and smoking, high blood pressure, ulcers, benign fatty tumors, and major injury than those who had seen less combat. Among the consequences of this were higher divorce rates, lower life satisfaction, and poorer health among combat than noncombat veterans. On the other hand, veterans exposed to herbicides had higher incidences of skin rashes, body aches, fatigue, benign fatty tumors, and other physical problems. Fertility patterns among veterans with higher exposure levels to combat and herbicides were similar to those with lower exposure levels. However, the incidence of miscarriages among the spouses of Vietnam veterans who had been exposed to Agent Orange and among spouses who had smoked during pregnancy were 40 percent higher than for those in the control group.[34]

In late November of 1988, Dr. Vernon Houk of the CDC called Dr. Michael Gochfeld, editor of *Environmental Research*, and castigated him for publishing the American Legion study. Dr. Gochfeld offered to provide space for Houk in a subsequent issue should he wish to submit a written rebuttal. Houk never sent Gochfeld a written critique. However, the Science Panel of the White House Agent Orange Working Group, of which Dr. Houk was a member, issued scathing critiques of the American Legion study to the press and select members of Congress. Its reviews of the study stated that the sample was worthless because of the low response rate (52 percent of the Legionnaires sampled had filled out and returned the questionnaires). AOWG also dismissed the use of self-reports in the study, and again asserted that military records were useless for any sound epidemiological study. AOWG also questioned the personal integrity and professional competence of the Stellmans and Sommer.

The Stellmans and Sommer defended their methodology and findings, and again pointed out that some of their findings were congruent with those reported in the CDC's own Vietnam Experience Study. For example, the demographic characteristics of veterans in the two studies and the incidences of post-traumatic stress disorder as well as other health problems were strikingly similar. In later written congressional testimony, the Stellmans stated:

> In most scientific fields, whenever a multitude of studies converge on similar results the various researchers are usually pleased; they rarely wage war on other investigators. Just the opposite has happened here.
>
> The personal and professional attacks which the CDC has carried out on [us] are reminiscent of the attacks which the tobacco industry carried out in the 1950's on the American Cancer Society and . . . the late Dr. E. Cuyler Hammond, when his large-scale prospective studies . . . began to show links between cigarette smoking and lung cancer.
>
> The . . . tobacco industry's strategy then, and the CDC's today, was to characterize the study methodology as so fundamentally flawed that not a single result can be believed. . . . We . . . have already responded to these criticisms in detail. . . . To summarize it briefly, CDC's characterization of

our methodology is factually wrong in many respects, and their criticisms
are riddled with faulty logic and contradictions. We were, in fact, quite
astonished at the sloppiness with which some reviewers misstated our
study goals and design.

. . . [T]he methodological attacks are mere smokescreen. . . . Dr. Houk
and his colleagues are attempting to escape the . . . boomerang which
their challenge ought to evoke, namely, does the CDC regard as unreason-
able the American Legion Study's conclusion that men who fought for
their country at the extreme peril of their own lives might now, as a direct
consequence, be suffering emotional stress, have psychological problems,
have combat-related illnesses, and use veteran health facilities? Only the
CDC spokespersons can explain why their public statements and criticisms contradict these reasonable expectations, whereas the printed findings of the CDC study confirm them.[35]

The Stellmans ended their testimony by saying that they had worked
with the CDC many times over the years and that they held the agency
in high esteem. Both Stellmans noted that they had strong collegial ties
with some of CDC epidemiologists, including several who had studied
under them as students in graduate school. "We prefer to believe," they
wrote, "that, like the Vietnam Experience Study, this attack is merely an
'oddment,' and that it does not reflect the high scientific and professional standards that characterize an important American health agency."[36]

A Landmark Court Decision

In January 1989, a presidential decree elevated the VA to cabinet status
and designated it the Department of Veterans Affairs (DVA). Newly
elected President George Bush a month earlier had announced his nomination for filling the top spot in the DVA: Edward Derwinsky. A veteran
of World War II in which he had served as an infantryman in the Pacific,
Derwinsky had been a twelve-term congressman from Illinois and had
recently lost his seat in an Illinois redistricting plan. During his years in
the House, Derwinsky had not been particularly active on veterans'
issues, though he was a recognized member of the American Legion,
Veterans of Foreign Wars, Catholic War Veterans, and Polish Legion of
American Veterans.

Derwinsky's nomination caused only a minor stir in the Senate,
whose task it would be to confirm him. Sonny Montgomery, chair of the
House Committee on Veterans' Affairs, said that he thought Derwinsky
would be an effective advocate of veterans and would defend the DVA
against pending budget cuts. Derwinksy himself explained his views on

veterans' issues without raising significant opposition and, on the question of Agent Orange, testified that he had "an open mind." On March 3, the Senate confirmed Derwinsky as the new director of the DVA.[37]

The Agent Orange controversy was now in a lull as both sides regrouped. CDC's position—that a valid Agent Orange study was impossible since so few veterans had been significantly exposed—buttressed the prevailing attitude within VA, now the DVA, that the problem was more political than real. This sentiment was shared by the White House Agent Orange Working Group (AOWG), the Congressional Office of Technological Assessment (OTA), and the Senate and House Committees on Veterans' Affairs. Alvin Young of AOWG felt that the CDC research, along with the earlier Ranch Hand findings as reported by the Air Force, was decisive. "The trail on Agent Orange," he observed, "has grown cold."[38] Agent Orange claimants, on the other hand, pointed to the research by the American Legion, the NCI and University of Kansas, the New Jersey Agent Orange Commission, and others, but for the moment seemed to have lost the initiative.

All this changed abruptly on May 3, 1989 when California federal court Judge Thelton Henderson ruled on a suit filed by Vietnam Veterans of America (VVA) and the National Veterans Law Center (NVLC). (Mary Stout, who had served in Vietnam as an Army nurse, had by this time been elected to succeed Bobby Muller as president of VVA.) The suit challenged the standards of proof required by the DVA of veterans claiming injury from Agent Orange.[39] In October of 1984, Congress had passed the Veterans' Dioxin and Radiation Exposure Compensation Standards Act. This act mandated that the VA (hereafter referred to as the DVA) pursue thorough epidemiological studies of the effects of herbicide exposure. It noted that there was "some evidence" that certain diseases were associated with exposure to dioxin, namely, chloracne, porphyria cutanea tarda (a rare liver disease), and soft tissue sarcoma (a form of cancer). The act also disputed the DVA's long-standing insistence on scientific proof as a precondition for compensation of Agent Orange claimants. It stated:

> It has always been the policy of the Veterans Administration and is the policy of the United States, with respect to individual claims for service connection of diseases and disabilities, that when, after consideration of all the evidence and material of record, there is an approximate balance of positive and negative evidence regarding the merits of an issue material to the determination of a claim, the benefit of the doubt in resolving each such issue shall be given to the claimant.[40]

Though the act clearly identified the principles by which the DVA should decide claims for service connection—"preponderance of the evidence" and "benefit of the doubt"—the DVA nevertheless continued to apply the scientific standard of "cause and effect" in the Agent Orange cases. VVA's lawsuit noted that, by 1989, the DVA had ruled on 33,272 claims from Vietnam veterans who felt they had been harmed by exposure to Agent Orange. The DVA had denied all but 5 of them, and all 5 of the favorable rulings had been cases of chloracne. In its lawsuit, VVA and the NVLC contended that the DVA in making these rulings had ignored its own guidelines and the principles reaffirmed in the 1984 Dioxin Exposure Act, and therefore had decided the cases in a wrongful manner.

Judge Henderson agreed. In a forty-eight-page decision, Judge Henderson ruled that the DVA had too strictly defined a standard of proof in the Agent Orange cases. In the section entitled, "Conclusion and Remedy," Judge Henderson wrote:

> We hold that the [DVA] misinterpreted two important provisions of the act. The [DVA] both imposed an impermissibly demanding test for granting service-connection for various diseases *and* refused to give veterans the benefit of the doubt in meeting that demanding standard. These errors compounded one another, as they increased both the *type* and the *level* of proof needed for veterans to prevail during the rule-making proceedings. We find that these errors, especially compounded with one another, sharply tipped the scales against veteran claimants.
>
> As the act was passed amidst "substantial uncertainty" over the health effects of Agent Orange, we do not find that these errors were harmless; there is a substantial possibility that the errors shaped the conclusions reached by the [DVA in deciding these cases]. Accordingly, we hereby invalidate the portion of the dioxin regulation which denies service-connection for all other diseases but chloracne. . . . We also void all benefit denials made under section 311 (d) and remand this matter to the [DVA] for further proceedings not inconsistent with this opinion. (emphasis in original)[41]

Senator Thomas Daschle was delighted with the ruling. "The decision is extremely significant, for it confirms that what Vietnam veterans, scientists, many of my colleagues, and I have been saying for years," he said on the floor of the Senate. The judge, he continued, "made the same decision any rational person would, given the strength of the scientific evidence and the government's own policy of giving the benefit of the doubt to veterans. . . ."[42]

The question of how to respond to Judge Henderson's ruling became one of Derwinsky's first major policy decisions. The stakes were enormous. If upheld on appeal, Henderson's ruling ultimately would force the DVA to completely rewrite its regulations regarding claims for compensation concerning those veterans who believed Agent Orange had harmed them. Further, the department would have to review its negative verdicts on more than 33,000 claims. On May 11, Derwinsky faced reporters and rendered his decision: in a stunning reversal of DVA policy, he accepted Judge Henderson's ruling and declined to appeal it in a higher court. In a letter to Attorney General Richard Thornburgh and VVA president Mary Stout, the first woman to head a nationally chartered veterans' organization, Derwinsky explained:

> I have reviewed the court's opinion, as has my staff. I have made the decision not to seek appeal. I intend to proceed immediately with action to promulgate regulations in a manner that is consistent with the opinion of the court. It is my opinion that an appeal would not be in the best interests of the [Bush] administration or the veterans' coummunity served by this department.[43]

To persons and groups advocating compensation for the Agent Orange claimants, Derwinsky's decision was more momentous than Henderson's ruling had been a week earlier. "There is a better chance now than ever before that Congress will move to resolve this long-term and controversial issue," Stout told reporters. "This victory . . . vindicates our diligent and dedicated efforts to seek justice for Vietnam veterans." And Rep. Lane Evans (D-Ill.) of Vietnam Veterans in Congress lauded Derwinsky's stand:

> Secretary Derwinsky took a big step in ensuring that the Veterans Administration would be a kinder and gentler bureaucracy. I salute him. . . . I also want to salute the Vietnam Veterans of America for bringing the suit in the first place, although I find it regrettable that they had to go to the federal courts to get the Veterans Administration to live up to the law of the land.[44]

Agent Orange and an American Family

Having accepted the California court's ruling, the question now became one of what the DVA's policy should be. Derwinsky hired retired Admiral Elmo Zumwalt, Jr., as a special consultant on Agent Orange issues, and he also directed the DVA's Advisory Committee on the Health-Related Effects of Herbicides to begin an assessment of the literature, disease by disease, for correlational evidence. Those supporting the Agent Orange claimants viewed the selection of Admiral Zumwalt as a very positive sign. Zumwalt's son, a Vietnam veteran, died of cancer of the lymphatic system, and both Zumwalt and his son, Elmo Zumwalt III, in a book written before the latter's death, attributed the cancer to Agent Orange exposure.[45]

Ironically, the decision to use Agent Orange in the area of operation in which Zumwalt III had served had been made by his father. From 1968 to 1970, Admiral Zumwalt was the commander of the riverine or "brown water" Naval forces that patrolled the coastal waters and the Mekong River of Vietnam's delta region. Zumwalt III, then a lieutenant (junior grade), had requested an assignment in Vietnam and, after several weeks of patrolling near Da Nang, had asked to be reassigned to the Mekong Delta in order to serve under his father's command. In part to show that he was receiving no favoritism, he volunteered there for patrol boat duty and for the more dangerous missions. One of these missions took him far upriver into Cambodia—officially American troops were not permitted to cross the border—where his boat ambushed some North Vietnames sampans carrying weapons into South Vietnam. Admiral Zumwalt later wrote of the significance of the event:

> Elmo's unauthorized but successful ambush demonstrated that the intelligence we received gave us only part of the story. Our agents had identified the infiltration routes along major rivers, but the Vietcong and North Vietnamese were clever enough to switch to lesser routes. Largely as a result of Elmo's ambush, I ordered our river boats into the mouths of the smaller canals and creeks.[46]

With Admiral Zumwalt's decision to shift operations to the narrow rivers and canals near the Cambodian border, patrolling became increasingly dangerous. Viet Cong guerillas frequently ambushed patrol boats from the dense vegetation along the narrow waterways. As casualties rose, Admiral Zumwalt sought strategies for reducing the numbers of ambushes and casualties, including some method for clearing the shore lines of vegetation. Subsequently, Admiral Zumwalt requested Operation Ranch Hand missions for the Mekong Delta. Zumwalt explains:

> [At] the time I got there, the one thousand small craft . . . were just doing routine patrolling, because the Viet Cong had been pretty cleared up from [coastal and major river] areas. When I made the decision to move them up . . . along . . . the Cambodian border, then it became a very high risk operation.
>
> . . . The casualties were running at the rate of about 6 percent a month. Which meant that the average young man had about a 70 to 75 percent chance of being killed or wounded during his year there. We just simply had to reduce those casualty rates and Agent Orange, which the Army had been using for three years in the jungles with no observed ill effect,

was the obvious choice. . . . And it reduced our casualties to less than a percent a month.[47]

In deciding to spray Agent Orange in the delta region, Admiral Zumwalt had no indication that the herbicide might be harmful to human health. His first awareness of a potential problem came later when the military restricted and then eliminated the Ranch Hand program altogether. He states:

> Well, my view is that not even the chemical companies knew [back then] of its carcinogenic effect. I think the chemical companies did know that it was causing some problems with skin chloracne and that sort of thing. The chemical companies were urged by the government to come up with something quickly that could be used. And they assured the government that, in their judgment, it was noncarcenogenic and the government assured those of us in the field that it was. But the compelling reason for that was that everybody agreed that we had to reduce casualties. Therefore, we couldn't take the time for the normal definitive research to be done.[48]

Lt. Zumwalt thus spent his tour in Vietnam patrolling some of the more heavily sprayed areas in the Mekong Delta. In March 1977, his son, Elmo Zumwalt IV, was born with a brain dysfunction and learning disabilities. In 1979 he and his wife became aware, through reports on television and in the newspapers, that other Vietnam veterans who had children with birth defects believed that their exposure to Agent Orange during the war might be responsible. Zumwalt III recalled having been exposed but at that time did not see a link between his exposure and his son's birth defects. Then in January 1983, he himself was diagnosed as having non-Hodgkin's lymphoma. He later wrote:

> I had seen Agent Orange defoliation nearly everywhere I had patrolled, but from the air the extent of it was dramatic—trees were stripped of leaves, thick jungle growth was reduced to twigs, the ground was barren of grass. In the 11 months I was in Vietnam, I had often washed in the waters into which Agent Orange had drained and had eaten local produce which I suspect had been doused with the chemical.
>
> I remember developing a skin rash while in the Sea Float area. . . . [A]t the time, I was thankful for the defoliation. It meant the enemy could not attack Sea Float without great cost to itself.
>
> Dad and I began a flurry of activity to learn as much as we could. We telephoned cancer specialists around the country. . . . [W]e went to the National Cancer Institute . . . where they discovered that the cancer had spread throughout my lymphatic system and had invaded my spleen, my bone marrow and probably my liver. . . . [They] offered some good news: [my kind of cancer] moves slowly, the median survival time . . . is eight

years. There was, however, a dark side: my type of lymphoma was always fatal.[49]

The Zumwalts did not go to the VA for medical care because, in the words of Admiral Zumwalt, "we were convinced that it was submarginal."[50] They sought help instead from cancer treatment centers at University Hospital in Denver and the University of California Medical Center in San Diego. Attorneys representing the veterans in the Agent Orange lawsuit against the manufacturers of Agent Orange approached Zumwalt III and asked him to participate in the lawsuit. They thought he would make a highly credible witness. Zumwalt III declined, wishing to make the most of his remaining time with his family. In February 1985, Zumwalt III was found to have Hodgkin's disease—a fast-moving, aggressive form of lympatic cancer—in addition to non-Hodgkin's lymphoma. Since the cancer had spread to several parts of his body, only radical chemotherapy could be used to retard its growth. The therapy, however, failed to stop the growth of his cancer and also destroyed his bone marrow, necessitating a bone marrow transplant. As his immune system weakened, Zumwalt III had to live for awhile in an eight-by-ten foot sterile cubicle at Seattle's Fred Hutchinson Cancer Reserach Center.

The Zumwalts carefully studied the medical literature. At first they were skeptical that that a relationship existed between exposure to Agent Orange and subsequent health problems and birth defects. They began to change their minds after they read the studies. The younger Zumwalt told a reporter in 1986:

> I am a lawyer and I don't think I could prove in court, by the weight of the scientific evidence, that Agent Orange is the cause of all the medical problems. . . . But I am convinced that it is.
>
> . . . I realize that what I am saying may imply that my father is responsible for my illness and [my son's] disability. I have the greatest love and admiration for Dad as a man, and the deepest respect for him as a military leader. I do not doubt for a minute that the saving of American lives was always his first priority. Certainly thousands, perhaps even myself, are alive today because of his decision to use Agent Orange.[51]

In the same *New York Times* interview, Admiral Zumwalt, stated:

> Knowing what I now know, I still would have ordered the defoliation to achieve the objectives it did, of reducing casualties. But that does not ease the sorrow I feel for Elmo, or the anguish his illness, and [my grandson's] disability, give me. It is the first thing I think of when I awake in the morning, and the last thing I remember when I go to sleep at night.[52]

Elmo Zumwalt III died of cancer August 14, 1988.

A Congressional Inquiry

Congress and the director of the DVA each has the power to extend a presumption of service connection: the policy that the DVA should automatically assume that certain diseases originated during military service. No extension of presumption was forthcoming from Congress in the Agent Orange claims before the DVA. In 1984, Congress had passed the Compensation Standards Act that reiterated the principle of giving veterans the benefit of the doubt when both positive and negative evidence existed. However, neither the House nor the Senate Committee on Veterans Affairs had backed Senator Thomas Daschle's proposals that would have rendered a presumption for non-Hodgkin's lymphoma, porphyria cutanea tarda, and soft-tissue sarcoma. (The DVA already had a provision for service connection in cases of chloracne.)

To begin with, some in Congress had accepted the DVA position that scientific proof should be produced prior to compensating Agent Orange claims. Further, Michael Gough and later Helen Gelband, both of the Office of Technological Assessment (OTA), advised Congress on current scientific opinion. They contended that herbicide exposure by ground troops had been insignificant, and that the Ranch Hand findings exonerated Agent Orange in the group they thought had been most heavily exposed. House Committee chairman Sonny Montgomery (D-Miss.) seemed persuaded by these arguments and therefore opposed extending presumption for Agent Orange exposure. On the other side, Senate Committee chairman Alan Cranston (D-Calif.) had not supported Daschle's legislation either. Because Cranston had been such a vigorous advocate for Vietnam veterans on the readjustment counseling issue a decade earlier, his lack of initiative on this issue puzzled those who sought presumption in Agent Orange cases.

In 1984, Senator (then Representative) Daschle had hired Laura Petrou as his legislative assistant who would concentrate full time on the Agent Orange issue. It was her job to monitor the ongoing research, especially that being done by the Air Force and CDC, to assist in developing legislation, and to work with the House Committee (and, after 1987, with the Senate Committee). She says of the politics in Congress concerning Agent Orange legislation:

> There has never been anyone in the committees, in the leadership, who was pushing hard as an advocate for Agent Orange. And they always wanted control of [Agent Orange legislation]. Even if Montgomery's name was on it, they did things behind the scenes to water it down.
>
> In the beginning, [Cranston] was one of the strongest supporters of Agent Orange legislation. . . . [W]hen Daschle was in the House, [Cranston]

was pretty supportive. . . . Not as much as Daschle, but he was very sympathetic. By the time we had gotten over to the Senate [in 1987], Cranston was not interested in Agent Orange anymore.

. . . Lots of meetings went on between Daschle, [Senator John] Kerry [D-Mass.], and Cranston when we were putting together the bill. We often got signals that Cranston . . . was inclined to do what Daschle and Kerry wanted, but that his staff was dead set against it and advised him he shouldn't do it. . . . I think his staff director, Jon Steinberg, saw Daschle as a threat to him and Cranston's leadership position. . . . Daschle wasn't on the committee and [Steinberg] didn't want [Daschle] to have too much power outside of it.

. . . Daschle was a very, very aggressive leader on Agent Orange and veterans' issues in general, and there were people who didn't like his aggressive style. . . . If [Cranston] had been willing to be a strong support-er of Agent Orange legislation, we wouldn't have needed to be. . . . He could have been the author of the [presumption] bill like the committee chairman frequently is.[53]

As the Air Force and the CDC had progressed with their studies, Daschle's office had begun to receive information that everything was not on the up-and-up. Petrou states: "We got a lot of anonymous phone calls from people. VA nurses, people at the Air Force, and all over the place, people started calling and saying, 'There's a whole lot more going on here.'" As Daschle's office had received documentation that someone at the AOWG had sanitized the 1984 Air Force Ranch Hand conclusions, word now filtered in that CDC scientists were not in agreement that the military records were useless, and that the decision to brand them as such had been made at a much higher level.

Representative Ted Weiss (D-N.Y.), chair of the House Subcommittee on Human Resources and Intergovernmental Relations, took it upon himself to launch an investigation into the CDC decision to discontinue its Agent Orange study. The hearings commenced on July 11, 1989, and he called in a full range of witnesses from the CDC, the DVA, and the American Legion study. The purpose of the hearings, Weiss explained in his opening remarks, was to determine "exactly what happened . . . [and] if the CDC study was part of a concerted effort to cover up the truth about Agent Orange, and if CDC was guilty of incompetence."[54]

Among those Weiss questioned extensively was Dr. Vernon Houk of the CDC. The first questions he had for Dr. Houk concerned the compo-sition of the White House Agent Orange Working Group (AOWG) and its authority over the CDC study. Houk testified that the AOWG had the mission of overseeing and coordinating federally funded research on Agent Orange, but did not have the authority to tell CDC scientists how to conduct the research or interpret their findings. Houk stated that he himself was a member of AOWG's Science Panel, which was composed of scientists employed by various federal agencies including the VA, Departments of Agriculture, Defense, State, and Labor, and the Environmental Protection Agency.[55]

Having established that AOWG had no authority to direct CDC on how to conduct the Agent Orange study, Weiss then sought to determine if AOWG had in fact interfered with the scientists' work at CDC. Although this questioning covered several topics, Weiss' interrogation concerning the selection of "spray path" widths for recording nearby troop movements typified the testimony:

Weiss: Did the [AOWG] science task force debate the issue of the spray paths?

Houk: Yes.

Weiss: What did they decide?

Houk: We accepted spray path by fixed wing. We accepted the HERBS tapes based upon the data that we had from the National Academy of Sciences that they were very accurate. The limitations of the service tapes which Mr. [Richard] Christian put together were very explicitly contained in his report and we accepted what those were. . . .

Weiss: Now on January 13, 1986, the White House Agent Orange Working Group Science Task Force decided that the spray width would be 2 kilometers; right?

Houk: We proposed the—

Weiss: The spray path would be 2 kilometers?

Houk: We proposed 2 miles within a path—2 kilometers.

Weiss: Two kilometers, right? That was the White House Agent Orange Working Group Science Task Force that made that decision; correct?

Houk: In concurrence with OTA.

Weiss: OK. Now did in fact CDC end up using the 2 kilometer spray path as its criterion?

Houk: Yes. We did assessment based upon either two or six and then ultimately came to using two.

Weiss: What I don't understand is, if CDC is doing this study and the [AOWG] Science Task Force is supposed to be monitoring or overseeing, how does the process get reversed so that the working group makes a determination on this particular issue and the CDC then follows its recommendations? Isn't that sort of reversing?

Houk: . . . No, they would make scientific recommendations to us and OTA made scientific recommendations to us. We would take those recommendations into consideration in the ultimate design of the study.[56]

Weiss continued the same line of questioning concerning who made the decision to cancel the Agent Orange study:

Weiss: OK, now the letter which I'm going to enter into the record . . . is dated October 28, 1987, from Dr. James Mason, the Assistant Surgeon General, to Mr. Don Newman, . . . Chair, Domestic Policy Council, [AOWG]. The bottom paragraph on page 1 says "Based on the review of the study results, both AOWG . . . and OTA concluded that a scientifically valid Agent Orange Exposure Study is not possible." Dr. Mason was in charge of CDC at that time; isn't that correct?

Houk: He was in charge of CDC and our recommendation to the two groups was that it was not possible to do a study. They concurred with the recommendation.

Weiss: Accordingly, Dr. Mason goes on to say, " . . . AOWG has instructed CDC to begin the process of cancelling the contracts and closing out all activities to the Agent Orange Exposure Study."

Houk: Yes.

Weiss: [I]t seems to me that the AOWG and OTA concluded, based on the review of study results, that a scientifically valid Agent Orange exposure study was not possible and that AOWG made the decision to cancel.

Houk: We made the recommendation. . . . We had people as our contractors that were doing very little, being paid, and we were pressing for someone to give us a decision following our recommendation that we could cancel the contracts.[57]

Rep. Weiss noted, and Dr. Houk concurred, that the AOWG Science Panel had made a number of assumptions about how long dioxin lasts in the bodies of humans who have been exposed to it. The CDC researchers had conducted a pilot study on Ranch Hand subjects in 1987 and from these findings estimated that dioxin had a "half-life" of seven years, that is, half of the dioxin absorbed by the body would have decomposed naturally within seven years. Weiss read from a document indicating that, in the opinion of one CDC scientist, the dioxin half-life study was so flawed that attempts to validate exposure from it using blood tests would have "a substantial likelihood" of failure. Weiss and Houk discussed the matter:

Houk: That may have been a personal opinion of his, but was not shared.

Weiss: This is from the senior statistician of the Agent Orange Project to Dan McGee, Director, Agent Orange project, not as a matter of personal opinion. This is a written document. . . .

Houk: I think that is a matter of personal opinion because the dioxin measurement in blood is an extremely well-standardized procedure. . . .

Weiss: So your senior statistician didn't know what he was talking about?

Houk: That's right. My staff are not subjected to review of their internal documents. They are scientists and can state their own opinons

freely. . . . I think he has been proven wrong and I discussed with
him that it would be inappropriate for a senior laboratory scientist
to comment on the inadequacies of a very elegant statistical design
and analysis.[58]

Weiss then turned to a January 1989 report from the CDC Vietnam
Experience Study. The report, Weiss said, stated that Vietnam veterans
in that study had lowered sperm counts and a higher incidence of abnormal sperm cells than their controls. The CDC concluded that this could
not have been attributable to Agent Orange since so few troops had been
exposed to the herbicide. Weiss quizzed Houk about these findings:

Weiss: You found that exposure assessment could not be done, not that
           veterans had not been exposed to the herbicide; isn't that so?
Houk: No. The few veterans there were of Army ground troops that were
           exposed would make the numbers of people who had abnor-
           malities in their sperm counts very highly unlikely due to Agent
           Orange.
Weiss: So it is your position now that the study was not cancelled because
           you couldn't in fact assess exposure but that it was canceled be-
           cause the troops were not exposed?
Houk: It was not done. We could not do a scientifically valid study for two
           reasons. One, we could not use the military records to assess
           exposures. . . . And from what we found in the validation study,
           exposures would be too few to be able to get a big enough cohort
           together to do them. . . .
Weiss: Not that there was not sufficient exposure.
Houk: That's right.
Weiss: You couldn't assess it.
Houk: That's right.
Weiss: So then again, I ask you, when you say that CDC found that few
           Army ground crews were heavily exposed to dioxin-contaminated
           herbicides, that that's simply not true as a statement; isn't that so?
           That's not what your study found? . . . You found that—
Houk: You could not use military records, yes.
Weiss: . . . OK, so how did that statement get into the report?
Houk: I'll have to take a look at that in the context and submit to you in
           writing.
Weiss: Has the CDC been able to explain in any way why Vietnam veter-
           ans have lowered sperm counts and altered sperm shapes?
Houk: No.[59]

Weiss then addressed the issue of how the AOWG's interpretation of
the CDC findings might have been applied to other federally funded
research. In particular, he had in mind the cancellation of a follow-up

study proposed by the VA after its 1987 research had detected higher levels of cancer among Marines who had served in Vietnam.

> *Weiss:* In a 1987 study of soft tissue sarcoma among Vietnam veterans, the [VA] reported that it had planned to conduct an elaborate computer match of troop movements and Agent Orange spray records, but canceled the computer match because: "An expert government panel has subsequently determined that military records alone could not be used to locate troops. . . ." The expert Government panel it refers to is the Agent Orange Working Group.
>
> *Houk:* I don't believe that. I think it is referring to the subpanel of the Agent Orange Working Group Science Panel. . . .
>
> *Weiss:* So the Science Panel made that determination that it could not be done even though the [VA] reported that it could do it? . . . What would have been wrong with the VA's attempt to conduct a computer match?
>
> *Houk:* If they wanted to do it, nothing.
>
> *Weiss:* But in fact, you turned it down. They cancelled it because of the White House [AOWG] Science Panel saying it wasn't going to work.[60]

Among others testifying at the hearings was former CDC epidemiologist, Dr. Dennis Smith. Smith had joined the CDC in 1984 to work on the Agent Orange study and had remained a member of the Agent Orange research team through 1987. Dr. Smith spoke of the enthusiasm felt by the team during 1984 and of the political problems that quickly engulfed them. His written testimony stated:

> At first, everyone was quite confident that the exposure index could be a good approximation of dosage received by the participants. As we created more complex models, the suspicion arose that we were trying to hide something through more complex exposure scores; to some extent this was true: certain parameters of the higher models could be adjusted to minimize certain effects, maximize other effects. . . . [S]ubtle promotion of certain parameters could markedly affect (or markedly mask) estimation of true exposure.
>
> . . . By December of 1985 I had become quite concerned about what was happening at the Agent Orange Projects: it was evident that the exposure index effort, in which we had devised many different models through the help of many different individuals . . . , was unproductive: there were too many factions that wanted different types of exposure indices, and no one had interest in agreeing with other factions—despite the fact that . . . the exposure indices were quite reasonably correlated with one another.[61]

In oral testimony, Smith claimed that the CDC research team, of which he was a part, made up some data to assess the utility of the "hits" method in determining exposure. Unfortunately, he continued, the fabricated data became intermingled with the actual data, and was mistakenly used in some of CDC's estimations of exposure. He stated:

> There were several data bases of troop locations. There were true sets of points in those data sets and there were falsified sets of points. The reason we had the falsified sets of points was so we could test out the models that we were using—our exposure models. But, at one point, people lost track of what was true and what was false.
>
> To this day I believe that what was done in the adipose tissue study was based on some of the data points that were put in for convenience.[62]

Dr. Smith also testified that the decision to track troop movements near spray swaths using battalions—units of 1,000 men rather than company-sized units of 200 men as called for in the original study protocol—had been made prior to exhausting the possibilities of using company data. Smith had been the person at the CDC who received the Department of Defense data on troop movements from Richard Christian. He told the subcommittee that the data supplied by Christian to the CDC were more than adequate to make a determination of troop movements on a company basis. The change to battalion level in tracking troop movements had the effect, Smith stated, of washing out the effect of exposure in the study. He also criticized the CDC's assumption that dioxin had a half-life of seven years in interpreting the use of blood samples, and contended that there was a great deal of discussion about this in the research team. He said he expressed his concerns to higher-ups in writing several times, but received "very little response."[63] Concerning the trend in these decisions and the assumptions concerning dioxin in the blood, Smith concluded:

> I think the purpose of those assumptions was to defeat the concept that they could complete the scientific study—yes—in that many words. And that was the reason that it was scientifically impossible.[64]

Dr. Phillip Landrigan, the Director of Environmental and Occupational Medicine at Mt. Sinai School of Medicine in New York and a consultant for the CDC throughout the Agent Orange studies, listened to the testimony of the witnesses who spoke prior to his appearance. When his turn came to testify, he told the committee:

> Quite frankly I find the events which have transpired today to be sad. I served with pride in the U.S. Public Health Service. I look back fondly on

220 Benefit of the Doubt

my 15 years in the CDC. I came in through an elite group at CDC which was called the "Epidemic Intelligence Service," the group which has been described again and again by people like Berton Rouche in his book "Eleven Blue Men." This group has stamped out smallpox, tracked Legionnaire's Disease, eradicated measles, and controlled rubella.

I find it very sad that the Centers for Disease Control, the agency which invented the term "shoe leather epidemiology," a term which is supposed to imply that CDC investigators literally wear out the soles of their shoes in the pursuit of epidemiologic truth, has failed in this case to exert themselves to find the truth in [the case of] Vietnam [veterans].[65]

A Presumption of Service Connection

The DVA Advisory Committee on the Health-Related Effects of Herbicides—directed by DVA Secretary Derwinsky to review the scientific literature and provide him with policy recommendations—began with non-Hodgkin's lymphoma. The committee was made up of researchers from various backgrounds. Whatever their preferences about what the policy ought to be concerning the Agent Orange claimants, they knew that their actions would come under intense scrutiny.

The committee collected more than ninety studies and reports which considered the relationship between non-Hodgkin's lymphoma and herbicides containing 2,4,5-T or 2,4-D.[66] The committee proceeded on an informal, ad hoc basis. It divided up the studies among its members and instructed them to review the assigned research, assess its validity, and summarize the findings. On the basis of these reviews, the committee divided the studies into four categories: valid positive (the study is scientifically sound and reports a link between the chemical and non-Hodgkin's lymphoma); valid negative (sound study but finds no link between the herbicide and the disease); valid inconclusive (sound study with inconclusive findings); and invalid (scientifically useless study). The committee classified four of the studies as valid positive, fourteen as valid negative, and eleven as valid inconclusive. The rest, they concluded, were invalid.

Following the stipulations in Judge Henderson's ruling, Derwinsky directed the committee to assess the literature for "statistical association." This criterion required an "observed coincidence in variations between exposure to the toxic substance and the adverse health effects [that] is unlikely to be a chance occurrence or happenstance." In other words, the committee was to determine if the incidence of non-Hodgkin's lymphoma among research subjects was consistently greater than expected by chance alone. This standard was considerably less strict than the "cause and effect" relationship used earlier by the DVA for

Agent Orange claims. Derwinsky's instructions asked the committee to make a judgment about the likely effect of the herbicide's compounds on human health. The committee wrestled with the criteria and semantics for making such a decision. Would the presence of one valid positive suffice? Would the number of valid positive studies have to outweigh the number of valid negative ones? How would they assign weights to the relative merit of the studies?

The commitee met on October 31, 1989, to reach a conclusion. In a public meeting, committee members fumbled about for some consensus over the association between the herbicide compounds and non-Hodgkin's lymphoma. Oklahoma Agent Orange Foundation director Mike Sovick, who attended the meeting, recalls:

> Dr. [Theodore] Colton . . . said that the committee [did] not have the expertise in a half-day to balance all the studies in a public hearing. . . . The committee staff person, Fred Conway, suggested that [they go] with . . . their gut reactions. . . . Dr. [James] Whitlock said [there are] "no animal data [but] maybe there is an association." Dr. [Warren] Sinclair used the words "could not rule out an association." . . . Dr. [George] Lathrop said there was "no evidence" of an association. Oliver Meadows, who was chair of the full committee, [proposed a] "nonassociational" [conclusion]. Colonel [Eileen] Bonner said that an association was "not likely." Dr. Colton's gut reaction was that he was "not convinced" of an association. Dr. [James] Neel was not present, but he left a note and his note, the essence of his note, was "it is as likely as not there is an association."
>
> Then a vote was taken. There were two positives and three votes against. (Five of the nine members voted; two asserted there is an association and three concluded there is not) . . . If you take the Neel vote and add it in, then you essentially have no consensus . . . , three-to-three.[67]

After more cautious discussion, the committee crafted a statement that expressed their lack of a consensus. One of them scrawled the decision on the meeting room blackboard and then xeroxed a handwritten copy for distribution to observers at the hearing. In its entirety, it read:

> The Committee does not find the evidence sufficient at the present time to assert (the word "assert" was marked through and replaced by the word "conclude") that there is a significant statistical association between exposure to p.oxy.h. (phenoxy herbicides) and NHL (non-Hodgkin's lymphoma). However, the committee cannot rule out such an association either. (parenthetical information added)

The committee had kicked the decision back to Derwinsky, who now could rule either way.

On November 24, 1989, Derwinsky announced that although he wished to resolve the matter quickly, he would await the outcome of the CDC Special Cancers study, due to be completed by the spring of 1990, before making a final decision on non-Hodgkin's lymphoma. "It is logical," he said in a statement released to the press, "to wait a few extra months for the results of the CDC study." Representatives of several veterans groups reacted angrily. "Sufficient studies have already been conducted," declared Miles Epling, commander of the American Legion, "It's time for action. . . . Based on our previous experience with the CDC, any study generated by them would be suspect in our minds."[67]

The CDC's findings were ready by March 29, 1990. The study assessed the incidences of six types of cancer among subjects who were Vietnam veterans and those who were not. CDC officials announced that they had found a higher incidence of non-Hodgkin's lymphoma among Vietnam veterans in the study than among their controls. Among Vietnam veterans, the rate of non-Hodgkin's lymphoma was 1.5 per 10,000 and, for the control group, 1.0 per 1,000. "We more or less rule out chance," Daniel Hoffman, assistant director of CDC's Center for Environmental Health, explained to reporters, "We think it's a true increase, but the reason for it, we don't know." Secretary Derwinsky wasted little time pondering the findings. The DVA, he announced to reporters, would extend a presumption of service connection to those Vietnam veterans suffering from non-Hodgkin's lymphoma. "Remember, this is a kinder, gentler administration," he said, "So our assumptions are more liberal."[68]

DVA's Committee on the Health-Related Effects of Herbicides meanwhile was pondering a second set of studies, this time dealing with soft-tissue sarcoma—cancers found in muscle and connective tissues. Seeking to avoid the delay and the near-miss that characterized the committee's recommendation on non-Hodgkin's lymphoma, Admiral Elmo Zumwalt, Jr., in his capacity as special advisor to Derwinsky, decided to be more aggressively involved in these deliberations. He had reviewed the scientific literature himself, and the problem now, he felt, was not one of science but of bureaucratic inertia. Zumwalt explains:

> First, I've been a part of the government long enough to know how the bureaucracy fights against unfavorable determination. So I give very little weight to what the Veteran's Administration has said or to what the Centers for Disease Control has said. I know that their institutional bias is to never admit that the government errs.
>
> . . . The generic problem, I think, is one that includes not only Agent Orange and the atomic tests, but also I would add to it others such as our

treatment of our Japanese Americans in World War II. And that is that it takes a long, long time to persuade a government to admit a mistake. It took us 50 years nearly in the case of our Japanese citizens. It took us a quarter of a century in the case of the atomic tests. And it may take us that long in the case of Agent Orange.

. . . You know, interestingly enough, such exotic diseases as MS (multiple sclerosis) are presumed to be service connected, even though there isn't a shred of medical evidence to establish that. The difference being that the government doesn't have anything to defend and the numbers are so small that it is not a cost factor. One of our big problems here is in the Bureau of the Budget's reluctance to see these additional costs.[69]

Admiral Zumwalt addressed the committee. He criticized their earlier deliberations on non-Hodgkin's lymphoma as lacking any consistent set of standards or epidemiological principles for ordering and evaluating the studies. He spelled out for the committee a formal, step-by-step process for evaluating the studies and providing policy recommendations. He prepared a summary from a special report he had prepared for Derwinsky. Zumwalt's report reviewed a wide range of studies and named twenty-eight conditions, mostly cancers, including soft-tissue sarcoma, which he felt ought to be service connected. To keep the heat on the committee, Zumwalt then held a news conference to make public his views.[70]

The committee's ruling this time was more straightforward: it ruled that those exposed to dioxin are more likely than not at a greater risk of developing soft-tissue sarcomas. On May 19, 1990, Derwinski accepted the committee's recommendation and provided a presumption of service connection to Vietnam veterans having soft-tissue sarcomas. Senator Thomas Daschle hailed the decision as "a major victory—one that Vietnam veterans have awaited for a long time." "I hope this is the beginning of the end of the ordeal Agent Orange victims have suffered," he said.[71]

Epilogue

On August 9, 1990, the House Committee on Government Operations released its offical report on the hearings held by Rep. Ted Weiss and the Subcommittee on Human Resources and Intergovernmental Relations. The executive summary of the report asserted that the White House Agent Orange Working Group (AOWG) and the Office of Management and Budget (OMB) had acted to quash both congressional legislation to compensate Agent Orange claimants and the CDC Agent Orange study mandated by Congress. By 1990, these were not new allegations. What was new to the public was the documentation provided in the report, which established the who, the what, and possibly the why for these actions.

The report showed that the focus of AOWG, established under President Jimmy Carter, changed under the Reagan administration. The White House by this time, the report said, had become fearful that the federal government would be liable for expensive compensation payments, not only to Vietnam veterans but also to civilian victim groups in the United States who had been exposed on the homefront to the same chemical compounds used in the manufacture of Agent Orange. These concerns were expressed in a series of memos unearthed by the House Committee. For example, on December 6, 1983, Mike Horowitz of OMB wrote a memo to Attorney General Edwin Meese. Horowitz stated that proposals before Congress to compensate Agent Orange claimants and veterans of the Second World War exposed to radiation "have enormous fiscal implications, potentially in the hundreds of billions of dollars. . . . It is therefore extremely important that we organize our position and response. . . ."[72]

A second memo on January 17, 1984, from Horowitz to David Stockman, President Reagan's budget director, said of Rep. Thomas Daschle's proposed legislation:

> The bill will make it far more difficult to stop broader victims compensation schemes involving hazardous wastes and substances. Dioxin—the toxic ingredient in Agent Orange—is a major issue in this area (Love Canal and Times Beach are largely dioxin exposure cases); we will be in the tenuous position of denying dioxin exposure compensation to private citizens while providing benefits to veterans for in many instances lower levels of exposure. (parenthetical material in original quote)[73]

Likewise, on February 6, 1984, Horowitz warned Edwin Meese of the sticky political problems raised by the requests for compensation by the "atomic veterans" of World War II:

> Many residents near test sites received cumulative exposures far in excess of the single doses to which veterans were exposed. These residents will undoubtedly demand compensation for these far greater levels of cumulative exposure. . . . The bill will certainly be used by anti-nuclear extremists as providing credibility for their alarmist claims on the dangers to the public from nuclear weapons facilities, nuclear reactors, transportation of nuclear materials, underground testing etc. This may have serious national security ramifications.[74]

The report also provided several exchanges between OMB and the White House concerning the CDC Agent Orange study. For example, Sarah Ducich of OMB sent Debbie Steelman of the White House staff a memo on July 18, 1986. The CDC at the time was pondering the study protocol for linking the "hits" method exposure index with blood tests for dioxin. Ducich wrote to the White House:

> The decision should take into account the legal implications of the blood test (the risks associated with testing individuals and the potential that claims against the government would be made by individuals who have higher than "normal" dioxin levels in their blood). I have discussed these issues briefly with Justice attorneys who would be available to evaluate the pilot study proposal for legal risks. Any evaluation should be done prior to the next AOWG meeting so that the information may be used in the decision on the pilot study.[75]

Ducich's memo—written before the CDC had finalized the protocol for the study—cautioned that "it is important that testimony and other public comments not associate the measurement of dioxin in blood with causation." It also urged the White House to contact the director of the CDC and encourage him to "be explicit that developing a measure of dixoin content in blood is neither a link to cause of exposure nor proof of a cause and effect relationship between dioxin and disease."[76]

The dissenting opinion by House committee members rejected the thrust and particulars of the report. The rebuttal read in part:

> After subpoenaing virtually every imaginable document prepared, reviewed or witnessed by the White House regarding Agent Orange, the most the Committee Report can tell us is that the White House opposed legislation which presumed that simple exposure alone to Agent Orange constituted a service-connected disability meriting compensation. We are then asked to believe that this opposition provided the impetus for its plot to cover up the truth about Agent Orange. This conclusion is simply not supported by the facts. . . . [T]he practical effect of the White House's legislative position was to oppose spending billions of tax dollars to compensate for an event that virtually no scientist has linked to long-term disabilities.
>
> . . . We suspect that the real motivation behind the . . . Subcommittee Chairman's zealous attack on the White House is to lay the groundwork for his final recommendation and real goal: writing Republican Presidents out of the Constitution. By recommending that all scientific research conducted in the future be done independently from the White House or other "political" organizations, this goal is made clear.[77]

Meanwhile, on March 9, 1990, Vietnam Veterans of America (VVA) had partitioned itself into two separate entities: the VVA Foundation, consisting of Bobby Muller and a handful of compatriots with whom he had founded the organization some ten years earlier, and VVA, the 30,000 member organization headed by its elected president, Mary Stout. The split represented the culmination of a divide that had existed from the origins of VVA as a membership organization in 1979. Simply put, Muller and the founders had a very different orientation toward the tasks at hand than the Vietnam veterans attracted as members to the organization. Perhaps nothing captured the disagreement between them better than the trip to Hanoi in 1981 by a VVA delegation. Muller saw America's policy in Vietnam as flawed and sought healing through reconciliation with his former enemies; the bulk of VVA'a membership renounced the overtures to Hanoi as an extension of antiwar politics. Muller wished to pursue these foreign policy issues, and most of the membership wanted to focus on Agent Orange and POW/MIA issues. The separation of founding fathers from the membership organization allowed each to pursue its own path.

Muller by this time had made a number of trips to Vietnam and a visit to the "killing fields" of Cambodia. It was time, he thought, for Vietnam veterans to move beyond their experience in war to its implications for the future. He states:

Our first trip, in 1981, was the first trip of Vietnam veterans going back. . . . It was a tremendous, tremendous experience. To be able to go back. People got a little bit upset about it but fuck them. . . . One of the things the [VVA] Foundation [has been doing] is providing sponsorship for these trips. Basically in 99 percent of the cases, guys came back from there, returned from Vietnam, incredibly advanced on a personal basis. There is no better therapy in the world. It's incredible. . . . On a personal basis, have you gone back?

[I answered "no."]

You really ought to . . . , you should. And I would just urge you if go back, go to Cambodia. Because as much as Vietnam was, you know, its own story, nothing changed life, I don't think, like Cambodia did. That is incredible. Genocide is an experience which is on a totally different order from a war. And as mind-boggling as it was to go to the killing fields and have, you know, 10,000 skulls in one area piled up, and went through these fields with bones, bones, bones, you know, I'm rolling around in my wheelchair in bones! I'm crushing them underneath here. [Muller points to the wheels of his wheelchair.] It's just fucking mind-boggling. The torture center put a chill in me the way nothing has. You see the racks, these torture devices, with blood stains still on them and on the floor. Pictures of everything that was done. Mind blowing.

The most affecting part of the trip was meeting people. And in their eyes, recognizing an entire society. . . . You really ought to go back. You really ought to go back. I telling you, it's . . . you know, aside from everything else, when you think of Vietnam, you're thinking of it from the context of what your reference points are. You know, whatever images, et cetera, from your own [tour in Vietnam]. You go back, and you totally replace it. With a whole new set of feelings and images and thoughts. You recognize . . . [pause].

And the people will love you. You know, you realize right away that the war was fought for the hearts and minds of the people, right? It's the Americans whose hearts and minds are captive to the Vietnam experience! Not the Vietnamese! [laughs] Oh, this was long ago in history. Hey, this is just another page. It was just another page. Between the French, huh? The Japanese, huh? The Chinese . . . [laughs] It was just another fucking page! Just another page! You know, Hey, you're American, how are you? You know? You understand?[78]

Notes

1. Richard Severo and Lewis Milford, *The Wages of War: When America's Soldiers Came Home—From Valley Forge to Vietnam* (New York: Simon and Schuster, 1989), 403.
2. Ibid., 396.
3. Richard Christian, personal interview with author, 15 January 1991, Washington, D.C.
4. Severo and Milford, *The Wages of War*, 405.
5. Christian, personal interview, 15 January 1991.
6. Ibid.
7. Severo and Milford, *The Wages of War*, 408.
8. Christian, personal interview, 15 Janaury 1991.
9. Severo and Milford, *The Wages of War*, 408.
10. Ibid., 409.
11. Iver Peterson, "Study of Effects of Agent Orange on Veterans is Stalled in Dispute," *New York Times*, 19 May 1986, A1, A19.
12. Ibid.
13. Michael Gough, *Dioxin, Agent Orange: The Facts* (New York: Plenum, 1986), 93–94. Also, Michael Gough, personal interview with author, 8 March 1989, Washington, D.C.
14. "Researchers Report Finding Telltale Sign of Agent Orange," *New York Times*, 18 September 1986, A28.
15. Phillip Shabecoff, "Herbicide Exposure Linked to Greater Risk of Cancer," *New York Times*, 20 August 1986, A5. See also Sheila Hoar et al., "Agricultural Herbicide Use and Risk of Lymphoma and Soft-Tissue Sarcoma," *Journal of the American Medical Association* 256 (1986):1141–1147.
16. Linda Martin, "Herbicide for Lawns is Linked to Cancer," *New York Times*, 20 October 1986, C5.
17. Ibid.

18.   Ben Franklin, "Veterans of Vietnam Found to Have High Death Rates," *New York Times*, 11 February 1987, A20.

19.   "Dioxin Levels Found in Vietnam Veterans Termed Not Unusual," *New York Times*, 25 July 1987, A8.

20.   Phillip Boffey, "Lack of Military Data Halts Agent Orange Study," *New York Times*, 1 September 1987, A1, C5.

21.   Ibid.

22..   Phillip Boffey, "Cancer Deaths High for Some Veterans," *New York Times*, 4 September 1987, A10. See also Patricia Breslin et al., "Proportionate Mortality Studies of U.S. Army and U.S. Marine Corps Veterans of the Vietnam War," *Journal of Occupational Medicine* 30 (1988):412–419.

23.   Lawrence Hobson, telephone interview with author, 22 March 1989, Washington, D.C.

24.   Severo and Milford, *The Wages of War*, 412.

25.   Warren Leary, "Vietnam Veterans' Health: No Worse than Others," *New York Times*, 13 November 1988, A13. See also *Journal of the American Medical Association* (1988).

26.   House Committee on Goverment Operations, *Oversight Review of CDC's Agent Orange Study*, Hearings before the Subcommittee on Human Resources and Intergovernmental Relations, 1st sess., 11 July, 1989 (Washington, D.C.: U.S. Government Printing Office), 130.

27.   "New Doubts Raised on Agent Orange," *New York Times*, 23 March 1988, A19. See also Richard Albanese, *United States Air Force Personnel and Exposure to Herbicide Orange* (Brooks Air Force Base, Tex.: USAF School of Aerospace Medicine, 1988).

28.   Senator Thomas Daschle, "Agent Orange: The Air Force Does It Again," *Congressional Record—Senate* (Washington, D.C.: U.S. Government Printing Office, 9 March 1990), S2550. This document contains the full summary of Sen. Daschle's contention of wrongdoing by Air Force investigators.

29.   Donald Newman, "Clearance of All Studies and Press Releases by the Domestic Policy Council Agent Orange Working Group," 1 April 1988. Obtained from Senator Daschle's office.

30.   Laura Petrou, "Newman Memo to Members of the Agent Orange Working Group," 7 June 1988. Obtained from Senator Daschle's office.

31.   Ben Franklin, "Study Finds Vietnam Combat Affecting Veterans' Health," *New York Times*, 12 November 1988, A7. See also the entire issue of *Environmental Research* 47 (1988), especially, Steven Stellman, Jeanne Stellman, and John Sommer, Jr., "Combat and Herbicide Exposures in Vietnam among a Sample of American Legionnaires," 112–128; Jeanne Stellman, Steven Stellman, and John Sommer, Jr., "Social and Behavioral Consequences of the Vietnam Experience among American Legionnaires," 129–149; and Steven Stellman, Jeanne Stellman, and John Sommer, Jr., "Health and Reproductive Outcomes maong American Legionnaires in Relation to Combat and Herbicide Exposure in Vietnam," 150–174.

32.   House Committee on Goverment Operations, 158–159.

33.   Ibid.,

34.   Ibid.,

35.   Ibid., 184–185.

36.   Ibid., 187.

37.   "Derwinsky Confirmed as Veterans' Secretary," *New York Times*, 3 March 1989, A26.

38. Colonel Alvin Young, personal interview with author, 6 March 1989.

39. See Nehmer v. U.S. Veterans Administration, 712 F. Supp. 1404, 1418 (N.D. Cal., 1989).

40. Veterans' Dioxin and Radiation Exposure Compensation Standards Act, Public Law 98–542, October 24, 1984, 98 Stat. 2727. Quoted from Admiral Elmo Zumwalt, Jr., *Report to the Secretary of the Department of Veterans Affairs on the Association between Adverse Health Effects and Exposure to Agent Orange*, May 5, 1990.

41. "Victory: VVA Wins A/O Judgment," *Veteran* 9 (June, 1989): 6.

42. Ibid., 11.

43. Ibid., 22–23.

44. Ibid., 23.

45. Elmo Zumwalt, Jr. and Elmo Zumwalt III, with John Pekkanen, *My Father, My Son* (New York: McMillian, 1986). See also Zumwalt and Zumwalt, "Agent Orange and the Anguish of an American Family," *New York Times Magazine*, 24 August 1986, 32–40, 49, 58.

46. Zumwalt and Zumwalt, "Agent Orange," 36.

47. Admiral Elmo Zumwalt, Jr., telephone interview with author, 4 April 1989, Alexandria, Virginia.

48. Admiral Zumwalt, telephone interview, 4 April 1989.

49. Zumwalt and Zumwalt, "Agent Orange," 36–37.

50. Admiral Zumwalt, telephone interview, 4 April 1989.

51. Zumwalt and Zumwalt, "Agent Orange," 38.

52. Ibid.

53. Petrou, personal interview with author, 28 March 1991, Washington, D.C..

54. House Committee on Goverment Operations, *Oversight*, 2.

55. Ibid., 49.

56. Ibid., 50–51.

57. Ibid., 54, 58.

58. Ibid., 59, 67.

59. Ibid., 68–69.

60. Ibid., 70–71.

61. Ibid., 89–90, 92.

62. Ibid., 104.

63. Ibid., 105.

64. Ibid., 108.

65. Ibid., 223.

66. Notes and transcripts of the meeting were made available to me by Michael Sovick, Oklahoma Agent Orange Foundation.

67. Michael Sovick, personal interview with author, 1 December 1989, Norman, Okla.

68. Bill McAllister, "VA Chief Delays Decision on Agent Orange Claims," *Washington Post*, 25 November 1989, A3.

69. Susan Okie and Bill McAllister, "CDC Finds No Linkage of Agent Orange, Cancer," *Washington Post*, 29 March 1992, A10.

70. Admiral Zumwalt, Jr., telephone interview, 4 Arpil 1989.

71. Bill McAllister, "Agent Orange Linked to 28 Diseases, Zumwalt Says," *Washington Post*, 17 May 1990: A4.

72. Bill McAllister, "U.S. Revises Agent Orange Stance," *Washington Post*, 19 May 1990, A5.

73.   House Committee on Government Operations, *The Agent Orange Cover-up: A Case of Flawed Science and Political Manipulation*, Twelfth Report, together with Dissenting Views. Report 101–672, August 9, 1990 (Washington, D.C.: U.S. Government Printing Office), 28.

74.   Ibid.

75.   Ibid., 29.

76.   Ibid., 31.

77.   Ibid.

78.   Ibid., 41–42.

79.   Robert Muller, personal interview with author, 27 March 1991, Washington, D.C.

9

TOWARD A SOCIOLOGY OF
VETERANS' ISSUES

Like veterans of previous wars, Vietnam veterans had pressing, immediate needs in readjusting to civilian life. To remedy this, leaders among
them and their allies formed organizations to articulate the problems,
energize constituent groups, and extract concessions from relevant power structures. They were opposed by others reluctant or unwilling to
concede to them. Such is the nature of social movements, namely, challenges to existing arrangements or beliefs. Social movements often encounter resistance, and struggles ensue among protagonists and
antagonists for material and cultural dominance. In this chapter, I will
detail the sociological thinking that led me to tell the story of "Vietnam
veterans since the war" in the manner that I did, and to develop the
implications of this story for understanding social movements in general
and veterans' issues in particular.

The Social Construction of Science

The story of Vietnam veterans presented in this book is not typical
sociological fare. Most sociologists would probably say that the style in
which I have recounted the story is neither sociological nor scientific. I
take exception to this charge. I consider myself a sociological storyteller,
a label that calls for some explanation. What does the telling of stories
have to do with sociology, and how does it square with sociology as a
science? Answering these questions requires a review of what science is
and how it fits into the scheme of sociological work.

To begin with, virtually all sociologists consider sociology to be a
science. Most of them think so because of the methods used in generat-
ing sociological knowledge. A clear majority of sociologists are "positivists" or "modernists." This means they assume that the world,
including the social world, operates according to natural laws that await
discovery by competent, impartial observers. According to this view,

231

scientists, whether of the social or physical variety, attempt to detect the regularities in and construct theories about the phenomena of interest to them. They derive hypotheses from these theories that they then test with systematically collected data. The purpose is to develop theories that correspond as identically as possible to the inherent patterns of the natural and social world. Unfortunately, the term *positivism* in sociology also is more narrowly associated with quantitative research using computerized statistical analyses, the more abtruse the better.

Storytelling is not necessarily incompatible with positivism, but in practice it clearly is. I therefore associate storytelling with a different view of sociology and science. To select from one of several applicable labels, storytelling is an artifact of the constructivist perspective within sociology. Other terms compatible with the constructivist perspective, at least in spirit and direction, are *postmodernism, deconstructionism, ethnomethodology and the documentary method,* and *reflexive sociology.*[1] Sociologists Malcolm Spector and John Kitsuse first advanced the constructivist approach for the study of social problems, and constructivist Naomi Aronson, among others, detailed how this perspective contains an alternative view of how science works.[2] What these approaches share is a critique of the principles of positivism, arguing instead that scientific facts themselves are socially constructed. Unlike positivists, who think the crucial relationship in science is between observer and the world's objective regularities, these sociologists argue that the crucial relationship lies among scientists themselves and others interested in their claims.

The sociology of knowledge approach to science, known in some sociological circles as the "strong programme," has varied historical influences but may be traced in recent times to historian Thomas Kuhn's work, *The Structure of Scientific Revolutions.*[3] Kuhn argued that the status of any scientific theory depends upon the presence or absence of successful social movement activity by its adherents. Aronson writes of this position:

> [C]laims-making is the essence of scientific work. As individuals, or even research teams, scientists cannot make discoveries, they can only make claims to discovery. For a claim actually to count as a discovery, other scientists must accredit it by recommending that it be published in a reputable journal and by citing it in their own articles. . . . [N]o matter how personally compelling the insights of an individual researcher, only the scientific community can judge the validity of his or her contribution to the advance of knowledge.
>
> . . . Successful claims-making, in both the social and scientific arenas, involves—at the very least—skilled documentation, the ability to command the attention of the appropriate audiences, and access to resources needed to defend claims against criticism. Indeed . . . successful scien-

tists, rather than conforming to the . . . norm of disinterestedness, display a tenacious attachment to their ideas—not unlike, perhaps, the zeal of a moral reformer.[4]

Constructivists themselves are not of a single mind. Sociologist Joel Best has identified two groups within the constructivist camp: "Contextual" constructivists see it as their prerogative to pass judgment on the claims and activities of claims makers; "strict" constructivists, on the other hand, confine themselves to reporting claims making without comment on how "true" they are.[5] This simple distinction belies an enormous epistemological divide between the two—and more generally, between positivists and proponents of the "strong programme"—and carries far-reaching implications for how their analyses ideally should be done. The key epistemological issue concerns whether one can know the world or only socially constructed versions of it, and may be debated endlessly.

As a contextual constructivist with only a passing interest in this debate, I suggest a pragmatic solution. Proceed with the insight that individual scientists do not work in a social vacuum. Recognize that they make claims to others about things they have discovered and that they negotiate with each other about the meaningfulness of these findings. Admit that this is so whether we are talking about how scientists see a psychiatric diagnosis, the greenhouse effect, or cold fusion. In each case, the goal is to move disputed claims along a path toward acceptance as a taken-for-granted fact. This calls for the ability to command the attention and respect of other professionals within one's specialty, and the skills and resources necessary to marshal this effort. Political and personal considerations, rather than interfering with the process, are an unavoidable, integral, and fascinating part of it. It is at this point, potentially at least, that the agendas of the "strong programme" and the constructivists of both stripes converge: The task is to describe in detail the claims and counterclaims of protagonists and antagonists, and to trace the "natural history" of scientific claims from their origin to their later status as accepted facts or discredited theories. This calls for a variety of descriptive strategies, including sociological storytelling.

The positivist platform, because of its close identity with quantitative research, contains at least one plank that devalues and demeans storytelling. Positivists argue that explanation is preferable to description and "mere" storytelling. Description concentrates on the details and nuances of selected observations, whereas explanation strives for summary statements that subsume detail and nuance. The more detail and nuance subsumed, the more powerful the explanation; conversely, the more detail presented, the "mere-er" the story. There is a simple value implicit in this position: Generalized explanation is more desirable than detailed description. One might therefore ask, Why is it desirable to explain anything? As French sociologist Bruno Latour has eloquently argued, explanation is preferable if one seeks "distancing" for purposes of prediction and control.[6] If the purpose is understanding and empathy, then detailed, richly textured description may be equally deserving or even preferable.

Constructivists, of course, are not alone in their preference for "thick" description in sociology.[7] During the first half·of the twentieth century, for example, Robert Park and Ernest Burgess, and sociologists trained by them at the University of Chicago, established the use of case studies and case histories in sociological research.[8] More recently, sociologists such as Barney Glaser and Anselm Strauss, John Lofland, and Norman Denzin have articulated the principles of scientific research for qualitative methods.[9] These sociologists share an emphasis on "grounded theorizing," to use the term provided by Glaser and Strauss, namely, a process of building theory through the intensive use of specially collected descriptive data. These approaches illustrate that one need not force a choice between detailed description and generalized explanation. The desire to produce informed, empirically based generalizations may be a central motive behind thick descriptions and sociological storytelling. It identifies thick description and storytelling as scientific work and distinguishes them from the work of journalists and other storytellers who do not consider their efforts to fall within the realm of science.

So what status does scientific knowledge have? It is at this point that strict constructivists part company with many nonpositivist social scientists. The strict constructivist makes no claim to special, privileged, more valid knowledge.[10] Some contextual constructivists, deconstructionists, and ethnomethodologists (and of course most positivists) have other ideas about this. On this point I side with the strict constructivists. A sociological story told in the constructivist tradition lies on the table as a set of claims for the reader to assess. My story has no privileged status, though I consider it both sociological and scientific. I do not ask ask the reader to believe it because the canons of science lend it legitimacy. The constructivist perspective provided me direction in selecting what to look at and how to write about it. Following theoretical and rhetorical preferences, I have used a variety of tools from my argument chest to draw the reader into the story.[11] Personal experiences fueled my interest and lent intensity. The book contains the story as I, a professional sociologist, understand it. The story's scientific utility lies in its ability to inform the reader about the experiences of Vietnam veterans and the theories of social movements.

A Constructivist Approach to Social Problems

The telling of the story of Vietnam veterans since the war falls within a symbolic interactionist perspective that views social problems as social constructions, a stance developed most notably by Malcolm Spector and John Kitsuse. Their position has two lines of argument: (1) The proper focus of a sociology of social problems is upon the actions and strategies of interested persons and interest groups who seek to certify a condition as a social problem. This removes the sociologist from the role of asserting whether a condition is or is not problematic and shifts the analysis to the social activity surrounding a putative condition. (2) The constructivist approach assumes that there is no necessary connection between how problematic a condition "actually is" and whether people consider it a social problem. For example, people may deny that a "truly problematic" condition is a social problem, or may simply overlook it because no one has brought it to their attention. Hence, a constructivist analysis should identify the protagonists, explore their claims and counterclaims, and reconstruct the sequence of events that make up the life course of a social problem.

This approach marks a departure from "objectivist" or "common-sense" thinking about social problems, which is the standard view among sociologists and probably most segments of the American public as well. "Social problems" is a popular sociology course at most universities, and a goodly number of sociologists assert that "social problems" is one of their areas of professional expertise. Commonly, professional social scientists and lay people alike think of social problems as "problematic conditions." Sociologists who teach social problems focus on some conditions that they claim "really are" problems. Likewise, if respondents of a survey were to state that "unemployment" and "drugs" are our most pressing social problems, most people would say this occurs because the incidence of joblessness and the consumption of illegal narcotics really are on the rise and are creating more hardship than before. Similarly, conditions that really are less pressing, most would say, create less awareness of them as social problems, and that things we no longer consider social problems actually have diminished in seriousness.

Spector and Kitsuse identify two unfortunate consequences of objectivist analyses by fellow sociologists who equate the study of social problems in sociology with the factual existence of problematic conditions:

> First, [sociologists] often mistake their own participation in certifying a small range of claims for a mandate to make authoritative statements in

areas where they have no recognized competence. For example, on what basis can a sociologist claim the authority to comment on the question of the addictive qualities of marijuana or its genetic effects?

Second, they inevitably put themselves in the position of borrowing findings from other disciplines whose reliability and validity they cannot evaluate. Richard Fuller, commenting more than a quarter century ago, saw clearly that this left the sociologist "open to the charge of professional fakery, i.e., the sociologist took his information and ideas from all the other sciences, and then proceeded to pass moral judgments on what ought to be done." His solution was to abandon the pretense that the sociologist "could hold himself out as an authority on everything from technological unemployment to dementia praecox. . . . [The sociologist] need not be an expert on social problems, but an expert on the sociology of social problems."[12]

Constructivists therefore consider claims about social conditions, rather than the conditions themselves, as social problems. Spector and Kitsuse state:

[W]e define social problems as the activities of individuals and groups making assertions of grievances and claims with respect to some putative conditions. The emergence of a social problem is contingent upon the organization of activities asserting the need for eradicating, ameliorating, or otherwise changing some condition. The central problem for the theory of social problems is to account for the emergence, nature, and maintenance of claims-making activity and responding activity.

. . . [T]he significance of objective conditions for us is the assertions made about them, not the validity of those assertions as judged from some independent standpoint. . . . [W]e assert that even the condition itself is irrelevant to and outside our analysis. We are not concerned whether or not the imputed condition exists. If the alleged condition were a complete hoax—a fabrication—we would maintain a noncommittal stance toward it unless those to whom the claim were addressed initiated their own analysis and uncovered it as a hoax.[13]

This statement characterizes the strict constructivist position preferred by Spector and Kitsuse. This stance has come under fire, most effectively perhaps from fellow subjectivists Steve Woolgar and Dorothy Pawluch. They contend that analyses by strict constructivists have an Achilles heel: At their most persuasive, they imply that some "true" conditions—never explicitly stated—vary from those articulated by the claims makers.[14] Joel Best, the principal architect of contextual constructivism, elaborates:

[A] standard constructionist explanation might proceed: although social condition X remained unchanged, X became defined as a social problem when people began making claims about it. . . . Constructionists are careful to identify claims as putative conditions . . . , implying that the nature of social conditions is irrelevant (and perhaps unknowable); yet they typically assume that they know the actual status of the social condition (as an unchanging phenomenon).[15]

Contextual constructivism therefore remains focused on the claims while admitting some knowledge about social conditions. Best explains:

Suppose we study a campaign against "crime in the streets." . . . A strict constructivist might note the claims-makers' references to higher crime rates or rising fear of crime . . . without making any assumptions that there were really increases in crime or the fear of crime. In contrast, a contextual constructionist might look at official crime statistics or polls measuring fear of crime—even if the claims-makers never referred to statistics or polls. Suppose, for instance, that claims-makers campaigned against increasing crime at a time when there was no increase in the crime rate. A contextual constructivist might well choose to make something of the discrepancy between the claims and other information about social conditions.[16]

I wrote this book as a contextual constructivist who draws many insights from the work of Spector and Kitsuse. Illustrations of constructivism's theoretical implications may be found in parts of my story about the health problems of Vietnam veterans. It is useful for purposes of developing these examples to distinguish the terms *disease, illness,* and *sickness.* Disease refers to a condition that impairs bodily functions. The perception that something is wrong is known as illness. Sickness occurs when appropriate medical authorities confirm that an individual has a disease and therefore may legitimately report feeling ill. These distinctions invite the recognition that sickness and its consequences may differ from a person's biological state. Although sickness may have some biological basis, not all diseased people are permitted to act sick and some people who are permitted to act sick are not diseased. In disputes about whether someone is sick, and about the extent and source of the sickness, the assumptions, values, and interests of several institutions come into play. In contemporary society, these include science, health care delivery systems, and the courts. As we have seen, the Veterans Administration (VA), later redesignated, the Department of Veterans' Affairs (DVA), is the health care delivery system and institution empowered to certify the illnesses of veterans as sicknesses.

Two schools of thought are relevant to this characterization of disease, illness, and sickness. The objectivist school presumes that self-evident diseases exist in the "real" world. When these diseases afflict enough persons, the evidence accumulates and invites discovery of such diseases as sicknesses. Though not dismissing political considerations entirely, objectivists believe that the task is methodological: If medical and governmental authorities develop and employ appropriate scientific principles, the facts will emerge and, to a significant extent, speak for themselves. In contrast, the constructivist approach denies any necessary connection between injury and disease and the likelihood of recognition. Here the certification of sicknesses is an inherently political process: Interested persons and interest groups advocate ideas about what is problematic, focus on certain kinds of evidence, and use available resources to establish claims. Constructivists contend that interested parties must work diligently and effectively to elevate disputed claims to the status of taken-for-granted fact. If no such parties emerge, or if interested parties are ineffective, the claims simply remain disputed.[17]

The description in Chapters 2 and 3 of the placement of post traumatic stress disorder (PTSD) in the American Psychiatric Association's *Diagnostic and Statistical Manual* (*DSM-III*) allows us to see the politics of diagnosis and disease in an especially clear light. PTSD is in *DSM-III* because a core of psychiatrists and Vietnam veterans worked consciously and deliberately for years to put it there. They ultimately succeeded because they were better organized, were politically active, and enjoyed more lucky breaks than their opposition. At issue here was the question of what constitutes the normal experience or reaction of soldiers to combat. *DSM-II* subsumed emotional distress during and after combat under the psychiatric syndromes of depression, alcoholism, and schizophrenia. Clinicians agreeing with this position regarded a soldier's combat experiences as incidental to a syndrome's onset and later treatment. Other psychiatrists departed from the offical diagnoses available in *DSM-II*. They identified the same symptoms in combat veterans as "war neurosis' or "post-Vietnam syndrome." These working diagnoses called for the clinician to take seriously the patient's combat experience. This orientation shifted the focus of the disorder's cause from the particular details of the individual soldier's background and psyche to the nature of war itself. Its advocates claimed that soldiers disturbed by their combat experiences were not abnormal; on the contrary, it was normal to be traumatized by the abnormal events of war.

However, if we were to ask these participants to comment on what they did and why they succeeded, they would probably add the the victory was also "just," that the official diagnosis now is "as it should be" because "that is the way it is" in the world of disease and bodily disorder. Their accomplishment, they would say, was to make plain what had not been seen before. In telling the story, I have sought not to adopt an ironic stance toward such a view or to suggest that this diagnosis, and diagnoses in general, are "merely" social constructions or the result of self-interested hegemony. Rather, in telling the story, I contribute another case to those which help us understand in detail how objective knowledge, and medical knowledge in particular, is produced, secured, and subsequently used to create other objective realities, such as, in PTSD, acknowledgment of war's horrors, populations of treated clinical cases of PTSD, and patients entitled to insurance coverage. At no time was the dispute over the question of whether diseases and disorders existed. Instead, it turned on whether one disorder, PTSD, existed and had yet to be discovered.

In the Agent Orange controversy, a small number of Vietnam veterans complained of illnesses of unknown and disputed origin. Civilian medical authorities diagnosed cancers and other disabling or life-threatening conditions. Some veterans sought help from the VA to confirm suspicions that exposure to Agent Orange in Vietnam caused the diseases. This scenario seemed unlikely to VA physicians and costly to VA administrators. Interested parties—the VA, the chemical companies who manufactured the herbicide, and other governmental agencies—assessed the enormous liability potential of the Agent Orange claims and sought to control the developing definition of the problem by discrediting the claimants and overseeing the research. Hence, the inquiries of veterans had no effective representation in the institutional arena that certifies the illnesses of veterans as sicknesses. The issue remained obscure until covered in a television documentary. The WBBM-TV news team operated under different organizational and methodological contraints than those of VA officials. The documentary blurred the distinction between illness and sickness by protraying the veterans' story sympathetically and by revealing the uncertainty in the medical community outside the DVA about Agent Orange's safety.

Latent disorders—diseases in which there is a substantial time lag between exposure and consequence—are especially useful in illustrating the politics of facts and certification. Uncertainty creates special personal, organizational, and political problems.[18] For starters, the time lag between exposure and consequence strains the methods of science, medicine, and law to the point where it is difficult to establish evidence. Simply finding and identifying the victims may be a formidable task. The controversy often becomes a convenient and symbolic medium for venting other anatagonisms. Organizations, communities, and government entities may become embroiled in disputes over blame and responsibility. Interest groups may form as advocates of different kinds of perspectives and evidence. When this occurs, participants may obtain contradictory conclusions by asking the same question in different domains, and conflicts may emerge over whose version will be accepted as true. In the protracted period of suffering and haggling, frustration and delusion may become a prominent feature of protagonists and antagonists alike. The case of Agent Orange encompasses all these considerations.

Theoretical Interpretations of Social Movements

Sociologists use the term *social movements* to refer to organized challenges directed at changing the status quo. "Progressive" social movements seek to introduce new ideas or arrangements or to further ones that have already been initiated; "conservative" movements redirect attention back to previously accepted ideas or arrangements. In general, sociologists think of social movements as political activity that extends beyond the conventional politics associated with elections. For example, social movements often involve efforts to critique existing arrangements and beliefs, energize and politicize potential members, and extract concessions from privileged groups and reluctant power structures. These may include strategies such as court suits, consciousness-raising events, boycotts, demonstrations, and other nonrountine but legal challenges, or may extend to unlawful activities and even violence.

As with other topics discussed in this chapter, there are two basic schools of thought in sociology about the dynamics of social movements. The classical or "strain" perspective—akin to the objectivist approach to social problems and disease—asserts that social movements occur when a flaw in the system—for example, a loss of congruence within a set of social arrangements or between an arrangement and supporting beliefs—harms an identifiable category of persons. As the "strain and pain" reach intolerable proportions, afflicted people band together and demand that something be done about the problem. Social movement participants are drawn together, strain theorists claim, because members of the afflicted category are all affected through a shared link to the source of the strain. Therefore, they may proclaim legitimately that their misfortunes are social problems rather than personal troubles. One may find examples of this position in the works of sociologist Neil Smelser and historian John Higham.[19] Although they may quibble over the details, Smelser, Higham, and other structural strain theorists focus on the origin of the discontent and agree that it lies in the malfunctioning of the social system.

The second school of thought contains a broad spectrum of positions: relative deprivation, rising expectations, resource mobilization, constructivist, and public arenas theories. The single contention unifying these positions is that there is no necessary connection between the harshness of objective conditions and the likelihood of social movement activity. Relative deprivation and rising expectations theorists, for example, observe that the modal responses to extreme hardship are apathy or, at the other extreme, short bursts of violent, nonproductive behavior. Sustained political action occurs, they say, when afflicted persons have hope. Among the deprivation theorists, this takes place as people note their relative, rather than their absolute, disadvantage and impute unfairness. Rising expectations theorists assert that improvements in social conditions raise hopes and thereby increase dissatisfaction, leading in turn to political action.[20] In the former, the perception of injustice and collective action are not tied to how harsh conditions are but to relative comparisons of them; in the latter, political action occurs as conditions improve and hope rises, not when conditions are at their worst.

Resource mobilization, constructivist, and public arenas theories do not focus on the sources or reasons for discontent but rather on the characteristics of issues and groups that may aid or hinder political mobilization. For example, resource mobilization theorist Anthony Oberschall writes:

> The minimum conditions of collective protest are shared targets of hostility . . . augumented . . . by more deeply rooted sentiments of collective oppression, common interests, and community of fate. These minimum conditions give rise . . . to only short-term, localized, ephemeral outbursts and movements of protest such as riots. For sustained resistance or protest an organizational base and continuity of leadership is needed. The organizational base can be rooted in two different types of social structure. The collectivity might be integrated and organized along viable traditional lines based on kinship, village, ethnic or tribal organization, or other forms of community, with recognized leaders and networks of social relations. . . . [Or], the collectivity might have a dense network of secondary groups based on occupational, religious, civic, economic, or special interest associations with leaders . . . and networks of social relations following associational ties. Both of these principles of social organization . . . produce . . . links and sentiments within the collectivity that can be activated for the pursuit of collective goals and the formation of conflict groups.[21]

The point here is that it is much more difficult to mobilize afflicted persons who have few prior associational ties than those who are already affiliated through social networks. In short, strain among the unaffiliated, no matter how intense, is unlikely to produce a viable social movement. Strain is a necessary but insufficient condition.

The necessity of certifying one's point of view moves us squarely into the domain of those who see social problems as social constructions and the products of social movements.[22] Constructivist explanations emphasize the attributes of collective definition over those of collective action favored by resource mobilization theorists. They describe the process through which social problems are identified and through which personal problems become public issues. Problematic conditions, worthy or not, constructivists contend, do not speak for themselves. They require someone to recognize, articulate, and champion them.

Public arenas theory falls within the constructivist approach but urges us to move a step beyond these observations. Developed most extensively by sociologists Stephen Hilgartner and Charles Bosk, this perspective focuses on the arenas within which the struggles take place, the "carrying capacities" of these arenas, and the "surplus compassion" among targets of influence. Hilgartner and Bosk write of their point of departure:

> As a first step to understanding the nature of the process of collective definition, it is necessary to note that there is a huge "population" of potential problems—putative situations and conditions that could be perceived as problems. This population . . . is highly stratified. An extremely small fraction grows into social problems with "celebrity" status, the dominant topics of political and social discourse. . . . The fates of potential problems are governed not only by their objective natures but by a highly selective process in which they compete with one another for public attention and societal resources.
>
> . . . The collective definition of social problems occurs not in some vague location . . . but in particular public arenas . . . [including] the . . . branches of government, the courts, made-for-TV movies, . . . the news media . . . , direct mail solicitations, . . . the research community, . . . professional societies, and private foundations. It is in these institutions that social problems are discussed, selected, defined, framed, dramatized, packaged, and presented to the public.
>
> . . . [E]ach [arena] has a carrying capacity that limits the number of social problems that it can entertain at any one time. . . . [T]he prime space and prime time for presenting problems are quite limited. It is this discrepancy between the number of potential problems and the size of the public space for addressing them that makes competition among problems crucial and central to the process of collective definition.[23]

This approach pays attention not only to the competition for space within arenas of public discourse but also to the limits of compassion among relevant segments of the population. Hilgartner and Bosk argue:

Carrying capacities exist . . . also at the individual level. . . . [M]embers of the public are limited not only by the amount of time and money they can devote to social issues, but also by the amount of "surplus compassion" they can muster for causes beyond the immediate concerns of persons of their social status. "Master statuses" guide people's selections of the social conditions that trouble them; underemployed black males, white male business executives, middle-class white mothers of small children inhabit very different day-to-day realities, and they tend to have differing social concerns. Once the priorities of their master status have been addressed, there may be very little surplus compassion left over for social issues with less personal significance.[24]

Hence, public arenas theory considers a problem in terms of both its own "shelf life" and other issues with which it competes. A problem's shelf life, or natural history, refers to how new or old a formulation it is, how fresh its current packaging is, and how many times its advocates have presented it to relevant segments of the public. Comparisons with other problems note the number of similar claims that, taken together, might constitute a "class" of problem definitions. The number and salience of recognized problems affect the space available for new ones. If space is limited, new claims must displace existing ones or else create new carrying capacities. There often is a curvilinear relationship between exposure and sympathy: Massive or repetitive bombardments initially increase awareness and sympathy, and then tail off in success as compassion fatigue sets in and "dedramatizes" an issue or an entire class of related issues. Likewise, a new and novel claim may sweep aside older, staler problem definitions, and so forth.

The content of problem definitions, not surprisingly, affects the likelihood of their acceptance. Problem definitions that are compatible with broad cultural themes stand a better chance of survival than those that pose fundamental critiques. Sociologist William Gamson refers to this phenomenon as the "strategy of thinking small."[25] Similarly, Hilgartner and Bosk note that sophisticated, subtle analyses travel more poorly than "stock explanations," which tap widely shared and highly stylized political myths.[26] In American society, definitions using individuals as the unit of analysis and asserting individual responsibility for a state of affairs receive easier play than those cast at the group or societal level.

The packaging of themes often is as important as their content. Advocates who find ways to present problem definitions with simple yet captivating imagery are more likely to triumph than those whose claims are substantively compelling but unexciting. Simple dramatic problem definitions also play better on television, whose forte is short, self-contained stories with a high degree of visual impact. Historic events, legal bouts, and individual cases that serve as clear, symbolic distilla-

tions of otherwise complex confrontations are especially useful in per-
suading relevant segments of the public or in focusing institutional review of a problem definition.

We may draw an illustration of the public arenas model from the story
of Vietnam Veterans Against the War (VVAW) presented in Chapter 1.
The period of 1967 to 1972 was one of intense social movement activity.
VVAW came into existence within an already substantial antiwar movement. The antiwar movement jostled with the counterculture movement, the black liberation movement, and the gay liberation movememt
for attention. This cacophony of social movement activity diminished
both the avenues open to VVAW within the arenas of public discourse
and the receptiveness among segments of an American public already
saturated with criticism. Charges and countercharges already clogged
the media with claims about the morality and wisdom of America's
policy in Vietnam. Decision makers and segments of the population
already were divided and committed.

Likewise, the arenas within which Vietnam veterans might potentially
have had standing, the military and the major veterans' organizations—
the American Legion, Veterans of Foreign Wars, and Disabled American
Veterans—were strongholds of support for the war. These organizations
were also hostile toward Vietnam veterans, particularly those who had
misgivings about the war and American policy. Many veterans who had
misgivings nonetheless were reluctant to speak out for fear of devaluing
their service in Vietnam or of being identified with antiwar radicals,
whom they despised. Hence Vietnam veterans and their families proved
to be reluctant targets of mobilization by any organization.

VVAW's claims about the war and America's military policy and conduct in Vietnam flew in the face of prevalent cultural and political
themes. As we have seen, VVAW highlighted combat atrocities and
suggested that Americans uncomfortable with that should bring the war
to an immediate end. Leaders of the antiwar movement, as we saw in
the march on Central Park in 1967 and Dewey Canyon III in 1971, often
were anxious to spotlight veterans willing to protest against the war or,
as we saw in the 1970 Winter Soldier Investigation, to advise and help
them in publicizing war atrocities. Predictably, many segments of the
population responded to these efforts by placing the blame on the individual soldier—the Vietnam veteran and especially the Vietnam veteran
protesting the war—rather than on the war itself.

How successful was this strategy? Clearly, the opinions of Vietnam
veterans did not carry privileged status among important segments of
the population. Psychiatrist Robert Lifton, and later VVAW, presented
"structural critiques" of the war. They argued that the psychological
processes that allow a soldier to do his job in the combat zone—to kill
enemy soldiers—also contain an "atrocity producing capacity," accentu-

ated in this instance by peculiar aspects of the Vietnam war. Reports of atrocities by Vietnam veterans clashed with idealized notions about war among substantial portions of the public. The subtleties of Lifton's argument often were either lost on or rejected outright by many who heard it, and VVAW's antics, especially the use of guerrilla theater, struck many who observed them as unworthy caricatures.

It is instructive here to compare VVAW's efforts in Operation RAW and Dewey Canyon III. In both instances, VVAW's participants relied on their status as veterans to gain exposure and sympathy and hoped this status would confer legitimacy upon their message. Hence, they dressed in remnants of military garb worn in Vietnam, vivdly reenacted atrocities, and provided testimonials for bystanders and the media. Although their route from Morristown, New Jersey, to Valley Forge, Pennsylvannia, has historical significance, it did not lend itself well to involvement in or by the systems of power and persuasion. Very few people heard of Operation RAW although sympathetic reporters for the *New York Times* covered it.

No so with Dewey Canyon III. Staged in Washington, D.C., as the first act of a much larger antiwar demonstration to take place a week later, VVAW quickly grabbed center stage of the nation's capital for itself. For the first time in a protest by VVAW, the status of veteran counted with people that mattered. Since the veterans slept illegally in tents on the mall, there were dramatic encounters and legal turmoil each night about their presence. Sympathetic congressmen and other politicians became involved in the proceedings, provided hearings, and added legitimacy. VVAW probably could not have attracted such sustained attention from the media and powerful people had it held the event anywhere else.

Finally, in Dewey Canyon III, VVAW stumbled onto the single most dramatic moment in its history, the ceremony in which veterans flung onto the steps of the capital their Purple Hearts for wounds received in combat and decorations for valor and meritorious service. The medal turning-in ceremony arguably stands as one of the most poignant symbols of the Vietnam war. The imagery of war veterans hurling their medals back at the government that had awarded them was stark and powerful. VVAW netted very little surplus compassion but, within overburdened arenas of discourse, captured the nation's attention in one dramatic episode.

Veterans as Social Movement Constituencies

Categories of individuals sharing some characteristic in common constitute potential groups, that is, people who may develop group consciousness and engage in collective action. This possibility exists when category members acquire distinctive sets of experiences by virtue of their common location in the social and historical process.[27] A common location limits the range of potential experiences, provides the substance of life events that members do experience, and typecasts the way they experience these events. For instance, draft-age males in wartime form a category that experiences the era's events differently than do females and males who are much younger or older, and those who serve in the military develop additional unique experiences. Members of such categories do not always develop a strong identification with each other, that is, develop group "consciousness," or form active political groups, but the potential to do so is there. Veterans, because they share military service, constitute a potential group. Of course, veterans also are simultaneously members of many additional categories defined in terms of gender, age, race or ethnicity, class, occupation, religion, and other social characteristics and life circumstances. All these traits may compete for a veteran's attention and any of them could become his or her master status.

Under what circumstances is veteran's status likely to become a characteristic around which successful group formation takes place? Theoretical considerations detailed above lead us to anticipate collective action among veterans when their military and war experiences are unique and intense, when veterans as a category also have characteristics that ease organization and mobilization, and when leaders and organizations solve the dilemmas of access, theme, drama, and discourse in public arenas. Sociologists John Modell and Timothy Haggerty have proposed a scheme for assessing the social impact of war that is relevant for our purposes here. They state:

> We propose a . . . framework . . . resting on the proposition that war represents, at once, a temporary reorganization and rejustification of the role structure of the society, and a shuffling (often substantial) of the individuals who occupy those roles. War, of course is far too varied an activity to allow easy sociological generalization. . . . [T]he relevant dimension . . . is the extent to which they ask people in general (and individuals in particular) to become something that they have not previously been. While much interest has focused on the reorganization of personality in the face or war, it ought to be understood in interaction with the less traumatic modification in the role reorganization that war causes. Not only must new members for the military (with particular skills or capacities) be secured from the civilian population, but new, often speedier paths must be devised within the military for filling critical roles that cannot be filled laterally from the civilian population.[28]

Hence, expansions and contractions in the military, particularly in response to war, may draw large numbers of persons, typically males, into military ranks. Once recruits are in the military, intense resocialization usually occurs to reorganize their personalities so that they may fill unaccustomed positions or perhaps perform acts—such as killing other humans—that previously were taboo. Likewise, alterations often take place in the structure and operation of the military and its career trajectories. These changes may be especially typecast if they affect the members of pre-existing groupings—age cohorts, social classes, racial groups, occupational specialties, or military subcultures—more favorably or harshly than others. Similarly, contractions at the end of the war may discharge veterans who find that they have fallen behind their contemporaries who did not serve, or may favor some groups more than others among those who did serve.

Wars and the conduct of them vary tremendously and make classification difficult. However, it is useful to ask if the kind of war fought might affect the formation of groups among its veterans. The French sociologist Bernard Boëne has examined wars with an eye toward their "functional uniqueness," that is, the extent to which their social characteristics call for a military markedly different from civilian organizations.[29] War, he says, may be simply defined as "violence + organization + legitimacy" in the pursuit of political goals. Variations in the conduct of war stem from varying proportions of these components. This is of interest to us because a typology of wars may suggest patterns in the experiences of those who participate in them and hence in the patterns of mobilization among veterans following these wars.

Boëne identifies several schemes for classifying wars and discusses one in detail having three subcategories: "primitive," complex, and abstract or inhibited warfare. He defines primitive wars, which have the archetype of military organization, as ones that employ weapons of limited destructive capability and restrict the violence largely to the combatants themselves.[30] Role expectations here may be simply defined: Rank-and-file combatants should display "a minimum amount of courage" along with generous amounts of "stamina, loyalty and good will"; leaders, in addition, should be competent, poised, and charismatic. Since not all can be, militaries hedge their bets by installing social distance before combat between officers and enlisted personnel "to enhance the former's status and prestige." The military faces at least three organizational imperatives beyond these individual expectations: It must promote conditions that instill cohesion among the combatants, orient primary group dynamics toward common goals, and resolve the practical tasks of resocialization, training, and support. Boëne concludes:

> [T]he dimension of violence is largely dominant here, and calls for an organization . . . that is highly distinctive (especially if the comparison is with contemporary, developed Western societies). . . . [H]owever . . . not

all aspects of military organization in primitive warfare are primarily or exclusively influenced by violence, and therefore mostly without parallel on the outside. Some aspects (planning, coordination, management, legitimation, exchanges with the environment) are oriented to friendly elements . . . and resemble those to be found in civilian organizations. . . . The relative weight of such non-unique social characteristics is inversely related to the proximity of both enemy and danger: they become dominant in base or garrison life.[31]

Complex warfare, to continue the typology, is grander in scope than primitive warfare. It involves significant proportions of the population as participants and may approach "total war," a societal fight to the death where anything goes. As such, civilians often are deliberately attacked and may suffer higher casualty rates than those in the military. Unlike primitive wars, of which one finds examples in past centuries and in the present one, complex wars are found only in modern times. Military organization in the nineteenth century served as a model for emerging civilian administration in France and Prussia and later for all large-scale economic concerns. Boëne asserts:

Armed services . . . pioneered the way which has led to the reign of instrumental rationality now common to nearly all spheres of activity. . . . As a result, military uniqueness . . . tends to decline substantially: the traditional virtues and style of the "primitive" warrior are clearly not much help . . . to military staff personnel. . . . [As] technology becomes a significant factor . . . the proportion of non-exclusively combatant roles, those which have counterparts in civilian life, increases sharply over the long term: in the U.S. Army . . . it rose from 6.8 per cent in the Civil War to 71.2 per cent in Korea.

. . . The influence of technology can be felt by those who are closest to combat: ever more powerful weapons and sustained firepower compel the combatants to scatter and hide on the battlefield, which obviously effects changes in the leadership style. . . . The new . . . "liberal" leadership style . . . reflects a situation in which the leader cannot fully . . . control the performance of his subordinates, and therefore depends on their good will. . . . Beyond a certain threshold of technological and logistic density, the man in uniform is no longer the prime instrument of combat: it is no accident if the trends just described have in most cases manifested themselves in navies and air forces long before they became apparent in armies.[32]

Boëne identifies the third category, abstract or inhibited warfare, with weapons of mass destruction, especially nuclear arms but also chemical and bacteriological arsenals. Here the political return from waging war declines as the risks to winner and loser alike increase astronomically.

Ironically, the superpowers neutralize each other and avoid direct warfare with each other except for primitive wars conducted with or through intermediaries. Faced with the threat of annihilation, nations must devote a large portion of the military to constant readiness as a deterrent to nuclear, chemical, or biological attack. Boëne summarizes the effect on military organization:

> In a nutshell, the dilution of traditional militariness reaches unprecedented levels. The powerful inhibition of actual war by mass-destruction weapons has largely eliminated individual and collective uncertainty, battle hazards and the transgression of civilian taboos: destiny braved, lives lost and lives taken. The "traditional" quality of military life is now only briefly revived during exercises and manoeuvres, the intensity of which cannot always conceal their artificial character. . . .
> Yet military uniqueness cannot, and should not completely fade away. Core elements of it, unparalleled in civilian life, persist: obedience, loyalty . . . , unlimited liability for service, with all the limitations of civil liberties they imply. . . . In these, the permanent and sacred character of the external security function finds expression, heightened rather than weakened in contemporary circumstances.[33]

These observations make clear that the veterans of any conflict are not a homogeneous category and are not likely to form a single group. Internal divides abound between former officers and enlisted personnel, between combat troops and rear-echelon staff, and among military occupational specialties by branch of service. Veterans of different wars, especially of wars that vary in type and in the age cohorts of soldiers who participated, may organize into separate and conflicting groups. However, regardless of the type of war, military organizations have characteristics distinct from those found in civilian organizations: Only in the military does the job description ask participants to fight and, if necessary, to die for the organization. In recognition of this, veterans' organizations at times ask potential adherents to overlook their many other differences and unite in common fraternity.

The politics of veterans' issues associated with the wounds of war includes additional concerns. Soldiers risk injury and death for the nation, and the society cannot easily repay them for this service. Compensation and other benefits recognize this altruism and stand as visible symbols of collective gratitude or even guilt. Nonetheless, veterans of all America's wars have encountered pitfalls in requesting medical treatment and compensation for service-connected injuries and disease. I propose three reasons for this. First, the military in time of war often uses new weaponry and other inventions that have unforeseen consequences. This occurs because technological innovation proceeds more rapidly than the cultural or structural adjustments to them,[34] and because the effects of combat on its participants are poorly understood. The repercussions include unanticipated diseases and injuries that the medical world is ill equipped to handle. Many veterans therefore exhibit illness and injuries that challenge the limits of existing medical knowledge. This may result in an increase in medical innovation and change, the systematic misdiagnosis and improper treatment of veterans' illnesses, or both.

Second, veterans often encounter difficulties more than a year after discharge that nonetheless are caused by experiences or conditions in the military. Latent disorders, as we have seen earlier, are diseases where there is a substantial time lag between the precipitating event and the emergence of debilitating symptoms. These diseases fall outside the criterion of temporal coincidence for service connection and make the determination of cause and effect very difficult. The time lag between exposure and consequence strains the ability to establish evidence. Even in dramatic instances of disease, observers may pose rival explanations for what has occurred with no way to judge among them.

Finally, in the years following a war, conflict often arises as veterans adjust to civilian life and the populace shoulders its debt to veterans. The "free-rider" principle helps explain why this takes place. The principle predicts the likely reactions when the costs of a policy are specific while the benefits are diffuse, or vice versa.[35] Specifically, during wartime, a nation meets military manpower needs through altruistic service by patriotic soldiers. When the war ends, the patriotic service remains "priceless"—that is, the society cannot reimburse the veterans for it at "market value"—but medical care and compensation for veterans carry specific price tags and compete for priority in limited budgets. The veterans are, in a sense, infinitely deserving, while resources are finite. Hence, the certification of sicknesses among veterans—in the constructivist view, an inherently political process in any circumstance—often is bitterly contested as altruistic service clashes with fiscal constraints and political realities.

Vietnam Veterans as Social Movement Constituencies

The scope of the Vietnam war was small compared to World War II. In Bernard Boëne's terminology, the former was a primitive war and the latter a complex one. However, the level of mobilization between 1964 and 1975, the official years of the Vietnam era, was significant. Almost three million men and about seven thousand women served in the

Southeast Asia theater of operation, and another six million served in the military elsewhere during that time. The nine million personnel of the Vietnam era are about three-fourths the roughly thirteen million mobilized during World War II. Perhaps the two most important features of this mobilization were generational. Those asked to serve in Vietnam were the sons and daughters of the World War II generation. Hence, comparisons with World War II were inevitable. Also, because it was a controversial primitive war, not everyone had to respond in order to meet the manpower needs, and not everyone wanted to. There were significant differences in social class between those persons of the same generation who served in Vietnam and those who did not. Unlike World War II, the Vietnam war was one in which those from the lower social classes bore the brunt of the call for service.

Psychologists Joel Brende and Edwin Parson, who specialize in the treatment of war neurosis, assert that the crucial divide here is between "good wars" and "bad wars." The terms reflect the orientation by significant segments of the public about the necessity, justness, purpose, and conduct of a war. Good wars enjoy strong and near unanimous support and sacrifice by segments of the public. Although good wars do not necessarily produce contented veterans, they do have the characteristics that ease a veteran's adjustment to civilian life: The clear sense of mission and purpose provide a compelling context for military service and, afterwards, for making sense of war experiences. Bad wars, conversely, make veterans' readjustment difficult. Brende and Parson state:

> Bad wars are "undeclared" wars; they are wars no one wants to take responsibility for. These are wars that such institutions as the Congress of the United States choose not to sanction fully. . . . In good wars the soldier feels that his is a legitimate mission; what he does in the war is shared symbolically with the entire country. However, in bad wars, what the soldier does in the war falls squarely on his shoulders. He alone bears the burden for killing, for it is unshared, unshareable. . . . [T]he soldier moves through the war experience adrift, and hence without a useful personal perspective that would aid him in formulating and weaving his own "tapestry of meaning."[36]

This good war–bad war distinction reared its head after Vietnam in both institutional and interpersonal activities. For example, the story of Senator Alan Cranston's bill to help Vietnam veterans—discussed in Chapters 2 and 3—lays bare the intergenerational conflicts among veterans of World War II and the Vietnam War. The "Class of '46," as World War II veterans were called, dominated the Department of Veterans Affairs (DVA), Congress's House Committee on Veterans Affairs, and the major veterans organizations. The American Legion, Veterans of

Foreign Wars (VFW), and the Disabled American Veterans (DAV) vigorously opposed this legislation and ensured its defeat on five occasions during the 1970s. The war experiences of World War II and Vietnam veterans differed markedly, as did their opinions about the rightness and wrongness of the Vietnam War and related notions about the "normal" experience of a soldier during and after combat.

Of course, similar divides existed among Vietnam veterans themselves. A 1975 Gallup poll asked a sampling of Vietnam veterans about the justness of the war's purpose. Fifty-one percent said that Vietnam had been a just war. These veterans felt that America's lack of unity in its will to win had botched the war, and they were angry at left-wing politicians and those who had opposed the war. Forty-nine percent felt that American intervention in Vietnam had not been a just war; this group of veterans was angry at right-wing politicians and those who had beaten the drums of war. Although they saw different culprits, both groups of veterans shared one sentiment: They felt betrayed. I suspect that Agent Orange serves as a potent symbolic issue because it taps this theme. Claims about its application in Vietnam and about stonewalling and coverups since then by the DVA, the Centers for Disease Control, and the White House Agent Orange Working Group all imply betrayal of those who fought by the government that they had served.

However, it is the story of the National Vietnam Veterans Memorial, discussed primarily in Chapter 6, that rivets our attention on the good war–bad war distinction. The memorial recognizes that the warriors of an unsuccessful war nonetheless displayed many of the same virtues as the participants in a good war—self-sacrifice, courage, loyalty, and honor. Yet how does a society commemorate an ignominious defeat? Sociologists Robin Wagner-Pacifici and Barry Schwartz have addressed this question and analyzed the National Vietnam Veterans Memorial. They write:

> When the cause of a lost war is widely held to be immoral or at best needless, then, in James Mayo's words, "defeat . . . cannot be forgotten and a nation's people must find ways to redeem those who died for their country to make defeat honorable. This can be done by honoring the individuals who fought rather than the country's lost cause." This commemorative formula . . . has been expressly invoked to justify the marking of the Vietnam War. . . . [Likewise] [w]hen Israeli officials speak in ceremonies occasioned by the Lebanon War, they extol its soldiers in words that are vivid and inspiring. Their remarks on the war are vague and pointless. . . . The dualism of cause and participant is similarly dramatized in the American South. Confederate Memorial Day ceremonies throughout the South vary . . . but one thread unites them all . . . , the determination to honor the Confederate soldier, without mention of seces-

sion and slavery. It was this same principle . . . that President Reagan's supporters invoked to justify his visit to honor Nazi Germany's war dead.[37]

This separation of warriors from their cause is not easily achieved. As Warner-Pacifici and Schwartz ask, "When . . . is tragedy no longer a tragedy? When is a war memorial no longer a war memorial? . . . Is there some essence of 'war memorialness' and can people identify it?"[38] War memorials usually seek to portray the heroic themes of battle in epic dimensions. They achieve this through structures having vertical dominance, grandness of size, and lightness of color. They feature prominent characteristics of the commemorated war and provide realistic depictions of combat. The Vietnam Veterans Memorial, by design, lacks these characteristics. Built below ground level, it simply bears in polished black granite the names of those who died. As we have seen, opposition to its construction centered mainly on this issue: Its opponents sought a memorial of white marble built above the ground with the American flag and words of triumph despite defeat. However, success in building the memorial and in gaining enthusiastic acceptance for it among segments of the population stemmed from its focus on those who served without resolving the politics of why they served.

Many accounts, including some of mine, have emphasized the uniqueness of the problems faced by Vietnam veterans. However, comparisons drawn solely between World War II and Vietnam War may overstate the uniqueness of the Vietnam experience. Journalist Richard Severo of the *New York Times* and attorney Lewis Milford make the case that World War II, with its broad-based support, victorious culmination, and largesse in veterans' benefits, was the exception rather than the rule among our nation's wars.[39] Their point is well taken. For example, Brende and Parson write of World War I returnees:

There are widespread accounts in 1919 of the bitterness of World War I veterans. . . . [These] veterans were bitter toward those who did not serve, toward those employers who were indifferent, and those in government who didn't seem to care. Moreover, they were angry because they had given all they had and had received very little, if anything, in return. They were embittered toward those "happy speech makers" who . . . used the occasion of the war to build their own personal gain and platforms of power. The angry veteran would have found it rather difficult to fight again: "They said, 'The next war, if they want me, they'll have to burn the woods and sift the ashes.'"[40]

Severo and Milford thus argue that World War I and especially the Korean War provide more appropriate control groups for assessing the

Vietnam experience. Korean war veterans, for example, fought in a limited war that ended in a stalemate. A skewed sample of draft-age males
participated, and toward the end of the war, the military used a one-year
rotation system. Military psychiatrists grappled with the problem of
"combat fatigue," and following the war, much attention focused on the
presumed susceptibility of American prisoners of war to "brainwash-
ing." Psychologist (and Vietnam veteran) Robert Fleming concludes a
similar contrast by asserting:

> Little mention has been made of the Korean War and those who fought
> there. If people remember anything, it is most likely the events of the first
> year of the war— . . . the movement of armies up and down the Korean
> peninsula. The last two years were a stalemate in which half as many men
> were maimed or killed as had been in the first twelve months. . . . The
> soldiers called it a "half-ass war"—a war in which hills were taken and
> given back the same day, and men died in a deadly game called "King of
> the Mountain. . . ." The American public, however, cared little about
> what was happening there. . . .

> Similarly, the public paid little attention to the Korean war veteran, and he
> called little attention to himself. A review of the literature reveals a dearth
> of references on the Korean War veteran. If any veteran in American
> history deserves the title of the forgotten veteran, it is the Korean War
> veteran.[41]

Theoretical Implications from Readjustment after Vietnam

This study of Vietnam veterans since the war provides three broad
implications for theories of social problems and social movements. The
first concerns the "natural history" of a social problem, the second,
the "bias" contained in decision rules used within various arenas, and
the third, the "bureaucratic resistance" to change found in large-scale
organizations.

The simplest model of a social problem's natural history is emergence,
rise to prominence, culmination, and decline, all in direct response to
concerted activity by interested persons and interest groups. In short,
claims makers bring what they see as a problematic condition to the
attention of relevant parties, there is some negotiated resolution, and
the issue declines in salience as claims makers cease their activity. Of
course, not all social problems follow this pattern. Research also has
documented that protagonists may struggle unsuccessfully to advance a
cause—they may fail outright, or be pre-empted or co-opted—and that

claims makers may mount a series of challenges, thereby giving a problem's history a cyclical pattern. The stories told here show that the natural history of a problem may be exceedingly complex. The simple model does not match the natural history of Vietnam veterans since the war, in part because there is no "one" Vietnam veterans' issue. Rather there is the general issue of readjustment following the war; various activists and groups defined the problem differently.

The controversies over PTSD, the National Vietnam Veterans Memorial, and Agent Orange therefore all address the readjustment process but differ markedly in substantive and strategic content. Here, changing casts of claims makers articulated the problems of Vietnam veterans in different arenas and with degrees of success. Further, we have seen that the protagonists on one issue sometimes became antagonists on later issues, and vice versa. Max Cleland and Senator Alan Cranston championed the readjustment counseling bill, but later were lukewarm on the issue of Agent Orange. Likewise, although generational differences between World War II and Vietnam veterans entered into all these controversies, the veterans of the two wars at times did successfully emphasize commonalities rather than differences. The American Legion, which opposed readjustment counseling for Vietnam veterans during the 1970s, later provided the single largest contribution for the memorial and sponsored a major Agent Orange study. These observations imply that researchers should avoid defining too narrowly the "boundaries" of a social problem under study. An episode corresponding to the simple model might be part of a larger cyclical pattern, or as with readjustment among Vietnam veterans, one that recurs as an issue in a series of events or settings.

The second implication concerns decision rules, or the explicit guidelines used by organizations or professions for rendering judgment about contested issues. These rules carry a bias or preference for reaching a decision about what to say or do amidst doubt. These biases vary and give the advantage to certain types of conclusions. Claims makers therefore often find it useful to switch arenas when the decision rules in one carry a bias contrary to their interests. The story of Agent Orange provides an ideal incident for exploring how one may derive different answers by asking the same question in different domains.

For instance, the null hypothesis—the proposition that the effect under investigation is not produced by the suspected cause—guides scientific research. The null hypothesis in Agent Orange research was that dioxin did not produce cancers in exposed subjects or birth defects in their offspring. By focusing on the null hypothesis, scientific research favors type II errors (failure to reject a false null hypothesis) over type I errors (rejection of a true null hypothesis).[42] If an error is going to be made, scientific investigators would rather incorrectly "fail to reject" a false null hypothesis than incorrectly reject a true one. Hence, it is a greater sin in scientific studies of phenoxy herbicides to conclude that dioxin harms health, when it actually does not, than to conclude that dioxin is not harmlful to humans when it actually is.

Medical diagnoses carry the opposite bias. Two types of errors may result here also. Physicians may diagnose well persons as sick or consider diseased as healthy. In the United States, physicians are socialized to believe that it is less of a sin to diagnose a well person as sick than to fail to detect disease in a diseased person.[43] Two considerations mediate this posture. First, medical knowledge retains a firm base in current scientific consensus. Physicians who act otherwise run the risk of being labeled quacks or of being sued. Second, organizational contexts in which directives endorse a position regarding etiology, diagnosis, or treatment may reverse the tendency to suspect harm until doubt is removed.[44] This also may occur when the diagnosed sickness implies organizational culpability for treatment and compensation. Although treatment and compensation take place in separate administrative channels in the DVA, the cause of an injury or disease takes on significance in the care of veterans beyond that usually required for diagnosis and treatment. Here, the patient's needs and interests may become divorced from those of the organization. Certainly it is necessary to ask in such cases, Can the organization afford to define people who report having illnesses—and hence who may be diseased—as sick?

The legal system provides yet a third set of criteria for establishing cause and effect in personal injury suits. Rules allow for the introduction and evaluation of several kinds of evidence including, but not limited to, scientific and medical evidence.[45] The basic principle in a civil suit is "preponderance of the evidence." A verdict may be reached when the evidence simply is tipped in either direction.[46] The judicial regulation of hazards recognizes two relevant standards of liability: strict liability and negligent liability.[47] Strict liability assigns legal responsibility whether the defendant was careless or not. Hence, the decision rule under strict liability is: If, in the judgment of the court, the probability that the defendant's activity caused the plaintiff's injury is greater than 50 percent, find for the plaintiff; otherwise, find for the defendant. Therefore, if a legal case is wrongfully decided, it is as likely to favor an undeserving plaintiff as an undeserving defendant.

The stories told here show that claims makers are savvy to these variations and work to use them to their advantage. For instance, the DVA's own regulations stated that veterans should be given the benefit of the doubt in cases of uncertainty. However, by adopting the scientific standard of proof as a precondition for treating and compensating Agent Orange claimants, the agency drastically tightened its decision rules.

Apparently, it preferred to err in favor of failing to provide care, than to extend treatment for which it might not actually be liable. The lawsuit filed by the National Veterans Law Center and Vietnam Veterans of America reversed the bias in DVA's Agent Orange policy by forcing the agency to use its more generous "benefit of the doubt" clause. This insight underscores clearly the process by which facts are produced and certified.

Finally, the controversies recounted here also point to a significant amount of tenacious bureaucratic resistance, if not concerted efforts to discredit and derail initiatives toward change. Claims makers in social movements devoted to the concerns of Vietnam veterans have demanded both normative and structural changes. The former are changes in the way we think about veterans' issues; the latter are alterations in the arrangements for allocating resources to meet veterans' needs. As we have seen, it requires effective organization and effort to implement either kind of change. However, not all initiatives for change meet similar resistance. Contests in which one group can achieve success only by displacing established persons, interests, and groups—zero-sum conflicts—are the most likely to encounter stiff opposition.

Students of formal organizations sometimes use the concept of the "lazy monopoly" to explain the inertia of large organizations facing demands for change.[48] The lazy monopoly typically has control over a service or product, and the absence of competition accentuates organizational recalcitrance. Its executives are slow to improve the quality of the product, change their policies, alter the structure of the organization, or assume responsibility for past mistakes. They prefer instead to lose clients or personnel who criticize the organization. As we have seen, the world of veterans' issues comprises primarily the DVA, the House Committee on Veterans' Affairs, and the major veterans' organizations. At one time or another they all preferred to lose Vietnam veterans as clients rather than capitulate to demands that would, they feared, "upset the applecart." Some policymakers also fretted that the protest might spread to other "victim groups." In these instances, claims makers find it necessary to mount initiatives that force change from sources outside the organization itself. Hence, the judicial system, diverse research communities, and countervailing government agencies often provide the leverage for change in controversies of the sort we have seen here.

Concluding Thoughts

Whether of good wars or bad wars, veterans have responded in varying degrees to efforts by organizational leaders to mobilize them. That veterans often seek commonality with other veterans is hardly surprising. Shared life-threatening situations provide the stuff of lifelong associations. Sociologist Glen Elder and his associates, notably psychologist Elizabeth Clipp, have studied the life course of World War II veterans using a longitudinal sample. Their research focuses on the role of reunions with comrades in readjusting to civilian life. Reviewing the now sizable literature on why soldiers fight, Elder and Clipp conclude:

> Combat soldiers fight and die for each other, not primarily for an abstraction such as "one's country." . . . Repeatedly, surveys of soldiers on the battlefields of World War II tell a story of felt obligation to fighting mates, a commitment to fulfilling expectations even under fearful circumstances. . . . When comrades fall in battle, their bonds of mutual obligation and loyalty make survivors especially vulnerable to self-blame and guilt. Deaths in battle are unpredictable events and symbolize the out-of-control nature of combat experience, yet they occur among men who believe they are their "brother's keeper. . . ."
>
> The bonding of comradeship endures through survivors who vow to remember the men who died. Not all survivors can tolerate the pain of remembrance . . . but men who sustained the memory were likely to do so through periodic assemblies of the battle unit. Memories of this kind can be kept alive through the years by talking about recollections in the company of people who once knew each other well—members of the patrol or company itself. It is through this collective memory and conversation that veterans find meaning in their military pasts and affirm the primordial ties of comradeship. Remembrance of the fallen cements relations among those who once knew and cared from them.[49]

Intense combat experience and the loss of comrades therefore may be powerful motives for group formation among veterans, which supersede all other social characteristics. Among some, as Elder and Clipp note, the memories may be too painful and lead instead to a complete withdrawal from any associations that recall experience in the military. Nevertheless, Elder and Clipp find that veterans who have experienced significant combat and the loss of comrades are the ones most likely to maintain lifelong ties with military service organizations. Although many such organizations are social in nature, some are overtly political, at a minimum on issues that relate directly to the needs and interests of veterans: the recognition for service, treatment and compensation for disabilities, and pensions. They also represent a substantial parapolitical structure that other veterans' organizations or political groupings may tap for sympathetic support. It is virtually a given, for instance, that political candidates for office make stops along the campaign trail at the conventions and meetings of veterans' organizations. National security—phrased as defense of homeland and the American way—is a sacred shroud.

Philip Caputo was one of the first Vietnam veterans to write of his experiences in Vietnam and of his return home. A lieutenant in the Marine Corps, his story details the idealism that led him to volunteer and the realities of the Vietnam that eventually snuffed out his idealism. He writes of his return:

> I came home from the war with the curious feeling that I had grown older than my father, who was then fifty-one. It was as if a life-time of experi-ence had been compressed into a year and a half. A man saw the heights and depths of human behavior in Vietnam, all manner of violence and horrors so grotesque that they evoked more fascination than disgust. Once I had seen pigs eating napalm charred corpses—a memorable sight, pigs eating roast people.
>
> I was left with none of the optimism and ambition a young American is supposed to have, only a desire to catch up on sixteen months of missed sleep and an old man's conviction that the future would hold no further suprises, good or bad.
>
> I hoped there would be no more surprises. I had survived enough am-bushes and doubted my capacity to endure many more physical and emo-tional shocks. I had all the symptoms of "combat veteranitis": an inability to concentrate, a childlike fear of the darkness, a tendency to tire easily, chronic nightmares, an intolerance of loud noises . . . and alternating moods of depression and rage that came over me for no apparent reason. Recovery has been less than total.[50]

So one might say of Vietnam veterans since the war. There have been many developments, both positive and negative. Recovery has been less than total.

Notes

1. See, for instance, Bruno Latour, "The Politics of Explanation," in *Knowl-edge and Reflexivity*, ed. Steve Woolgar (London: Sage, 1988); Donald McCloskey, *The Rhetoric of Economics* (Madison: University of Wisconsin Press, 1985); Stephen Pfohl, *Predicting Dangerousness* (Lexington, MA: D.C. Heath, 1978); John Heri-tage, *Garfinkel and Ethnomethodology* (Worchester, Great Britain: Polity, 1984); and Laurel Richardson, "Value Constituting Practices, Rhetoric, and Metaphor in Sociology" (Paper presented at the American Sociological Association meetings, San Francisco, August, 1989).

2. See Malcolm Spector and John Kitsuse, *Constructing Social Problems* (Haw-thorne, NY: Aldine de Gruyter, 1978); and Naomi Aronson, "Science as a Claims-making Activity: Implications for Social Science Research," in *Studies in*

the Sociology of Social Problems, ed. Joseph Schneider and John Kitsuse (Norwood, NJ: Ablex, 1984), 1–24.

3. Thomas Kuhn, *The Structure of Scientific Revolutions* (Chicago: University of Chicago Press, 1970).

4. Aronson, "Science," 5–6, 9.

5. See John Kitsuse and Joseph Schneider, "Preface," in *Images of Issues: Typifying Contemporary Social Problems*, ed. Joel Best (Hawthorne, NY: Aldine de Gruyter, 1989), xi–xiii, and Best, *Images of Issues*, 244–249.

6. Latour, "Politics of Explanation," 157–164.

7. I borrowed this term from Clifford Geertz, *The Interpretation of Cultures* (New York: Basic Books, 1973), 26. Geertz argues that "the essential task of theory building . . . is not to codify abstract regularities but to make thick description possible, not to generalize across cases but to generalize within them" (quoted in Robin Wagner-Pacifici and Barry Schwartz, "The Vietnam Veterans Memorial: Commemorating a Difficult Past," *American Journal of Sociology* 97 (1991):377.

8. For an overview of Robert Park and Everett Burgess's ecological theory and case studies of Chicago's "ecological niches" by their students and colleagues, see James Short, Jr., *The Social Fabric of the Metropolis: Contributions of the Chicago School of Urban Sociology* (Chicago: University of Chicago Press, 1971).

9. Barney Glaser and Anselm Strauss, *The Discovery of Grounded Theory* (Chicago: Aldine, 1967); John Lofland, *Analyzing Social Settings* (Belmont, CA: Wadsworth, 1971); and Norman Denzin, *The Research Act: A Theoretical Introduction to Sociological Methods*, 3rd ed. (Englewood Cliffs, NJ: Prentice-Hall, 1989).

10. See Joseph Gusfield, "On the Side: Practical Action and Social Constructivism in Social Problems Theory," in *Studies in the Sociology of Social Problems*, ed. Joseph Schneider and John Kitsuse (Norwood, NJ: Ablex, 1984), 31–51.

11. I borrowed this phrase from Richardson, "Value Constituting Practices."

12. Spector and Kitsuse, *Constructing Social Problems*, 77–78. The quotation from Richard Fuller in the cited material from Spector and Kitsuse is from Richard Fuller, "The Problem of Teaching Social Problems," *American Journal of Sociology* 44 (November, 1938):415–435.

13. Spector and Kitsuse, *Constructing Social Problems*, 75–76.

14. Steve Woolgar and Dorothy Pawluch, "Ontological Gerrymandering: The Anatomy of Social Problems Explanations," *Social Problems* 32 (1985): 214–27.

15. Best, *Images of Issues*, 245.

16. Ibid., 247.

17. See Spector and Kitsuse, *Constructing Social Problems*; Aronson, "Science"; and Armand Mauss, *Social Problems as Social Movements* (Philadelphia: J.P. Lippincott, 1975).

18. See Stephen Couch and J. Stephen Croll-Smith, "The Chronic Technical Disaster: Toward a Social Scientific Perspective," *Social Science Quarterly* 66 (1985):564–75.

19. See Neil Smelser, *The Theory of Collective Behavior* (New York: Free Press, 1963); and John Higham, *Send These to Me: Jews and Other Immigrants in Urban America* (New York: Atheneum, 1975).

20. See Ralph Turner and Lewis Killian, *Collective Behavior* (Englewood Cliffs, NJ: Prentice-Hall, 1972); Ted Gurr, *Why Men Rebel* (Princeton, NJ: Princeton University Press, 1970); and James Davies, "The J-Curve of Rising and Declining Satisfactions as a Cause of Some Great Revolutions and a Contained Rebellion,"

in *Violence in America: Historical and Comparative Perspectives*, ed. H. D. Graham and Ted Gurr (New York: Signet, 1969), 671–709.

21. Anthony Oberschall, *Social Conflict and Social Movements* (Englewood Cliffs, NJ: Prentice-Hall, 1973), 119. See also John McCarthy and Mayer Zald, "Resource Mobilization and Social Movements: A Partial Theory," *American Journal of Sociology* 82 (1977):1212–41.

22. See Herbert Blumer, "Social Problems as Collective Behavior," *Social Problems* 18 (1971):298–306; Spector and Kitsuse, *Constructing Social Problems*; and Mauss, *Social Problems*.

23. Stephen Hilgartner and Charles Bosk, "The Rise and Fall of Social Problems: A Public Arenas Model," *American Journal of Sociology* 94 (1988):57–59.

24. Ibid., 59–60.

25. William Gamson, *The Strategy of Social Protest*, 2nd ed. (Belmont, CA: Wadsworth, 1990).

26. Hilgartner and Bosk, "Rise and Fall of Problems," 64.

27. For a classic statement of the link between categories (quasi-groups) and groups, see Ralf Dahrendorf, *Class and Class Conflict in Industrial Society* (Palo Alto, CA: Stanford University Press, 1959). For an application to age cohorts, see Wilbur Scott and Harold Grasmick, "Generations and Group Consciousness: A Quantification of Mannheim's Analogy," *Youth and Society* 11 (1979):191–213.

28. John Modell and Timothy Haggerty, "The Social Impact of War," *Annual Review of Sociology* 17 (1991):205–24.

29. Bernard Boëne, "How Unique Should the Military Be? A Review of Representative Literature and Outline of a Synthetic Formulation," *Archives of European Sociology* 31 (1990):3–59. The definition of war appears on p. 27.

30. Ibid., 29–30.

31. Ibid., 30.

32. Ibid, 34–35.

33. Ibid., 39.

34. William Ogburn originally developed the thesis, known as "cultural lag theory," that technological innovations are adopted and implemented more rapidly than are the norms for dealing with their consequences. See Ogburn, *Social Change: With Respect to Culture and Original Nature* (New York: Viking, 1939), 200–201.

35. See James Buchanan, "The Potential for Taxpayer Revolt in American Democracy," *Social Science Quarterly* 59 (1979):692. The free-rider principle states: "If the benefits of an action are . . . well-defined while the costs . . . are generalized, . . . individuals will act without regard to the costs involved. . . . Conversely, if the costs are . . . well-defined while benefits are . . . generalized, . . . individuals will . . . refrain from taking certain actions."

36. Joel Brende and Erwin Randolph Parson, *Vietnam Veterans: The Road to Recovery* (New York: Signet, 1985), 86.

37. Wagner-Pacifici and Schwartz, " Vietnam Veterans Memorial," 380.

38. Ibid., 381.

39. Richard Severo and Lewis Milford, *The Wages of War: When American Soldiers Came Home—From Valley Forge to Vietnam* (New York: Simon and Schuster, 1989).

40. Brende and Parson, *Vietnam Veterans*, 86.

41. Robert Fleming, "Post Vietnam Syndrome: Neurosis or Sociosis?" *Psychiatry* 48 (1985):126.

42.   For a full discussion of this issue, see William Hays, *Statistics for the Social Sciences* (New York: Holt, Rinehart and Winston, 1973).

43.   For a discussion of the decision rules in science and medicine, see Thomas Scheff, "Decision Rules and Types of Error, and Their Consequences in Medical Diagnosis," in *Medical Men and their Work*, ed. Eliot Freidson and Judith Lorber (Chicago: Aldine, 1972), 309–23.

44.   For an example, see Constance Nathanson and Marshall Becker, "Professional Norms, Personal Attitudes, and Medical Practice: The Case of Abortion," *Journal of Health and Social Behavior* 22 (1981):198–211.

45.   See Murray Levine and Barbara Howe, "The Penetration of Social Science into Legal Culture," *Law and Policy* 7 (1985):173–98.

46.   See David Kaye, "Statistical Significance and the Burden of Persuasion," *Law and Contemporary Problems* 46 (1983):13–23.

47.   See Talbot Page, "On the Meaning of the Preponderance Test in Judicial Regulation of Chemical Hazard," *Law and Contemporary Problems* 46 (1983):267–83.

48.   See Albert Hirschman, *Exit, Voice, and Loyalty: Responses to Decline in Firms, Organizations, and States* (Cambridge, MA: Harvard University Press, 1970); and John Seidler, "Priest Resignations in a Lazy Monopoly," *American Journal of Sociology* 44 (1979):763–83.

49.   Glen Elder and Elizabeth Clipp, "Wartime Losses and Social Bonding: Influences across 40 Years in Men's Lives," *Psychiatry* 51 (1988):180.

50.   Philip Caputo, *A Rumor of War* (New York: Ballantine Books, 1977), 4.

BIBLIOGRAPHY

Books and Book Chapters

American Council on Science and Health (ACSH). *The Health Effects of Herbicide 2,4,5-T*. New York: ACSH, 1981.

American Psychiatric Association (APA). *Diagnostic and Statistical Manual, Mental Disorders*. Washington, D.C.: APA, 1952.

———. *Diagnostic and Statistical Manual of Mental Disorders*. 2d ed. Washington, D.C.: APA, 1968.

———. *Diagnostic and Statistical Manual of Mental Disorders*. 3d ed. Washington, D.C.: APA, 1980.

Aronson, Naomi. "Science As a Claims-Making Activity: Implications for Social Science Research." In *Studies in the Sociology of Social Problems*, ed. Joseph Schneider and John Kitsuse, 1–24. Norwood, N.J.: Ablex, 1984.

Atkinson, Rick. *The Long Grey Line*. New York: Pocket Books, 1989.

Bayer, Ronald. *Homosexuality and American Psychiatry: The Politics of Diagnosis*. New York: Basic Books, 1984.

Best, Joel, ed. *Images of Issues: Typifying Contemporary Social Problems*. Hawthorne, N.Y.: Aldine de Gruyter, 1989.

Blank, Arthur Jr. "Irrational Responses to Post-Traumatic Stress Disorder and Viet Nam Veterans." In *The Trauma of War: Stress and Recovery in Viet Nam Veterans*. ed. Steven Sonnenberg, Arthur Blank, Jr., and John Talbott, 71–98. Washington, D.C.: APA, 1985.

Bonior, David, Stephen Champlin, and Timothy Kolly. *The Vietnam Veteran: A History of Neglect*. New York: Praeger, 1984.

Bourne, Peter. *Men, Stress, and Vietnam*. Boston: Little, Brown, 1970.

Brende, Joel, and Erwin Randolph Parson. *Vietnam Veterans: The Road to Recovery*. New York: Signet Book, 1985.

Caputo, Philip, *A Rumor of War*. New York: Ballantine, 1977.

Cecil, Paul Frederick. *Herbicidal Warfare: The RANCH HAND Project in Vietnam*. New York: Praeger, 1986.

Cleland, Max. *Strong at the Broken Places*. Atlanta: Cherokee, 1986.

Conrad, Peter, and Joseph Schneider. *Deviance and Medicalization: From Badness to Sickness*. St. Louis: C.V. Mosby, 1980.

Council on Scientific Affairs. *The Health Effects of "Agent Orange" and Polycholrinated Dioxin Contaminants*. Chicago: American Medical Association, 1981.

Dahrendorf, Ralf. *Class and Class Conflict in Industrial Society*. Palo Alto, CA: Stanford University Press, 1959.

Davies, James, "The J-curve of Rising and Declining Satisfactions as a Cause of Some Great Revolutions and a Contained Rebellion." In *Violence in America: Historical and Comparative Perspectives*, ed. H. D. Graham and Ted Gurr, 671–709. New York: Signet, 1969.

Denzin, Norman. *The Research Act: A Theoretical Introduction to Sociological Methods*. 3d ed. Englewood Cliffs, N.J.: Prentice-Hall, 1989.

Egendorf, Arthur. *Healing From the War: Trauma and Transformation after Vietnam*. Boston: Houghton Mifflin, 1985.

Egendorf, Arthur, Charles Kadushin, Robert Laufer, George Rothbart, and Lee Sloan. *Legacies of Vietnam: Comparative Adjustment of Veterans and their Peers*. Washington, D.C.: U.S. Government Printing Office, 1981.

Figley, Charles, and Seymour Leventman, eds. *Strangers At Home: Vietnam Veterans Since the War*. New York: Praeger.

Gamson, William. *The Strategy of Social Protest*. 2d. ed. Belmont, CA: Wadsworth, 1990.

Geertz, Clifford. *The Interpretation of Cultures*. New York: Basic Books, 1973.

Glaser, Barney, and Anselm Strauss. *The Discovery of Grounded Theory*. Chicago: Aldine, 1967.

Goodwin, Jim. "The Etiology of Combat-Related Post-Traumatic Stress Disorders." In *Post-Traumatic Stress Disorder: A Handbook for Clinicians*, ed. Tom Williams, 1–18. Cincinnati, Oh.: Disabled American Veterans, 1987.

Gough, Michael. *Dioxin, Agent Orange: The Facts*. New York: Plenum, 1986.

Grinker, Roy and John Spiegel. *Men Under Stress*. Philadelphia: Blakiston, 1945.

Gurr, Ted. *Why Men Rebel*. Princeton, N.J.: Princeton University Press, 1970.

Gusfield, Joseph. "On the Side: Practical Action and Social Constructivism in Social Problems Theory." In *Studies in the Sociology of Social Problems*, ed. Joseph Schneider and John Kitsuse, 31–51. Norwood, N.J.: Ablex, 1984.

Hays, William. *Statistics for the Social Sciences*. New York: Holt, Rinehart & Winston, 1973.

Heritage, John. *Garfinkel and Ethnomethodology*. Worchester, Great Britain: Polity, 1984.

Higham, John. *Send These to Me: Jews and Other Immigrants in Urban America*. New York: Atheneum, 1975.

Hirschman, Albert. *Exit, Voice, and Loyalty: Responses to Decline in Firms, Organizations, and States*. Cambridge, MA: Harvard Unviersity Press, 1970.

Horowitz, Mardi. *Stress Response Syndromes*. New York: Aronson, 1976.

Kardiner, Abram. *War, Stress, and Neurotic Illness*. New York: Paul B. Hoeber, 1947.

Kitsuse, John, and Joseph Schneider. "Preface." In *Images of Issues: Typifying Contemporary Social Problems*, ed. Joel Best, xi-xiii. Hawthorne, N.Y.: Aldine de Gruyter, 1989.

Kormos, Harry. "The Nature of Combat Stress." In *Stress Disorders among Vietnam Veterans: Theory, Research and Treatment*, ed. Charles Figley, 3–22. New York: Brunner/Mazel, 1978.

Krystal, Henry, and William Niederland, eds. *Psychic Traumatization*. Boston: Little, Brown, 1971.

Kuhn, Thomas. *The Structure of Scientific Revolutions*. Chicago: University of Chicago Press, 1970.

Kuramoto, Frank. "Federal Mental Health Programs for the Vietnam Veteran." In *Strangers At Home: Vietnam Veterans Since the War*, ed. Charles Figley and Seymour Leventman, 293–304. New York: Praeger, 1980.

Kurtis, Bill. *Bill Kurtis on Assignment*. Chicago: Rand-McNally, 1983.

Latour, Bruno. "The Politics of Explanation." In *Knowledge and Reflexivity*, ed. Steve Woolgar. London: Sage, 1988.

Lifton, Robert Jay. *Home From the War: Neither Victims Nor Executioners*. New York: Basic Books, 1973.

Lofland, John. *Analyzing Social Settings*. Belmont, CA: Wadsworth, 1971.

MacPherson, Myra. *Long Time Passing: Vietnam and the Haunted Generation*. New York: Signet, 1984.

Mahedy, William. *Out of the Night: The Spiritual Journey of Vietnam Vets*. New York: Ballantine, 1986.

Mauss, Armand. *Social Problems as Social Movements*. Philadelphia, PA: J.P. Lippincott, 1975.

McCloskey, Donald. *The Rhetoric of Economics*. Madison, Wis.: University of Wisconsin Press, 1985.

Modell, John, and Timothy Haggerty. "The Social Impact of War." In *Annual Review of Sociology*, ed. W. Richard Scott and Judith Blake, 205–224. Palo Alto, CA: Annual Reviews Inc., 1991.

Moskos, Charles, Jr. *The American Enlisted Man*. New York: Russell Sage Foundation, 1970.

———, "The Military." In *Annual Review of Sociology*, ed. Alex Inkeles, James Coleman, and Neil Smelser (eds.), 55–77. Palo Alto, CA: Annual Reviews Inc., 1976.

Murphy, Edward. *Vietnam Medal of Honor Heroes*. New York: Ballentine, 1987.

Oberschall, Anthony. *Social Conflict and Social Movements*. Englewood Cliffs, N.J.: Prentice-Hall, 1973.

Ogburn, William. *Social Change: With Respect to Culture and Original Nature*. New York: Viking, 1939.

Pfohl, Stephen. *Predicting Dangerousness*. Lexington, Mass.: D.C. Heath, 1978.

Scheff, Thomas. "Decision Rules and Types of Error, and Their Consequences in Medical Diagnosis." In *Medical Men and their Work*, eds. Eliot Freidson and Judith Lorber (eds.), 309–323. Chicago: Aldine, 1972.

Schuck, Peter. *Agent Orange on Trial: Mass Toxic Torts Disasters in the Courts*. Cambridge, MA: Harvard University Press, 1986.

Scott, Wilbur. "Vietnam Veterans Against the War: the Politics of Antiwar Protest." In *Perspectives on Social Problems*, ed. James Holstein and Gale Miller, 229–253. Greenwich, CT: JAI Press, 1992.

Scruggs, Jan, and Joel Swerdlow. *To Heal a Nation: The Vietnam Veterans Memorial*. New York: Harper and Row, 1985.

Severo, Richard and Lewis Milford. *The Wages of War: When America's Soldiers Came Home—From Valley Forge to Vietnam*. New York: Simon and Schuster, 1989.

Short, James, Jr. *The Social Fabric of the Metropolis: Contributions of the Chicago School of Urban Sociology.* Chicago: University of Chicago Press, 1971.

Smelser, Neil. *The Theory of Collective Behavior.* New York: Free Press, 1963.

Spector, Malcolm, and John Kitsuse. *Constructing Social Problems.* Menlo Park, CA: Cummings, 1977, and (2d edition) Hawthorne, N.Y.: Aldine de Gruyter, 1987.

Steiner, Gilbert. *The State of Welfare.* The Brookings Institution: Washington, D.C., 1971.

Thayer, Thomas. *War Without Fronts: The American Experience in Vietnam.* (Boulder, CO: Westview Press, 1985.

Turner, Ralph, and Lewis Killian. *Collective Behavior.* Englewood Cliffs, N.J.: Prentice-Hall, 1972.

Wilcox, Fred. *Waiting for an Army to Die: The Tragedy of Agent Orange.* New York: Random House, 1983.

Wilson, John. *Identity, Ideology and Crises: The Vietnam Veteran in Transition: A Preliminary Report on the Forgotten Warrior Project.* Cincinnati, Oh.: Disabled American Veterans, 1977.

Zumwalt, Elmo, Jr., and Elmo Zumwalt III, with John Pekkanen. *My Father, My Son.* New York: McMillian, 1986.

Journal Articles and Professional Papers

Archibald, Herbert, D.M. Long, and Read Tuddenham. "Gross Stress Reaction in Combat—A 15-Year Follow-up." *American Journal of Psychiatry* 119 (1962): 317–322.

Archibald, Herbert, and Read Tuddenham. "Persistent Stress Reaction Following Combat: A 20-Year Follow-up." *Archives of General Psychiatry* 12 (1965): 474–481.

Bey, Douglas, and Walter Smith. "Organizational Consultation in a Combat Unit." *American Journal of Psychiatry* 126 (1971): 401–406.

Bloch, H. Spencer. "Army Psychiatry in the Combat Zone—1967–1968." *American Journal of Psychiatry* 126 (1969): 289–298.

Blumer, Herbert. "Social problems as Collective Behavior." *Social Problems* 18 (1971): 298–306.

Boëne, Bernard. "How Unique Should the Military Be? A Review of Representative Literature and Outline of a Synthetic Formulation." *Archives of European Sociology* XXXI (1990): 3–59.

Breslin, Patricia, Han Klang, Yvonne Lee, Vicki Burt, and Barclay Shepard. "Proportionate Mortality Studies of U.S. Army and U.S. Marine Corps Veterans of the Vietnam War." *Journal of Occupational Medicine* 30 (1988): 412–419.

Buchanan, James. "The Potential for Taxpayer Revolt in American Democracy." *Social Science Quarterly* 59 (1979): 691–696.

Couch, Stephen, and J. Stephen Croll-Smith. "The Chronic Technical Disaster:

Toward a Social Scientific Perspective." *Social Science Quarterly* 66 (1985): 564–575.

Elder, Glen, and Elizabeth Clipp. "Wartime Losses and Social Bonding: Influences across 40 Years in Men's Lives." *Psychiatry* 51 (1988): 177–198.

Fleming, Robert. "Post Vietnam Syndrome: Neurosis or Sociosis?" *Psychiatry* 48 (1985): 122–139.

Fuller, Richard. "The Problem of Teaching Social Problems." *American Journal of Sociology* 44 (1938): 415–435.

Galston, Arthur. "Herbicides: A Mixed Blessing." *BioScience* 29 (1979): 85–90.

Haley, Sarah. "When the Patient Reports Atrocities: Specific Treatment Considerations of the Vietnam Veteran." *Archives of General Psychiatry* 30 (1974): 191–196.

Helzer, John, Lee Robins, and D.H. Davis. "Antecedents of Narcotic Use and Addiction: A Study of 898 Vietnam Veterans," *Drug and Alcohol Dependence* 1 (1976): 83–90.

———. "Depressive Disorders in Vietnam Returnees." *Journal of Nervous and Mental Disease* 168 (1976): 177–185.

Hilgartner, Stephen, and Charles Bosk, "The Rise and Fall of Social Problems: A Public Arenas Model." *American Journal of Sociology* 94 (1988): 53–78.

Hoar, Sheila et al. "Agricultural Herbicide Use and Risk of Lymphoma and Soft-Tissue Sarcoma." *Journal of the American Medical Association* 256 (1986): 1141–1147.

Horowitz, Mardi, and George Solomon, "A Prediction of Delayed Stress Syndromes in Vietnam Veterans." *Journal of Social Issues* 31 (1975): 67–80.

Kaye, David. "Statistical significance and the burden of persuasion." *Law and Contemporary Problems* 46 (1983): 13–23.

Lacey, Pamela, and Vincent Lacey. "Agent Orange: Government Responsibility for the Military Use of Phenoxy Herbicides." *Journal of Legal Medicine* 3 (1982): 137–178.

Levine, Murray, and Barbara Howe. "The Penetration of Social Science into Legal Culture." *Law and Policy* 7 (1985): 173–198.

McCarthy, John, and Mayer Zald. "Resource Mobilization and Social Movements: A Partial Theory." *American Journal of Sociology* 82 (1977): 1212–1241.

Nathanson, Constance, and Marshall Becker. "Professional Norms, Personal Attitudes, and Medical Practice: The Case of Abortion." *Journal of Health and Social Behavior* 22 (1981): 198–211.

Page, Talbot. "On the Meaning of the Preponderance Test in Judicial Regulation of Chemical Hazard." *Law and Contemporary Problems* 46 (1983): 267–283.

Richardson, Laurel. "Value Constituting Practices, Rhetoric, and Metaphor in Sociology." Paper presented at the American Sociological Association meetings, San Francisco, August 1989.

Scott, Wilbur. "Competing Paradigms in the Assessment of Latent Disorders: The Case of Agent Orange." *Social Problems* 35 (1988): 145–161.

———. "PTSD in DSM-III: A Case in the Politics of Diagnosis and Disease." *Social Problems* 37 (1990): 294–310.

———. "PTSD and Agent Orange: Implications for a Sociology of Veterans' Issues." *Armed Forces and Society* 18 (1992): 592–612.

Scott, Wilbur and Harold Grasmick. "Generations and Group Consciousness: A Quantification of Mannheim's Analogy." *Youth and Society* 11 (1979): 191–213.

Seidler, John. "Priest Resignations in a Lazy Monopoly." *American Journal of Sociology* 44 (1979): 763–783.

Shatan, Chaim. "The Grief of Soldiers in Mourning: Vietnam Combat Veterans' Self Help Movement." *American Journal of Orthopsychiatry* 45 (1973): 640–653.

Shatan, Chaim, John Smith, and Sarah Haley. "Proposal for the Inclusion of Combat Stress Reactions in DSM-III." Paper for the DSM-III Task Force of the American Psychiatric Association, June 1976.

Shatan, Chaim, Sarah Haley, and John Smith. "When Johnny Comes Marching Home: Combat Stress and DSM-III." Paper presented at the annual meeting of the American Psychiatric Association, Toronto, May 1977.

Shatan, Chaim. "Stress Disorders and *DSM-III.*" Letter to members of the Vietnam Veterans Working Group. March 5, 1978.

Shils, Edward, and Morris Janowitz, "Cohesion and Disintegration in the Wehrmacht in World War II." *Public Opinion Quarterly* 12 (1948): 280–315.

Stellman, Jeanne, Steven Stellman, and John Sommer, Jr. "Social and Behavioral Consequences of the Vietnam Experience among American Legionnaires." *Environmental Research* 47 (1988): 129–149.

Stellman, Steven, Jeanne Stellman, and John Sommer, Jr. "Combat and Herbicide Exposures in Vietnam among a Sample of American Legionnaires." *Environmental Research* 47 (1988): 112–128.

———. "Health and Reproductive Outcomes maong American Legionnaires in Relation to Combat and Herbicide Exposure in Vietnam." *Environmental Research* 47 (1988): 150–174.

Tshirley, Fred. "Dioxin." *Scientific American* 254 (1986): 29–35.

Wagner-Pacifici, Robin, and Barry Schwartz. "The Vietnam Veterans Memorial: Commemorating a Difficult Past." *American Journal of Sociology* 97 (1991): 376–420.

Woolgar, Steve, and Dorothy Pawluch. "Ontological Gerrymandering: The Anatomy of Social Problems Explanations." *Social Problems* 32 (1985): 214–227.

Newspaper and Magazine Articles

"Agency to Yield on Herbicide Issue." *New York Times*, 16 October 1982, A6.

Ayres, R. Drummond, Jr. "Air Force Reports No High Death Rates Among Defoliant Sprayers." *New York Times*, 2 July 1983, A9.

Bernstein, Carl. "Viet Vets Camped on Mall Resemble Basic Training Outfit." *Washington Post*, 22 April 1971, A-14.

Bird, David. "Veterans Divided on Damages Pact." *New York Times* 10 May 1984, A24.

Blumenthal, Ralph. "Judge Withdraws from Suit over Agent Orange." *New York Times*, 14 October 1983, B7.

————. "Judge Speeds Up Agent Orange Suit." *New York Times*, 13 November 1983, A31.

————. "Test Cases Chosen for Herbicide Trial." *New York Times*, 12 December 1983, B28.

Boffey, Phillip. "Agent Orange: Despite Spate of Studies, Slim Hope of Answers." *New York Times*, 30 November 1982), C1, C7.

————. "Lack of Military Data Halts Agent Orange Study." *New York Times*, 1 September 1987, A1, C5.

————. "Cancer Deaths High for Some Veterans." *New York Times*, 4 September 1987, A10.

Burgess, John, and Eugene Robinson. "Overflowing Joy over Ex-Hostages' Return Not Shared by All Americans." *Washington Post*, 28 January 1981, A29.

Burnham, David. "Dow Says U.S. Knew Dioxin Peril of Agent Orange." *New York Times*, 5 May 1983, A18.

Cameron, Juan. "Carter Takes on the Budget Monster." *Fortune*, January, 1977, 83–84.

Cannon, Lou. "Reagan & Co.: White House No Longer Pulling Together in the Traces." *Washington Post*, 15 November 1982, A3.

Cannon, Lou, and Pete Earley. "Embattled VA Chief Steps Down." *Washington Post*, 5 October 1982, A1, A7.

Carhart, Tom. "Insulting Vietnam Veterans." *New York Times*, 24 October 1981), A23.

Childs, Charles. "From Vietnam to a VA Hospital: Assignment to Neglect." *Life*, 22 May 1970, 24D-33.

Claiborne, William,and Sanford Unger. "Judge Lifts Ban on Vets, Scolds U.S." *Washington Post*, 23 April 1971, A1.

"Compromise on Vietnam Memorial." *Washington Post*, 25 March 1982, B3.

"Derwinsky Confirmed as Veterans' Secretary." *Washington Post*, 3 March 1989, A26.

"Dioxin Levels Found in Vietnam Veterans Termed Not Unusual." *New York Times*, 25 July 1987, A8.

"Dioxin: Quandary for the '80's." *St. Louis Post-Dispatch*, 14 November 1983, 1–2.

Domjan, Laszio, Marjorie Mandel, Jo Mannies, and Margaret Freivogel. "Dioxin in Missouri: How It Happened." *St. Louis-Post Dispatch*, 14 November 1983, 1–18.

Earley, Pete. "Many Are in Line to Take on a Tough Job." *Washington Post*, 22 October 1982, A19.

————. "Agent Orange Compensation Gains Favor." *Washington Post*, 9 March 1983), A3.

————. "Study Panel Cautious on Viet Sprays." *Washington Post*, 25 February 1984, A1, A2.

————. "Agent Orange Settlement Divides Vietnam Veterans." *Washington Post*, 5 August 1984, A3.

Earley, Pete, and Lou Cannon. "Army Official in Line to be VA Chief." *Washington Post*, 5 November 1982, A1, A6.

"Events Listed in Salute to Viet Veterans." *Washington Post*, 10 November 1982, A20.

Fishman, Charles. "Memorial's First Names Unveiled." *Washington Post*, 22 July 1982, E3.

Forgey, Benjamin. "Vietnam Vet Memorial Action." *Washington Post*, 5 March 1982, B9.

———. "Monumental 'Absurdity.'" *Washington Post*, 6 March 1982, C5.

———. "Commission Acts on Vets Memorial Design." *Washington Post*, 10 March 1982, B6.

———. "Monumental Problems." *Washington Post*, 17 July 1982, C1, C10.

———. "Hart's Vietnam Statue Unveiled." *Washington Post*, 21 September 1982, B1, B4.

———. "Vietnam Memorial Clears Last Major Hurdle." *Washington Post*, 14 October 1982, A1, A2.

"Four Veterans Defend Visit to Vietnam." *New York Times*, 29 December 1981, A3.

Franklin, Ben. "Veterans of Vietnam Found to Have High Death Rates." *New York Times*, 11 February 1987, A20.

———. "Study Finds Vietnam Combat Affecting Veterans' Health." *New York Times*, 12 November 1988, A7.

"Fullbright Panel Hears Antiwar Vet." *Washington Post*, 23 April 1971, A4

Harris, Art. "Town Struggles with Toxic Legacy." *Washington Post*, 10 January 1983, A3, A8.

Hodge, Paul. "Vietnam Vets' Memorial May Begin in Two Weeks." *Washington Post*, 19 February 1982, A18.

Hornblower, Margot. "A Sinister Drama of Agent Orange Opens in Congress." *Washington Post*, 27 June 1979, A3.

———. "Vietnam Veterans Divided Over Agent Orange Battle." *Washington Post*, 9 August 1984, A3.

Horowitz, Rick. "Maya Lin's Angry Objections." *Washington Post*, 7 July 1982, B1, B6.

"Inside: the VA." *Washington Post*, 9 March 1984, A17.

Jackson, Donald. "Confessions of 'Winter Soldiers.'" *Life*, 9 July 1971, 22–27.

Johnson, Haynes. "America Has Been Liberated Too—Freed of Its Pent-Up Emotions." *Washington Post*, 21 January 1981, A27.

———. "A Capital Welcomes Its Heroes, With Emotion." *Washington Post*, 28 January 1981, A1, A25.

Kihss, Peter. "U.S. Adding 42 Centers for Veterans of Vietnam." *New York Times*, 26 July 1981, A6.

Kilpatrick, James. "The Names." *Washington Post*, 21 September 1982, A19.

Leary, Warren. "Vietnam Veterans' Health: No Worse than Others." *New York Times*, 13 November 1988, A13.

Lifton, Robert. "Why Civilians are War Victims." *U.S. News and World Report*, 15 December 1969, 25.

Lin, Maya. "The Vietnam Memorial." *New York Times*, 14 July 1981, A24.

Manear, Edward. "Poison or Not?" *Washington Post*, 14 January 1983, A14.

Martin, Linda. "Herbicide for Lawns is Linked to Cancer." *New York Times*, 20 October 1986, C5.

McAllister, Bill. "VA Chief Delays Decision on Agent Orange Claims." *Washington Post* 25 November 1989, A3.

———. "Agent Orange Linked to 28 Diseases, Zumwalt Says." *Washington Post*, 17 May 1990, A4.

———. "U.S. Revises Agent Orange Stance." *Washington Post*, 19 May 1990, A5.

McCombs, Phil. "Maya Lin and the Great Wall of China: The Fascinating Heritage of the Student Who Designed the Vietnam Memorial." *Washington Post*, 3 January 1982, F1, F9-F13.

———. "Reconciliation: Ground Broken for Shrine to Honor Vietnam Veterans." *Washington Post*, 27 March 1982, A1, A14.

———. "Veterans Honor the Fallen, Mark Reconciliation." *Washington Post*, 14 November 1982, A1, A18, A20.

Molotsky, Irvin. "White House Withdraws Support of Long Islander to be V.A. Head." *New York Times*, 21 March 1981, A10.

"Most Ex-POW's Polled Dislike Vietnam War Memorial Design." *Washington Post*, 12 October 1982, C2.

"New Doubts Raised on Agent Orange." *New York Times*, 23 March 1988, A19.

"New V.A. Chief Says Veterans of Vietnam Not Neglected." *New York Times*, 16 July 1981, A13.

"No Major Diseases Cited in Agent Orange Sprayers." *New York Times*, 25 February 1984, A12.

Okie, Susan, and Bill McAllister. "CDC Finds No Linkage of Agent Orange, Cancer." *Washington Post*, 29 March 1992, A10.

"Personalities." *Washington Post*, 5 February 1982, B2.

Peterson, Bill. "The Welcome." *Washington Post*, 26 January 1981, A1, A12.

Peterson, Iver. "Vietnam Veterans Parade in Shadow of 52 Hostages." *New York Times*, 1 February 1981, A22.

———. "Study of Effects of Agent Orange on Veterans is Stalled in Dispute." *New York Times*, 19 May 1986, A1, A19.

Prochnau, Bill. "VFW Lines Up with Viet Vets on Agent Orange." *Washington Post*, 23 November 1982, A1, A4.

"Prospective V.A. Chief Withdraws over Cutbacks." *New York Times*, 29 April 1981, A25.

"Protest: A Week Against the War." *Time*, 3 May 1971, 11.

Quindlen, Ann. "A Vietnam Veteran Stills Audience with Rebuke." *New York Times*, 30 May 1979, B1, B3.

"Researchers Report Finding Telltale Sign of Agent Orange." *New York Times*, 18 September 1986, A28.

Robinson, Douglas. "100,000 Rally at U.N. Against Vietnam War." *New York Times*, 16 April 1967, A1.

Russakoff, Dale. "U.S. Offers to Buy Poisoned Homes of Times Beach." *Washington Post*, 23 February 1983, A1, A2.

Severo, Richard. "Herbicides Pose a Bitter Mystery in U.S. Decades after Discovery." *New York Times*, 29 May 1979, A1, A18.

Shabecoff, Phillip. "Herbicide Exposure Linked to Greater Risk of Cancer." *New York Times*, 20 August 1986, A5.

"Shadows of Vietnam: The Trip to Hanoi . . ." *Washington Post*, 9 January 1982, A22.

Sherwood, Brian. "Time to Remember our Vietnam Heroes." *New York Times*, 3 February 1981, A18.

Sinclair, Ward. "Vietnam Memorial: Another Symbol of Frustration for Vets." *Washington Post*, 26 May 1980, A3.

"Student Wins War Memorial Contest." *New York Times*, 7 May 1981, A20.

Sullivan, Ronald. "Veterans for Peace Simulate the War." *New York Times*, 5 September 1970, A6.

―――. "War Protestors Meet Opposition." *New York Times*, 6 September 1970, A8.

Thomas, Jo. "Cancer Victims Seeking U.S. Aid, Say A-Bombs Caused Disease." *New York Times*. 9 June 1979, A12.

―――. "Stakes High as Senate Examines Cancer in Troops at Atom Tests." *New York Times*, 20 June 1979, A1, A24.

Unger, Sanford. "Vets Can Use Mall, Court Quickly Rules." *Washington Post*, 20 April 1971, A-12.

Unger, Sanford, and William Claiborne. "Vets Camp on Mall Banned by Burger." *Washington Post*, 21 April 1971, A1, A8.

"V.A. Assailed on Delayed Agent Orange Study." *New York Times*, 16 September 1982, A25.

"VA Opposes Agent Orange Bill." *Washington Post*, 27 April 1983, A21.

Van Eckert, Wolf. "The Making of a Monument." *Washington Post*, 26 April 1980, C1, C7.

"Veteran Exposed to Atomic Tests Given Benefits." *New York Times*, 27 November 1979, A18.

"Veterans' Agency Opposing Measures on Toxic Chemical." *New York Times*, 23 June 1983, A21.

"Vets Disobey Court Order, Sleep on Mall." *Washington Post*, 22 April 1971, A1.

"Victory: VVA Wins A/O Judgment." *Veteran*, 9 (June, 1989), 6, 11, 22–23, 28.

Waters, Sheila, "Time to Remember our Vietnam Heroes, *New York Times* (February 3, 1981): A18.

Weinraub, Bernard. "Now, Vietnam Veterans Demand Their Rights." *New York Times*, 27 May 1979. sec. 6, 30.

―――. "Vietnam Invites 4 U.S. Veterans to Visit Hanoi." *New York Times*, 13 December 1981, A1, A24.

―――. "Vietnam Veterans Take an Emotional Journey to Hanoi." *New York Times*, 19 December 1981, A3.

―――. "Hanoi Aide Welcomes Study of Herbicide Impact." *New York Times*, 23 December 1981, A10.

―――. "4 Veterans End Vietnam Trip Nervous about Return to U.S." *New York Times*, 25 December 1981, A2.

Wilkerson, Isabel. "'Art War' Erupts Over Vietnam Veterans' Memorial." *Washington Post*, 8 July 1982, D3.

Wolfe, Tom. "Art Disputes War: The Battle of the Vietnam Memorial." *Washington Post*, 13 October 13 1982, B1, B3, B4.

"Yesterday . . ." *Washington Post*, 5 February 1982, A25.

Zumwalt, Elmo, Jr., and Elmo Zumwalt III. "Agent Orange and the Anguish of an American Family." *New York Times Magazine*, 24 August 1986, 32–40, 49, 58.

Personal and Telephone Interviews with Author

David Addlestone, personal interview, 10 August 1988, Washington, D.C.
Steven Bentley, personal interview, 25 October 1988, Dallas, Texas.
Ken Berez, personal interview, 27 March 1991, Washington, D.C.
Arthur Blank, Jr., personal interview, 23 October 1988, Dallas, Texas.
David Bonior, personal interview, March 8, 1989, Washington, D.C.
William Brew, personal interview, 12 August 1988, Washington, D.C.
David Carter, personal interview, 13 February 1989, Norman, Oklahoma.
Richard Christian, personal interview, 15 January 1991, Washington, D.C.
Max Cleland, telephone interview, 27 January 1989, Atlanta, Georgia.
William Crandell, telephone interviews, 16 January 1989 and 23 January 1989, Albany, New York.
Stuart Feldman, telephone interview, 7 May 1991, Washington, D.C.
Charles Figley, telephone interview, 10 November 1988, Lafayette, Indiana.
Richard Fuller, personal interview, 7 March 1989, Washington, D.C.
Michael Gough, personal interview, 8 March 1989, Washington, D.C..
Eric Hamburg, personal interview, 12 August 1988, Washington, D.C.
Sarah Haley, personal interview, 25 October 1988, Dallas, Texas, and telephone interview, 9 November 1988, Somerville, Massachusetts.
Lawrence Hobson, telephone interview, 22 March 1989, Washington, D.C.
Richard Kilmer, telephone interview, 18 April 1989, Louisville, Kentucky.
Michael Leaveck, personal interview, 10 August 1988, Washington, D.C.
Rusty Lindley, telephone interview, 17 April 1989, Washington, D.C.
William Mahedy, telephone interview, 22 November 1988, San Diego, California.
Guy McMichael, personal interview, 9 March 1989, Washington, D.C.
Shad Meshad, personal interview, 24 October 1988, Dallas, Texas.
Robert Muller, personal interview, 27 March 1991, Washington, D.C.
Laura Petrou, personal interview, 28 March 1991, Washington, D.C..
Harold Pincus, personal interview, 9 August 1988, Washington, D.C.
Chaim Shatan, personal interview, 24 October 1988, Dallas, Texas.
Jack Smith, telephone interviews, 22 December 1988, 29 December 1988, and 12 September 1989, Cleveland, Ohio.
Michael Sovick, personal interviews, 17 March 1989, 1 December 1989, and 6 December 1989, Norman, Oklahoma.
Jonathon Steinberg, personal interview, 12 August 1988, Washington, D.C.
Barton Stichman, personal interview, 10 August 1988, Washington, D.C.
John Talbott, telephone interview, 24 February 1989, Baltimore, Maryland.
John Terzano, telephone interviews, 9 April 1991 and 11 Arpil 1991, Washington, D.C.
Tom Williams, personal interview, 25 October 1988, Dallas, Texas.

John Wilson, personal interview, 24 October 1988, Dallas, Texas.
Alvin Young, personal interview, 6 March 1989, Washington, D.C.
Elmo Zumwalt, Jr., telephone interview, 4 April 1989, Arlington, Virginia.

Government Documents

Albanese, Richard. *United States Air Force Personnel and Exposure to Herbicide Orange*. Brooks Air Force Base, TX: USAF School of Aerospace Medicine, 1988.
Cleland, Max. Testimony before the Subcommittee on Veterans' Affairs, Senate Committee on Labor and Public Welfare, Vol. 6, January 27, 1970.
Daschle, Thomas, U.S. Senator. "Agent Orange: The Air Force Does It Again," *Congressional Record—Senate*. Washington, D.C.: U.S. Government Printing Office, March 9, 1990, S2550-S2558.
Davis, Miriam, and Michael Simpson. *Agent Orange: Veterans' Complaints and Studies of Health Effects*. Issue Brief Number IB83043 Washington, D.C.: Library of Congress, 1983.
Department of the Army (DA). *Employment of Riot Control Agents, Flame, Smoke, Antiplant Agents, and Personnel Detectors in Counterguerilla Operations*. Training Circular TC3–16. Washington, D.C.: DA, 1969.
Environmental Protection Agency. "Rebuttable Presumption against Registration and Continued Registration of Pesticide Produrts Containing 2,4,5-T." *Federal Register* 43 (April 21, 1978).
Feldman, Stuart. *Sunbelt States Reap G.I. Bill Bonanza: Eastern and Midwestern Vietnam Veterans Lose Scholarship Opportunities*. Report prepared for the National League of Cities, United States Conference of Mayors, Washington, D.C., 1977.
Lifton, Robert Jay. "Guilt of the Survivor, A Profile of the Vietnam Veteran." Testimony before the Subcommittee on Veterans' Affairs of the Committee on Labor and Public Welfare, United States Senate, Vol. 6, January 27, 1970.
MacLeod, Colin. *Report of 2,4,5-T: A Report of the Panel on Herbicides of the President's Science Advisory Panel*. Washington, D.C.: U.S. Office of Science and Technology, 1971.
Newman, Donald. Memo entitled "Clearance of all studies and press releases by the Domestic Policy Council Agent Orange Working Group." April 1, 1988. Obtained from office of Senator Thomas Daschle.
Petrou, Laura. Memo entitled "Newman Memo to Members of the Agent Orange Working Group." June 7, 1988. Obtained from office of Sennator Thomas Daschle.
U.S. Congress, House Committee on Veterans Affairs. *Veterans' Benefits in the United States: A Report to the President by the President's Commission on Veterans' Pension*. House Commission Print No. 235, 84th Cong., 2nd sess. 1956).
U.S. Congress, House Committee on Government Operations. *Oversight Review of CDC's Agent Orange Study*, Hearings before the Subcommittee on Human Resources and Intergovernmental Relations, 1st sess., July 11, 1989. Washington, D.C.: U.S. Government Printing Office.

U.S. Congress, House Committee on Government Operations. *The Agent Orange Coverup: A Case of Flawed Science and Political Manipulation*, Twelfth Report, together with Dissenting Views. Report 101–672. August 9, 1990. Washington, D.C.: U.S. Government Printing Office.

U.S. General Accounting Office (USGAO). *U.S. Ground Troops Were in Areas Sprayed with Herbicide Orange*. FPCD-80–23. Washington, D.C.: USGAO, 1979.

Zumwalt, Admiral Elmo, Jr. *Report to the Secretary of the Department of Veterans Affairs on the Association between Adverse Health Effects and Exposure to Agent Orange*. May 5, 1990.

INDEX

AAAS (American Association for the Advancement of Science), 81

Agent Orange
American Legion study of, 203–206
atomic veterans and, 107–109
Boffey's article on, 166–167
broadening of issue of, 90–92
Centers for Disease Control's study of, 166, 191–196
change in lawsuit against manufacturers of, 178–181
Combat Development and Test Center and, 76–77
combat experience and, 204–205
compensation for exposure to, 176–177
components of, 77
congressional inquiry and, 213–220
controversy of, 101–102
Council of Vietnam Veterans and, 83–87
court decision regarding, 207–209
debate of, 82–83
Department of Veterans Affairs and, 206–209, 213
disability claims and, 75–76, 89–90
documentary on, 87–88
early research on, 87–88

end of lawsuit against manufacturers of, 184–1857
end to studies of, 199–202
first complaints of, 81
General Accounting Office report and, 116–117
Gough report and, 118–119
government and, 105–107
HERBES tapes and, 88, 116
"hits" method of studying, 192–193, 194, 199
House Committee on Government Operations report and, 223–225
latent disorders and, 239–240
lawsuit against manufacturers of, 91, 102–105, 114–116, 129–131, 151–154, 167–170
presumption of service connection and, 119–122, 213, 220–223
Public Law 96–151 and, 164
Ranch Hand and, 77–81, 82, 202–203
restriction of, 81–82
Ryan lawsuit and, 109–110
"self-report" method of studying, 203, 205
Severo's article on, 106–107
spraying missions using, 76–81, 116–117
2,4-D study and, 198–199
Veteran's Administration's study of, 106, 165–166, 191